MICRO ECONOMICS

MICRO ECONOMICS

Dr. M. JOHN KENNEDY
M.A., M.Com., PhD., M.B.A.,

Associate Professor,
Dept. of Economics (Center for Research),
Arul Anandar College,
Karumathur, Madurai-625514.

Himalaya Publishing House
ISO 9001:2015 CERTIFIED

First Edition : 1999
Reprint : 2001, 2003, 2005, 2006, 2008
Reprint : 2009, 2010, 2012, 2013, 2014
Reprint : 2015, 2016, 2019, 2022
Reprint : 2023

Published by : Mrs. Meena Pandey
for **HIMALAYA PUBLISHING HOUSE PVT. LTD.,**
"Ramdoot", Dr. Bhalerao Marg, Girgaon, Mumbai - 400 004.
Phone: 022-23860170, 23863863; **Fax:** 022-23877178
E-mail: himpub@bharatmail.co.in; **Website:** www.himpub.com

Branch Offices :

New Delhi : "Pooja Apartments", 4-B, Murari Lal Street, Ansari Road, Darya Ganj, New Delhi - 110 002.
Phone: 011-23270392, 23278631; Fax: 011-23256286

Nagpur : Kundanlal Chandak Industrial Estate, Ghat Road, Nagpur - 440 018. Phone: 0712-2721215, 2721216

Bengaluru : Plot No. 91-33, 2nd Main Road, Seshadripuram, Behind Nataraja Theatre, Bengaluru - 560 020.
Phone: 080-41138821; Mobile: 09379847017, 09379847005

Hyderabad : No. 3-4-184, Lingampally, Besides Raghavendra Swamy Matham, Kachiguda, Hyderabad - 500 027.
Phone: 040-27560041, 27550139

Chennai : No. 34/44, Motilal Street, T. Nagar, Chennai - 600 017.
Mobile: 09380460419

Pune : "Laksha" Apartment, First Floor, No. 527, Mehunpura, Shaniwarpeth (Near Prabhat Theatre), Pune - 411 030.
Phone: 020-24496323, 24496333; Mobile: 09370579333

Cuttack : Plot No. 5F-755/4, Sector-9, CDA Markat Nagar, Cuttack - 753014, Odisha. Mobile: 09338746007

Kolkata : 3, S.M. Bose Road, Near Gate No. 5, Agarpara Railway Station, North 24 Parganas, West Bengal - 700 109. Mobile: 09674536325

Printed at : M/s. Sri Sai Art Printer, Hyderabad. On behalf of HPH.

PREFACE

This book is primarily meant to serve as a standard, comprehensive and complete text-book for the B.A. B.B.E., students of Madurai Kamaraj, Manonmonium Sundaranan Barathian, Barathidasan, Mahatma Gandhi and Chennai Universities.

The text is organised into 32 chapters. I have taken special care to explain difficult concepts in an easy and concise way. In preparing this book, I have referred to many standard reference texts of a number of authors. I gratefully acknowledge my intellectual debt to all of them.

I express my thanks to Rev. Fr. P.S. Arul S.J. Rev. Fr. G. Lawrence Amal Raj S.J. Principal and Secretary, Rev. Fr. Anto Vice-Principal, and all my department colleagues, for their helpful suggestions. I shall be failing in my duty if I do not express my deep sense of gratitude to E. Pandiaraj (Dena Bank, Madurai) for his encouragement in the preparation of this book. Last, but not the least, I thank my publisher Himalaya Publishing House for the quick and neat execution of the work.

Suggestions for improvement are welcome.

M. John Kennedy

CONTENTS

PART ONE: INTRODUCTION

PART TWO: THEORY OF CONSUMER BEHAVIOUR

PART THREE: THEORY OF PRODUCTION

PART FOUR: THEORY OF PRODUCT PRICING

*** PART ONE ***

INTRODUCTION

1

DEFINITION OF ECONOMICS

"The instability of the economy is equalled by the instability of economists."

— John H. Williams

PRELUDE

Economics is a social science, a classified body of knowledge concerning human relationships clustered about man's effort to earn a living.[1] Economics is quite an old discipline. That is why Prof. Samuelson remarks that Economics is the **"Oldest of the arts, the newest of the sciences, indeed the queen of the social sciences."**

The origin of the subject could be traced to the works of the Greek Philosopher Aristotle who confined the study of economics to household management and acquiring, guarding and making proper use of wealth. It is important to note that the word 'Economics' has been derived from the Greek words 'oikos' (a house) and 'nemein' (to manage). Thus economics means managing a household with limited funds. Adam Smith's magnum opus book "An Enquiry into the Nature and Causes of Wealth of Nations" published in the year 1776, laid the strong foundation for the growth of Economics. So Adam Smith is rightly called the "Father of Economics." Although there is a plethora of definitions, there is no concensus among economists about a precise definition of economics.

---

1. Clifford L. James, *Principles of Economics,* 9th edn., Barnes & Noble Books, New York, 1968, p.1.

Zeuthan's remark that 'economics is an unfinished science' still holds.

WEALTH DEFINITION

The early classical economists defined economics mainly as a study of wealth. To his famous treatise, Adam Smith gave the suggestive title 'An Enquiry into the Nature and Causes of Wealth of Nations." The spirit of Smith's enquiry is reflected in the writings of his successors like J.B. Say, Nassu senior, J.S. Mill and W.S. Jevons. For example, according to J.S. Mill "Economics investigates into the nature of wealth and the laws of production and distribution." The term wealth was taken as "riches or abundance of money or scarce goods having exchange value". The atmosphere of the Industrial Revolution marked by unprecedented material prosperity and accumulation of wealth should naturally justify the scope which these economists assigned to economics.

CRITICISM OF WEALTH DEFINITION

Wealth definition gave rise to serious misconceptions at the hands of some literary writers of the 19th century like John Ruskin, Thomas Carlyle, Charles Dickens, William Morris and Mathew Arnold. Economics was branded as the bread-and-butter science; the gospel of mammon, a science that taught selfishness and love for money; a dark and dismal science, a bastard science, a pig science and so on.

At a time when Christianity was spreading fast and religious sentiments were strong, they thought that the study of economics was bound to pollute, ethical values in life. The Bible was a major source to these writers. In the Bible it is said that "It is easier for a camel to go through the eye of a needle than for a rich man to enter the kingdom of God". Therefore rich people have no place in the kingdom of God. Since economics teaches us how wealth is to be acquired, it is against the will of God.

Prof. Kirzner rightly remarks, "The unworthiness of political economy in public opinion stemmed directly from its explicit preoccupation with so degrading a subject-matter as wealth."[2]

1. Too much Emphasis on Wealth

As mentioned earlier, literary writers and religious followers strongly voiced their protest against the study of economics because of its too much attachment to wealth.

But actually this criticism arises because of the narrow interpretation of wealth. Adam Smith treated economics as political economy and therefore

2. Kirzner, I.M. — *The Economic Point of View,* Affiliated East-West Press Pvt. Ltd., New Delhi, 1967, p. 49.

emphasised the importance of wealth from a national angle. If wealth is looked upon as money alone, it will give a wrong picture.

2. Restricted Meaning of Wealth

The classical definition considered wealth as, material goods only, like table, radio, sweets etc. Non material services of drivers, singers, teachers are not taken as wealth. But in modern days wealth denotes both goods and services.

3. Concept of Economic Man

Classical wealth definition was based mainly upon the assumption of an 'economic man' who had no consideration for love, affection, sympathy, patriotism etc. In other words, an economic man was supposed to give attention to economic activities only. But in reality human behaviour cannot be properly understood and analysed unless the other motives are also given due weightage.

4. No Mention of Man's Welfare

Wealth definition explains the wealth-getting and wealth-spending activities of man. It pays no attention to the equity principle which is of paramount importance to maximise the welfare of the society.

5. Economic Problem

Wealth definition is silent over the basic economic problem of meeting unlimited wants with scarce means. In other words, the central problem of economics, is not at all touched by wealth definition.

6. Defective Logic

Logic is the science of reasoning. The science of logic states that a word whose meaning is nebulous should not be used to define another; on the basis of this argument we may say that since the meaning of 'wealth' is not clear, a definition based on the word 'wealth' is also not scientific and correct.

WELFARE DEFINITION

Adam Smith's wealth definition made economics a dismal science. Alfred Marshall was the first neo-classical economist to rescue economics from ridicule, condemnation and misunderstanding. Carlyle and Ruskin considered economics as merely a bread and butter science and a 'gospel of mammon.' Marshall therefore re-oriented economics and placed it on the pedestal of glory in his classic work 'Principles of Economics', published in 1890.

Marshall, in his definition, shifted the emphasis from wealth to human welfare. According to him wealth is simply a means to an end in all activities, the end being human welfare.

In Marshall's[3] own words, "Political Economy or Economics, is a study of mankind in the ordinary business of life; it examines that part of individual and social action which is most closely connected with the attainment and with the use of the material requisites of well being." He adds that economics "is on the one side a study of wealth; and the other and more important side, a part of the study of man."[4] Thus Marshall gave primary importance to man and secondary importance to wealth.

Prof. A.C. Pigou,[5] an ardent follower of Marshall also gave a similar definition.

"The range of our enquiry becomes restricted to that part of social welfare that can be brought directly or indirectly into relation with the measuring rod of money."

MERITS OF MARSHALL'S DEFINITION

The following merits are claimed in favour of the Marshallian Welfare definition.

1. A Classificatory Definition

The basic argument advanced in favour of Marshallian definition is that it clearly classifies welfare into material welfare and non-material welfare. On the basis of the role and behaviour of man in the society they are classified into ordinary and extraordinary. Likewise economic actions are bifurcated into individual and social actions.

2. Rescues Economics from the grip of being called "Dismal Science"

In Marshallian definition, the emphasis has been shifted from wealth to welfare. It shows the way to maximise human welfare. Just as medicine helps to improve the health of man, economics provides a helping hand to improve his material welfare. No wonder Prof. Pigou has compared economics with the science of medicine. Thus economics is rescued from its dismal character.

---

3. A. Marshall, *Principles of Economics,* 8th Edition, MacMillan, London 1982, p.1.
4. *Ibid.*
5. A.C. Pigou, *Economics of Welfare,* MacMillan, London 1952, p.11.

3. Clear about the Scope of Economics

According to this definition, economics is a social science. It is not a pure science like physics or chemistry. Moreover it is also not an art. It is one among the social sciences. But because of the measuring rod of money economics is superior to other social sciences.

4. Clear on the Scope of Economics

This definition is also very clear on its scope. It deals only with the material activities of man in his ordinary business of life. It is not interested in the activities of eccentric people like misers or abnormal persons like sadhus or saints.

Criticism of Welfare Definition

Lionel Robbins led a frontal attack on the welfare definition in his immortal work "An Essay on the Nature and Significance of Economic Science" published in 1932. In the words of Robbins, "The materialist definition of economics misrepresents the science as we know it."

1. Material and Non-material Welfare

Robbins begins his attack by pointing out that economists should not narrow down the scope of economics by confining their attention to the study of material welfare alone. The services of teachers, actors, singers, lawyers etc. do promote welfare and such welfare may be termed as non-material welfare. The above-mentioned services have much economic significance because they are scarce in relation to demand and possess value.

2. Objection to Welfare

Robbins objects not only to the word 'material' but also to the very idea of 'welfare.' For the neo-classical economists, economics is concerned with the causes of material welfare. According to Robbins, there are certain material activities which do not promote welfare. The manufactures of intoxicants such as wine and opium are certainly economic activities. But they are not conducive to human welfare.

3. Classificatory Definition

According to Robbins, the materialist definition is classificatory rather than analytical. Materialist definition classifies human activities into 'economic' and 'non-economic', 'productive' and 'unproductive', 'material welfare' and 'non-material welfare.' Materialist definition considers only those human activities which are undertaken to promote material welfare.

All other human activities though they contribute to welfare are excluded from the scope of economics.

4. Welfare cannot be Measured

The neo-classical economist's idea of welfare is based on cardinal utility. But utility is a psychological entity which cannot be measured. It varies from person to person, place to place and time to time. Therefore the concept of welfare based on measurable utility is elusive in character.

5. Welfare involves Value Judgement

Robbins considers welfare definition as involving value judgements because it prescribes policies which are likely to increase welfare. But he considers economics as neutral between ends. Value judgement is within the province of a philosopher and not that of an economist. The function of an economist is to explore and explain and not to advocate and condemn. To Robbins, economics must remain neutral between ends just as mechanics stand neutral between rival schemes of railway construction.

6. Economics is a Social Science

Robbins disputed the Marshallian conception of economics as a 'Social Science' — "a study of man as they live and move and think in the ordinary business of life." According to Marshall, the activities of an individual living in seclusion like a Himalayan Sadhu or Robinson Crusoe fall outside the orbit of economics. Robbins on the other hand regards economics as a human science. Economics is as much concerned with an exchange economy as with the activities of a recluse like Robinson Crusoe. The central problem in economics, according to Robbins, is the allocation of scarce means among alternative ends.

SCARCITY DEFINITION

After rejecting the materialist definition of Marshall, Lionel Robbins formulated his own conception of economics in his book "The Nature and Significance of Economic Science" in 1932.

In the words of Lionel Robbins,[6] "Economics is the science which studies human behaviour as a relationship between ends and scarce means which have alternative uses." He deduced his definition from four fundamental characteristics of human existence.

1. Unlimited Wants

"Ends" refers to human wants which are boundless but the resources available to satisfy these wants are limited. Some wants are inborn but others are acquired through customs and conventions. When one want is satisfied another crops up. Multiplicity of wants calls forth ceaseless efforts for their satisfaction.

---

6. L. Robbins — *The Nature and Significance of Economic Science,* London, Macmillan, 1969, p. 16.

2. Scarcity of Means

The resources (time or money) at the disposal of a person to satisfy his wants are limited. The external world does not offer full opportunities for their complete achievement. If things are available in abundance just like free goods, the economic problem will not arise. But as Prof. Meyer says "Alladin's lamps exist only in Arabian fairy tales."

Scarcity does not mean absolute scarcity, but relative scarcity, i.e., scarcity in relation to demand. Scarcity is a ratio, not an absolute fact. The supply of a commodity may be small, but if nobody demands it, we shall not call it scarce in the economic sense. Thus, rotten eggs, though much fewer than good ones are not scarce in the economic sense. Foodgrains though supplied in millions of tonnes may be scarce in the market as the demand is greater.

3. Alternative Uses of Scarce Means

Economic resources are not only scarce but are also versatile. If the resources cannot be put to alternative uses, the question of choice will not arise. We may use land for raising crops or for building houses. We cannot do both. If we choose one thing, we must give up others.

4. The Economic Problem

When the means at the disposal of a person are limited and the resources can be put to several uses and when wants can be graded on the basis of intensity, the behaviour necessarily takes the form of choice.

In the words of Robbins, "When time and the means for achieving ends are limited and capable of alternative application, and the ends are capable of being distinguished in order of importance, then behaviour necessarily assumes the form of choice".[7] Further he writes, "We have been turned out of paradise, we have neither eternal life nor unlimited means for gratification."[8]

Thus the choosing of one is at the cost of another. In order to make choice scientific, some form of pricing process is inevitable. Robbin thus reduced economics to a theory of pricing process or valuation theory.

Economic Problem and Technical Problem

An economic problem is different from a technical problem. A technical problem arises when the question is as to the best method of accomplishing some one end. Suppose we decide to build a canal, the

7. Robbins, *op. cit.*, p.14.
8. *Ibid.*, p.15.

problem of how to build a canal with given resources is technical. But if in view of our limited resources, the question is whether we should spend the available funds on building a canal or constructing a railway line or building a museum, our problem becomes an economic one. In a technical problem, the end is one and the means are many. In an economic problem the ends are many and the means are limited."[9]

In the words of Prof. Milton Friedman,[10] "Economics is the science of how a particular society solves its economic problems. An economic problem exists whenever scarce means are used to satisfy alternative ends. If the means are not scarce there is no problem at all, there is Nirvana. If the means are scarce but there is only a single end, the problem of how to use the means is a technical problem. No value judgements enter into its solution; only knowledge of physical and technical relationship."

MERITS OF ROBBINS' DEFINITION

This definition has demolished the old structure of economics based on "material welfare." In its place, it has erected an altogether new structure with two fundamental stones, viz., the scarcity of means and the multiplicity of ends.

1. Economic Problem

According to Robbins, economic problem arises due to (*i*) unlimited wants (*ii*) scarce means and (*iii*) versatility of means. It is scarcity that leads to choice.

2. Analytical

Marshallian definition is classificatory because it uses such vague expressions like 'material welfare' and 'material requisites of well-being.' Robbins' definition is considered to be more satisfactory and scientific because it is analytical and it focuses attention on a particular aspect of behaviour, namely, the form imposed by the influence of scarcity.

3. It is Universal in Application

Robbins definition is universal in the sense that it is applicable to all nations and all economic systems. In the words of Eric Roll "It exists in the one man community of Robinson Crusoe, in the patriarchal tribe of central

9. Jathar and Beri — *Elementary Principles of Economics,* 10th edn., Oxford University Press, New Delhi, 1969, p.3.
10. *Price Theory,* Kalyani Publications, New Delhi, 1988, p. 6.

Africa, in medieval and feudalist Europe, in modern capitalist America and in communist Russia."[11]

4. A Positive Study

According to the neo-classical economists, a human activity must possess two qualifications to be included in the subject matter of economics (*i*) it must create material goods, and (*ii*) material goods must contribute to human welfare. But Robbins emphasized that economics is a science, "Economics is entirely neutral between ends. Economics is not concerned with ends as such.[12] The ends may be noble or ignoble. They may be material or immaterial. They may be economic or non-economic. Thus according to Robbins, economics is a science concerned with what is and not what ought to be.

5. Scope of Economics

Prof. Robbins has widened the scope of economics. Robbins viewed production of potatoes as much as economic activity as production of 'philosophy' if it involved alternatives and choices.

6. Opportunity Cost

The direct outcome of the scarcity definition is the concept of 'opportunity cost' which is vital in the field of Economic Analysis.

7. The Concept of Scale of Preferences

The concept of scale of preferences is also implicit in the scarcity definition of Robbins. In real life, an individual is confronted with the problem of illimitable wants with scarce means. In such a situation an individual will choose the one that will give him a greater amount of satisfaction. This implies that he has a scale of preference, a kind of list of his unsatisfied wants arranged in the order of satisfaction. A commodity near the top of the list would give him more satisfaction than a lower one. Few people are consciously aware of having a scale of preference, though most are aware that some wants are more pressing than others.[13] For the purpose of economic theory, however, it is necessary to assume that every one has a scale of preferences which is implied in the scarcity definition.

CRITICISM OF ROBBINS' DEFINITION

Robbins' definition is based on two foundation stones — multi-plicity of wants and scarcity of means. Prof. Macfie is so much impressed with the

11. Eric Roll — *Elements of Economic Theory,* Faber & Faber, London, 1945, p.16.
12. Robbins, *Op. cit.*, p. 24.
13. *Ibid.*, p.148.

scarcity definition that he is led to remark "What he (Robbins) has said cannot be resaid. To me it appears final within its scope." But Robbins is not without critics, Robbins' critics, namely R.W. Souter, Lindley Fraser, Barbara Wootton, T. Parson, criticised him mainly for ignoring the normative aspect of human behaviour and for making economics an 'obscure science.'

1. It is Too Narrow and Too Wide

D.H. Robertson,[14] feels Robbins' definition 'at once too narrow and too wide.' It is too narrow because it excludes such topics as defects of economic organisation which lead to idle resources. It is too wide to admit the army commander and the cricket captain a place in his field both of whom are concerned with allocation of scarce means which have alternative uses. Therefore, Robbins' definition is applicable even to non-economic problems thereby making the scope of economics too wide.

2. Old Wine in a New Bottle

According to critics, Robbins has not discovered anything new. His definition is only just like old wine in a new bottle. The concept of scarcity which occupies a pride of place in economic theory had already been discussed by physiocrats and classical writers. Robbins himself quotes the contributions of Wicksteed, Stigler and Chandler towards this concept. But this argument is true only to a limited extent. Though the concept was in existence for long, the way he has handled the concept is really admirable.

3. It offers only Light but not Fruit

Robbins has made economics a positive science. A positive science is concerned with what it is and not what ought to be. In such a case, economics will give us only light and not fruit.

4. The Welfare Concept can also be traced in Robbins' Definition

Robbins has been criticised for ignoring the welfare aspect in his definition. As Boulding has remarked "Prof. Robbins in defining economics as a valuation problem seems to deprive economics of the right to study welfare." According to Robbins, the scarce means are to be adjusted to the multiple ends in such a manner as to secure the maximum which is nothing else than the maximum welfare. Thus welfare has entered through the back door in Robbins' definition.

---

14. D.H. Robertson — *Lectures on Economic Principles,* Vol. I, Asia Publishing House, Bombay, 1957, p.23.

5. Artificial Distinction between Ends and Scarce Means

Robbins has also been criticised for creating an 'artificial scheme' between 'ends' and 'means.' According to him ends are tendencies to which people conduct themselves and which can be defined and understood. It excludes the concept of purpose which is fundamental to human action.

6. Robbins' Conception of Economics is Confined to Micro Analysis

Robbins' definition is essentially micro in character. It is concerned with how an individual faces unlimited ends with scarce means. But economics is not concerned with individualistic ends and means alone. Economic problems are mostly social in character rather than individual. But Robbins does not recognise the macro-economic character of Economics.

7. It Ignores Growth Economics

The scope of economics grows by leaps and bounds every day. Economics of today is different, from the economics of yesterday. It is a growing science. Recently, the economics of growth and development has become an integral part of economics. But Robbins in his definition does not pay any attention to this aspect of economics. Robbins discussed only the allocative aspect of resources without giving importance to the growth aspect.

8. Economics of Abundance

According to Robbins, economic problem arises due to scarcity. But economic problems may also arise due to plenty rather than scarcity as had happened during the great depression of 1930s. Moreover Prof. Kenneth Galbraith, a noted American economist in his book, "The Affluent Society", states that scarcity is not a problem in America. So that the conventional scarcity idea has only little relevance.

9. Not applicable to Underdeveloped Countries

Robbins definition provides no solution to the problems of under-developed countries. A peculiar feature of many under developed countries is that the resources are not scarce, but they are either under utilised, or unutilised or misutilised. Robbins simply assumes the resources as given and analysed their allocation among alternative uses.

10. Role of Deduction

Robbins gave undue importance to the methodology of deduction in his analysis. Some economists question the validity of this analysis. As

Prof. Fraser remarks "Deduction without induction is empty and induction without deduction is blind."

11. Rationality Assumption

Robbins assumes rationality on the part of economic units in their behaviour. But this assumption is unrealistic and questionable. In actual practice, man is influenced more by customs and habits than by rational outlook.

COMPARISON BETWEEN ROBBINS' AND MARSHALL'S DEFINITION

Basically there is not much difference between scarcity and welfare definitions. It is said that "we all talk about the same things, but we have not yet agreed what it is we are talking."

Similarities

1. Wealth and Scarce Means

Robbins' and Marshall's definitions are similar in the sense that there is no fundamental difference between wealth and scarce means. Marshall called wealth as "requisite of well being." Robbins termed it as 'scarce means.'

2. Primary Importance to Man

Both definitions assigned primary importance to man. According to Marshall, the aim of wealth is to improve human welfare. To Robbins, economics dealt the relationship between ends and scarce means which have alternative uses. Thus the ultimate aim of the two is the study of human beings.

3. Rationality

Both definitions consider rationality on the part of a human being. According to Marshall, the aim of a rational man is to maximise his welfare. But Robbins thinks that the aim of rational man is to maximise his satisfaction. There is not much difference between satisfaction and welfare. Prof. Pigou regards satisfaction as a prelude to welfare.

Differences

Scarcity Definition of Robbins	*Welfare Definition of Marshall*
1. According to Robbins, economics includes both economic and non economic activities.	According to Marshall, economics deals only with those economic activities which promote welfare
2. Robbins considers economics as a human science.	Marshall admits economics as a social science.
3. Scarcity definition believes in the positive aspect of economics.	Welfare definition believes in the normative aspect of economics.
4. This definition is analytical.	This definition is classificatory.
5. Applicable to all economies.	Applicable only to capitalist econo-mies.

MODERN DEFINITION

After 65 years of Lionel Robbins' publication of "The Nature and Significance of Economic Science" the nature and scope of economics has widened. It is no longer a value theory or a theory of resource allocation as imagined by Robbins. The credit for revolutionising the study of economics surely goes to Lord J.M. Keynes. Keynes defined economics as the "study of the administration of scarce resources and the determinants of income and employment."

According to the Prof. Benham Economics is "a study of the factors affecting the size, distribution and stability of a country's national income."

Recently Prof. Samuelson[15] has given a definition based on Growth aspects which is known as the Growth definition.

"Economics is the study of how people and society end up choosing, with or without the use of money, to employ scarce productive resources that could have alternative uses to produce various commodities and distribute them for consumption, now or in the future, among various persons or groups in society. Economics analyses the costs and the benefits of improving patterns of resource use."

The Main Features of Growth Definition

Firstly, it is applicable even in a barter economy where money measurement is not possible.

Secondly, the inclusion of time element makes the scope of economics dynamic.

15. P.A. Samuelson, ***Economics,*** 11th edn., McGraw-Hill, 1983, p. 2.

Thirdly, this definition possesses universality in its application. Thus we may conclude that though in a sense it is similar to Robbins' definition, it is an improvement over Robbins' scarcity definition.

QUESTIONS

1. "Economics is a Science of Wealth." — Discuss.
2. "Economics is a study of mankind in the ordinary business of life." (Marshall) — Comment.
3. "Economics is a science of material welfare." — Write a short note on it.
4. "Whatever economics is concerned with, it is not concerned with the causes of material welfare as such." (Robbins) — Discuss.
5. Critically examine Marshall's definition of Economics.
6. "Economics is the science of choice." — Elucidate.
7. "Economics is the science which studies human behaviour as a relationship between ends and scarce means which have alternative uses." — Explain.
8. Show the superiority of Robbins' definition over Marshall's definition.
9. Do you accept the contention that welfare concept has entered Robbins' definition through the back door?
10. Discuss the various definitions of Economics.
11. Explain Robbins' definition of Economics.

❖ ❖ ❖

2

METHODS AND NATURE OF ECONOMIC LAWS

"Economists are the failed priests of our generation."

— Louis Rukeyser, 1983.

The term 'methodology' refers to the way in which economists proceed with the study of a subject matter. In other words, methodology implies the logical process of discovering and demonstrating the truth.

Every science has its own methods of investigation. Two kinds of methods have been developed by different schools of thought.

1. The Deductive method, and the
2. Inductive method.

During the 19th century, there was a bitter controversy between the Classical School of Britain and the Historical School of Germany on the relative uses and merits of deductive and inductive reasoning. The major champions of the classical school are David Ricardo, Malthus, J.S. Mill, N.W. Senior etc. The Historical School comprised of Carl Knies, Roscher, Hildebrand etc. The controversy over methodology went on till Schmollar and Alfred Marshall brought about a compromise. In fact, induction and deduction are two different forms of logic both of which are used to establish the truth.

1. DEDUCTIVE METHOD

Deduction proceeds from the general to the particular while induction proceeds from the particular to the general. In the words of Gee Wilson "By deduction in logic is meant reasoning or inference from the general to the particular, or from the universal to the individual. Induction is the process of reasoning from a part to the whole, from particular to general or from the individual to the universal."[1]

Deductive method is also known as analytical, abstract or *a priori* method. Under this method starting with a few assumptions, hypotheses or postulates are made. On the basis of these assumptions, certain testable hypotheses are framed. The hypotheses are then tested against the observed facts. The hypotheses confirmed by the facts are accepted as tentative theories. If a theory so formulated stands the test of time, it becomes a law such as the law of diminishing returns, law of demand etc.

Let us illustrate deductive reasoning by a simple example. Take the universal law of diminishing marginal utility. It simply states that the larger the stock of a commodity the less, is its marginal utility. From this simple self-evident law, a number of inferences can be drawn by deductive reasoning. The first inference is that rich people derive small amount of utility from money than the poor people. The second inference is that the rich can bear more of the tax burden. Similarly, the law of demand is also based on the law of diminishing marginal utility. The larger the stock of a commodity, the less will be its marginal utility; so people will buy more of a commodity only when the price is lowered. Similarly a number of additional observations can be made.

There are two methods of deductive reasoning.

(*i*) Mathematical, and

(*ii*) Non-mathematical,

The classical economists followed the non-mathematical method of deduction, while Cournot, Pareto and Edgeworth have extensively used the mathematical deductive approach in their analysis. Of the two, the latter is strongly gaining momentum.

MERITS OF DEDUCTIVE METHOD

The following are the main advantages of the deductive method of economics.

---

1. Gee Wilson, *Social Science Research Methods,* 1950.

1. Simplicity

The deductive method is extremely simple and easy to follow because it avoids the difficulty of collecting statistics which is a complicated affair. From a few basic facts of human nature, we can deduce a number of economic laws. For example, according to the law of diminishing marginal utility, the utility of money for the rich is lower than the utility of money for the poor. Therefore in order to achieve equality in income, progressive tax system is suggested. But the principle of progressive taxation is deduced from the law of diminishing utility through deductive reasoning.

2. Limited Use of Experimentation

It is not possible for the economist to conduct controlled experiments in a laboratory. The experimentation in physical sciences like physics and chemistry are precise. But experimentation in economics is not only a complicated affair but also an unreliable one. The data required for the experimentation are not only available but also inadequate. So, the next best alternative is to follow deductive reasoning. Prof. Boulding rightly calls this method as "intellectual experimentation."

3. Universal Application

The theories derived from deductive analysis are more widely applicable than the theories based on induction. The theories based on deductive principle are applicable to all places and at all times. For example the law of diminishing returns and the law of equimarginal utility are suitable to all persons and to all countries.

4. Complementary

It is generally argued that deductive analysis is complementary to inductive analysis. If inductive method fail to deliver goods, it is the deductive method that has to come to our rescue.

In the words of Prof. Cairns,

"The method of deduction is incomparable when conducted under proper checks, the most powerful instrument of discovery ever wielded by human intelligence."

5. Lack of Bias

Deduction does not give scope to the researcher, or investigator to influence the final result with his personal favour or prejudice. In other words deductive analysis is impartial, unbiased and neutral.

6. Precision

Deductive method also gives precise and clear cut results as it involves the use of logic and mathematics. Deductive method is also known as the mathematical method. Today an economist with a knowledge of econometrics is able to draw inferences in a short span of time and make analogies with other generalisations and theories.

7. Effectiveness

Deductive method is also useful to make predictions about the future. We can predict what consequences are likely to follow under certain given conditions. For example, if the price of a commodity falls, we can easily predict a greater demand for that commodity, while the supply of the same commodity will fall.

8. Suitability

The deductive method is much more suitable in those complex economic phenomenon where cause and effect are inextricably mixed up. It is with the help of reasoning alone that certain right conclusions can be made about human behaviour.

We may conclude with Professor Koopmans[2] that "the theories that have become dear to us can very well stand by themselves, as an impressing and highly valuable system of deductive thought, erected on a few premises that seem to be well chosen first approximations to a complicated reality."

DEMERITS OF DEDUCTIVE METHOD

In spite of its various plus points this method suffers from a number of weak spots also. The major attack on this method was levied by the Historical School which flourished in Germany. The mistakes of the classical economists were not in the method, but their unsound premises. According to the Historical School of Economics, theories without facts are baseless.

1. Lack of Reliability

The deductive method is based on assumptions. *Ceteris Paribus* is assumed throughout the process of reasoning. Classical economists developed their theories on unsound premises. For example, they believed that self-interest alone motivates human behaviour. This is obviously not true. Therefore, Professor A.P. Lerner called deductive method as "arm chair" method and suggested that it should be properly guarded against its failings.

---

2. T.C. Koopmans — *Three Essays in the State of Economic Science,* McGraw Hill Book Co., 1957.

2. Dogmatism

The adherents of deductive analysis claim that economic laws are universal and eternal in their application. This makes economics dogmatic.

3. Dangerous

Deductive method based on wrong premises is dangerous when universal validity is claimed for such generalisations. For example, J.B. Say's famous law of market, claims universal validity. The law states "supply creates its own demand." Therefore there will not be over-production in the market. If the government frames policies on the basis of this law it may prove to be disastrous.

4. Abstraction

In deduction there is too much of abstraction. It is very difficult for ordinary people to follow this method. It requires a high degree of knowledge in logic and abstraction which every beginner may not possess. Therefore theoretical models with little empirical content are termed as "intellectual toys" having no connection to reality.

2. INDUCTIVE METHOD

This method is also known as the historical, empirical or 'a posteriori' method of economic analysis. When this method is employed, a mass of data relating to the problem to be studied must be collected. These facts are collected and then used as a basis for generalisations. The inductive method is sometimes employed to check the findings of economic theory developed by the deductive method.

The inductive method involves four stages:

(*i*) Observation,

(*ii*) Formation of hypothesis,

(*iii*) Generalisations, and

(*iv*) Verification.

According to Prof. Boulding[3] inductive method involves two forms. (1) Experimental Method, and (2) Statistical Method.

Experimental Method

This method is popular in physical sciences like physics, chemistry and biology. It has limited and narrow scope in economics. Since the economist lacks controlled experiment as in laboratories, he is unable to conduct suitable experiments. Moreover economics deals with human behaviour, where such type of experiments are not possible.

3. K.E. Boulding, *Economic Analysis,* 4th edn., Harper & Row, New York pp., 10-11.

As Prof. Albert L. Meyer[4] states "Human beings have wills of their own and resent being treated as guinea pigs for the purpose of social experimentation. Therefore the alternative is the statistical method."

Statistical Method

The statistical method is concerned with the framing of generalisations on the basis of statistical data collected from the various sectors of the economy. Recent developments in statistics have made this approach more popular. The researchers use statistical data and establish, cause and effect relationships between variables. The Engel's Law of Family Expenditure, Malthusian Theory of Population, Cobb-Douglas Production Function etc., have been derived from inductive statistical reasoning.

MERITS OF INDUCTIVE METHOD

1. Reliability

The generalisations arrived through this method are more reliable than those of the deductive method. The empirical study reduces the gap between theory and practice. The adoption of the inductive method has provided certain basic laws in economics. For example, the study of family budgets led to the formulation of Engel's law of consumption which states that as income increases, the proportion of income spent on food item decreases.

2. Check on Deduction

The inductive method is sometimes used to check the findings of economic theory developed by the deductive method.

3. Dynamic Approach

Inductive method is helpful in analysing the dynamic phenomena of economics.

4. Framing Government Policies

The conclusions arrived at by inductive reasoning can be tested on the basis of facts. Such results are vital in framing government policies in various fields.

5. Scientific in Character

Since inductive methods extensively use statistical tools, there is the possibility of arriving at results which are nearer to reality. Moreover as the sample size increases, the accuracy of the result also increases.

---

4. Albert L. Meyers, *Elements of Modern Economics,* World Press, Calcutta, 1956, p. 2.

DEMERITS OF INDUCTIVE METHOD

1. Possibility of Bias

The propositions derived through this method are based upon the data collected by investigation. If the investigator has certain ethical or ideological predilections of his own, the inductive method may lead to biased conclusions.

2. It is a Difficult Method

The method of induction is difficult in nature. It is very difficult for beginners to collect data, analyse them and derive some sensible conclusions out of them.

3. Costly Method

It is a costly method as collection of data and an analysis of them require much investment.

4. Inapplicability

In many cases, the inductive method is inapplicable due to the plurality of causes and intermixture of results.

5. Limited Scope for Verification

Since the propositions obtained through this method are based on a few facts, the universal application is not very much valid.

Complementary of the Two Methods

The modern economists are of the view that both are not competitive but complementary in economic analysis. They argue that theories without facts are barren while facts without theories are meaningless.

As Schmoller remarked "Induction and deduction are both needed for scientific thought as the right and left foot are both needed for walking."

Wagner also thinks in the same direction when he says, "true solution of the context about method is not to be found in the selection of deduction or induction but in the acceptance of deduction and induction." Prof. Samuelson also remarks "properly understood, theory and observation, deduction and induction cannot be in conflict."

3. NATURE OF ECONOMICS

Economists are sharply and divergently divided on the question whether economics can be regarded as a science or as an art. But some choose a middle path stating that it is both a science and an art.

ECONOMICS AS A SCIENCE

Science is a systematised body of knowledge which traces the relationship between cause and effect. Prof. Robbins considers economics as a science. According to him, the last three letters of the word 'Economics' i.e., 'ics' indicate a clear proof that it is a science like physics, mathematics, and dynamics. "Economics thus derives its name from the fact that it is a science rather than an art."[5]

In the words of Poincare "Science is built up of facts as a house is built up of stones; but all accumulation of facts is no more a science than a heap of stones is a house."

The main features of a science are that:

1. It is a systematised study of a subject,
2. It establishes the cause and effect relationship of a fact,
3. Its laws are universal in nature.

Science is quantitative but the basis of art is qualitative. Science is precise and descriptive; art is vague and suggestive. Science seeks facts while art craves for beauty. Moreover scientific study is impersonal and objective while the appreciation of the art is deeply personal and subjective.[6]

The following arguments are advanced to consider economics as a science.

1. Systematised Study

The first essential feature of a science is that it should be a systematised study. The scientific method of study consists of three important steps.

(*i*) observation,

(*ii*) reasoning, and

(*iii*) verification.

Likewise in economics also theories have been formulated after the relevant matters are systematically collected, classified and studied. Moreover it is systematically divided into five components, namely, consumption, production, exchange, distribution and public finance.

---

5. M. Briggs and P.A. Jordan, *A Textbook of Economics,* 10th edn., University Tutorial Press, Ltd., London, 1965, p. 2.
6. V. Ganapathi, *Principles of Economics,* Emerald, Madras 1984, p. 12.

2. Scientific Law

A Science is not a mere collection of facts, but it establishes a relationship between cause and effect. Laws in physics and chemistry trace this cause and effect relationship very clearly. For example, two atoms of hydrogen and one atom of oxygen will form water, all other things being equal. Likewise, Newton's law of gravitation explains how things tend to move downwards if nothing prevents them. In economics, the law of demand states that other things being equal, a fall in the price of a commodity leads to an extension in demand and vice versa. Here fall in price is the cause and extension, in demand is its effect. Thus the second requirement for a science is also fulfilled.

3. Experiments

In physical sciences, experiments can be conducted in laboratories. In economics, laboratory is the economy in which several laws and theories can be tested. The various economic systems like capitalism, socialism and mixed economy are the experiments of economics. Likewise, price mechanism is an experiment in a free enterprise economy which shows how resources are effectively allocated without a central planning authority. Likewise various monetary and fiscal policies can be tested in the economy to identify their role in the economy.

4. Measuring Rod of Money

According to Marshall, the measuring rod of money has conferred a special status to economics like other physical sciences and even a status superior to that of other social sciences. To use Marshall's words,[7] "Just as the chemist's fine balance has made chemistry more exact than most other physical sciences; so this economist's balance (money) rough and imperfect as it is, has made economics more exact than any other branch of social science."

5. Universal

The last requirement for a science is that its laws should be universal. In economics also, the law of demand, the law of diminishing returns etc., are universal in nature.

ARGUMENTS AGAINST ECONOMICS TO SHOW THAT IT IS NOT A SCIENCE

The following arguments are posed to show that economics is not a science.

---

7. A. Marshall, *Principles of Economics,* 8th edn., Macmillan London, 1982, p. 12.

1. Conflicting Views

There is a popular saying "Lay six economists end to end and you will never reach a conclusion." Some economists argue that economics is not a science because economists disagree. According to Mrs. Barbara Wootton "whenever six economists are gathered, there are seven opinions."[8]

But this can be easily refuted; doctors disagree and no one denies and says that physiology and anatomy are not sciences.

2. The Laws of Economics are not Universal

Economic laws are not universal in nature. The laws which are applicable to capitalistic countries are not applicable to socialistic countries. The laws which are valid in a developed economy may not fit in with a developing economy.

3. Economic Laws are not Exact and Precise

Unlike physical laws like gravitation, economic laws are not exact and precise. Most of the economic laws will operate only if the qualifying statement 'other things being equal' is valid. Physical sciences except biology deal with lifeless matters like liquid, gas, electricity etc. But economics deals with human beings whose actions are not only varied but are also inconsistent. The inexactness in economics arises due to various reasons.

1. The economy in which we live is complex.
2. The laboratory experimentation is not possible.
3. The economist may be influenced by his personal bias and prejudices.

4. Difficulty in Making Prediction

According to Marshall, "the laws of economics are to be compared with the law of tides rather than with the simple and exact law of gravitation." The tides in the sea are the highest on the night of the full moon. As the size of the moon decreases, the height of the tides also goes on declining. Thus, by looking at the size of the moon, we can forecast when the tides in the sea will be the highest, but such a forecast can also prove to be entirely wrong. Likewise economic laws are only statements of tendencies and are only approximate. In many cases the law may not operate.

But economists argue that economics is a science because it satisfies the attributes of a science. Even though economics is not as exact as physical sciences, the views of Wootton is not be acceptable to economists.

---

8. Mrs. Barbara Wootton, *Lament for Economics* (1938), p. 14.

"Economists are under the suspicion of being charlatans and they cannot afford to arrogate honourable titles to themselves. In the increasingly common application by theoretical economists of the term science to their studies, there is an element of wish fulment."[9]

ECONOMICS AS AN ART

The systematic application of scientific principles is an art.

According to J.N. Keynes "An art is a system of rules for the attainment of given end."

In the words of an Italian economist, Luigi Cossa, "A science teaches us to know, an art teaches us to do. Science lays down certain principles while art puts these principles into practice. In a word, science explains and expounds; art directs; art imposes precepts or proposes rules."

In this sense, economics is an art. Economics provides solutions to many of the problems. The law of Equimarginal utility helps a consumer to solve his problem of getting maximum satisfaction with limited means. The doctrine of consumer's surplus helps a Finance Minister in the field of taxation. Keyne's theory of employment provides a solution to unemployment. As Prof. Pigou rightly remarks "Economics is not only light giving but also fruit bearing."

But many economists consider economics as a science. Marshall prefers to call economics as "a science pure and applied rather than a science and an art." In his zeal to give economics the status of a pure science, Robbins has said "The function of an economist is to explore and explain and not advocate and condemn." According to Robbins, the role of an economist is to explore and explain economic effects, but the question of value judgement should be left to the politicians and moral authorities.

But a rational and scientific approach will consider its science and art aspects. The science of economics will not be much use unless it offers not only light but also fruit. The study of economics will be a waste if it fails to offer solutions to various problems of the economy. As Prof. Marshall rightly remarks "Nothing that is wrong in practice is ever right in theory." We may conclude in the words of Cossa "Science requires art; Art requires science, each being complementary to the other." Thus economics is both a science and an art.

9. B. Wootton, *Op. cit.*

4. NATURE OF ECONOMIC LAWS

Every science uses terms such as hypothesis, theory and law.[10] A hypothesis attempts to explain some facts. If the hypothesis can explain new facts and is not contradicted by new discoveries, it is promoted to the rank of a theory. Theory establishes relationships between cause and effect. If a theory continues to stand the test of time and experience, a law may be formulated.

Like all sciences, economics has its own laws. A law is a statement of casual relationship between two sets of phenomena, one is a cause and the other is an effect. A set of generalisations drawn by economists are called the Laws of Economics.

For example, the Law of Demand states that as price falls demand expands and vice versa. Engel's Law of Family Expenditure states that as income increases the proportion of income spent on food items decreases. Greshm's Law states that "bad money drives good money out of circulation." Other important laws are, law of diminishing marginal utility, law of equi-marginal utility, the law of variable proportions etc. In the words of Marshall:[11]

"Economic laws, or statements of economic tendencies, are those social laws which relate to branches of conduct in which the strength of the motives chiefly concerned can be measured by a money price."

According to Robbins "Economic laws are statements of uniformities which govern human behaviour in the allocation of scarce resources between given ends."

FEATURES OF ECONOMIC LAWS

1. Economic Laws are Conditional

According to Prof. Seligman 'economic laws are essentially hypothetical'.[12] Economic laws are conditional or hypothetical and their validity depends upon the fulfilment of certain conditions. That is why all economic laws are qualified by the statement, "other things being equal." The law of demand states that people would buy more at a lower price than at a higher price. This is true only if "Other things remain equal" that is income, taste, prices of substitutes etc. remain unaltered.

---

10. K.P.M. Sundaram — *Micro Economics,* 6th edn., Sultan Chand & Sons, New Delhi, 1990, p. 111.
11. A. Marshall — *Principles of Economics,* 8th edn., Macmillan, London, 1982, p. 27.
12. E.R.A. Seligman, *Principles of Economics,* Macmillan, New York, 1905, p. 25.

2. Economic Laws are Relative

The economic laws are of two types:

(*a*) Universal laws, and

(*b*) Relative laws.

***(a)* Universal Laws**

Some economic laws are universal in nature. They are axiomatic in character. The statements like 'saving is a function of income', 'human wants are unlimited' etc., are universally valid. Likewise, the law of demand and supply are applicable to all countries and at all times.

***(b)* Relative Laws**

But all economic laws are not like axioms and hence universally valid. For example, the laws which are applicable to a free enterprise economy cannot be applied to a communist economy. Laws which are applicable to developed countries cannot be applied to developing countries. Laws which hold good at certain times will not be effective during other times. The examples of such laws are the laws of tariff, banking, commerce etc.

As Hildebrand[13] rightly remarks

"A uniform code of economic legislation cannot be indifferently applied to all countries at all epochs of their development. An attempt must be made to adapt it to the varied conditions of time and place."

3. Economic Laws are Less Exact

The laws of physical and natural sciences are exact and definite. Physical sciences deal with lifeless matter which always behave in the same way; hence their laws are exact and certain. They are immutable.

But economic laws are not so precise as those of physics or chemistry. This is because the economist's laboratory is the economy where he has to rely in a great measure on logic or intuition which are subject to variations from economist to economist. As rightly pointed out by Prof. Schumpeter "Economic laws are much less stable than are the 'laws' of physical sciences... and they work out differently in different institutional conditions." Causes for the inexactness of Economic laws, are

1. Non-availability of the laboratory method,
2. Men are not similar in their tastes or purchasing power,
3. Differences in bias and ideologies exist among persons.

---

13. P.L. Mehta, *Essentials of Microeconomics,* Sultan chand & Sons, New Delhi, 1988, p. 21 (Quoted).

4. Economic Laws Resemble Biological Laws

Economics is more allied to biology than to physics. This is mainly because both economics and biology deal with life and not with matter. But in one respect economics is in a worse position than biology, in that the use of experimentation is almost impossible in economics.[14]

5. Economic Laws are Statements of Tendencies

According to Prof. Marshall, economic laws are statements of tendencies. They state that under certain conditions certain things will take place. Economic laws do not give any certainty that they 'must' happen. Economic laws are only probabilities and not certainties.

Physical and natural sciences are predictable. The law of gravitation tells us how different objects are attracted downwards by the force of gravity. Likewise, a given quantity of oxygen and hydrogen would give us water. But this is not the case in economics. As Marshall suggested "The laws of economics are to be compared with the laws of the tides, rather than with the simple and exact law of gravitation." The laws of tides explaines how there is a rise and fall of tides twice a day under the influence of the sun and the moon and how there are strong tides on new and fullmoon days. Thus the science of tides can predict when the tide will probably be the highest on any day at a particular place; but its operation may be obstructed by many unforeseen circumstances, such as heavy rainfall or strong winds. Similarly, in human activities also, there are many unforeseen circumstances as a result of which the expected course of action may not happen.

6. Economic Laws are More Exact than the Laws of Social Sciences

Samuelson considered economics as the queen of social sciences. Economic laws are more exact than the laws of other social sciences like ethics, sociology, politics etc. This is because, in economics, economic activities can be measured with the measuring rod of money.

7. Economic Laws and Government Laws

The laws of government must be obeyed. The government laws are enacted by the legislature and enforced by the executives. If the citizen violates these laws, he is punished. Economic laws are not commands. There is no question of obeying or disobeying the economic laws. Economic laws are indicative and not imperative. For example, a consumer who violates the law of demand cannot be punished. Government laws can be mended, amended or ended but economic laws are permanent.

---

14. K.P.M. Sundaram, *Op.cit.,* p. 12.

8. Economic Laws and Moral Laws

Moral law is a law of human conduct and states what we ought to do or what we ought not do. 'Respect your elders', speak the truth are some moral laws. If a person violates or breaks a moral law, he may not be punished by the government. But it may create hatred against him by the other members of the society. Economic laws do not dictate what is good or what is bad. They simply give information.

5. POSITIVE AND NORMATIVE APPROACHES

There are two kinds of sciences — a positive science and a normative science.

Economics has been recognised as a positive science from its inception. A positive science is concerned with "What is" and a normative science with 'What ought to be.' As R.T. Bye says, "positive science confines itself to an accurate description of a phenomenon, it explains what it is, how it works and what are its effects."

According to J.N. Keynes[15] a positive science may be defined as "a body of systematised knowledge concerning what is; a normative or regulative science is a body of a systematised knowledge relating to the object of what ought to be and concerned with the ideal as distinguished from the actual."

The statement "It is impossible to break up atoms" is a positive statement. This statement is positive because it can be refuted by empirical observations. The statement "Scientists ought not break up atoms" is a normative statement. This statement is normative because it involves value judgements. To put it in other words, the positive science seeks to understand, explain and predict. It cannot be used to determine whether an outcome is good or bad. In short, positive science describes while normative science evaluates."

According to Milton Friedman, positive economics deals as to how an economic problem is solved, while normative economics on the other hand deals with how economic problem should be solved.

POSITIVE SCIENCE: ENGLISH CLASSICAL VIEW

The English Classical School considered economics as a purely positive science. Positive economics studies the actual economic entities and relationships among them. In other words, it simply examines cause and

15. J.N. Keynes, *The Scope and Method of Political Economy* (4th ed.), Agustus M. Kelley, New York, 1965, pp. 34-35.

effect relationships. But it remains strictly neutral as regards ends. Robbins, Senior and Friedman are the main champions of positivism. In the words of Robbins "The role of the economist is more and more conceived as that of the expert who can say what consequences are likely to follow certain actions but who cannot judge as an economist the desirability of such an action." Therefore these economists argue that economists are not the competent persons to pass value judgements."

ARGUMENTS IN FAVOUR OF POSITIVE SCIENCE

The following arguments are advanced in favour of economics as a positive science.

1. It is Based on Logic

Logical enquiry is a rational enquiry. According to Robbins, economics is a positive science as it is based on logical reasoning. With the help of logic, the relationship between cause and effect can be ascertained. For example, positive economics examines the merits and demerits of direct and indirect taxes. But it cannot pronounce value judgements as to which one is the best.

2. It is Based on the Principles of Specialisation of Labour

The modern economy is based on division of labour. Each work is entrusted to a specialised group of workers. The production and sale of opium may be frivolous or pernicious to health and therefore morally unjustifiable, but economists have no right to give value judgements because this particular activity satisfies human wants and involves economic activity. According to Robbins, the role of economists should be confined only to economic activities, and other areas may be left either to politics or ethics.

3. Fear of Confusion

If 'positive economics' is combined with 'normative economics' ultimately it may lead to confusion. For example, if the economists explain the nature of income distribution and at the same time tell us what type of income distribution should be adopted it will complicate the problem.

4. More Uniformity

According to Robbins the study of what ought to be will cause perpetual disagreement and controversy in the subject. This may hamper the progress of the science.

5. More Neutrality

It is said that a man cannot serve for two masters. If an economist deals with both the questions, what is, and what ought to be, he cannot be neutral. If ethics is included in economics, the economist will be put in a very awkward position.

NORMATIVE SCIENCE: GERMAN HISTORICAL VIEW

Marshall, Hawtrey, Fraser, Wolf and Paul Streeten are the main advocates of Normative science.

According to these economists, economics is otherwise known as the science of human welfare and as such welfare can be maximised only when economics attains a normative character. Prof. Marshall rightly remarks "Economics will be barren and useless unless it studies the causes which promote material welfare."

The advocates of normative economics do accept the positive character of economics but they say an economist cannot ignore the value judgement of economics. As Prof. Pigou says "An economist's impulse is not the philosopher's impulse, knowledge for the sake of knowledge, but rather the physiologist's impulse, knowledge for the healing that knowledge may help to bring."[16]

Normative economics depends on 'value judgement.' As Prof. Hawtrey remarks "Economics cannot be dissociated from ethics."[17] Under normative economics disagreement among economists is inevitable.

According to Lipsey "Disagreements over normative statements cannot be settled merely by an appeal to facts."[18]

Marshall was a strong critic of the poverty of the masses and gave sanction to inter-personal comparison of utility on humanitarian grounds. As pointed out by Pigou, Marshall believed that "economic science is chiefly valuable neither as an intellectual gymnastic nor even as a means of winning truth for its own sake, but as a hand-maid of ethics and a servant of politics."[19] Thus economics is not only "light-giving", but also "fruit-bearing." Prof. Fraser also rightly remarks "An economist who is only an economist is like a poor pretty fish."

---

16. A.C. Pigou — *The Economics of Welfare,* Macmillan, London, 1952, pp. 4-5.
17. R.C. Hawtrey — *The Economic Problem,* Longmans, Green & Co. New York, 1960, p. 184.
18. Richard G, Lipsey — *An Introduction to Positive Economics,* ELBS, 1969, p. 5.
19. Pointed out by A.C. Pigou — *Memorials of Alfred Marshall,* Kelley & Millman, New York, 1956.

ARGUMENTS IN FAVOUR OF NORMATIVE SCIENCE

1. Man is not only Logical but also Sentimental

While explaining the positive nature of economics, Robbins gave much importance to logic and completely ignored the sentimental aspects of man. Economists like other human beings have heart, flesh and blood. They know the miseries and sufferings of mankind. They are in a better position to suggest policy recommendation.

2. Wrong Argument of 'Equilibrium is Equilibrium'

According to Robbins, "There is no penumbra of approbation around the theory of value. "Equilibrium is just equilibrium."

According to critics, it is wrong to assume that equilibrium is just equilibrium. In the words of Fraser "Economics is something more than a value theory or equilibrium. "There is no doubt about the statement that the existence of huge unemployment is the result of excess supply of labour over demand. But it is the responsibility of the economists to suggest ways and means to solve this social evil.

3. Necessity of Value Judgement

Economic policies in the real world affect some people favourably and others unfavourably. Moreover in modern times planning is inevitable for developing countries. For planning economists use value judgements on the desirability of various projects. The task of value judgement should not be left to the politicians and social reformers only.

4. A Means of Social Betterment

Various economists have developed policy measures to develop the economy. For example, Adam Smith stressed the necessity of *Laissez faire.* Malthus warned the excess of over population. J.S. Mill pleaded for the imposition of taxes on unearned incomes. Lord Keynes suggested policy measures to remove unemployment and so on.

BOTH A POSITIVE AND A NORMATIVE SCIENCE

According to Robbins "The gulf between positive economics and normative economics is so wide that no human ingenuity can bridge it."

But this argument is not correct. The economist can bridge this gulf considerably. The modern economists accept that economics is both a positive science and a normative science. They argue that optimum utilisation of the resources would not be the only aim but also the achievement of some desirable objectives such as more and just distribution of economic power and opportunities. Marshall and his followers firmly believed that economics and ethics are interwined. As Wootton rightly remarks. "It is very difficult to divert their discussions completely of all normative significance."

Thus economics is both a positive and a normative science.

QUESTIONS

1. State the advantages and disadvantages of inductive method in economic analysis.
2. What is the inductive method?
3. Show how deductive method is better than inductive method in economics.
4. Distinguish between positive and normative economics.
5. Distinguish between inductive and deductive method analysis.
6. Explain the difference between positive and normative economics.
7. Examine inductive and deductive methods of analysis used in economics.
8. What are the limitations of economics laws?
9. What are the characteristics of economic laws?
10. Economic laws are similar to the laws of tides — why?
11. Discuss the claims of Economics to be regarded as a science.
12. "There is no penumbra of approbation around the theory of value. Equilibrium is just an equilibrium." — (Robbins) — Discuss.

❖ ❖ ❖

3

MICRO ECONOMICS AND MACRO ECONOMICS

"We are not ready to suspect any person of being defective in selfishness."

— Adam Smith

Micro economics and Macro economics are the two main pillars of modern economic theory. Another name for micro economics is price theory. The corresponding name for macro economics is income theory.

Although the two branches of economics existed side by side for centuries, the division became transparent only during the 1930s. The terms "micro economics" and "macro economics" were first coined and used by a Norwegian economist Ragnar Frisch of Oslo university in 1933. The prefixes 'micro' and 'macro' have been derived from the Greek words — 'mikros' meaning small and 'makros' meaning large.

MEANING OF MICRO ECONOMICS

Micro economics owes its origin to the classical economists. It originated with Adam Smith and culminated with Alfred Marshall. Marshall's 'Principles of Economics' is an outstanding example of micro economic analysis. Other notable economists who made their distinctive contribution to micro economics are E.H. Chamberlin, Mrs. Joan Robinson and J.R. Hicks.

'Micro' means a small part. Thus micro economics is the study of the economic actions of individuals and small group of individuals. The small group of individuals may be households, firms and industries consisting of several firms. Micro economics explains how and why these units make decision.

Micro economics, which is the heir to the traditional "principles of economics," deals primarily with the determinations of relative prices and allocation of resources among competing ends under full employment conditions.[1]

In the words of Roy J. Ruffin[2] "Micro economics studies the economic decision making of firms and individuals in a market setting, it is the study of the economy in the small."

In everyday economic life, things are bought and sold, people decide where and how many hours to work. Business managers decide what to produce and how this production is to be organised. These activities result in transactions that take place in markets where buyers and sellers come together. People engaging in transactions are motivated to do the best they can for themselves with the limited resources at their disposal. Economic decision makers use marginal analysis to determine their best course of action.

Micro economics studies how business firms operate under different competitive conditions and how the combined actions of buyers and sellers determine prices in specific markets. Since micro economics splits up the entire economy into smaller parts for the purpose of intensive study, it is also known as "slicing method." The subject matter of micro economics fundamentally covers the following areas:

(*i*) Theory of 'value-product pricing' and 'Factor pricing' and

(*ii*) Theory of economic welfare.

IMPORTANCE OF MICRO ECONOMICS

Micro economics is the kingpin of economic analysis. It has both theoretical and practical validity. In the words of Keynes, "Micro economics is a necessary part of one's apparatus of thought."

1. To understand the working of the Economy

The basic merit of micro economics is that it is useful for understanding the operations of an economy. It tells us whether the particular economic unit functions optimally or not.

1. Robert Y. Ahw, *Micro Economics, Theory and Applications,* John Wiley & Sons, New York, 1976 p. 3.
2. *Principles of Economics,* Brown Higher Education, 4th edition, p. 5.

Micro economics has long been used to deal with environmental problems. It is used to explain marriage, divorce, fertility, crime, and even suicide patterns. Micro economic theories of voluntary agreements are used in legal judgements and to determine compensation for personal injuries. The expansion of micro economics into other social sciences has caused economics to be called the "imperialist" social science.[3]

2. Price Determination and Allocation of Resources

Micro economics is useful in the determination of price and allocation of resources among competing ends. A demand and supply model is frequently used in economic analysis. The model states that price is determined by the combined forces of demand and supply. Demand and supply determine the point of equilibrium. At the equilibrium price, the quantity demands equals the quantity supplied. If price falls then the quantity supplied will be less than the quantity demanded.

3. Helpful in Analysing and Framing an Economic Policy

Economic policies are framed with the help of micro economics. Price mechanism provides a helping hand in this respect. The effect of direct and indirect taxes on various sections of a society can be easily found by an analysis of micro economics. Micro analysis will also state whether the subsidy is justified or not in the interest of the farmers in the country.

4. Optimum Utilisation of Factors of Production

Micro economics helps the consumers to achieve a maximum level of satisfaction. Likewise it helps the producers to reap maximum profits.

In order to achieve maximum satisfaction, a rational consumer follows the principle of substitution. He substitutes one commodity for another till the ratio of marginal utilities equals the ratios of prices of the various commodities.

Mathematically, a consumer maximise satisfaction when

$$\frac{MU_A}{P_A} = \frac{MU_B}{P_B} = \ldots = \frac{MU_B}{P_n}$$

where MU is the marginal utility and P is the price. The subscripts A, B ... n indicate the respective commodities.

Likewise, a producer will maximise his profit when the ratio of marginal product of the factors of production equals the ratio of their prices.

---

3. Roy J. Ruffin, *op. cit.*, p.6.

$$\text{Thus} \quad \frac{MP_L}{P_L} = \frac{MP_C}{P_C} = \dots \frac{MP_n}{P_n}$$

Where MP is the marginal product and P is price. Subscripts L, C ... n indicate the respective factors of production.

5. Linear Programming

Linear programming as a tool in micro economics is useful to a producer in numerous ways. It helps him to know which factor supply is in abundance and which supply is scarce in quantity. This enables a producer to combine the factors of production in an optimum manner and increases his income. Linear programming also analyses the best possible production process among the alternative production processes to achieve maximum income.

6. Predictions

Economic laws are based on predictions. This does not mean that price theory will enable us to predict the future. Rather it will enable the possessor to make conditional predictions.

It shows that if something occurs, then a set of results will follow. For example the Law of demand states that if price falls, demand expands and vice versa.

7. Helpful to Managerial Economics

Micro economic principles help the business executive while making managerial decisions. By applying the tools of economic theory, the firm can estimate the demand and the cost of its product.

8. It is the Basis of Welfare Economics

Micro economics is the basis for welfare economics. The subject of welfare economics is the well-being of persons as consumers and producers. The aim of welfare economics is to maximise social welfare. This maximisation of social welfare is possible only under perfect competition. But under monopoly, oligopoly, or monopolistic competition there is excess capacity and misallocation of resources.

In the words of Prof. Lerner, "Micro economics helps in suggesting ways and means of eliminating wastages, in order to bring maximum social welfare."

9. In the Field of International Trade

In the field of international trade also micro economic tools are very helpful. The main areas in international trade which require the help of micro economics are devaluation, gains from international trade, balance of payments disequilibrium and the determination of the foreign exchange rate. The relative elasticities of demand for each other's product determines the gains from international trade. In case of devaluation, if the demand for the product of the exporting country is elastic, then it will gain from devaluation. The disequilibrium in the balance of payments occurs due to the gap between the demand for and the supply of foreign currency. The demand for and supply of foreign exchange determines the rate of exchange in a free market economy.

LIMITATIONS OF MICRO ECONOMICS

Professor R.A. Bilas points out that, while price theory is useful, one should not be blinded by the theory. It is simply a tool of analysis for the economist to go along with other tools such as history, statistical methods and mathematics.

1. Assumption of Full Employment

Micro economics is mainly based on the assumption of full employment in the economy. "To assume full employment", according to Keynes "is to assume out difficulties away." But in reality full employment is an exception rather than the rule. As such the validity of micro economic theories is doubtful.

2. Free Enterprise Economy

Micro economic models are based on the assumption of a free enterprise economy in which the market mechanism plays a vital role. It also assumes the policy of *laissez faire* on the part of the government. But after the Great Depression of the 1930s *laissez faire* policy has lost its importance. This makes the study unrealistic.

3. Complex Economic Activity

Another serious limitation is that it is concerned with the behaviour of individual elements of the economic organism and not with the organism as a whole. The major policies of the government such as monetary policy and fiscal policy produce considerable effect in the complex economic system. But these policies do not come within the purview of micro-economics, but are studied under macro-economics. As Boulding says "Description of a large and complex universe of facts like the economic system is impossible in terms of individual items." Thus the study of micro economics portrays an imprecise picture of the economy.

4. Inadequate and Misleading

Micro economics is not only inadequate but also misleading. It is not necessary that the principles which are applicable in the case of a particular household, firm or industry may also be equally applicable to the economy as a whole. There are situations when simple micro economic aggregation leads us to different conclusion than what is revealed by macro economics. This is not a paradox but a kind of confusion or fallacy called by logicians the "fallacy of composition."

A fallacy of compositions is the assumption that what is true for each part taken separately is also true for the whole or, in reverse, that what is true for the whole is true for each part considered separately.

A classic example of the fallacy of composition would be say that the best way to escape a fire in a crowded movie theatre is to run to the exit. If one person runs from his or her seat to the exit, that person will escape unharmed. If all people run from their seats to the nearest exit, few will escape unharmed.

MACRO ECONOMICS

Macro Economics is the child of the Great Depression of 1930s.

According to Prof. Brooman, "Macro economics is the obverse of micro economics." Macro economics is concerned with the economy as a whole or large segments of it.

Macro economics is interesting because it deals with important uses. But it is fascinating and challenging too, because it reduces complicated details of the economy to manageable essentials. In the language of a metaphor, macro economics is concerned with the study of an elephant as a whole, while micro economics studies the particular parts of it; while the former presents a bird's eye-view of the economy. The latter presents only a worm's eye-view confined to some specific parts of the economy. Modern macro economic theory is the outcome of the whole body of literature that has grown out of the income and employment theories initiated by Keynes in his General Theory.

Since, macro economics splits up, the economy into big lumps for the purpose of study, it is also called the Method of Lumping.

Definitions

It is the words of Samuel, A. Morley "Macro economics is the study of key economic magnitudes, such as prices, income and employment measured over the entire economy."[4]

4. Samuel A. Morley — *Macro Economics,* Holts-Saunders International editions, Japan, 1984, p. 3.

According to Prof. Rosalind Levacic[5]

"Macro economics is concerned with the determination of the broad aggregates, in the economy such as national product, employment, the price level and the balance of payments."

Richard G. Lipsey[6] lists of the problems of macro economics as follows:

(*i*) Problems relating to fluctuations in the level of employment of labour.

(*ii*) Problems relating to fluctuations in the average level of prices.

(*iii*) Problems relating to fluctuations in the general level of money wages.

(*iv*) Problems relating to the allocation of resources between the production of consumer goods and the production of capital goods.

(*v*) Problems relating to the rate of growth of production capacity.

(*vi*) Problems concerning the relation between international trade and the levels of employment.

DISTINCTION BETWEEN MICRO AND MACRO ECONOMICS

The main differences between micro economics and macro economics are the following:

1. Objectives

Micro economics deals primarily with the determination of relative prices and allocation of resources among competing ends under full employment conditions. Macro economics deals with the study of fluctuations in the levels of employment, aggregate income and the general price level, and of the ways of preventing such fluctuations. But as Prof. Fred R. Glahe[7] points out "whereas Micro Economics can be studied without any reference to macro economics, the converse is not true. Consequently, we must employ certain tools and theories of micro economics in our study of macro economics."

2. Differences in the Degree of Aggregation

The unit of study under micro economics is a part(s) a sector(s) etc. It deals with the behaviour of individual units, in particular consumers,

5. Rosalind Levacic, *Macro Economics,* EIBS, and Macmillan, London, 1983, p.1.
6. Richard G. Lipsey, *An Introduction to Positive Economics,* EIIS, London 1969, p. 542.
7. Fred R. Glahe, *Macro Economics — Theory and Policy,* 3rd edn., Harcourt Brace Jovanovich International edn. 1985, p. 2.

firms etc. The unit of study under macro economics is the whole economy. It deals with aggregates like savings and national income.

3. Differences in Subject Matter

The subject matter of micro economics in the determination of price, consumer's equilibrium, distribution and welfare etc. On the other hand, the subject matter of macro economics is full employment, trade cycle, economic growth, national income etc. In other words, macro economics is "bull dozer" economics which is designed to push large problems whereas micro economics is like a 'plough' which is designed to solve small problems.

4. Techniques of Analysis

Micro economics uses partial equilibrium analysis with certain assumptions. Macro economics on the other hand uses general equilibrium analysis to study the determination of aggregate price and output levels.

5. Assumptions

***(a)* National Output:**

In micro economics the total output of an economy is a variable. In macro economics the total output of the economy is given.

***(b)* Distribution of Output:**

In micro economics, the distribution of output, employment among the various sectors is given. In macro economics, the distribution of output, employment among different sector varies.

***(c)* Price Level:**

In micro economics, price level is a variable but relative prices are given. But in macro analysis, price level is given but relative prices are considered as variables.

In recent years, the boundary line between micro economics is becoming less and less distinct.

LIMITATIONS OF MACRO ECONOMICS

1. Firstly, there is the danger of excessive generalisation of individual experience to a system as a whole.
2. Secondly, Prof. Boulding points out that it is possible to add or substract apples or oranges but it is not possible to add or substract apples and sky scrappers. Therefore, it is not possible to derive aggregates of individual goods.

3. Thirdly, there are conceptual and practical difficulties in the formulation of macro economic variables.
4. Lastly, macro economics may not be helpful in analysing the sectoral behaviour of an economy.

INTEGRATION OF MICRO ECONOMICS AND MACRO ECONOMICS

In reality, a hard and fast line cannot be drawn between micro and macro economic analysis. Both approaches are necessary. In a sense, they are complementary and not competitive. The micro economic variables have an impact on macro variables and vice versa. Suppose we are interested in analysing the well-being of people. From the macro point of view, welfare will be maximised in a state of full employment of the available resources. From the micro point of view, economic welfare will be maximised in a state of optimum allocation of resources.

Some economists feel that even when we analyse macro economic problems, we should approach these problems from the micro economic point of view. These economists talk of micro foundations of macro economics.

This approach is called "the bottoms-up approach" as compared with the macro economic approach which is a tops-down approach."

A study of individual family budgets for example is very useful to understand the pattern of aggregate consumption of goods and services in the society. We can cite several other examples of micro foundations of macro economics. Thus the two branches of theory are mutually supportive. Most economic problems have both micro economic and macro economic dimensions.

We may conclude in the words of Samuelson[8]: "There is really no opposition between micro and macro economics. Both are absolutely vital. And you are only half educated if you understand the one while being ignorant of the other."

IMPORTANCE OF MACRO ECONOMICS

Economics today is very largely "The House that Keynes Built."

Macro economics has gained much popularity among the modern economists since the publication of Keynes' *General Theory of Employment, Interest and Money* in 1936. Prof. J.K. Mehta[9] feels that so long as men live

---

8. P.A. Samuelson, *Economics*, McGraw-Hill, New York 1983, p. 356.
9. J.K. Mehta, *Studies in Advanced Economic Theory,* S. Chand & Co., New Delhi, 1957.

in society, the economist cannot afford to neglect the study of its macro economy.

1. The study of macro economics is indispensable for understanding the functioning of an economy.
2. Macro economics is of great help in the formulation of economic policies.
3. It is helpful in the computation of national income and in the analysis of the problems relating to national income.
4. It is helpful in the study of growth and development of countries.
5. It is helpful in the study of the general level of taxation and public expenditure.
6. Macro economics enables us to study the nature and size of the material welfare of the nations.
7. Macro economics helps us to understand and analyse the performance of an economy.
8. It is also helpful in the development of economic theories.
9. Macro economic approach is of utmost importance to analyse and understand the effect of inflation and deflation.
10. Macro economics also explains macro economic paradoxes.

QUESTIONS

1. Distinguish between micro economics and macro economics.
2. Explain the merits and limitations of micro economics.
3. Examine the view that micro economics constitutes the most fundamental part of economic theory.
4. Explain the significance of macro economic analysis.
5. "The line between macro-economic and micro-economic theory cannot be precisely drawn. A true general theory of the economy would clearly embrace both." — (G. Ackley) discuss.
6. Explain the difference between 'Micro Economics' and 'Macro Economics.'
7. What is macro economics?
8. Examine the meaning and purpose of Micro Economic Analysis. Distinguish Micro Economic Analysis from Macro Economic Analysis.
9. Discuss the statement that Micro Economics is a study of interacting Units.
10. Indicate the importance of micro economics.

❖ ❖ ❖

4

ECONOMY — ITS VITAL PROCESSES AND BASIC PROBLEMS

"Name the greatest of all inventors — Accident."

— Mark Twain, 1875

WHAT IS AN ECONOMY?

The land on which we live is surrounded by factories, offices, farms, railways, bus stands, cinema houses, colleges, banks, hospitals, financial institutions etc. These units provide income and employment to the people. The income received from employment is utilised for the purchase of goods and services. Therefore an economy may be defined as a system which provides people with the means to work, and earn a living. The Indian Economy consists of all sources of production in agriculture, industry, transport, banking, communication etc. In the words of Sir John Hicks "An economy consists of nothing else but an immense cooperation of workers or producers to make things and do things which consumers want."[1]

THE VITAL FUNCTIONS OF AN ECONOMY

Feeding, digestion and growth are the vital processes of living beings. In the same way, every economy has its vital processes which are production,

1. J.R. Hicks, *The Social Frame Work — An Introduction to Economics,* 1971, pp. 17-18.

consumption and growth. Economies might differ in their organisation but all economies perform these three functions.

CENTRAL PROBLEMS OF AN ECONOMY

According to Robbins, human wants are unlimited, but the resources available to satisfy them are limited. If an economy has unlimited wants accompanied by unlimited resources to satisfy them, then there will be no economic problem. But, in reality, resources are limited and they have alternative uses. The various problems of choice faced by an economy may be classified into three broad categories (known as the Central problems of economy).

1. What to produce and in what quantities?
2. How to produce? and
3. For whom to produce?

These three problems are made well-known by Prof. Samuelson's phrase "What, how and for whom."

Production Possibility Curve

Prof. Samuelson in his book 'Economics' has introduced an ingenious device called 'production possibility curve.' The set of problems facing every economic system can be clearly analysed with this tool.

Human material wants are virtually unlimited or insatiable. But economic resources are scarce or limited. Therefore every society is faced with the basic problem of choosing and allocating its scarce resources among alternative uses.

Production possibility curve shows the menu of choice along which a society can choose to substitute one good for another assuming a given state of technology and given total resources.[2]

The production possibility curve illustrates three concepts: scarcity, choice and opportunity cost.

Modern economy produces thousands of products, and therefore choices before us are complex. In order to reduce the problem to its simplest form we consider the economy in which two goods 'butter' and 'guns' are produced with the available resources and technology.

Production possibility curve is based on the following Assumptions:

1. Only two goods x (butter) and y (guns) are produced in the economy.

---

2. P.L. Mehta — *Essentials of Micro Economics,* 1988, p. 28.

2. There is full employment of resources.
3. The resources are fixed in quantity. But they can be re-allocated from the production of one commodity to that of another.
4. The state of technology is given and constant.
5. The time period is short.

Let us illustrate the production possibility curve with the help of a production possibility schedule.

Table 4.1
Alternative Production Possibilities

Possibilities	*Butter (million quintals)*	*Guns (thousands)*
A	0	15
B	1	14
C	2	12
D	3	9
E	4	5
F	5	0

A schedule of a number of possibilities is given in the table 'A' being the extreme case where all guns and no butter is produced, and F being the opposite extreme where all resources go into the production of butter. In between these two extreme possibilities, some other possibilities exist. In between — at E, D, C and B — butter is being given up increasingly in return for more guns.

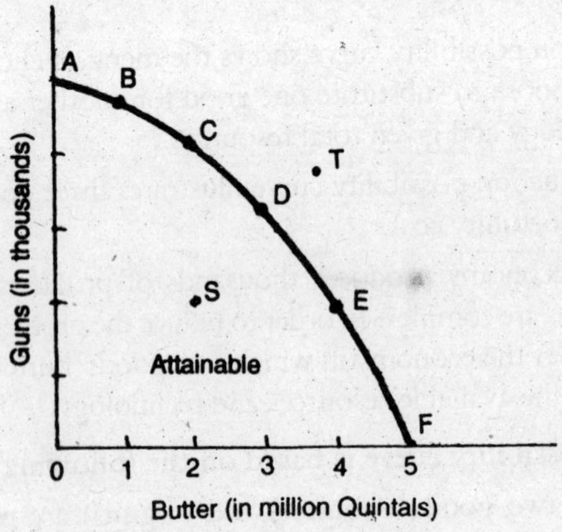

Fig. 4.1

In Fig. 4.1 X-axis represents butter and Y-axis represents guns we represent can the production possibility curve as shown in Fig. 4.1. Production possibility curve is also known as the transformation curve and production possibility frontier. The boundary line ABDCEF separates the areas of choice that are attainable in the period in question from those that are unattainable. The economy cannot be outside the curve and the economy being inside the curve would reflect waste, inefficiency and unemployment.

Since the total productive capacity is utilised, the problem is to choose the pattern of utilisation among the various alternatives available. Thus the production of butter requires the sacrifice of some guns and vice versa. The production possibility curve falls from left to right because when more resources are being utilised to get more of butter, some of the guns must be sacrificed.

In the words of Prof. Samuelson[3]: "A full employment economy must always, in producing one good, be giving up something of another. Substitution is the law of life in a full employment economy. The production possibility frontier depicts society's menu of choices." Based on the above curve the following observations may be made.

Table 4.2

Combination	*Position*	*Test of Efficiency*
B C D & F	On the production possibility curve	Technologically efficient.
S	Inside the production possibility curve	Technologically inefficient.
T	Outside the production possibility curve	Technologically infeasible.

Uses of Production Possibility Curve

The production possibility curve is used for many analytical purposes. Some of them are given below.

1. The Notion of Scarcity

The production possibility frontier provides a rigorous definition of scarcity. The resources available to mankind both human and non-human are scarce in relation to wants, and the solution lies in economising these resources.

According to Prof. Samuelson, "Economic scarcity refers to the basic fact of life that there exists only a finite amount of human and non-human resources, which the best technical knowledge, is capable of using to produce

3. *Economics*, McGraw Hill, 1983, p. 19.

only limited maximum amounts of each economic good as shown by the P P Frontier. And thus far, nowhere on the globe is the supply of goods so plentiful or are tastes so limited that the average family can have more than enough of everything it might fancy."[4]

2. The Problem of Choice

The concept of production possibility curve is useful to solve the problem of choice which is vital in economics. The problem of choice may be allocation of resources among various goods (guns or butter in our example) or consumption for the present generation (food, cloth etc.) and for the future generation (machines, dams, bridges etc.).

3. Solution of Central Problems

The production possibility frontier also helps us to make clear the three basic problems of economic life: What, How and For Whom.

SOME BASIC ECONOMIC PROCESSES AND PRODUCTION POSSIBILITY CURVE

1. Economic Development

The production possibility curve can be used to show the impact of economic development. To explain this let us relax the assumption of constant technology, and of the short period.

Before economic development, the nation is poor because of technological backwardness. Its productive capacity is also limited. Moreover it must devote all its resources to food, enjoying only a few comforts.

Suppose there is an improvement in technology. Assume that a new variety of seed is discovered which substantially increases the output. Then, it will be possible to produce more. The production possibility curve will shift out to the new curve (ppc_1) shown in Fig. 4.2(*b*). Now the nation goes from A to B (see Fig. 4.2 (*b*)), expanding its food consumption very little compared with its increased consumption of non-necessities.

4. Samuelson, *Ibid.*, p. 20.

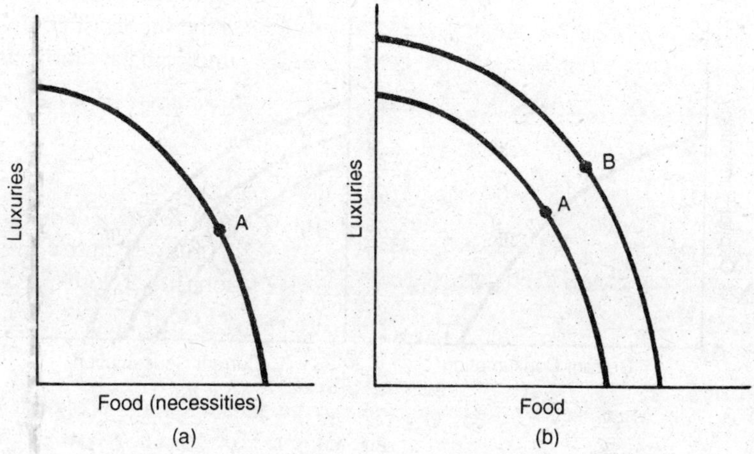

Fig. 4.2

2. Capital Formation

Every economy may face a dilemma whether to produce consumer goods for the present or to produce capital goods in order to produce more in future. If an economy invests some of its resources in the form of machinery, dams etc. it makes provision for capital formation. The impact of capital formation on the economy may be analysed with the production possibility curve.

Let us assume three nations I, II and III with same resource base and technology. But these nations have different investment patterns. Nation I diverts its resources for current consumption only. Nation II and III do invest, but the III nation invest more than the II nation. The impact of their investment patterns is shown in Fig. 4.3(*b*).

Fig. 4.3(*b*) shows that the production possibility curve for nation I has not moved at all. Nation III has shifted the production possibility curve to the maximum followed by nation II. But in respect of current consumption and capital formation nation III is better placed than nation II.

3. Unemployment

Let us assume that there is unemployment of resources in the economy. In this case there is idle labour force available in the economy. Such a position of large-scale unemployment is shown at point U. If the economy is properly managed, people can be put back to work. The movement to D will increase consumer goods without any decrease in capital goods. The

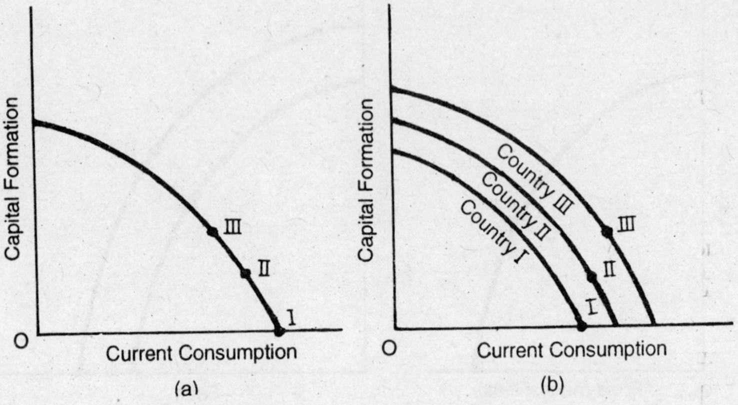

Fig. 4.3

movement to C will increase the supply of capital goods without any decrease in consumer goods. By moving to point D, supply of both the goods could be increased. To put it in simple terms, every point on the production possibility curve is superior to U.

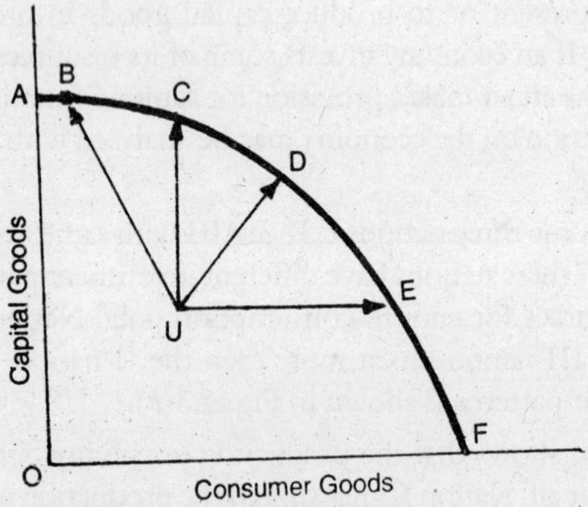

Fig. 4.4

QUESTIONS

1. What is an economy? What are the vital processes of an economy?
2. Discuss the central problem of an economy?
3. Write a note on production possibility curve.

❖ ❖ ❖

5

THE CONCEPT OF EQUILIBRIUM

"Equilibrium denotes in economics absence of change in movement, while in the physical sciences it denotes absence of movement itself."

—J.K. Mehta

MEANING

The concept of equilibrium is so important in economic theory that some economists call Economics as Equilibrium Economics.

The term 'equilibrium' has been derived from the Latin words, "acqui" meaning 'equal' and "libra" meaning 'balance.' Thus equilibrium means 'equal balance.' The term has been borrowed from physics. In physics, it means a state of balance. When two opposing forces balance each other on a particular object, then the object is said to be in a state of equilibrium. In economics, equilibrium implies a position of rest characterised by the absence of change.

In the words of Stigler[1]: "An equilibrium is a position from which there is no net tendency to move, we say net tendency, to emphasize the fact that is not necessarily a state of sudden inertia but may instead represent the cancellation of power forces."

According to Scitovsky[2]: "A market or an economy or any other group of persons and firms is in equilibrium when none of its members feels impelled to change his behaviour."

1. G.J. Stigler. The Theory of Price, Macmillan, London, 1966, p. 28.
2. Tiber Scitovsky, *Welfare and Competition*, Unwin University Books, London, 1971, p. 231.

The following diagram will make the concept clear.

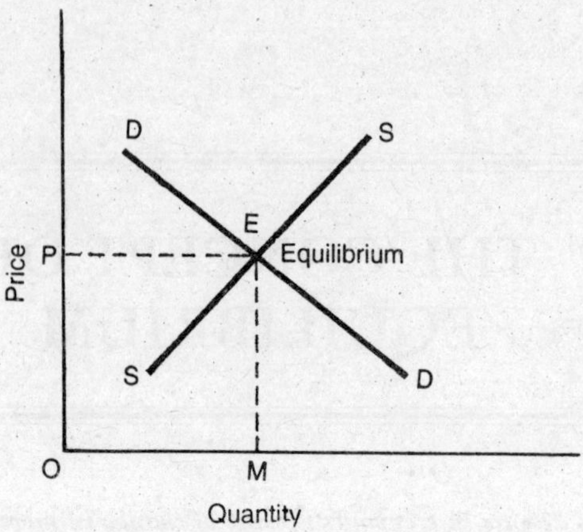

Fig. 5.1

In Fig. 5.1 DD is the demand curve and SS is the supply curve. The intersection of the curves determine the equilibrium values of price and quantity exchanged. In equilibrium the market is cleared; suppliers can sell the quantity that they want to sell and buyers can buy the quantity that they want to buy.

CLASSIFICATION OF EQUILIBRIUM

In economic analysis, equilibrium can be classified as follows:

1. Stable, Unstable and Neutral Equilibrium

Prof. Schumpeter[3] illustrates the three equilibrium positions with an analogy of a ball placed in three different positions. "A ball that rests at the bottom of a bowl illustrates the first case; a ball that rests on a billiard table, the second case, and a ball that is perched on the top of an inverted bowl, the third case."

In Fig. 5.2(*a*) the ball is resting at the bottom of the bowl. It is in stable equilibrium. If disturbed, the ball will again come back to its original position.

---

3. J.A. Schumpeter — *History of Economic Analysis*, George Allen & Unwin, London, 1954, p. 971.

In Fig. 5.2(*b*) the ball rests on a billiard table. It is in neutral equilibrium. If disturbed the ball will find its equilibrium at some other new place.

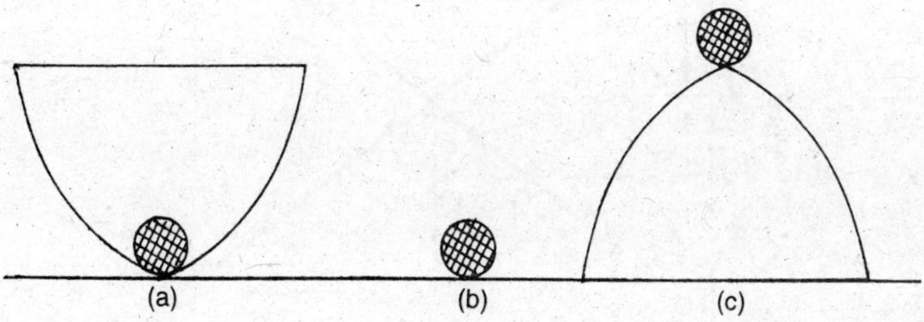

Fig. 5.2

In Fig. 5.3(*c*) the ball is balanced at the top of the inverted bowl. It is in unstable equilibrium. If disturbed, the ball will roll down either side of the bowl and will never return to its original position.

Prof. A.C. Pigou[4] has defined the three kinds of equilibrium in the following words: "A system is in stable equilibrium position if, when any small disturbance takes place, forces come into play to re-establish the initial position; it is in neutral equilibrium if, when such a disturbance takes place, no re-establishing forces but also on further disturbing forces are evoked so that the system remains at rest in the position to which it has moved; and is in unstable equilibrium if the small disturbance calls out further disturbing forces which act in a cumulative manner to drive the system from its initial position." He also gives proper analogies to illustrate the three kinds of equilibrium as "A ship with a heavy keel is in stable equilibrium, an egg lying on its side is in neutral equilibrium, an egg poised on one of its ends is in unstable equilibrium."

Similarly the three cases of equilibrium can also be analysed with the tools of demand and supply as used in economic analysis.

---

4. A.C. Pigou, *The Economics of Welfare*, Macmillan, London, 1952, pp. 794-795.

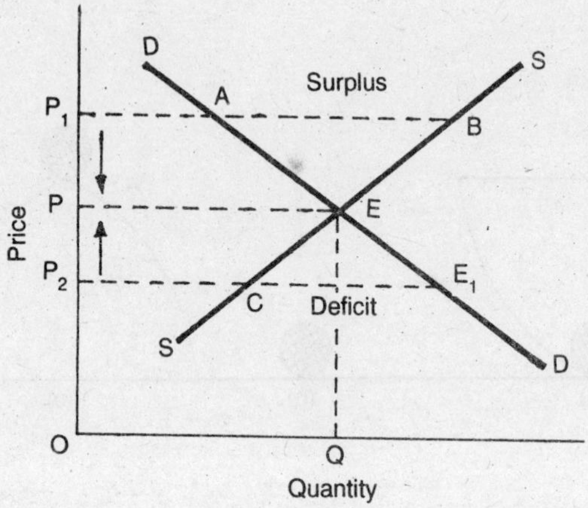

Fig. 5.3

In Fig. 5.3 the demand curve DD is negatively sloped and the supply curve SS is positively sloped. The equilibrium at point E determines the price OP and the quantity OQ where the supply and demand are in balance. It is the case of stable equilibrium. Suppose the market price is OP_1. At this price, the quantity supplied is P_1B, while the quantity demanded is only P_1A. There is a surplus quantity in the market to the extent of AB. This excess of supply over demand generates a downward pressure on price, indicated in the diagram by the arrow pointing downward from the horizontal line representing the price OP_1.

At prices below the equilibrium level, the quantity demanded exceeds the quantity supplied. At the price OP_2, there is a shortage to the extent of CE_1. This excess demand over supply generates upward pressure on price indicated in the diagram by the arrow pointing upward from the horizontal line representing the price OP_2. Clearly one or the other process will always be at work so long as price is not at equilibrium.

Unstable Equilibrium

If the demand curve is normal and the supply curve is a negatively sloping curve, unstable equilibrium occurs. This negatively sloping supply curve is rare and is caused by a decreasing cost of increasing production due to various internal and external economies enjoyed by the firm.

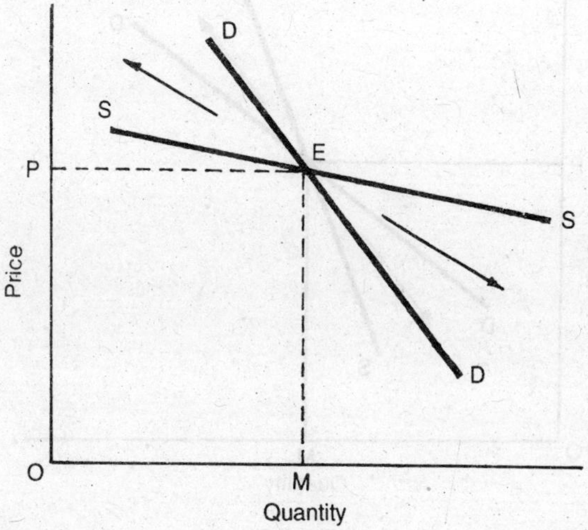

Fig. 5.4

In Fig. 5.4 the equilibrium point is E. OP is the price and OM is the quantity. An increases in price above OP will result in an excess of demand over supply. This shortage causes the price to rise higher and higher, that is away from equilibrium never returning to its original position. Likewise any decrease in price below OP will result in an excess of supply over demand. This excess supply will push the price further downwards, resulting in the movement all the more away from equilibrium. Thus E represents an unstable equilibrium position.

Another limiting case of unstable equilibrium is found when the supply curve is normal and the demand curve is positively sloping. This type of demand curve is true in the case of 'Giffen goods.' In the case of giffen goods demand increases as the price of the good increases and vice-versa.

In Fig. 5.5 the exceptional demand curve intersects the normal supply curve at E which determines the equilibrium price at OP and the equilibrium quantity at OM. An increase in price above OP will result in an excess of demand over supply. This excess of demand over supply will cause a further increase in the price. A decrease in price below OP will result in excess of supply over demand. This excess of supply over demand will cause a further fall in the price. Thus E in the above diagram is in unstable equilibrium as there is no likelihood of the original equilibrium position being ever restored.

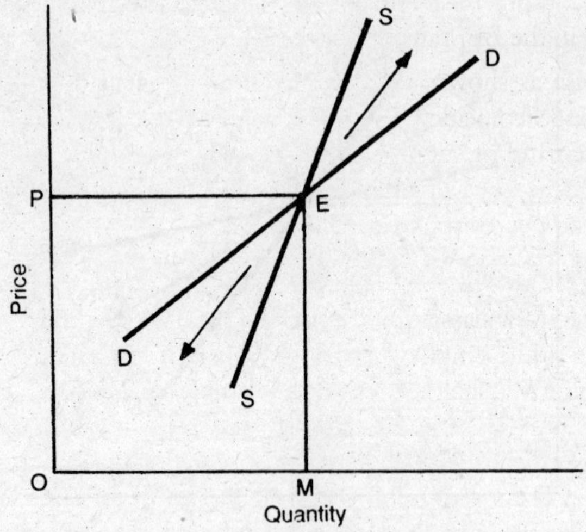

Fig. 5.5

Neutral Equilibrium

The position of neutral equilibrium arises when demand and supply curves coincide with a range of prices or a range of quantities. The Neutral equilibrium is illustrated in the following diagram.

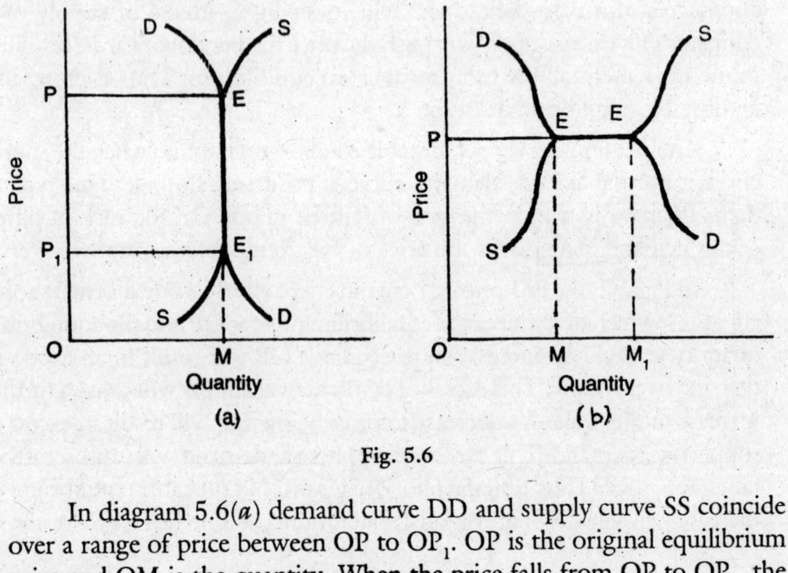

Fig. 5.6

In diagram 5.6(*a*) demand curve DD and supply curve SS coincide over a range of price between OP to OP_1. OP is the original equilibrium price and OM is the quantity. When the price falls from OP to OP_1, the equilibrium output OM remains unchanged. The market is in neutral equilibrium in the EE_1 range of price.

Likewise as shown in diagram 5.6(*b*) the demand curve DD and supply curve SS coincide with the range of output from OM to OM_1. A change in demand or supply within this range of output has no effect to alter the price level. The equilibrium price is thus neutral to changes in demand or supply from OM to OM_1.

Short-Run and Long-Run Equilibrium

The credit for classifying the period into short run and long-run goes to Marshall. While emphasising the importance of time element in the theory of value Marshall differentiated these concepts. The short-run is a period in which the number and plant size of the firms are fixed. In the short-run production can be altered only by changing the amounts of variable factors. In the short-run supply is adjusted to the changes in demand with the existing plant because the time is too short to change the scale of the plant. In the short-run demand plays a relatively major role in the determination of price, and such an equilibrium is known as short-run equilibrium.

In the long-run, the number of firms as well as the size of the plant is subject to variation. Since the size of the plant is variable, the existing firms making excess profits seek to expand their capacity, while the excess profits attract new firms into the industry. Entry of new firms, as well as the

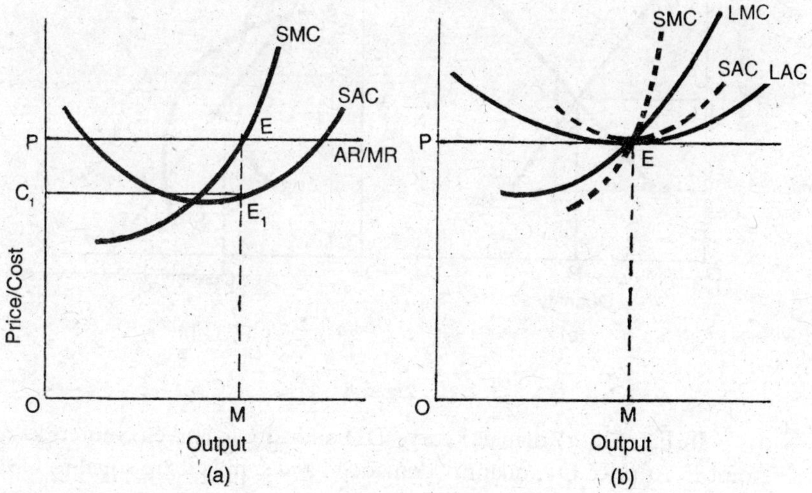

Fig. 5.7

adjustment of the productive capacity by the existing firms, will lead to the long-run equilibrium in which all the firms will be earning just the normal profits.

The short-run and long-run equilibrium of a firm under perfect competition is explained as follows:

Fig. 5.7(*a*) depicts the short-run equilibrium. Equilibrium is attained at the point where MC=MR. The firm is making abnormal profits as shown by the area PP_1E_1E. It is at this level of profit, that the firm has no tendency to deviate from it.

Fig. 5.7(*b*) indicates the case of long-run equilibrium. Equilibrium is established at the point E, where LMC =LMR=AR=AC. It is important to note here that all the firms are earning only normal profits.

Unique and Multiple Equilibrium

According to Prof. Stigler[5], "equilibrium may be unique or multiple. A position of unique equilibrium arises if there is a single set of prices and quantities which fulfil the conditions of equilibrium. Multiple positions of equilibrium exist when several different sets of prices and quantities will meet the equilibrium conditions."[5]

The following diagram clearly illustrates the concept.

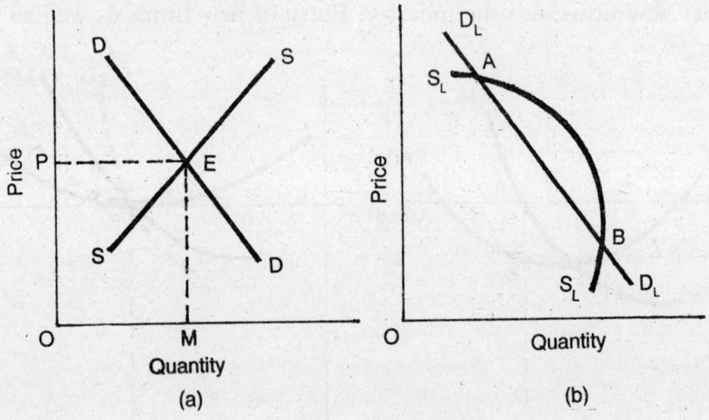

Fig. 5.8

In Fig. 5.8(*a*) demand curve DD and supply curve SS intersect at point E. At price OP, quantity demanded and supplied are equal to OM.

5. The Theory of Price, *op. cit.*, p. 27.

This equilibrium position satisfies one single price and one equilibrium quantity. This is the case of unique equilibrium.

In Fig 5.8(*b*) D_L is the demand curve for labour and S_L is the supply curve for labour. The supply curve of labour is backward bending based on the assumption that when income increases, beyond a certain level the workers will prefer more of leisure and less of work. The supply curve S_L intersects the demand curve D_L at two equilibrium points B and A. The multiple equilibrium position is extremely 'rare' and is purely a formal concept, while in the real world, the single equilibrium concept is common.

Static and Dynamic Equilibrium

According to Prof. Mehta,[6] "Static equilibrium is that equilibrium which maintains itself outside the period of time under consideration." Static equilibrium is related to the equilibrium of a static economy. In such a society there is no change in prices, output, incomes, tastes, technology etc.

It is a state of bliss which every firm, industry or factor wants to attain and once reached would not like to leave. A consumer is in equilibrium when he gets maximum satisfaction on the principle of equi-marginal utility. Any other allocation of his income other than this particular pattern will yield only lesser satisfaction. An industry is in equilibrium when all the existing firms are earning only normal profit. In such a situation there is no incentive for firms to leave or enter the industry. A factor unit is in equilibrium when it is employed in its highest paid occupation, so that its income is optimum. Prof. Boulding offers a mechanical analogy of a static equilibrium in the form of a ball rolling at a constant speed or better still of a forest in equilibrium where trees sprout, grow or die but where the composition of the forest, as a whole remains unchanged. Prof. Pigou also gives a similar analogy as follows: "Just as the drops of water that form a stream are always changing but its form remains the same, so do in a static state the factors change but they are not of any consequence."

Dynamic equilibrium is possible in a changing society where prices output, income, tastes, population, capital, technology etc. are changing. Over a period of time, there is a possibility of disequilibrium. The participants in a market are buyers and sellers. If some market participants disagree with the existing equilibrium position, their efforts will alter the existing equilibrium position and the state of disequilibrium sets in. Those participants, who are outside the orbit of equilibrium in their attempt to reestablish the equilibrium position throw others into disequilibrium. Thus

6. J.K. Mehta, *Advanced Economic Theory,* Macmillan Company of India Limited, 1971, p. 86.

a chain of reaction sets in, which ultimately brings the decision of all the participants in harmony and a new equilibrium position is established. According to Prof. J.K. Mehta 'when after a fixed period, the equilibrium state is disturbed, it is called dynamic equilibrium.'

Partial and General Equilibrium

Partial equilibrium is the counter part of micro economic analysis. Partial equilibrium analysis was popularised by the English economist, Marshall. According to Prof. Stigler: "A partial equilibrium is one which is based on only a restricted range of data; a standard example is the price of a single product, the prices of all other products being held fixed during the analysis." Partial equilibrium analysis studies the relationship between one or two variables, keeping all others constant.

For example, the law of demand states that other things remaining the same, when the price falls, demand expands. Here it is assumed that other determinants of demand except price remain constant. Likewise when we analyse the attainment of equilibrium of a firm, it is explicitly assumed that all other firms are in equilibrium.

General Equilibrium

General equilibrium was first systematically studied by the French mathematical economist, Leon Walras (1834-1910). General equilibrium analysis is concerned with the economy as an inter dependent of various economic variables. Prof. K.E. Boulding gives the example of three balls lying in a bowl. The equilibrium position of any one ball depends not only on the shape of the bowl and on its own size but also on the positions of the other two balls. General equilibrium analysis deals with the equilibrium of the whole organism in the economy — consumers, producers, resource owners, firms and industries. General equilibrium is achieved when all the organisms in the economy are in equilibrium.

General equilibrium analysis is highly mathematical in nature. Even simple examples require a good understanding of economic theories and a good familiarity with analytical tools.[7]

QUESTIONS

1. What is meant by equilibrium analysis? What is its importance in economic analysis?
2. Distinguish between "static equilibrium" and "dynamic equilibrium."
3. Define equilibrium. What are the various types of equilibrium?

---

7. D.N. Dwivedi — *Principles of Economics,* 1985, p. 61.

4. Distinguish between partial equilibrium and general equilibrium.
5. Write short notes on the following:
   1. Short-run and Long-run equilibrium.
   2. Stable, unstable and neutral equilibrium.
   3. Unique and multiple equilibrium.

❖ ❖ ❖

6

ECONOMIC STATICS AND DYNAMICS

"Each successive addition to the population brings a consumer and a producer."
— Henry Charles Carey 1840

The terms 'statics' and 'dynamics' are derived from the Greek words Statikos meaning 'Causing to stand' and Dynamikos meaning 'Causing to change.' Originally these concepts were used in physical sciences. August Comte (1798-1857) a theoretical physicist used these concepts in social sciences. The usage has been popularised by J.S. Mill in Economics. The credit for making a scientific distinction between the two terms goes to Prof. Ragner Frisch.

ECONOMIC STATICS

The term economic statics has different meanings in mechanics and economics. In mechanics it implies a state of rest in which there is no motion. A book lying on the table is a good example for this. In economics it implies a state in which the economic activity is continuous, regular, definite and smooth. In such a state all the economic activities go on without any fluctuations or inexactitude.

Static analysis is concerned solely with the equilibrium values of the variable of interest in the specified time period.[1] According to Prof. Pigou, "Just as the drops of water that form a stream are always changing but its

1. A. Asimakopulos, *Micro Economics*, first edn., Oxford University Press, New Delhi, 1979, p. 80.

form remains the same so do, in a static state, the factors change but they are not of any consequence." Clark maintains that, five kinds of generic changes are conspicuous by their absence in a static state. The size of population, the supply of capital, the methods of production, the forms of business organisation and the wants of the people remain constant, but the economy, continues to work at a steady pace. According to Schumpeter, it is "an economic process that merely reproduces itself." Thus economic statics refers to that type of economic analysis in which the time element does not enter as a variable. All variables in this type of economic analysis relate to the same period of time. The theory of product pricing is a good example for static analysis.

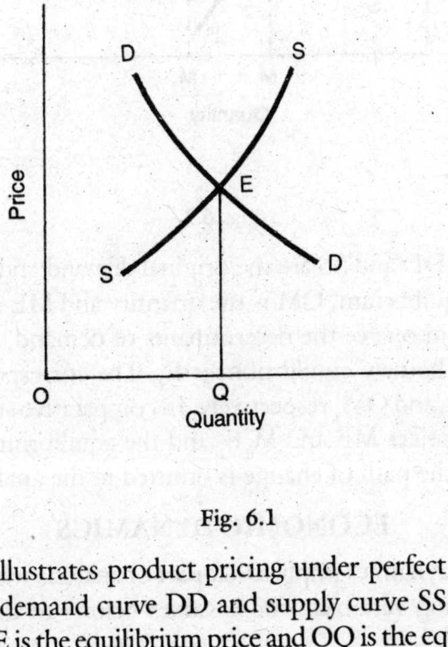

Fig. 6.1

Fig. 6.1 illustrates product pricing under perfect competition. The intersection of demand curve DD and supply curve SS gives the point of equilibrium. QE is the equilibrium price and OQ is the equilibrium quantity. This is a static analysis of price determination because all the relevant variables involved such as price, quantity demanded and supplied relate to the same point of time. Joan Robinson's Imperfect competition and Chamberlin's Monopolistic competition are important contributions in economic statics.

COMPARATIVE STATICS

Comparative statics is a method of comparing two equilibrium positions. Under comparative statics we analyse and compare the original equilibrium position and the new equilibrium position. The path of adjustment from one equilibrium to another equilibrium is not analysed.

This is just like comparing two 'still' pictures.

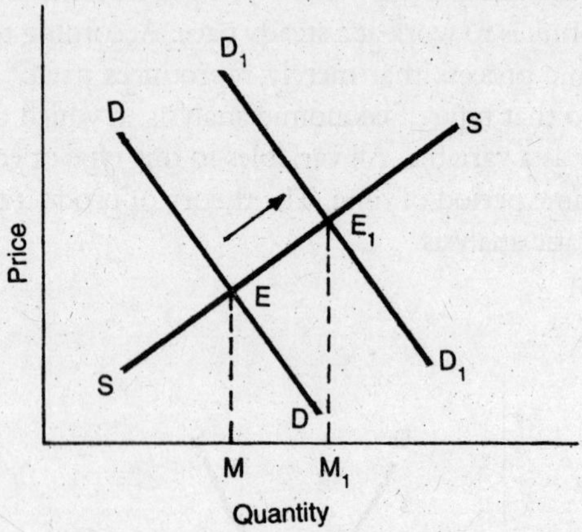

Fig. 6.2

In Fig. 6.2 DD and SS are the original demand and supply curves. E is the point of equilibrium, OM is the quantity and ME is the price. Now due to a change in one of the determinants of demand, the new demand curve is D_1D_1. The new equilibrium is E_1. The corresponding price and quantity are M_1E_1 and OM_1 respectively. In comparative statics we compare the equilibrium prices ME and M_1E_1 and the equilibrium quantities OM and OM_1. Thus the path of change is omitted in the analysis.

ECONOMIC DYNAMICS

Economic dynamics implies that part of analysis which considers the relationship among variables whose values belong to different points of time.

In the words of Prof. Hicks, economic dynamics refers to "those parts where every quantity must be dated."[2] In economic dynamics the time element enters explicitly in one form or the other. Some variables, of the relationships of this type of economic analysis will belong to different

2. J.R. Hicks, *Value and Capital,* The English Language Book Society, Oxford, 1979, p. 115.
3. R.R. Barthwal, *Micro Economic Analysis,* First edn., Wiley Eastern Limited, New Delhi, 1991, p.12.

time periods either with a 'lag' or with a 'lead' time.[3] For example, current supply of a commodity in the market may be related to its price in the previous year (or period) and when we use such a supply relationship together with the demand for the commodity, to determine its current price, then it will be dynamic economic analysis.

The study of economic dynamics is more realistic because it avoids the assumptions such as constant tastes, preferences, fashions, technology over time, perfect mobility of factors etc. Professor J. Mc Kenna has aptly remarked "comparative statics gives only a partial glimpse of the movement, for we have only two still pictures to compare, whereas true dynamics would give us a movie." Although dynamic analysis is informative, comprehensive and realistic its application is limited to growth theories, investment planning etc. A major part of economic theories are in the grip of economic statics.

Comparison between Economic Statics and Dynamics

1. Time Element

In static economics all economic variables relate to the same point of time. But in economic dynamics all variables are a function of time.

2. Process of Change

Static analysis is a transition from one equilibrium position to the other. It is not interested in the process of equilibrium. Dynamic analysis on the other hand explain the path of equilibrium. In terms of analogy while statics is a 'still' picture, dynamics is a movie.

3. Reality

Static analysis is based on the *ceteris paribus* assumption, some of which are highly unrealistic. Dynamic analysis on the other hand deals with economic variables susceptible to changes. Therefore its approach is nearer to reality.

4. Methodology

Economic statics is based on deductive analysis while Economic dynamics is based on inductive analysis.

QUESTIONS

1. Differentiate 'statics' from 'dynamics' in Economics. Which of these do you consider to be more general and fundamental?
2. Distinguish between Economic Statics and Dynamics.
3. Explain the terms 'static' and 'dynamic' in Economic analysis.
4. Explain economic statics, comparative statics and economic dynamics.
5. What is static economic analysis?

❖ ❖ ❖

PART TWO

THEORY OF CONSUMER BEHAVIOUR

7

LAW OF DEMAND

"Producers dance to the Consumer's tune."

— *Wonnacott*

INTRODUCTION

Meaning of Demand

Demand is essential for the Creation, Survival and Profitability of a firm. It is essential to distinguish between demand and desire. A beggar's demand for a Maruti car is only a desire and does not constitute a demand. A miser may possess enough money but he may not be willing to spend it. In this case also desire will not be called demand. Therefore demand is not merely a wish or desire but an effective demand, that is, desire backed by purchasing power, and willingness to buy.

In the words of Prof. J. Harvey,[1] "Demand in economics is the desire to possess something and the willingness and the ability to pay a certain price in order to possess it."

According to Stonier and Hague, "Demand in economics means demand backed up by enough money to pay for the good demanded."[2]

Demand is always at a price. As Prof. Benham[3] points out "The demand for a thing at a given price is the amount of it which will be bought per unit of time at that price."

1. *Modern Economics,* 3rd Edn., The Macmillan Press Ltd., London 1983, p. 58.
2. *A Textbook of Economic Theory,* ELBS, London, 1988, p.18.
3. *Economics,* 8th Edn., ELBS, London, 1967, p. 172.

Demand has the following Four Characteristics

1. Price: Demand is always related to price. It is meaningless to say that the demand for refrigerator in the market is one thousand. The person must state the price at which the consumer is prepared to purchase the said quantity of the commodity.

2. Time: Demand always means demand per unit of time, per day, per week, per month or per year.

3. Market: Demand is always related to the market. Market here simply refers to the contact between buyers and sellers. There is no need for a definite geographical area.

4. Amount: Demand is always a specific quantity which a consumer is willing to purchase. It is not an approximation, but is to be expressed numerically.

DEMAND SCHEDULE

A demand schedule is a list of prices and corresponding quantities. Since the demand schedule obeys the law of demand, price and quantity demanded vary inversely. The following is the hypothetical demand schedule of an individual.

Table 7.1

Price (P_x)	*Quantity demanded* (Q_x)
5	1
4	2
3	3
2	4
1	5

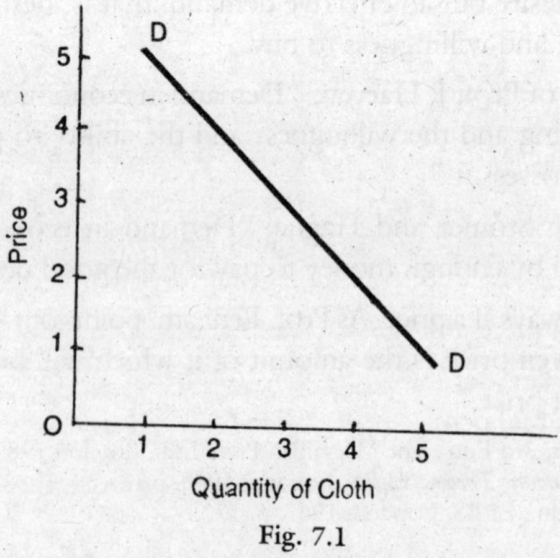

Fig. 7.1

The table given above can be converted into a demand curve. The vertical axis represents price and the horizontal axis measures quantity. Actually, the practice of measuring quantity on the horizontal axis and price on the vertical axis is a convention established by Prof. Alfred Marshall.

When the price is Rs. 3 the corresponding quantity of cloth demanded is 3 units. For every price, there will be a corresponding quantity. We can get a curve, by joining all the points. The curve is known as the 'demand curve'. This demand curve shows the relationship between the two variables, price and quantity. The demand curve is always so called, even when it happens to be a straight line.

Market Demand Curve

The market demand curve is the sum of the demand curves of all the consumers. It is to be noted that the demand curve for all consumers shows different slopes, different positions and different shapes. This is because of the fact that at certain prices some consumers will purchase very little, and some others a lot. As price increases or decreases, some consumers will vary their purchases very little and some will vary their purchases significantly.

For the sake of simplicity let us assume that there are two consumers in the market. Their demands and the market demand are shown in Table (7.2).

Table 7.2
Demand Curves for two Consumers and the Market Demand Curve

Price of x (in Rs.)	*Consumer I*	*Consumer II*	*Market Demand of x*
5	1	—	1
4	2	1	3
3	3	2	5
2	4	3	7
1	5	4	9

The above table shows that when the price is Rs. 5 the quantity demanded is 1 unit. When the price is Rs. 4 the quantity demanded is 3 units. Likewise when the price is Rs. 1 the quantity demanded will be 9 units. Thus the market demand schedule denotes an inverse functional relationship between price and quantity.

Thus the market demand curve is obtained by the horizontal summation of individual demand curves $D = D_1 + D_2$.

4. *Price Theory — A Provisional Test,* Kalyani Publishers, New Delhi, 1988, p. 15.

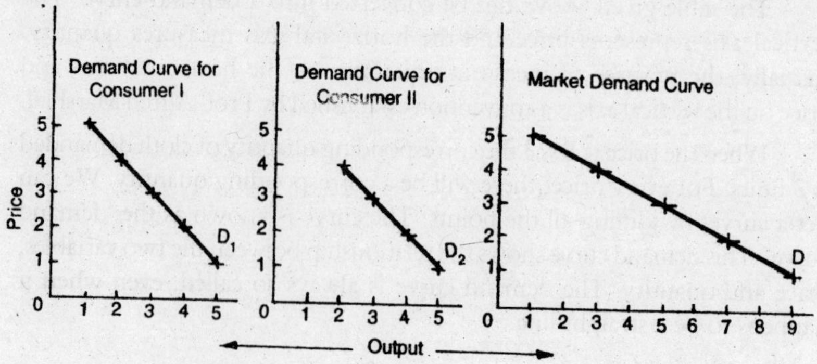

Fig. 7.2

Types of Demand: There are three kinds of demand,

1. Price Demand
2. Income Demand, and
3. Cross Demand.

1. Price Demand: Price demand refers to the various quantities of a commodity that a consumer would purchase at a given time in the market at various hypothetical prices.

2. Income Demand: Income demand refers to the various quantities of a commodity that a consumer would purchase at a given time in a market at various levels of income.

3. Cross Demand: The relationship between the prices of substitutes or complements and the quantity purchased of a related commodity is called cross demand.

LAW OF DEMAND

The inverse relationship between the price of a commodity and its quantity demanded per unit of time is referred to as the law of demand.

In Marshall's words "... the amount demanded increases with a fall in price and diminishes with a rise in price."

In the words of Prof. Samuelson, "Law of Demand states that people will buy more at lower prices and buy less at higher prices, other things remaining the same."

The phrase "other things being equal" is an important qualification; When we say "other things being equal" we assume,

1. No change in the consumer's income
2. No change in consumer's tastes and preferences
3. No change in the prices of substitutes and complements
4. No new substitutes for the goods have been discovered
5. People do not feel that the present fall in price is a prelude to a further decline in prices.
6. The commodity in question is not one which has a prestige value.

If any one of the above assumptions is violated, then the law of demand does not hold good.

WHY THE DEMAND CURVE SLOPES DOWNWARDS?

Most demand curves slope downwards to the right throughout their length, although, the slope may be much steeper in some parts than in others.

1. Law of Diminishing Marginal Utility

Marshall developed the law of demand on the basis of the law of diminishing marginal utility. The marginal utility curve can be converted into a demand curve. The theory states that each successive unit of a commodity gives lesser satisfaction than the preceding unit. Therefore the consumer will buy more only at a lower price. The demand curve slopes downwards because the marginal utility curve also slopes downwards.

2. Substitution Effect

When a commodity becomes cheaper, it tends to be substituted wholly or partly for other commodities. This is called substitution effect.

3. Income Effect

When the price of a commodity falls the real income of the consumer increases and vice versa. Having bought his old quantity of it, a part of the money is left unspent in the consumer's pocket, a part of which he is likely to spend on the same commodity. The resulting increase in the quantity demanded is called income effect.

Of the two effects the substitution effect is more certain than the income effect. In the case of superior goods both the effects work in the same direction and therefore the cumulative effect is an extension of demand when price falls. In the case of inferior goods, they work in opposite directions. The positive substitution effect is more powerful than the negative income effect, so that the demand will expand when price falls. But in the case of Giffen goods, the negative income effect outweighs the positive substitution effect. So the consumers will buy less at a lower price.

4. Entry of Buyers

When there is a fall in the price of any commodity the consumers who were not purchasing that commodity because of its higher price will now enter into the market and purchase some units of the commodity.

5. Less Urgent Uses

When a commodity becomes cheaper, it will be put to less urgent uses also. For example, if pure water is dear, we shall use it only for cooking but when it becomes cheaper, we shall use it for washing and for less urgent uses also.

EXCEPTIONS TO THE LAW OF DEMAND

Normally, the demand curve slopes downwards from left to right, showing that demand extends as price falls. But there are however some unusual demand curves which do not obey the law and the reverse occurs. A fall in price brings about a contraction of demand and a rise in price results in an extension of demand. Therefore the demand curve slopes upwards from left to right. It is known as an exceptional demand curve.

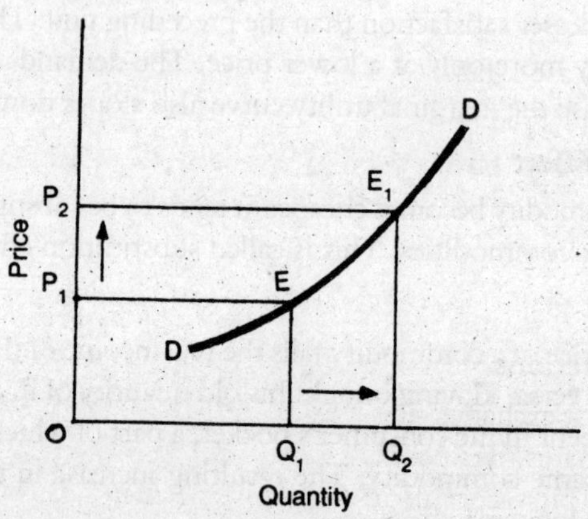

Fig. 7.3

In Fig. 7.3 DD is the demand curve which slopes upwards from left to right. It shows that when price is OP_1, OQ_1 is the demand and when the price rises to OP_2, demand also extends to OQ_2. Such upward sloping demand curves violate the basic law of demand.

According to Prof. Watson,[5] there are only two possible exceptions to the law of demand. Both of them are quite unimportant.

1. Giffen Paradox

The first exception is associated with the name of Sir Robert Giffen (1837-1910). He observed that, early in the 19th century a rise in the price of bread caused low-paid British wage earners to buy more bread and not less. These wage earners subsisted on a diet mainly of bread. When its price rose, they had to spend more money on a given quantity of bread and they could not buy as much meat as before. To maintain their intake of food, they bought more bread even at higher prices.

Marshall could not explain this phenomenon. It appeared to be a paradox to him. This paradox was solved by Prof. Hicks with his powerful tool of indifference curves. In the case of Giffen goods the negative income effect is more powerful than the positive substitution effect so that people will buy less when price falls and more when price rises.

2. Veblen Goods or Goods having 'Snob Appeal'

The second exception is associated with the name of Thorstein Veblen (1857-1929) and his doctrine of conspicuous consumption. Certain goods like diamonds, model gowns, may be wanted chiefly for ostentation, the desire to impress others.

In such a case a fall in price might make them lose some of their appeal and the quantity demanded might fall.

Although 'snob' buyers may leave the market when the price falls, it is likely that large number of new buyers would enter thereby adding to demand at these lower prices.[6]

Other Exceptions

1. Price Expectations

In the stock exchange market, people follow 'bull' and 'bear' tactics. If the price of shares rises people expect a further rise in its price in future and hence they buy more of it. Similarly when it falls, buyers wait for further decrease in price and hence, stop buying it.

2. Consumer's Psychological Bias or Illusion

Sometimes certain consumers buy more at a higher price due to sheer ignorance. There are many goods for which we do not know the quality

5. D.S. Watson. *Price Theory and Its Uses,* Fifth Edition, Khosla Publishing House, New Delhi 1986, p. 22.
6. J. Harvey, *op. cit.*, p. 85.

and we sometimes judge the quality by its price. In markets where prices act as "signals" of quality, people tend to assume that quality has gone up when prices are raised and hence may demand more of the commodity at a higher price. Similarly with the fall in price the consumer may contract his demand on his low quality bias. It is likely to happen in the case of reduction sales.

MOVEMENT ALONG AND SHIFT IN THE DEMAND CURVE

A movement along a demand curve refers to a change in the quantity demanded due to a change in its own price. The movement downwards is an extension of demand. The movement upwards is a contraction of demand.

The Fig. 7.4 shows that at point A, the price is OP_2 and quantity demanded is OQ_2. When price falls to OP_3 (movement along the demand curve A to C) the quantity demanded increases to OQ_3. If price rises to OP_1 (movement from A to B) quantity demanded decreases to OQ_1.

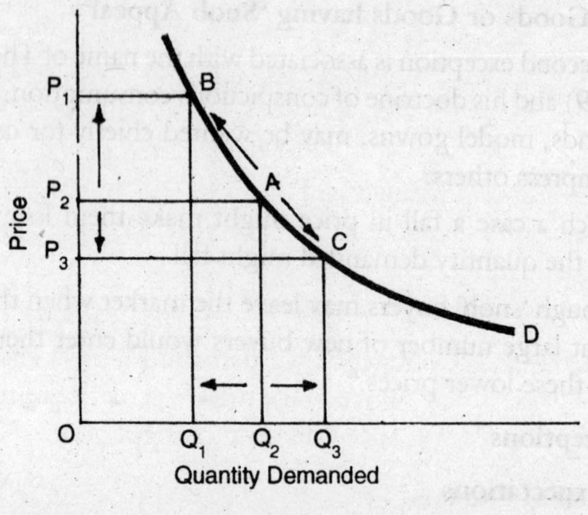

Fig. 7.4

A shift in the demand curve occurs with a change in the value of a variable other than its price in the general demand function.

An increase in demand due to changes in conditions of demand is shown by way of shifts in the demand curve.

On the left hand side of the diagram 7.5(*a*) the original demand curve is DD, the price is OP_1 and the quantity demanded is OQ_1. Due to a change in the conditions of demand (change in income, taste or change in prices of substitutes and complements) the quantity demanded decreases from OQ_1 to OQ_2. This is shown as a shift in the demand curve to the left. The new demand curve is D_1D_1.

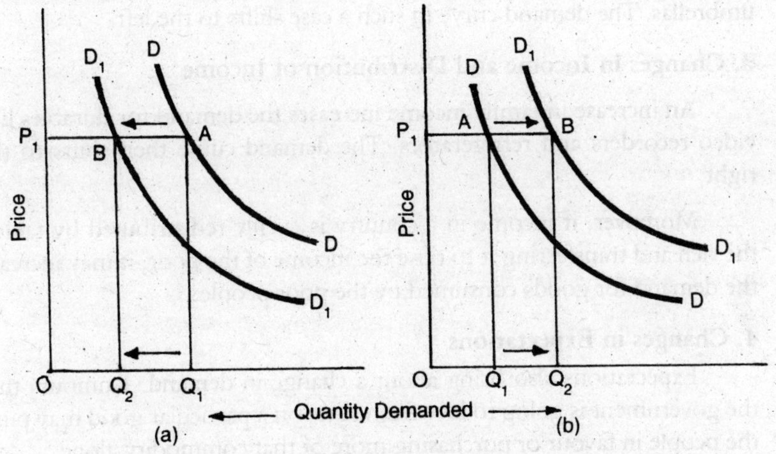

Fig. 7.5

On the right hand side of the diagram 7.5(b) the original price is OP_1 and the quantity demanded is OQ_1. Due to changes in the conditions of demand, the quantity purchased has increased to OQ_2. Thus the demand curve shifts to the right. It has now become D_1D_1.

'Extension' and 'Contraction' of demand follow a change in price. Increases and decreases in demand take place when price remains the same and the other factors bring about demand changes.

Determinants of Demand

According to D.S. Watson a change in demand is caused by changes in income, tastes and prices of substitutes and complements. The various determinants of demand are listed as follows.

1. Changes in Tastes and Fashions

The demand for some goods and services is very susceptible to changes in tastes and fashions. If a commodity becomes more fashionable a larger quantity of it may be bought at the old price or even at a slightly higher price. The fashion among ladies to keep their hair long or short brings about changes in demand for hair-pins, hair-nets etc. Similarly if tastes have deteriorated for a product, less of it will be demanded without any rise in its price.

2. Changes in Weather

An unusually dry summer results in a decrease in the demand for umbrellas. The demand curve in such a case shifts to the left.

3. Changes in Income and Distribution of Income

An increase in family income increases the demand for durables like video recorders and refrigerators. The demand curve then shifts to the right.

Moreover, if income in a country is evenly redistributed by taking the rich and transferring it to raise the income of the poor, it may increase the demand for goods consumed by the poor people.

4. Changes in Expectations

Expectations also bring about a change in demand. Rumours that the government is going to levy fresh taxes on a particular good may push the people in favour of purchasing more of that commodity alone.

5. Changes in Savings

Savings and demand are inversely related. If the marginal propensity to save becomes high the amount available for consumption will become less. The demand will therefore decrease.

6. State of Trade Activity

During the periods of boom and prosperity, the demand for all commodities tends to increase. On the contrary, during times of depression there is a general slackening of demand.

7. A Change in the Real Income

As money income increases, real income also increases. If the income goes to the rich, demand does not increase as much as it increases when such income benefits go to the poor. The simple reason is that the marginal propensity to consume of the rich is less than that of the poor.

8. Consumer Credit Policy

With a liberalisation in the credit policy of the banks or the hire-purchase system adopted by companies, the demand for VCRs, cars, houses etc. will increase.

9. Advertisement

In advanced capitalistic countries advertising is a powerful instrument affecting the demand in the market. In highly competitive markets a powerful competitive advertising campaign through TV, radio, newspapers etc. will move the producer's demand curve to the right and at the same time move the demand curve for competing goods to the left.

10. Taxation and Subsidy

If fresh taxes are levied or the existing rates of taxation on commodities are increased their prices go up. The demand for such commodities will decrease. On the other hand, if rebates and subsidies are given as in the case of khadi products during festival seasons, the demand will increase.

11. Change in the Value of Money

During times of inflation, the prices will rise. Therefore consumers will have to readjust their expenditure pattern so that the demand for certain things will have to be reduced and for others stimulated.

12. Change in Population

The demand for goods depends upon the size of population. An increase in population tends to increase the demand for goods and a decrease in population tends to decrease the demand. Moreover not only the size of the population but also the composition of population tends to affect the demand for a particular commodity.

Derivation of the Law of Demand from the Law of Diminishing Marginal Utility

The law of demand which states that more will be bought at a lower price and vice versa has been derived by Marshall from the law of diminishing marginal utility. As the consumer gets less and less utility from additional units of a commodity he will be willing to demand more units at a lower price. Therefore, the marginal utility curve slopes downwards from left to right. Naturally the demand curve based on marginal utility also slopes downwards from left to right. This can be easily shown by the following Fig. 7.6.

In Fig. 7.6(*a*) at OM_1 quantity, Marginal utility is MU_1. Now $MU_1=P_1$. At OP_1 price the consumer demands OM_1 quantity, similarly at OM_2 quantity, the marginal utility is MU_2. Now $MU_2=P_2$. At price OP_2 the consumer will buy OM_2. Similarly at OM_3 quantity, the marginal utility is MU_3. At P_3 the consumer will buy OM_3. Thus the downward curve as shown in Fig. 7.6(*b*) slopes downwards from left to right.

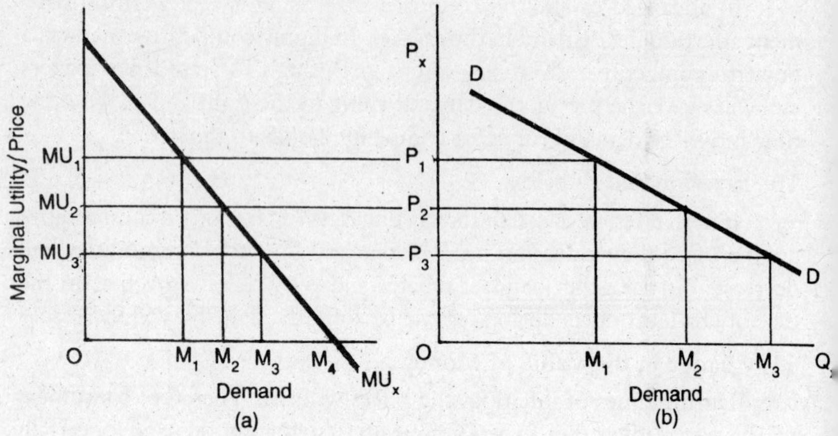

Fig. 7.6

QUESTIONS

1. Explain the determinants of market demand for a commodity.
2. What is exceptional demand curve?
3. Why does the abnormal demand curve slope upward?
4. Under what circumstances does the demand curve behave abnormally? Why?
5. Distinguish between extension of demand and increase in demand.
6. Why is demand curve downward sloping? Are there any exceptions?
7. Explain perverse demand curves.
8. State the Law of Demand. What are the exceptions to it?
9. Distinguish between complementary goods and substitutes.
10. What is the significance of the difference between 'a movement along the demand curve' and 'a shift in the demand curve'?

❖ ❖ ❖

8

CARDINAL UTILITY THEORY

"We never know the worth of water, till the well is dry."

— Thomas Fuller, 1732

The Cardinal Utility Theory was developed by classical economists, viz., Gossen (1810-1858) of Germany, William Stanley Jevons (1835-1882) of England, Leon Walras (1834-1910) of France, Karl Menger (1840-1921) of Austria.

Neo-Classical Economists, particularly Alfred Marshall (1842-1924) made significant refinements in the Cardinal Utility Theory. This led to the Cardinal Utility Theory being known as Neo-Classical Utility Theory or 'Marshallian Utility Theory.'

Meaning of Utility

Utility is the capacity to satisfy a human desire or serve a human purpose. In the words of S.C. Maurice[1] "utility is a consumer's perception of his or her own happiness or satisfaction."

Moreover 'utility' and 'usefulness' are not synonymous. A commodity may be regarded by society as useless or even positively undesirable. It may be frivolous, injurious or even pernicious, but if it satisfies an economic want, it possesses utility. For example, a cigarette will yield tremendous utility to a smoker, but zero or negative utility to a non-smoker. Therefore utility has no moral, legal, or ethical connotation.

1. *Economic Analysis Theory and Applications,* Universal Book Stall, New Delhi, 1988, p. 126.

Diamond rings and paintings by Picasso may be useless in the functional sense of the term, yet be of tremendous utility to brides and all connoisseurs.[2]

Since utility is 'subjective' and not 'objective', it is not susceptible to precise quantitative measurement. Utility is a relative phenomenon, which varies from person to person, from time to time and from place to place depending upon the intensity of people's respective needs. It also depends to a large extent on culture and civilisation.

Likewise, the term utility should not be confused with satisfaction. Utility implies 'expected satisfaction' whereas 'satisfaction' stands for realised satisfaction.' A consumer thinks of utility when he is contemplating the purchase of a commodity, though he obtains satisfaction only after the consumption of the commodity.

CARDINAL AND ORDINAL UTILITY

The controversy between cardinalist and ordinalist approaches to utility theory is not of recent origin.

There are some theories of utility that attach a significance to the magnitude of utility. These are known as cardinal utility theories.

The numbers 1, 2, 3 and so on are cardinal numbers. The cardinal utility theory states that it is measurable just as weight, temperature, and length. Utility is assumed to be measurable in subjective units called utils.

This mythical unit of satisfaction is merely a convenient pedagogical device which will allow us to quantify a thinking about human behaviour.[3]

Marshall assumed that utility is measurable in monetary units. The money price which we are willing to pay for an extra unit of a commodity is supposed to measure its utility.

Thus according to the concept of Cardinal Utility, utility can be measured and compared in terms of the number of units. For example,

An apple possesses 10 utils and

An orange possesses 5 utils

Here the utility of an apple is twice that of an orange.

Economists who believed in cardinal utility can be divided into two groups.[4]

2. C.R. McConnell and H.C. Gupta, *Economics, Principles, Problems and Policies,* Tata Mc-Graw Hill Publishing Company Limited, New Delhi, 1974, p. 161.
3. C.R. McConnell, and H. C. Gupta, *Ibid.*
4. G.S. Maddala — *Micro Economics Theory and Applications,* McGraw Hill, 1989, p. 90.

Nineteenth century economists such as Jevons, Walras and Marshall belonged to the first group. They considered utility to be not only measurable but also additive, that is if an orange gives 5 utils of utility and an apple gives 10 utils of utility then the utility of both an orange and an apple is 5 + 10 = 15 utils. Economists such as Edgeworth and Irving Fisher belonged to the second group. They argued that utility is measurable but not additive, that it depends simultaneously on all the amounts of the different goods consumed. The marginal utility a consumer derives from another ounce of butter depends on the consumer's current rate of consumption of other commodities such as bread or margarine.

The numbers 1st, 2nd, 3rd and so on are ordinal numbers. J.R. Hicks and R.G.D. Allen assumed that utility cannot be measured but can only be ranked. Utility in this case denotes rank ordering of preferences. That is, we can say whether the utility of an orange is less than, equal to, or greater than the utility of an apple.

Since ordinal utility theory requires fewer assumptions and has as much predictive power as the cardinal utility theory, economists have preferred the former to the latter following the law of parsimony. The law of parsimony, often called Occam's Razor is that if two theories have equal predictive power then the theory with fewer assumptions should be preferred.

• ASSUMPTIONS

The Cardinal Utility approach is based on the following explicit assumptions.

1. Rationality

The consumer is rational in the sense that he aims at maximising his utility subject to income constraint.

2. Cardinal Utility

Marginal utility analysis assumes utility as a quantifiable entity. According to Marshall, the amount of money which a person is willing to pay for a thing, instead of going without it, is the money measurement of utility.

3. Constancy of Marginal Utility of Money

Since money is the measuring rod of utility, the marginal utility of money must remain constant. If the marginal utility of money changes as income increases or decreases the measuring rod may behave like an elastic ruler. Then it becomes inappropriate to measurement.

As Prof. Tapas Majumdar[5] observes, "If money is supposed to provide the measuring rod of utility, then evidently, as with all measuring rods, its unit must be invariant; it must measure the same amount of utility in all circumstances."

But Marshall defended this assumption on the ground that the individual consumer's expenditure on any one thing is only a small part of his whole expenditure. Hence little variations in expenditure do not alter the marginal utility of money.

4. Utilities Are Independent

The marginal utility approach assumes that the satisfaction derived from the consumption of one good is the function of that good alone and not of another. In other words, the commodities which are supposed to enter the consumer's budget are neither substitutes nor complements.

Suppose there are 'n' commodities in the basket.

$$TU = (x_1, x_2, \ldots x_n)$$

with additive utility, we can write

$$TU = U_1 (x_1) + U_2 (x_2) + \ldots + U_n (x_n)$$

Where $U_1 (x_1)$ is the utility derived from the first good alone, and $U_2 (x_2)$ is the utility derived from the second good alone and $U_n(x_n)$ is the utility derived from the 'n'th good alone.

5. Diminishing Marginal Utility

The marginal utility of a commodity diminishes as a consumer possesses larger quantities of it.

$$MU_X = f(Q_X)$$

Marginal utility of a commodity x is a function of the quantity of x. The greater the quantity, the lesser is its marginal utility.

There are two approaches to explain consumer's behaviour in terms of cardinal utility.

1. Diminishing marginal utility.
2. Equi-marginal utility.

5. Tapas Majumdar, *The Measurement of Utility*, Macmillan Company Limited, London, 1966, p. 54.

THE LAW OF DIMINISHING MARGINAL UTILITY OR GOSSEN'S FIRST LAW

The tendency for the utility of successive units to decline is known in Economics as the Law of diminishing marginal utility. The Law of diminishing marginal utility is based on general observations of human behaviour. The assertion that products are characterised by diminishing marginal utility as consumption rises, is an empirical one.

Eyes become tired of beautiful pictures or scenes and ears are deadened by even the sweetest music in course of time.[6] The Law states that as we have more of a thing the less is the utility we derive from the additional increments of it. A German economist Gossen was the first to explain this Law.

Alfred Marshall[7] in his book 'Principles of Economics' gave a precise explanation of this law.

"The additional benefit which a person derives from a given increase of his stock of a thing diminishes with every increase in the stock that he already has."

Thus the law states that as a person consumes more of any good the total utility he derives increases but the increase in total utility is not proportionate to the increase in his consumption.

The law of diminishing marginal utility is also called the law of satiable wants since the want for a particular commodity will get satiated as the consumer has more and more of it and he will not like to have any more of it, after a certain stage.

Explanation

Suppose Mr X is hungry and eats oranges one by one. The first orange gives him great pleasure. By the time he starts taking the second, the intensity of his desire diminishes to a certain extent, and the second orange yields less satisfaction. The satisfaction derived from the third will be less than that of the second, that of the fourth less than that of the third and so on. In this way, the incremental utility will go on decreasing till it drops to zero, and if he takes more, the satisfaction may become even negative or disutility may creep in.

---

6. B.P. Tyagi — *Economic Analysis,* 1st Edn., Jaiprakash Nath & Company, p. 287.
7. A. Marshall — *Principles of Economics,* 8th Edn., Macmillan & Company, London, 1982, p. 79.

Zero utility means the consumer is not in need of the commodity any further. According to Watson, negative marginal utility means so many units of something, for example cats. It is reasonable for a person to have two cats for joy, whereas twelve are a nuisance.

Let us assume that the following table indicates the satisfaction derived by a person from successive units of consumption of oranges.

Table 8.1

Number of Oranges	*Total Utility*	*Marginal Utility*
1	6	6
2	11	5
3	15	4
4	18	3
5	20	2
6	21	1
7	21	0
8	20	–1

Total Utility

Total utility is the utility obtained from all the units consumed. If, a consumer consumes 'n' units of commodity X, then the utilities derived from 'n' units will be referred to as the total utility of 'n' units. If 5 oranges are consumed in our example, T.U. = (6+5+4+3+2) = 20 utility.

Marginal Utility

Marginal utility is the utility from an additional unit of consumption,

$$MU = \frac{\Delta TU}{\Delta C} \text{ where}$$

TU = total utility

C = consumption and

$\Delta C = 1$

or

Marginal utility of 'n' units of commodity X is the difference between the total utility of 'n' units and the total utility of 'n–1' units of the commodity.

Symbolically,

$$MU_n = TU_n - TU_{n-1}$$

where

MU_n = Marginal utility of n units,

TU_n = Total utility of n units,

TU_{n-1} = Total utility of n–1 units

The marginal utility of the 5th orange in our example is

$$MU_5 = TU_5 - TU_4$$

$$= 20 - 18 = 2$$

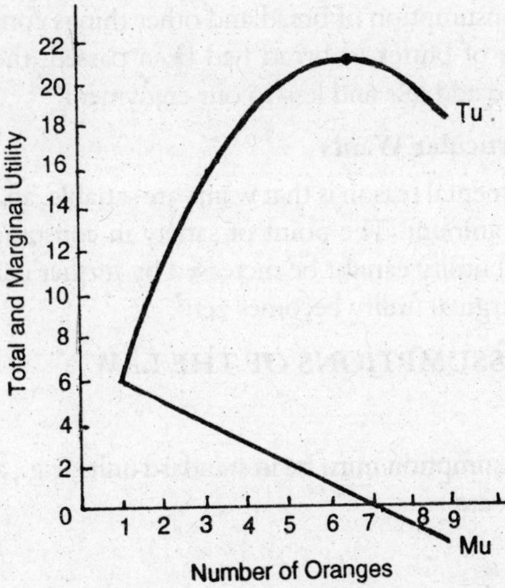

Fig. 8.1

Relationship Between Marginal Utility and Total Utility

Marginal Utility	*Total Utility*
1. Declines	1. Increases but at a diminishing rate
2. Reaches zero; and	2. Reaches maximum; and
3. Becomes negative.	3. Declines from the maximum.

As suggested by the word 'decreasing' in the law, it is the decreasing part of the marginal utility curve that is relevant. The law states that as more of a good is consu ned, the marginal utility of the good will eventually decline. Therefore, the law is consistent even with an increasing marginal utility at an early stage. But a stage will certainly come when the law of diminishing marginal utility will become operative.

The Figure 8.1 shows that when 7 oranges are consumed, the total utility is maximum, but marginal utility is reduced to zero.

REASONS FOR DIMINISHING MARGINAL UTILITY

Prof. K.E. Boulding points out two important reasons for the operation of the law of diminishing marginal utility.

1. Commodities are Imperfect Substitutes for one another

Commodities are not perfectly substitutable for one another. There are certain appropriate proportions in which commodities tend to be consumed, say bread and butter. If we increase the consumption of butter while keeping the consumption of bread and other things constant, when the best proportions of butter to bread had been passed, the successive doses of butter would add less and less to our enjoyment.

2. Satiability of Particular Wants

Another fundamental reason is that wants are satiable, and we cannot consume an infinite amount. The point of satiety in consumption is the point where the total utility cannot be increased by further consumption, and therefore the marginal utility becomes zero.

ASSUMPTIONS OF THE LAW

1. Reasonability

The unit of consumption must be in standard units, e.g., a cup of tea, a bottle of cool drink etc.

2. Homogeneity

All the units of the commodity must be identical in all aspects, like taste, quality, colour and size.

3. Continuity

The law holds good only when the process of consumption continues without any time gap. If a break is necessary it must be appropriately short.

4. Constancy

The law assumes that the consumer's taste, habit or preference must remain the same during the process of consumption. Likewise, the income, the prices of the commodity and its substitutes are constant.

5. Rationality

The consumer is assumed to be a rational economic man. Moreover the mental condition of the consumer remains normal during the process of consumption.

EXCEPTIONS TO THE LAW OF DIMINISHING MARGINAL UTILITY

There are certain exceptions to the law of diminishing marginal utility. But a closer analysis will show that these exceptions are apparent and not real.

1. Rare Collections

In the collection of 'curios' and antiques, stamps, old paintings, coins etc., the law of diminishing marginal utility does not hold good. In these rare collections, marginal utility increases as the number of collection increases. But two units of the same coin or stamp may not yield the same utility. The addition of coins or stamps of the same type will yield only diminishing utility. Therefore it is not a real exception to the law.

2. Abnormal Persons like Drunkards and Misers

The law does not apply to eccentric or abnormal persons like misers or drunkards. The additional doses of intoxication to a drunkard will yield increasing marginal utility. He may feel that each incremental dose takes him a step nearer to the gates of Heaven.

Likewise, a miser may get increasing marginal utilities from successive acquisitions of money. But this argument is also not correct because a drunkard or a miser is not a rational consumer and we do not study his irrational behaviour in economics.

3. Love of Display and Goods of Conspicuous Consumption

It is also said that the law of consumption does not apply to one's love of display of goods like jewellery diamonds or love of power. But since economics deals with the economic behaviour of man in average and normal activities, these are only exceptional tendencies which are not covered under the sphere of economics.

4. Stock of Other Goods

Sometimes it is argued that the utility of a commodity increases, if a large number of people begin to use it. Telephone is the example often cited in this connection. The utility of one's telephone increases, with increasing number of telephones in his place of residence. This is also to a certain extent not correct. Suppose all the families in the area possess telephones, any additional set to the same family will yield less satisfaction.

We may conclude in the words of Taussig "The tendency shows itself so widely and with so few exceptions that there is no serious inaccuracy in speaking of it as universal."

IMPORTANCE OF THE LAW OF DIMINISHING MARGINAL UTILITY

The Law of diminishing marginal utility is of great practical importance.

1. Basis of Economic Laws

Some important economic laws such as consumer's surplus, law of demand, elasticity of demand and the law of substitution are based on this law.

2. Taxation

This law is the basis for progressive taxation. Adam Smith was the first to explain the canon of 'Ability to pay' in taxation in his book 'Wealth of Nations.' On the basis of this law Prof. Pigou argued that the marginal utility of money for the poor person is higher than for the rich person. Therefore the progressive system of taxation, imposing a heavier burden on the rich, is a practical application of this principle in the field of public finance.

3. Socialistic Plea

The law of diminishing marginal utility is a powerful weapon in the hands of the socialists. Socialists argue for redistribution of income and wealth in favour of the poor. In keeping with the law, such a transfer will mean less loss of utility of the rich than the gain in utility to the poor.

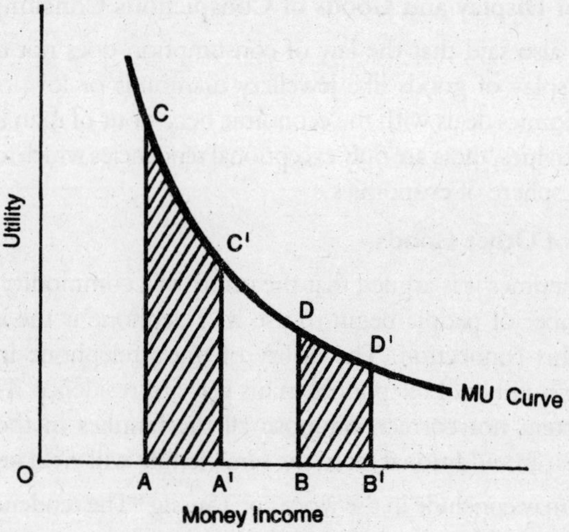

Fig. 8.2

Let us assume that there are two individuals in a society. OA is the poor man's income, OB' is the rich man's income. Let the rich man's income be reduced by B'B and let the same amount of money income be transferred to the poor man, so that his income rises by AA'. It is clear from the figure that the gain in utility ACC'A' is greater than the loss in utility BDD'B'.

4. Determination of Value

The law explains as to why an increase in the supply of a commodity makes its value fall. With an increase in supply the marginal utility of the commodity falls and hence its price also falls. So it is useful to the consumer and the businessman.

5. Downward Sloping Demand Curve

This law explains the reason for the downward sloping demand curve. As the quantity of a commodity increases, marginal utility falls and so the consumer will buy more of the commodity only at a lower price.

6. Diamond — Water — Paradox

The concept of diminishing marginal utility is useful to explain the divergence between value-in-use and value-in-exchange.

Water is more useful in life (value-in-use) but it has little value in exchange. It has no marginal utility because of its abundance.

Diamonds on the other hand are mere decorations and not useful to daily life, but diamonds being scarce have a very high marginal utility. Thus the law of diminishing marginal utility explains as to why diamonds are highly priced when compared to water. This puzzle is often referred to as diamond water paradox.

This paradox is explained with the help of the following Figure 8.3.

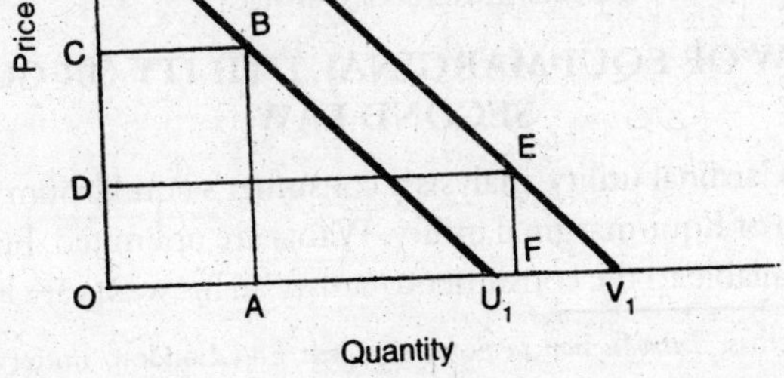

Fig. 8.3

UU_1 is the marginal utility curve for diamond and VV_1 is the marginal utility curve for water. The supply of diamond is OA and the supply of water is OF. The theory tells us that the marginal utility of diamond (AB) is higher than the marginal utility of water (FE). The total utility of water OFED is greater than the total utility of diamond OABC. Since price is related to marginal utility and not to total utility, the price of diamond is higher than the price of water.

7. Determination of Household Expenditure

This law is of paramount importance to the households to determine their optimum expenditure on a particular commodity. The households will carry on their expenditure up to the point where marginal utility is equal to price.

We may conclude in the words of Cairncross.[9] "It can be applied not only to things like butter and bread, railway journeys, men's hats, and so

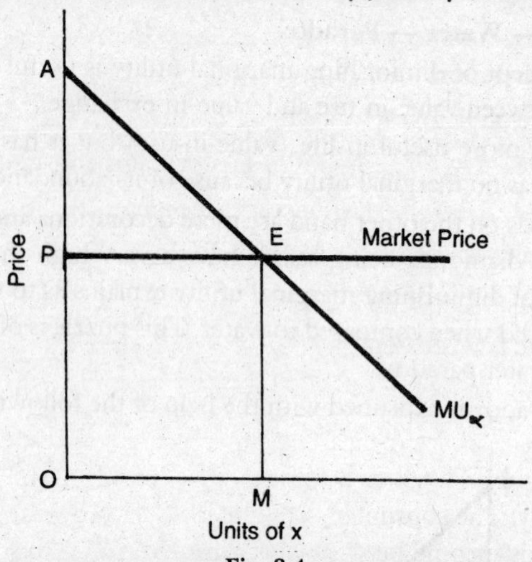

Fig. 8.4

on, but also to the lectures of economists, the speeches of politicians and even the number of suspects in detective stories."

THE LAW OF EQUI-MARGINAL UTILITY OR GOSSEN'S SECOND LAW

In the Cardinal utility analysis a consumer's equilibrium is explained with the help of Equi-marginal utility. Wants are unlimited, but the means which are available to the consumer to satisfy all his wants are limited. This

9. A. Cairncross, *Introduction to Economics,* 4th Ed., London, Butterworths, 1966, p. 221.

law guides the consumer to allocate his income among various commodities for getting maximum satisfaction.

The law of equi-marginal utility is also known as the law of substitution or the law of economy in expenditure or the law of maximum satisfaction or the principle of income allocation.

In the words of Prof. Marshall[10] "If a person has a thing which can be put to several uses, he will distribute it among these uses in such a way that it has the same marginal utility in all. For if it had a greater marginal utility in one use than another, he would gain by taking away some of it from the second use and applying it to the first."

Prof. J.R. Hicks[11] has stated "utility will be maximised when the marginal unit of expenditure in each direction brings in the same increment of utility."

Assumptions: The law is based on the following assumptions:

1. The consumer is rational in the sense that he wants to get maximum satisfaction.
2. The utility of each commodity is measurable in cardinal numbers.
3. The marginal utility of money remains constant.
4. The income of the consumer is given.
5. There is perfect competition in the market.
6. The prices of the commodities are given.
7. The law is based on the law of diminishing marginal utility.

Principle

Let us take a hypothetical consumer planning his expenditure. Suppose the consumer purchases two commodities X and Y. The respective prices are Px and Py. The consumer's income is Rs. 8. Now the question is, how to allocate his income between the commodities X and Y. The marginal utility schedules for X and Y are given below.

10. Alfred Marshall, *op. cit.,* p. 98.
11. J.R. Hicks, *Value and Capital*, Oxford University Press, 1979, p. 1.

Table 8.2

Units of money	*Marginal Utility of x*	*Marginal Utility of y*
1st Rupee	20	16
2nd "	18	14
3rd "	16	12
4th "	14	10
5th "	12	8
6th "	10	6
7th "	8	4
8th "	6	2

The consumer will spend his first rupee on commodity X because it gives him 20 units of utility which is the highest in his demand schedule. Likewise the consumer spends his second rupee on commodity X which will increase his total utility by 18 units. The consumer will spend the third rupee on X or Y, because both give the same level of utility. If he spends the third rupee on X, naturally the fourth rupee will be on Y, the 5th on X, the 6th on Y, the 7th on X and the 8th on Y. Altogether the consumer spends five rupees on X and three rupees on Y.

The marginal utilities of the last rupee spent on X and the last rupee spent on Y are equal with 12 utils each. In other words,

$$\frac{MU_x}{P_x} = \frac{MU_x}{P_y} = \frac{12}{1} = \frac{12}{1}$$

$$\text{Total utility} = TU_{x+y} = TU_x + TU_y$$

$$= (20+18+16+14+12) + (16+14+12)$$

$$= 122$$

Any other way of allocation of expenditure on the two commodities will reduce his total satisfaction. This fact is illustrated with the help of the following Figure 8.5 which is based on the Table (8.2).

Fig. 8.5 shows that when the consumer spends Rs. 5 on X and Rs. 3 on Y, the marginal utility of the last rupee on both the commodities is equal to 12 utils so that the consumer is in equilibrium.

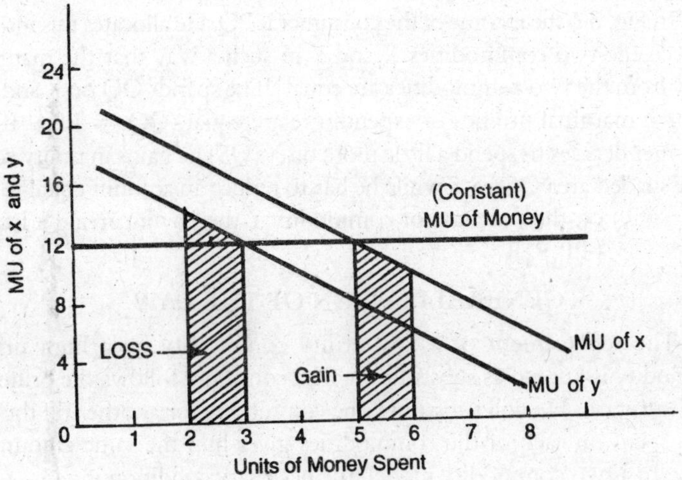

Fig. 8.5

Let us assume that the consumer spends one more rupee on X and as a result spends one rupee less on Y. The gain in utility is shown by the shaded area under the marginal utility curve of X. The loss in utility is shown by the shaded area under the other curve showing the marginal utility of Y. It is very clear from the diagram that the loss in utility is much greater than the gain in utility. Hence the earlier pattern of expenditure was the best.

AN ALTERNATIVE EXPLANATION OF THE LAW

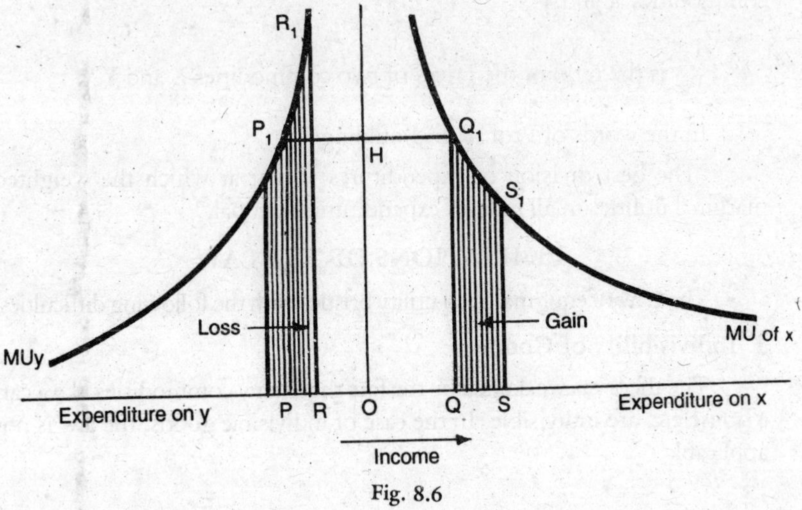

Fig. 8.6

In Fig. 8.6 the income of the consumer is PQ. He allocates this income between the two commodities X and Y in such a way that the marginal utility from the two commodities are equal. If he spends OQ on X and OP on Y the marginal utilities of expenditure are equal ($QQ_1 = PP_1$). If the consumer decides to spend a little more on X (QS) he gains in utility equal to the shaded area QQ_1S_1S while he has to reduce an amount equal to PR (QS = PR) on the purchase of commodity Y thereby incurring a loss in utility of area PP_1R_1R.

GENERALISATION OF THE LAW

The replacement of a low utility commodity by a high utility commodity is known as substitution. The consumer follows the principle of substitution. He will substitute one commodity for another till the last rupee spent on each of the commodities gives him the same amount of utility. In a two commodity model, the necessary condition is

$$\frac{MU_x}{P_x} = \frac{MU_y}{P_y}$$

or

$$\frac{MU_x}{MU_y} = \frac{P_x}{P_y}$$

Where $\frac{MU_x}{MU_y}$ is the ratio of the marginal utilities of the two commodities X and Y.

$\frac{P_x}{P_y}$ is the ratio of the prices of two commodities X and Y.

In the words of Prof. K.E. Boulding[12]

"The best division of expenditures is that at which the weighted marginal utilities in all lines of expenditure are equal."

LIMITATIONS OF THE LAW

The Law of equi-marginal utility bristles with the following difficulties.

1. Indivisibility of Goods

The theory is weakened by the fact that many commodities like a car, a house etc. are indivisible. In the case of indivisible goods, the law is not applicable.

2. The Marginal Utility of Money is Not Constant

The assumption that the marginal utility of money remains constant is not correct. The marginal utility of money increases with every decrease in its available stock.

3. The Measurement of Utility is Not Possible

Marshall states that the price a consumer is willing to pay for a commodity is its utility to him. But modern economists argue that, if two persons are paying an equal price for a given commodity, it could not mean that both are getting the same level of utility. Thus utility is a subjective concept which cannot be measured in quantitative terms.

4. Utilities are Interdependent

This law assumes that commodities are independent and therefore their marginal utilities are also independent. But in real life commodities are either substitutes or complements. Their utilities are therefore interdependent.

5. Indefinite Budget Period

According to Prof. K.E. Boulding, indefinite budget period is another difficulty in the law. Naturally the budget period is assumed to be a year. But there are certain commodities which are available for several succeeding accounting periods. It is difficult to calculate marginal utility for such commodities.

In conclusion, we may say that all prudent and rational persons are expected to act upon the law consciously or unconsciously.

As Chapman[13] puts it,

"We are not, of course compelled to distribute our incomes according to the law of substitution or equi-marginal expenditure, as a stone thrown into the air is compelled, in a sense to fall back to the earth, but as a matter of fact, we do in a certain rough fashion, because we are reasonable."

Importance

According to Prof. Marshall, "The applications of this principle extend over almost every field of economic activity."

---

12. K.E. Boulding, *Economic Analysis, op. cit.,* p. 528.
13. Chapman, S.J. *Outlines of Political Economy,* Longmans, Green & Company, London, 1912, p. 48.

1. It Applies to Consumption

Every rational human being wants to get maximum satisfaction with his limited means. The consumer arranges his expenditure in such a way that,

$$\frac{MU_x}{P_x} = \frac{MU_y}{P_y} = \frac{MU_z}{P_z}$$, so that he will get maximum satisfaction.

2. It Applies to Production

The aim of the producer is to get maximum output with least cost, so that his profit will be maximum. Towards this end he will substitute one factor for another till

$$\frac{MP_L}{P_L} = \frac{MP_c}{P_c} = \frac{MP_n}{P_n}$$ where,

MP_L = marginal product of labour

MP_C = marginal product of capital

MP_n = marginal product of n

P_L = Price of Labour

P_C = Price of Capital

P_n = Price of n

$$\text{or} \quad \frac{MP_L}{MP_c} = \frac{P_L}{P_c}$$

3. Distribution of Earnings Between Savings and Consumption

According to Marshall, a prudent person will endeavour to distribute his resources between his present needs and future needs in such a way that the marginal utility of the last rupee put on saving is equal to the marginal utility of the last rupee spent on consumption.

4. It Applies to Distribution

The General theory of distribution involves the principle of substitution. In distribution the rewards to the various factors of production, their relative shares are determined by the principle of equi-marginal utility.

5. It Applies to Public Finance

The principle of 'Maximum Social Advantage' as enunciated by Professors Hicks and Dalton states that, the revenue should be distributed in such a way that the last unit of expenditure on various programmes brings equal welfare, so that social welfare is maximised.

6. Expenditure of Time

Prof. Boulding relates Marshall's law of equi-marginal utility to the expenditure of limited time, i.e., twenty four hours. He states that a person should spend his limited time among alternative uses such as reading, studying and gardening, in such a way that the marginal utility from all these uses are equal.

CRITICAL EVALUATION OF MARGINAL UTILITY ANALYSIS

The weaknesses of the marginal utility approach are manifold.

1. Subjective Notion of Utility

According to cardinalists, utility is a measurable entity in cardinal numbers. But this assumption is not correct. Utility is a subjective psychological phenomenon which cannot be measured.

The cardinal measurement concept may be very useful to explain elementary economic behaviour. But when it is extended to an advanced analysis of consumer behaviour, it becomes a nuisance.

Prof. Hicks observes "It might be more convenient as a sort of scaffolding useful in erecting the building, but has to be taken down when the building has been completed."[14]

2. Utilities of Commodities are Not Independent

This approach assumes, that the utility to a consumer depends upon that commodity alone. In other words, the commodity has neither substitutes nor complements. But in actual life, utility depends upon the availability of substitutes and complements. The utility of a car depends upon petrol and that of tea depends upon the availability of coffee. Thus utilities are inter-dependent rather than independent.

3. Wrong Assumption of Constant Marginal Utility of Money

The assumption of constant marginal utility of money is untenable. As the consumer's money stock increases, the marginal utility of money decreases. So money cannot be used as a measuring rod, as its own utility changes.

4. Dual Effects of Price Effect

The fall in the price of a commodity, increases the quantity demanded of it. It is known as the price effect. With the fall in the price of the

14. Hicks J.R., *A Revision of Demand Theory,* Oxford Clarendon Press, 1959, p. 9.

commodity, the real income of the consumer increases. The increase in quantity demanded due to an increase in real income is known as income effect.

Moreover the consumer substitutes the cheaper commodities for some relatively costlier commodities. This is due to the substitution effect. Therefore price effect is the sum of the income effect and the substitution effect. The utility theory fails to explain how much increase is due to income effect and how much is due to the substitution effect. In the words of Hicks,[15] "The distinction between direct and indirect effects of a price change is accordingly left by the cardinal theory as an empty box, which is crying out to be filled."

5. Giffen Paradox

Marshall could not explain Giffen goods and it remained as a paradox to him. It is because of the presumption of constant marginal utility of money and his failure to recognise the existence of income effect.

In the case of Giffen goods the negative income effect is more powerful than the positive substitution effect, so that the consumer will buy less of a quantity when its price falls.

6. Assumption of a One Commodity World

The Marshallian Marginal utility theory is applicable to a only one commodity world. Moreover it fails to explain the demand for indivisible goods.

7. Assumes Too Much and Explains Too Little

Critics argue that Marshall's utility theory is based on a number of unrealistic assumptions. But it ends up as a totally inadequate and unrealistic theorem.

8. Rationality

The theory assumes rationality on the part of the consumer. Due to ignorance or advertisement, the consumer may be forced to choose a wrong choice.

9. Introspection

The marginal utility approach is based on introspection. As such it is not amenable to empirical verification.

---

15. J.R. Hicks, *Ibid.*, p. 14.

QUESTIONS

1. What is marginal utility? What sort of relation exists between total utility and marginal utility.
2. What is the relation between the Marginal Utility and price of a good?
3. What are the assumptions of law of diminishing marginal utility?
4. Examine the assumptions and shortcomings of marginal utility analysis.
5. Explain the law of diminishing marginal utility. Discuss the importance of the law.
6. Describe the law of equi-marginal utility.
7. According to Marshall, how does a consumer attain equilibrium?
8. "The application of the principle of substitution extends over almost every field of economic activity." Explain.
9. Distinguish between Cardinal Utility and Ordinal Utility.

9

INDIFFERENCE CURVE ANALYSIS

INDIFFERENCE CURVE ANALYSIS

The cardinal utility approach is basically criticized for its assumption that utility is a measurable entity. Many ordinalists, like Edgeworth, Slutsky, Hicks and Allen believe that measurement of subjective utility on an absolute scale is neither possible nor necessary. This skepticism about the measurement of utility forced them to evolve an alternative approach to analyze consumer behaviour. The culmination of this search is the indifference curve theory. This approach does not require that consumers be able measure utility in any specific units of measurement but does assume that consumers are able to rank their preferences for combinations of goods.

Assumptions

The heart of the ordinal utility approach to consumer behaviour is contained in five basic assumptions or axioms.

1. Complete

The completeness assumption states that the consumer has a definite order of preferences or rank ordering for every conceivable combination of commodities. The completeness assumption is sometimes called the trichotomy assumption for the following reason. Suppose there are two different combinations of goods, A and B. This axiom assumes that the consumer must state. "I prefer A to B" or I prefer "B to A" or "A and B are equally preferred." The consumer is not in a state of indecision. According to Hal R. Varian "one might imagine extreme situations involving life or death choices where ranking the alternatives might be difficult or even impossible but these choices are for the most part outside the domain of economic analysis."

2. Consistency or Transitivity

Along with complete ordering we expect that the consumer preferences are not self-contradictory or conflicting with each other. This is the assumption of transitivity (The technical name for consistency is transitive) This means that if A is preferred to B, and B and preferred to C, then A is preferred over C.

Symbolically,

If A >B, and B>C, then A>C.

3. Non Satiation

The third important assumption is that consumers always prefer more goods to less. It means that the consumer is not satiated atleast not in all goods. More precisely if bundle A contains atleast as much of every commodity as bundle B and more of atleast one commodity, then A is preferred to B.

"Parents of small children may occasionally observe behaviour that violates this assumption, but it seems plausible for most adult behaviour."

4. Substitutability

The goods consumed by the consumers are substitutable.

5. Optimality

Finally, the optimally assumption means the consumer tries to maximize utility given his income and market prices.

INDIFFERENCE SCHEDULE

An indifference schedule is a tabular list showing the various combination of x and y that the consumer would consider equivalent (i.e., equally satisfactory, of equal total utility or of indifference.)

Table 9.1

Indifference Schedule

Combinations	X (Oranges)	Y (Apples)	Satisfaction
A	2	15	k
B	5	9	k
C	7	6	k
D	17	2	k

It is obvious from this schedule that every combination of x and y gives equal satisfaction 'k' to the consumer.

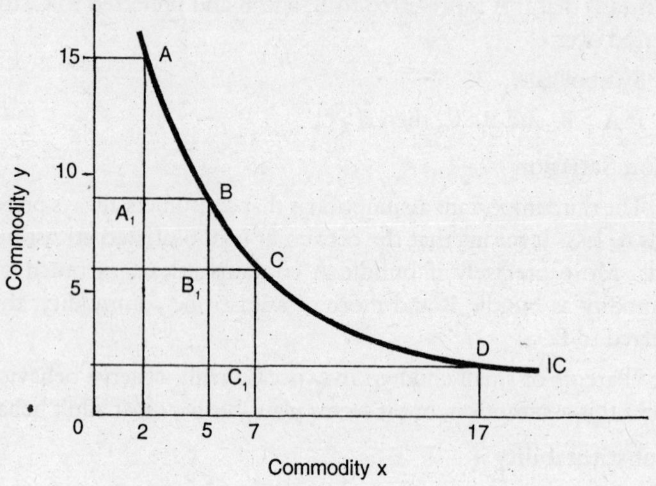

Fig. 9.1

Just as a demand curve may be constructed from a demand schedule, an indifference curve may be constructed from an indifference schedule.

The locus of all commodity combinations from which the consumer derives the same level of satisfaction forms an indifference curve. It can also be called an iso utility curve ("iso" means same) An indifference map is a set of indifference curves.

In the words of Koutsoyiannis

"An indifference curve is a locus of points-particular combinations or bundles of goods-which yield the same utility (level of satisfaction) to the consumes, so that he is indifferent as to the particular combination he consumes."

MARGINAL RATE OF SUBSTITUTION

The shape of an indifference curve provides useful information about preferences. Indifference curve replaces the concept of the marginal rate of substitution for the concept of marginal utility.

According to Leftwich[1] "The marginal rate of substitution of x for y (MRS_{xy}) is defined as the maximum amount of y the consumer is willing to give up to get an additional unit of x and still remain on the same indifference curve."

Thus, the marginal rate of substitution is just a fancy name for an acceptable trade off between two goods.

Diminishing Marginal Rate of Substitution

Table 9.1 and diagram 9.1 explains the concept of diminishing marginal rate of substitution.

Since y decrease as x increases, the change in y is negative (i.e., $-\Delta y$), so the equation is

$$MRS_{xy} = -\frac{\Delta y}{\Delta x} \text{ and}$$

$$MRS_{yx} = -\frac{\Delta x}{\Delta y}$$

However, as with price elasticity of demand the convention is to ignore the minus sign

ie., $MRS_{xy} = \frac{\Delta y}{\Delta x}$

In fig. 9.1 Oranges by X and Apples by Y, we have the following marginal rate of substitution

$MRS_{x \text{ for } y}$

$$\text{Between A and B: } \frac{AA^1}{A_1B} = \frac{6}{3} = 2.0$$

$$\text{Between B and C : } \frac{BB_1}{B_1C} = \frac{3}{2} = 1.5$$

$$\text{Between C and D: } \frac{CC_1}{C_1D} = \frac{4}{10} = 0.4$$

Thus, MRS_x for y diminishes with increasing x. This is the principle of diminishing marginal rate of substitution.

PROPERTIES OF THE INDIFFERENCE CURVES

Indifference curves are subjective and unique to each person. Nevertheless they have in common the following properties.

1. Higher indifference curve represent higher levels of satisfaction

The consumer is better off when he moves to a higher indifference curve. Consider the following Fig.9.2.

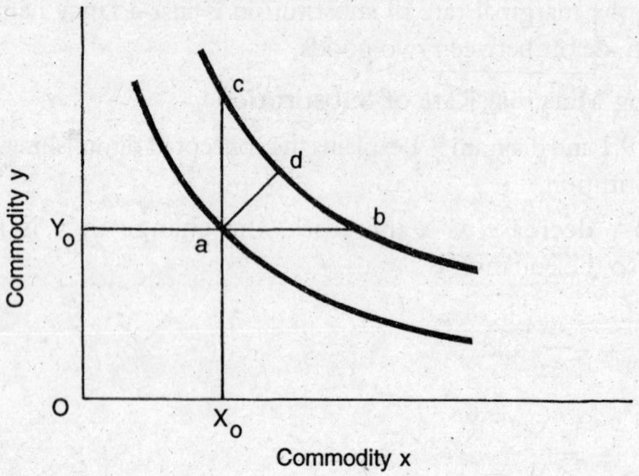

Fig. 9.2

The horizontal movement from a to b means a larger quantity of x by ab, quantity of y (OY_0) remaining the same. The vertical movement from a to c means increase in the quantity of y by ac, the quantity of x (OX_0) remaining the same. In case of the diagonal movement from a to d means larger quantities of both x and y. Thus bundle of goods on a higher indifference curve is preferred by the consumer. This is called "monotonicity" of preferences.

2. Indifference curves cannot intersect

Indifference curve cannot intersect each other because an intersection would indicate two difference levels of satisfaction which is impossible.

The combination C is preferable to B since C contains more of both X and Y, C however is indifferent to A which lies on the same indifference curve; B is also indifferent to A for the same reason Since both C and B are indifferent to A, by the transitivity of indifference relation C and B must be indifferent to each other. This however contradicts the fact that C is preferred to B. Accordingly indifference curves cannot intersect.

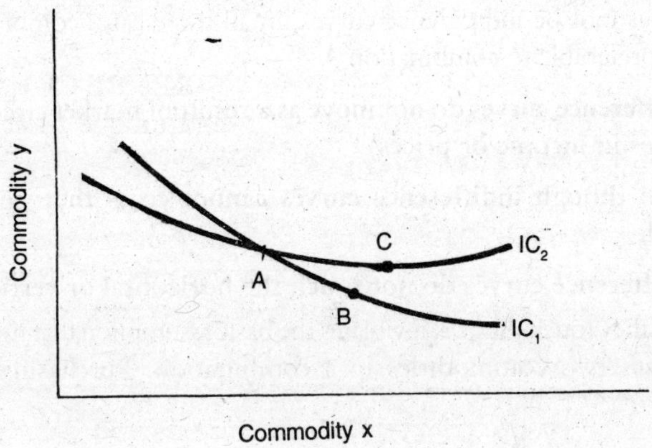

Fig. 9.3

3. There are an infinite number of indifference curves

In the commodity space there are an infinite number of points. In between two indifference curves, we can draw an infinite number of indifference curves. An indifference map, is merely a partial set of indifference curves shown for an expository purpose.

4. Indifference curve must have a negative slope

An indifference curve has a negative slope, which denotes that if the quantity of commodity (y) decreases, the quantity of the other (x) must increase, if the consumer is to stay on the same level of satisfaction. (a necessary consequence of the non satiety postulate).

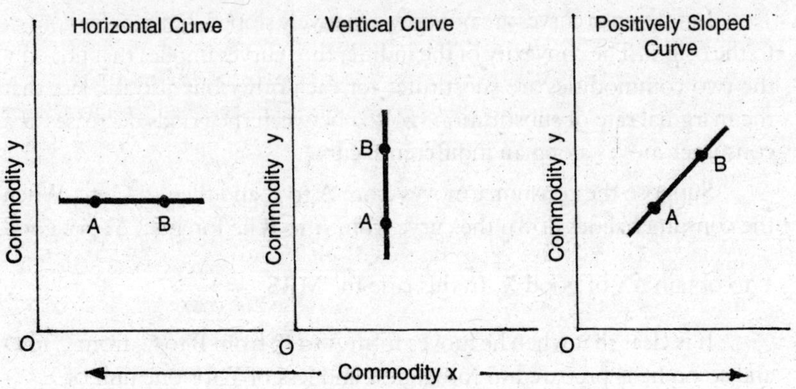

Fig 9.4

The curves that do not have negative slopes such as those shown in fig 9.4 cannot be indifference curves, in all three cases combination B is clearly preferable to combination A

5. Indifference curves do not move as a result of market circumstances (changes in income or prices)

6. Even though indifference curves cannot cross they need not be parallel.

7. Indifference curves do not touch the horizontal or vertical axis.

If they touch the axis, it violates the basic assumption that the consumer purchases two commodities in a combination. Purchasing only one

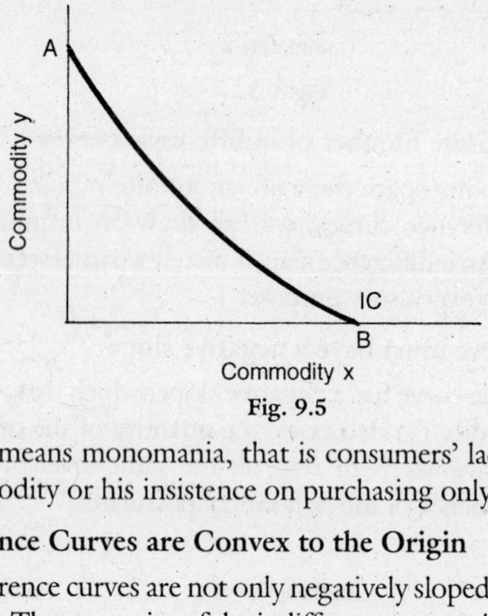

Fig. 9.5

commodity means monomania, that is consumers' lack of interest in the other commodity or his insistence on purchasing only one commodity.

8. Indifference Curves are Convex to the Origin

Indifference curves are not only negatively sloped, but are also convex to the origin. The convexity of the indifference curves implies that not only the two commodities are substitutes for each other but also the fact that the marginal rate of substitution (MRS) between the goods decreases as a consumer moves along an indifference curve.

Suppose the consumer moves from A to B and then to C etc. When the consumer slides down the curve from A to B he foregoes ΔY_1 of good Y to obtain ΔX of good X. In this case the $MRS_{xy} = \frac{\Delta y_1}{\Delta x}$

It is clear that when he moves from A to B, from B to C, from C to D and so on he is prepared to forego less and less of Y for one unit of X.

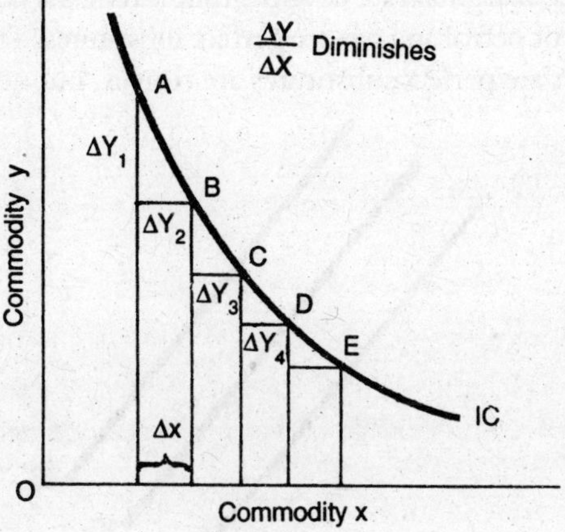

Fig. 9.6

Let us suppose that the indifference curve is not convex to the origin. (1) It may be concave to the origin. (2) It may be straight line.

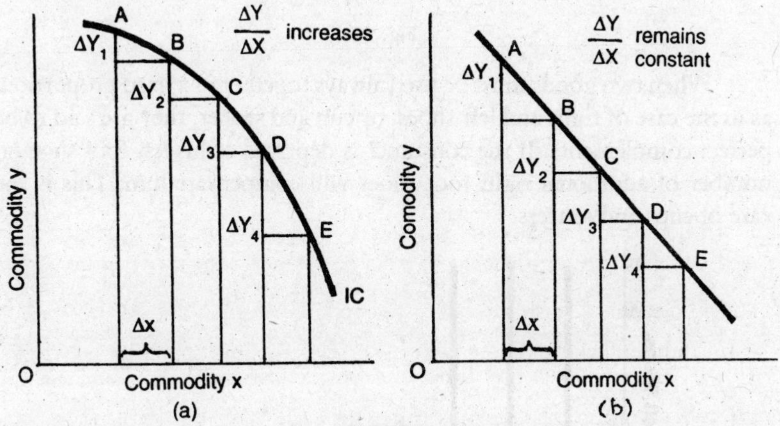

Fig. 9.7

Fig. 9.7 (*a*) shows that ΔY_2 is greater than ΔY_1 — that is marginal rate of substitution of X for Y increases.

Fig. 9.7 (*b*) shows that $\Delta Y_1 = \Delta Y_2$, that is the marginal rate of substitution of X for Y remains constant. Both the cases are against the normal behaviour of MRS (i.e., diminishing).

9. Indifference Curve for Substitute and Complementary Goods

The curvature of an indifference curve may be used to determine whether the commodities are substitutes or complements.

When two goods are completely interchangeable, they are perfect substitutes. The indifference curve for perfect substitutes will be a straight line because the marginal rate of substitution remains constant. Different brands of beer or petrol and gas are perfect substitutes. The preferences for two goods that are perfect substitutes are convex, but not strictly convex.

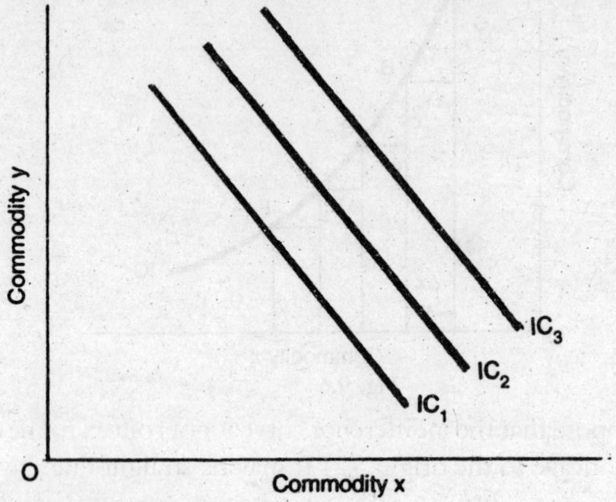

Fig. 9.8

When two goods must be used always together in a fixed proportion, as in the case of right and left shoes, or cup and saucer, they are said to be perfect complements. If the consumer is deprived of his left foot shoe no number of additional right foot shoes will compensate him. This is the case of cups and saucers.

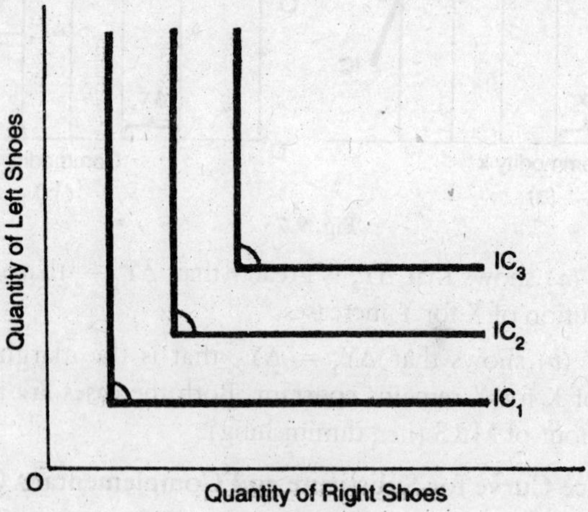

Fig. 9.9

The 90° angles in the indifference curves indicate that an increase in only one of the perfect complements does not increase the consumer's satisfaction. Thus the indifference curves are L-Shaped.

CONSUMER'S EQUILIBRIUM

A consumer is in equilibrium when he obtains maximum satisfaction from his expenditure on the commodities he wants to purchase. The main theme on which the theory of consumer behaviour is built is that a consumer attempts to allocate a limited money income among various available goods and services so as to maximise his satisfaction or utility.

ASSUMPTIONS

1. Indifference Map

The consumer has an indifference map which shows his scale of preferences for the various combinations of two commodities and it remains unchanged throughout the analysis.

2. Constant Income

He has a given amount of money to spend.

3. Perfect Competition

He is one of the many buyers and he knows the prices of all goods which are given and constant. Alternatively we can say that there is perfect competition in the market.

4. Homogeneity

All commodities are homogeneous and divisible.

5. Rationality

There is a rational behaviour on the part of the consumer who tries to maximise his satisfaction.

PRICE LINE OR BUDGET LINE

In order to study consumer's equilibrium it is necessary to understand his budget line. In the words of Prof. Maurice[2] "The budget line is the locus of combinations or bundles of goods that can be purchased if the entire money income is spent."

The price line indicates all the possible combinations of X and Y that a consumer can buy at a particular time, given the market prices and the consumer's income.

---

2. S.C. Maurice, *Economic Analysis Theory and Application,* 5th edn., Universal Book Stall, New Delhi, 1988, p. 141

Suppose our hypothetical consumer has a fixed income, say Rs. 8 to spend. Let us assume that he wishes to purchase two goods X and Y. The price of X is assumed to be Rs. 2, and that of Y, Re. 1. If he spends his entire income on X, he gets 4 units of X and no Y, or if he spends it on Y alone, he gets 8 units of Y and no X. The following table shows the various alternatives of X and Y that he could buy with Rs. 8.

Table 9.3

X *(units)*	Y *(units)*	*Total amount spend on* X + Y
4	0	Rs. 8 + 0 = 8
3	2	6 + 2 = 8
2	4	4 + 4 = 8
1	6	2 + 6 = 8
0	8	0 + 8 = 8

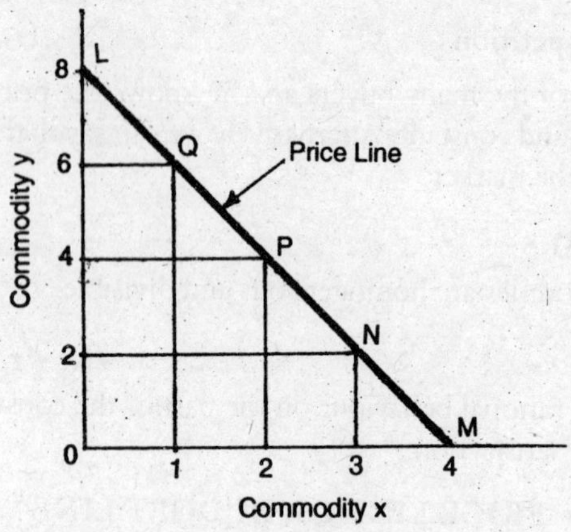

Fig. 9.10

In Fig. 9.10 Commodity X is measured along the horizontal axis and Y along the vertical axis. The line LM shows the various combinations of X and Y that could be bought with Rs. 8. The line LM is called the price line or budget line. Now the slope of the price line is measured as $\frac{OL}{OM}$.

At point Q the consumer is having 6Y and 1X and at point P he is having 4Y and 2X. The slope of LM line is the ratio of X price to Y price which is $2 = \frac{p_x}{p_y}$. Thus the slope of the price line is p_X. That is the slope of the price line or the budget line represents the ratio of the two prices under consideration.

It is obvious that the slope of the price line depends upon two factors.

1. The money income of the consumer and
2. Prices of the two goods he wants to buy.

MANY POSSIBLE PRICE LINES

Change in Consumer's Income

When the prices of two goods X and Y remain unchanged, so that $\frac{p_x}{p_y}$ remains constant, an increase in money income causes an outward parallel shift in the budget line. Similarly a decrease in money income, causes a parallel inward shift in the budget line.

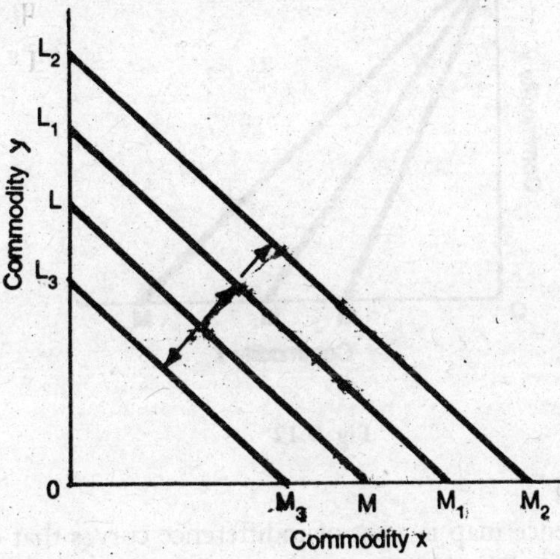

Fig. 9.11

Suppose the original price line is LM. Given the prices of the two goods and income, the consumer can buy OM of X commodity or OL of Y commodity. If his income increases the price line becomes L_1M_1. He can now buy OM_1 of X and OL_1 of Y. If his income increases further and the price line becomes L_2M_2, he can buy OM_2 of X and OL_2 of Y. Similarly when his income decreases, the income line will tend to shift downwards as L_3M_3.

Change in Price

A change in the price of any one of the two commodities results in a change in the slope of the price line.

Suppose the price of commodity X changes and the price of Y remains the same. When the price of X falls, the price ratio $\frac{Px}{Py}$ will tend to diminish. Now the price line changes from LM to LM_1 then to LM_2 etc. Conversely when the price of X tends to rise, the price ratio $\frac{Px}{Py}$ rises. Now the price line shifts from LM_2 to LM_1 and to LM.

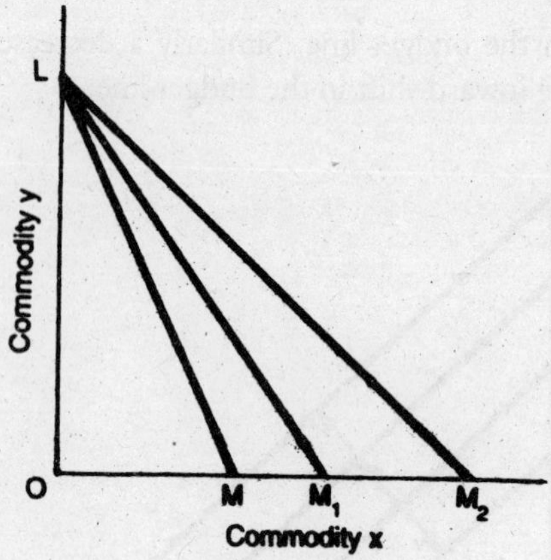

Fig. 9.12

Indifference Map

An indifference map is a set of indifference curves that describes a person's preference. The indifference map of a consumer shows all the properties of a normal indifference curve. All indifference curves slope downwards from left to right. Moreover they are convex to the origin. They do not touch any one of the two axes. Higher indifference curves represent higher levels of satisfaction. (Fig.9.13).

Conditions Necessary for Consumer's Equilibrium

1. The first condition is that the marginal rate of substitution must be equal to the ratios of commodity prices.

$$MRS_{xy} = \frac{MU_x}{MU_y} = \frac{P_x}{P_y}$$

2. Indifference curve should be convex to the origin.

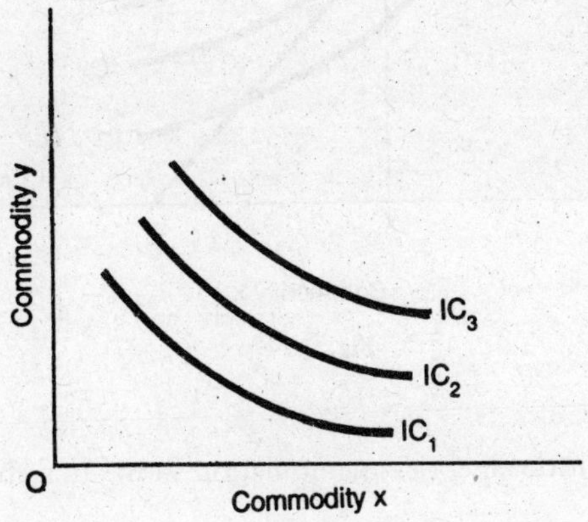

Fig. 9.13

Consumer's Equilibrium

Given the consumer's preference, i.e., indifference map, we are in the final stage of optimisation process, i.e., how much of X and Y does the consumer buy. The consumer's equilibrium represents the combination of goods purchased that maximises utility subject to the budget constraint. To obtain consumer's equilibrium we have to superimpose the budget line on the consumer's indifference map. The indifference map shows what is desirable. The budget line shows what is feasible. A consumer's equilibrium is a result of desirability and feasibility forces that a consumer is faced with. This is shown in fig.9.14.

The point of consumers' optimisation is attained at E, where indifference curve IC_2 is just tangent to the price line. At the point of tangency the slopes of the budget line (P_x/P_y) and of the indifference curve ($MRS_{xy} = MU_x/MU_y$) are equal:

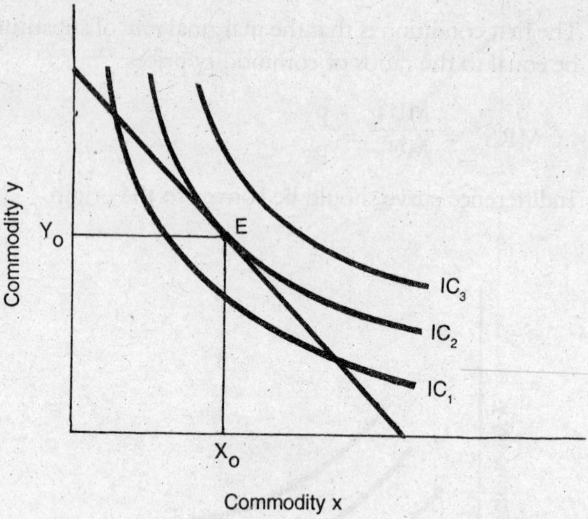

Fig. 9.14

$\frac{MU_x}{Mu_y} = \frac{P_x}{P_y}$. A little algebraic manipulation shows that this equation is equivalent to the marginal utility per rupee rule for equilibrium

$$\frac{MU_x}{P_x} = \frac{MU_y}{P_y}$$

Thus the first condition is denoted graphically by the point of tangency of the two curves. The second condition is implied by the convex shape of the indifference cruves. The choice (X_oY_o) is an optimal choice for the consumer.

INCOME EFFECT

Income effects are the adjustments people make because the purchasing power of the given income is altered when price changes.

The effect of a change in the consumer's income can be easily shown on an indifference curve.

14. W.J. Baumol, *Economic Theory and Operations Analysis,* Prentice-Hall of India Private Ltd., New Delhi, 1982, p. 211.

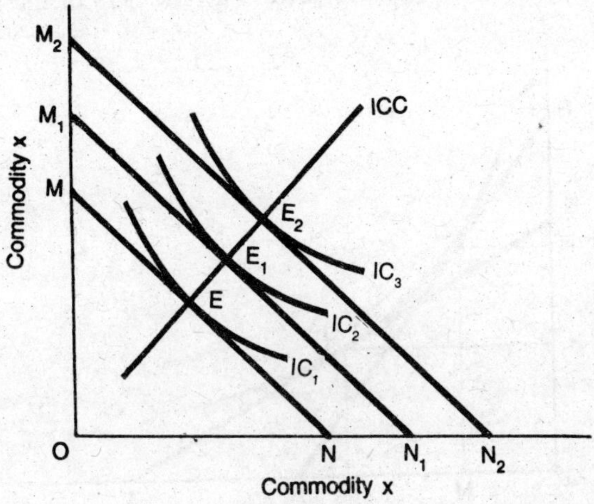

Fig. 9.15

In Fig. 9.15 the initial equilibrium position is at point E, where the indifference curve IC_1 is tangent to the price line MN. If income increases, then the budget line shifts from MN to M_1N_1 and then to M_2N_2. The corresponding equilibrium points will be E_1 and E_2 respectively. Income consumption curve (ICC) is derived by joining all equilibrium points E, E_1 and E_2 on the consumer's indifference map as income changes.

Generally, for normal goods income consumption curves (ICC) has a positive slope showing that as the consumer's income increases, his purchases of the two commodities will increase. But this need not be so in all cases.

SUBSTITUTION EFFECT

According to Stonier and Hague[3] "A substitution effect occurs, when the relative prices of goods change but the consumer's money income is altered in such a way that he is neither better nor worse off than he was before. His real income is the same. However, he has to rearrange his purchases in accordance with the new relative prices."

The substitution effect is based on the following assumptions:

1. The relative prices have changed making one commodity cheaper and the other commodity dearer.
2. Money income of the consumer does not change.

3. A.W. Stonier and D.C. Hague — *Op. cit.*, p. 67

The substitution effect is explained with the help of the following diagram.

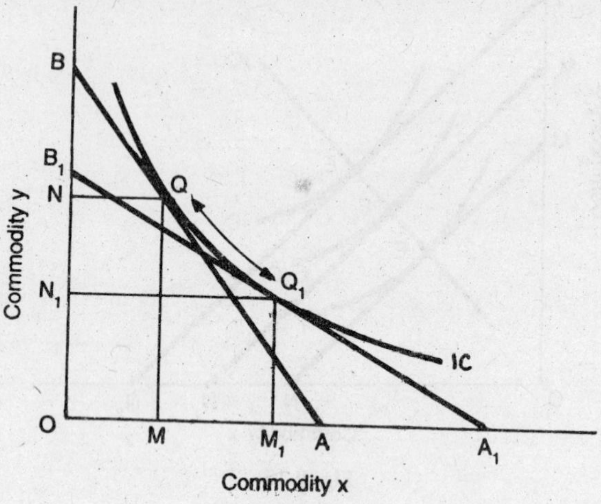

Fig. 9.16

In Fig. 9.16 AB is the original price-line. The point of equilibrium is at point Q where the price line is tangent to the indifference curve. He buys OM of X and ON of Y. Suppose the price of commodity Y increase and the price of commodity X falls relatively. Consequently the new price line will be B_1A_1. It touches the indifference curve at point Q_1 — the new equilibrium position of the consumer with relative changes in prices. Thus although the consumer remains on the same indifference curve, he is on it at a different position. Instead of being at point Q he is now at point Q_1. Here the consumer has reduced the consumption of commodity Y from ON to ON_1 and increased the consumption of commodity X from OM to OM_1. This move along the indifference curve from Q to Q_1 represents the substitution effect. The consumer though neither better off nor worse off, substitutes X which is now relatively cheaper for Y, which is now relatively dearer. When the consumer substitutes the consumption of one commodity for the other, it is known as the 'Substitution effect.'

PRICE EFFECT

Price effect is the change in the quantity consumed of goods and services due to a change in their relative prices.

To explain the price effect let us take a two commodity model in which the price of commodity X changes keeping the consumers' income, his tastes and preferences and the price of commodity Y constant.

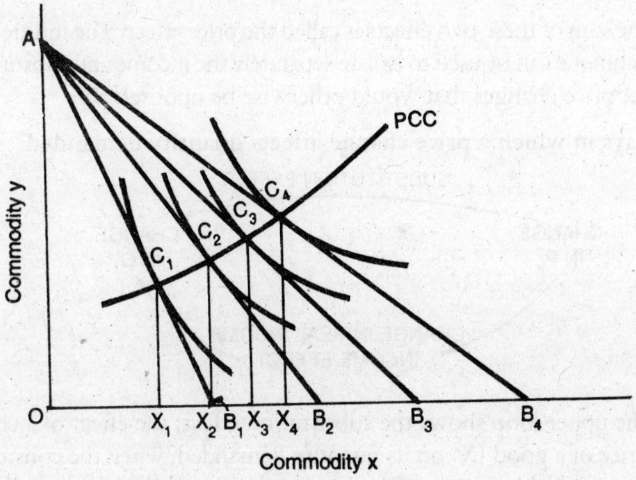

Fig. 9.17

In Fig. 9.17 as the price of X is successively lowered the budget line shifts from AB_1 to AB_2, AB_2 to AB_3 and AB_3 to AB_4 respectively. Given the budget line the consumer chooses the combination that is shown by the tangency of an indifference curve and the budget line C_1, C_2, C_3 and C_4 represent such equilibrium combinations. The curve connecting all the points of consumer's equilibrium as price changes is called the Price Consumption Curve. In the above figure the PCC has an upward slope. This indicates that when the price of X falls, consumer's real income increases. This enables him to buy more of both goods X and Y.

INCOME AND SUBSTITUTION EFFECTS OF A PRICE CHANGE

Economists divide the change in the quantity of a good purchased, resulting from a change in its price, into two components, viz., substitution effect and income effect.

Substitution Effect: The substitution effect is that portion of the change in quantity demanded due solely to a change in relative prices.

Income Effect: Income effects are the adjustments people make because the purchasing power of a given income is altered when price changes.

The sum of these two effects is called the price effect. The indifference curve technique can be used to isolate separately the income and substitution effects of price changes that would otherwise be unobservable.[4]

Two ways in which a price change affects quantity demanded

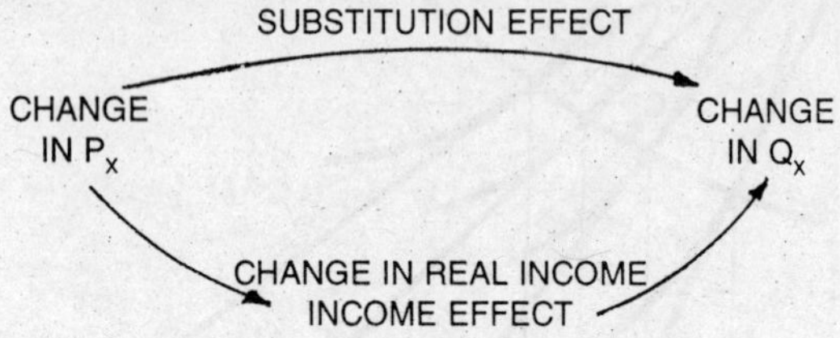

The upper loop shows the substitution effect; the effect of a change in the price of a good (X) on its quantity demanded, when the consumer's real income is held constant. The lower loop shows the income effect. It shows how a change in the price of an article leads to a change in the consumer's real income, which in turn affects the quantity demanded.

The splitting of the price effect into the substitution and income effects can be done in several ways, depending on what we would like to hold constant.

There are mainly two methods suggested in economic literature.

1. The Hicksian method,
2. The Slutskian method

The Hicksian Method

Let the consumer be in equilibrium initially at E_1 on indifference curve IC_1 and the budget line AB_1, where he consumes E_1X_1 of Y and OX_1 of X. Now let the price of X fall (income and the prices of other goods remain constant) so that the new budget line is AB_2. The new budget line AB_2 is tangent to IC_2 at point E_3. Thus a movement from E_1 to E_3 or an increase in the quantity demanded of X from X_1 to X_2 takes place.

Now we can ask the question[5]: "What would be the consumer's optimal bundle be, if he or she is faced with the new lower price of X but experiences no change in real income?" The answer is E_3 with X_2 units of good X demanded.

4. G.S. Maddala, *Micro Economics — Theory and Applications*. McGraw-Hill International Edition, 1989, p. 13
5. Robert Y. Ahw, *Micro Economics, Theory and Applications*, John Wiley & Sons, New York 1976, p. 81

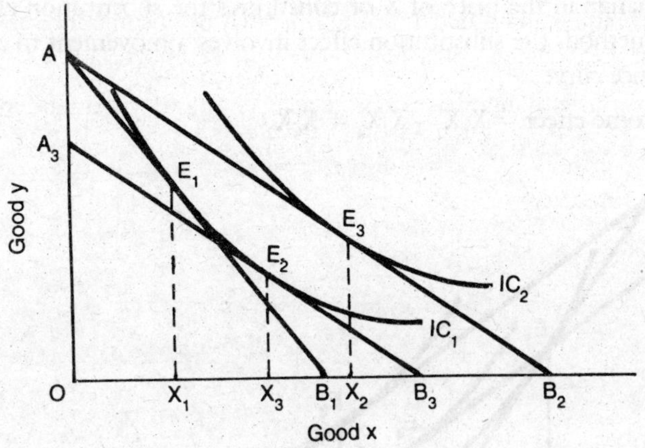

Fig. 9.18

Hicksian method of eliminating income effect is to reduce consumer's income, (by way of taxation), so that he returns to his original indifference curve, IC_1, keeping in view the new price ratio. This has been done by drawing a price line A_3B_3 parallel to AB_2 and tangent to indifference curve IC_1 at point E_2. Thus the movement from E_1 to E_2 or the increase in quantity demanded from X_1 to X_3 is solely in response to a change in relative prices. This is the substitution effect.

If we substract substitution effect X_1X_3, from the total price effect X_1X_2, we get the income effect.

Income effect = $X_1X_2 - X_1X_3 = X_3X_2$

The Slutskian Method

The Slutskian version of bifurcation of income effect and substitution effect is illustrated in Fig. 9.19.

The initial budget line is AB_1. The consumer is in equilibrium at point E_1 on indifference curve IC_1. When price of X falls, and other things remaining the same, the consumer moves to another equilibrium point E_3, on indifference curve IC_3. The movement from point E_1 to E_3 increases consumer's purchase of X by X_1X_2. This is the total price effect caused by the fall in price of X.

In an attempt to isolate the substitution effect, Eugen Slutsky suggests that as the consumer's real income is reduced he must be able to purchase his original consumption bundle (i.e., OX_1 of X and E_1X_1 of Y) at the new price ratio. Doing so would lead to the budget line A_4B_4, which passes through E_1 but is parallel to AB_2, thus reflecting the new price for X. Slutsky then argues that the movement along this budget line from E_1 to E_4 is due to the change in the price of X or constitutes the substitution effect. In Slutsky method, the substitution effect involves a movement to a higher indifference curve.

Income effect = $X_1X_2 - X_1X_4 = X_4X_2$

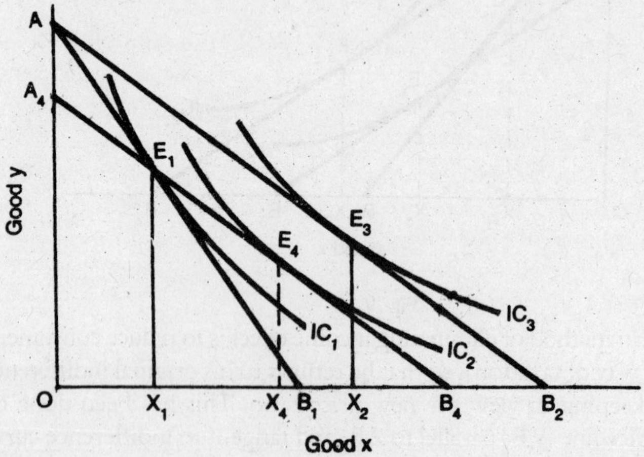

Fig. 9.19

Hicksian Approach Vs. Slutskian Approach

Slutskian approach is an attempt to hold the apparent real income constant in the sense that consumer is left with the income just sufficient to

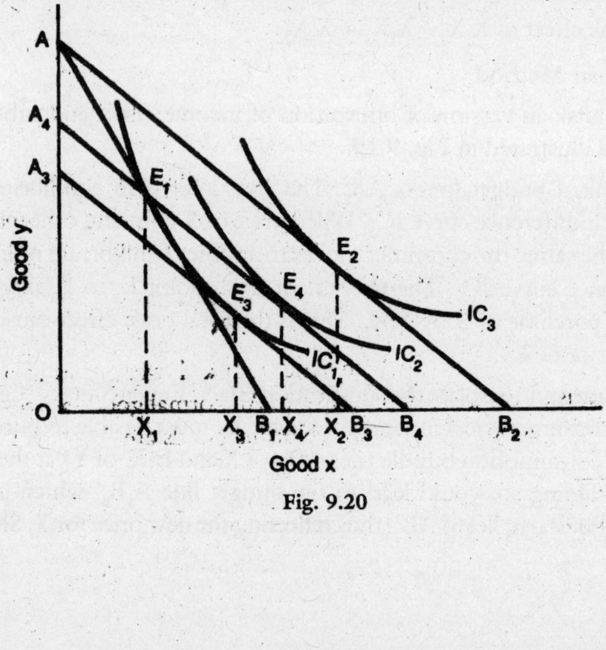

Fig. 9.20

purchase the original combination of the two goods. Hicksian approach holds constant the real income expressed in terms of the original level of satisfaction so that the consumer remains on the original indifference curve. Thus the Hicksian Substitution effect keeps utility constant rather than keeping purchasing power constant.

The measurement from E_1 to E_2 equals X_1X_2 of commodity X. Till this point there is no difference between the two approaches. But variations start beyond this point. According to the Hicksian approach, the movement from E_1 to E_3 is the substitution effect and movement from E_3 to E_2 is income effect. According to the Slutskian approach the movement from E_1 to E_4 is the substitution effect and movement from E_4 to E_2 is the income effect. The relationship between the price effect, the substitution and the income effect of the two approaches can be summed up as follows:

Table 9.3

Method	*Fall in the price of X*	*Total price effect*	*Substitution effect*	*Income effect*
1. Hicksian method	– Δpx	$X_1 X_2$	$X_1 X_3$	$X_3 X_2$
2. Slutskian method	– Δpx	$X_1 X_2$-	$X_1 X_4$	$X_4 X_2$

Table 9.3 shows that the fall in the price of X and the total price effect are same in the two approaches. But the substitution effect (X_1 X_4) is more under the Slutskian approach than it is under the Hicksian approach (X_1 X_3). Consequently, income effect (X_4 X_2) is less under the Slutskian approach than under the Hicksian approach (X_3 X_2).

As regards the comparative importance of the two methods, Hicksian method seems to be more scientific because the consumer remains on the same indifference curve due to a fall in the price of X, he becomes neither better off nor worse off as a result of the substitution effect. The Slutskian method is not theoretically defensible, because the movement involves between indifference curves and thus is not really a substitution effect.

To put it in the words of Baumol[6]: "While Hicksian approach is considered as a highly persuasive solution to the problem of splitting price effect into substitution and income effects, Slutskian approach is intuitively perhaps less satisfying."

6. W.J. Baumol, *Economic Theory and Operations Analysis,* Prentice-Hall of India Private Ltd., New Delhi, 1982, p. 211.

GIFFEN PARADOX

The law of demand, which states that at lower prices more would be bought, is a very general proposition. All normal goods as well as most of the inferior goods obey the law. However, there are certain types of inferior goods to which the general rule does not apply. Such goods are known as Giffen goods. In the case of Giffen goods, income and substitution effects work in the opposite direction and the income effect exceeds the substitution effect. This phenomenon causes a paradoxical situation, i.e., when the price of an inferior good increases, its quantity demanded also increases. This paradox is known as Giffen paradox.

It is named after Sir Robert Giffen (1837-1910), a famous British statistician and economist. Giffen claimed to have observed very poor workers increasing their consumption of cheap food like bread, when its price increased. The workers spent large portions of their income on bread, which was apparently an inferior good for them. When the price rose, the income effect would have been so strong as to force them to drop meat and other more expensive items of food from their diet. As, bread was still the cheapest food available, they have purportedly consumed more of it even though its price has risen.

Marshall[7] attributed this paradox to Robert Giffen. But there is no mention to this paradox in the voluminous writings of Giffen. Moreover, economists doubt whether Giffen paradox was actually observed. It is so difficult to find an example of Giffen good in the modern world that it must be concluded that the so-called Giffen paradox is very unlikely; it can therefore be regarded as a geometric curiosity with little empirical evidence.[8]

Three conditions are necessary for classifying goods as Giffen goods. Giffen goods are inferior goods; but not all inferior goods are Giffen goods.

1. It should be an inferior good having a relatively larger negative income effect.
2. The substitution effect of a price change must be relatively small.
3. It must be an inferior good which absorbs a large proportion of the consumer's income.

Originally, the consumer was in equilibrium at E_1. As the price of X is lowered the consumer moves from E_1 to E_3 and the quantity of X purchased decreases by X_2X_1. The movement from E_1 to E_3 can be split into two parts,

---

7. *Principles of Economics,* 8th Edn., Macmillan, London, 1982, pp. 109-110
8. David N. Hyman, *Modern Micro Economics,* Mosby College Publishing St. Louis 1989, p. 119.

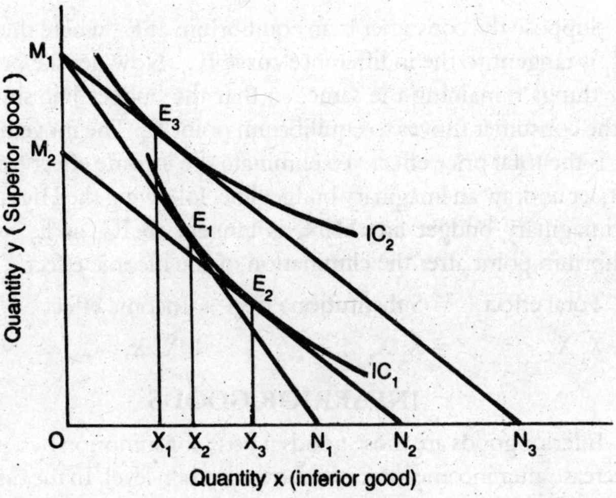

Fig. 9.21

the substitution effect which increases the quantity of X purchased by X_2X_3 units and the income effect which decreases the quantity purchased by X_3X_1 units. Since the decrease in quantity demanded due to the income effect is greater than the increase in quantity demanded due to the substitution effect, the total price effect of a decrease in the price of X is negative.

NORMAL GOODS

Normal goods are those that a person consumes more when income increases.

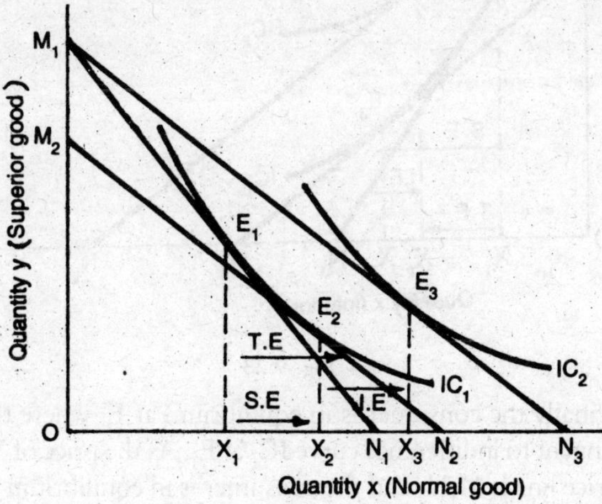

Fig. 9.22

Suppose the consumer is an equilibrium at E_1, where the budget line M_1N_1 is tangent to the indifference curve IC_1. Now, let the price of X fall, other things remaining the same, so that the budget line shifts to M_1N_3 and the consumer moves to equilibrium point E_3. The movement from E_1 to E_3 is the total price effect. To eliminate the income effect from the price effect, let us draw an imaginary budget line, following the Hicksian method. The imaginary budget line M_2N_2 is tangent to IC_1 at E_2, which is the equilibrium point after the elimination of the income effect.

Total effect = Substitution effect + Income effect

$X_1X_3 = X_1X_2 + X_2X_3$

INFAERIOR GOODS

Inferior goods are those goods whose consumption by a person tends to decrease after income increases above a certain level. In the case of inferior goods positive substitution effect is more powerful than the negative income effect and the net result would be an increase in the quantity of the goods bought, when its price falls.

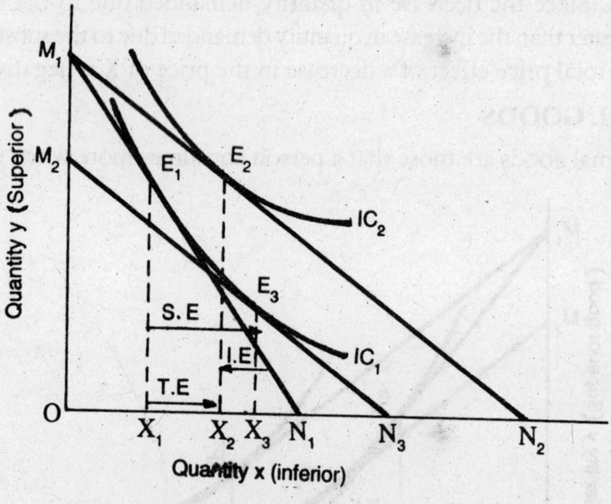

Fig. 9.23

Originally the consumer is in equilibrium at E_1 where the price line M_1N_1 is tangent to indifference curve IC_1 at E_1. As the price of X is lowered, the new price line is M_1N_2 and the consumer is in equilibrium at E_2, where the price line M_1N_2 is tangent to indifference curve IC_2. The movement from E_1 to E_2 is the total price effect. To eliminate the income effect from the price effect, let us draw an imaginary budget line M_2N_3 (following the Hicksian method), tangent to the original indifference curve IC_1 at E_3, which is the equilibrium point after the elimination of income effect. Consumer movement from E_1 to E_3 is due to an increase in the quantity consumed of X by $X_1 X_3$. The movement from X_3 to X_2 shows a negative income effect.

Income Effect = $X_1X_3 - X_1X_2 = -X_2X_3$

Thus in the case of inferior goods, the positive substitution effect (X_1X_3) outweighs the negative income effect (X_2X_3). This clearly shows that the law of demand applies to most of the inferior goods.

Substitution and Income effects of a price decline on quantity demanded, can be tabulated as follows:

Table 9.4

Type of Good	*Substitution effect*	*Income effect*	*Total effect*
Normal	Increase	Increase	Increase
Inferior (but not Giffen)	Increase	Decrease	Increase
Giffen	Increase	Decrease	Decrease

DERIVATION OF DEMAND CURVE

The individual consumer's demand curve can be derived from his price consumption curve. In fact, the individual demand curve and his price consumption curve give us the same information. But the demand curve gives it in a more direct manner.

The price consumption curve (PCC) traces the effect of a change in price on the quantity demanded. The process of deriving the individual consumer's demand curve from his price consumption curve is shown in Figure 9.24.

In Fig. 9.24 commodity A is measured along the horizontal axis, and money income is measured along the vertical axis. IC_1, IC_2 and IC_3 are indifference curves. Now the price of commodity A is successively lowered. Therefore LN, LQ and LR are the budget lines of the consumer. At first the consumer is in equilibrium at P_1 and purchases OM_1 quantity of A. If the total money income of the consumer is divided by the number of the units that can be bought with that money, we get per unit price of the good. At P_1, the price per unit of commodity A is OL/ON. At OL/ON price, the consumer buys OM_1 quantity of commodity A. Similarly at

OL/OQ price, he purchases OM_2 quantities of commodity A and at OL/OR price he purchases OM_3 quantities of commodity A.

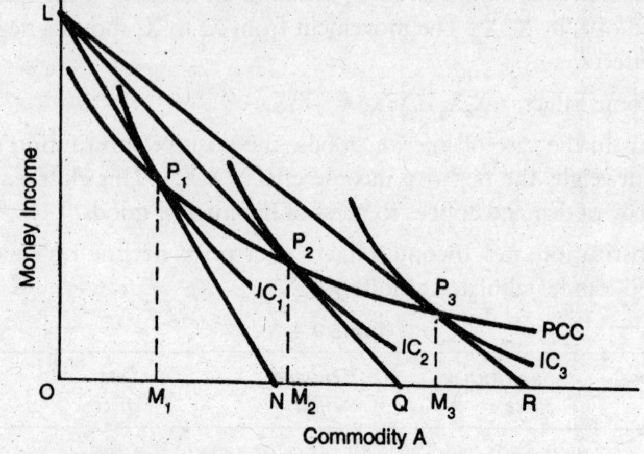

Fig. 9.24

The price consumption curve (PCC) connects all equilibrium points P_1, P_2 and P_3 at different prices.

The demand curve shows the price and quantity of goods purchased by the consumer. Now let us assume that the income of the consumer is Rs. 40 and ON = 8 units, OQ = 10 units and OR = 20 units. By using this information, the demand schedule can be represented as follows.

Table 9.5

Price-Demand Schedule for Commodity A

Budget line	*Price of A* $= \frac{\text{Total money income}}{\text{No. of units of A}}$	*Quantity of A demanded*
LN	OL/ON (40/8= Rs.5)	OM_1 = 8 units
LQ	OL/OQ (40/10 = Rs.4)	OM_2 = 10 units
LR	OL/OR (40/20 = Rs.2)	OM_3 = 20 units

With this demand schedule, we can construct the individual consumer's demand curve.

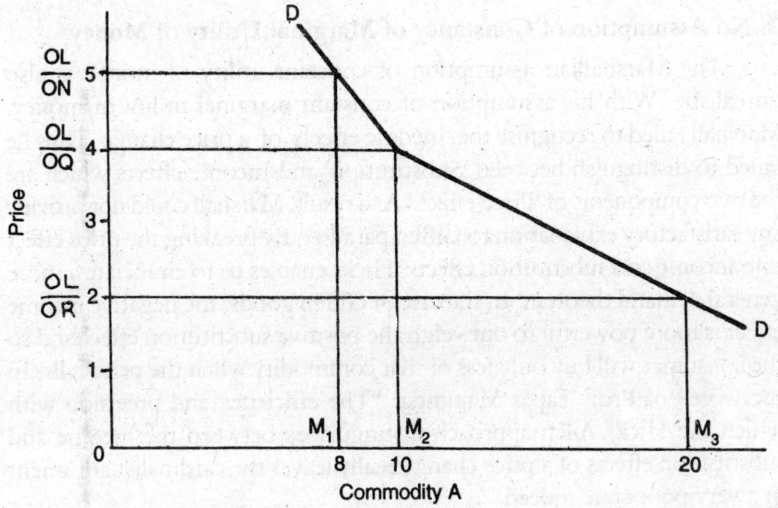

Fig. 9.25

Fig. 9.25 shows the individual consumer's demand curve. The market demand curve can be obtained by a horizontal summation of individual demand curves.

SUPERIORITY OF INDIFFERENCE CURVE ANALYSIS

The Hicks and Allen indifference curve has certain distinct and undeniable merits over the Marshallian utility analysis.

1. More Realistic Measurement of Utility

The Marshallian analysis of consumer behaviour is based upon the insecure foundation of the cardinal utility analysis which assumes that utility is measurable and additive. This according to Hicks and Allen is highly unrealistic and ambiguous. Since utility is a psychic-entity, it varies from person to person and from time to time.

The basic merit of the indifference curve technique is that, it is based on the ordinal utility function. It is not assumed that the consumer is capable of measuring the amount of utility attributable to any given increment of a commodity. All that is assumed is that "the consumer weighs in his mind the relative desirability of the different combinations of goods and services" and indicates whether one combination is preferred more or less or equally to another. Thus the indifference curve technique provides a more realistic measure of consumer's satisfaction compared to the original one provided by Marshall.

2. No Assumption of Constancy of Marginal Utility of Money

The Marshallian assumption of constant utility of money is also unrealistic. With his assumption of constant marginal utility of money. Marshall failed to recognise the 'Income effects' of a price change. Thus he failed to distinguish between 'Substitution' and Income effects which are the two components of 'Price-effect.' As a result, Marshall could not provide any satisfactory explanation to Giffen paradox. By breaking the price effect into income and substitution effects, Hicks enables us to enunciate a more general demand theorem. In the case of Giffen goods, the negative income effect is more powerful to outweigh the positive substitution effect and so the consumer will buy only less of that commodity when the price falls. In the words of Prof. Tapas Majumdar "The efficiency and precision with which the Hicks Allen approach distinguishes between the income and substitution effects of a price change really leaves the cardinalist argument in a very poor state indeed."

3. Analyses Multi-goods Model

Marshallian demand theory is based on a single commodity model. Marshall avoids the discussion of substitutes and complementary goods by grouping them together as one commodity. Hick's ordinal utility approach considers atleast two goods in one combination. Prof. Hicks explains the relationship between substitutes and complements of goods in a scientific way.

4. Less Restrictive

It has been asserted that Marshallian utility analysis assumes 'too much' while it explains 'too little'. The indifference curve analysis arrives at the same equilibrium condition for a consumer with less restrictive and fewer assumptions.

A consumer is said to be in equilibrium when the price line is tangent to the indifference curve. To put it in other words, the marginal rate of substitution is equal to the price ratio of the two commodities. Thus at E in our diagram.

$$\text{MRS of x for y} = \frac{\text{Price of x}}{\text{Price of y}} \quad \text{... (1)}$$

But MRS of x for y is nothing but the ratio between the marginal utility of x and the marginal utility of y.

$$\text{MRS of x for y} = \frac{\text{MU of x}}{\text{MU of y}} \quad \text{... (2)}$$

From (1) and (2) it follows that

$$\frac{\text{MU of x}}{\text{MU of y}} = \frac{\text{Price of x}}{\text{Price of y}}$$

which can be written as $\dfrac{\text{MU of x}}{\text{Price of x}} = \dfrac{\text{MU of y}}{\text{Price of y}}$

Thus the proportionality rule of consumer's equilibrium enunciated by Marshall can be explained through the indifference curve with less restrictive and fewer assumptions.

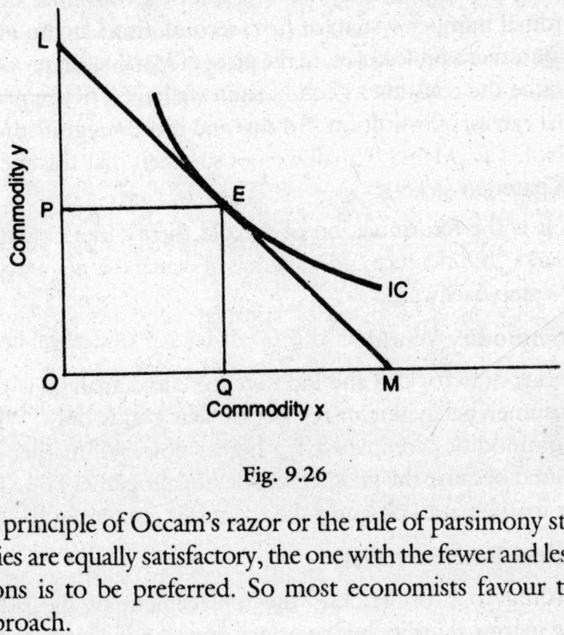

Fig. 9.26

The principle of Occam's razor or the rule of parsimony states that if two theories are equally satisfactory, the one with the fewer and less stringent assumptions is to be preferred. So most economists favour the ordinal utility approach.

5. Practical Importance

The indifference curve analysis can be used to analyse the effects of rationing and taxation on consumption and incomes of the people.

A CRITICAL EVALUATION

Some economists like D.H. Robertson, Frank H. Knight and W.E. Armstrong have strongly criticised the indifference curve theory.

According to Schumpeter "From a practical stand point, we are not much better off when drawing purely imaginary indifference curves than we are when speaking of a purely imaginary utility function."

1. Old Wine in a New Bottle

Prof. D.H. Robertson is of the view that indifference curve analysis is merely 'the old wine in a new bottle.' The analysis according to him, has simply substituted new concepts in the place of old ones.

In splitting the throat of diminishing utility, Hicks and Allen did not leave us destitute. They have given us in its place a creative concept known as the marginal rate of substitution. Instead of the concept of 'utility' we have the term 'preference.' Instead of the cardinal number system of one, two, three etc. which measures the strength of a consumer's device, we have the ordinal number system of first, second, third etc. to indicate the pattern of consumer's preferences. In the place of Marshallian proportionality rule to describe the consumer's equilibrium we have a new equation, viz., the marginal rate of substitution. All this and more suggests the question posed by Prof. J.K. Mehta: "Shall we not say then that this method is of Marshall in paretian jacket?"

Thus it is the reformulation of the old theory in a new grab. Prof. Knight remarks "Indifference curve analysis of demand is not a step forward, it is in fact a step backward."

2. Two Commodity World

A serious drawback of the indifference curve analysis is that it can analyse consumer behaviour in respect of two goods only. When more than two commodities are involved, a higher power of mathematics may have to be used because the geometrical device altogether fails. The use of high power mathematics obscures the economic content of the analysis.

3. Marshallian Base Essential

According to Prof. Hicks, "the replacement of the principle of diminishing marginal utility by the principle of diminishing marginal rate of substitution is not a mere translation; it is a positive change in the foundation of the theory of consumers' demand."[9]

But Prof. Armstrong rightly contends that it is impossible to arrive at the Hicksian principle of diminishing MRS without making use of the 'Marshallian Scaffolding" of the marginal utility. Why does the MRSxy

---

9. J.R. Hicks, *Value and Capital*, 2nd Edn., ELBS, 1979, p. 21.

diminish and the indifference curve becomes convex to the origin. As the consumer's stock of X increases the marginal utility of X in terms of Y falls and that of Y increases. Thus, Hicks has not been able to derive the fundamental concept of utility. By a stroke of terminological manipulation, the concept of utility has been relegated to the background, but it is there all the same. Thus it is obvious that "the principle of diminishing marginal rate of substitution is as much determinate or indeterminate as the poor law of diminishing marginal utility."

4. Fails to Explain Consumer's Behaviour when Risk and Uncertainty Arise

John Von Neumann and Oskar Morgenstern in their classic work 'The Theory of Games and Economic Behaviour' have demonstrated that an indifference curve is of no avail to explain the consumer's behaviour when risks and uncertainties are involved. Prof. Samuelson has termed the whole technique as non-operational.

5. Ignores Demonstration Effect

The indifference curve analysis takes no notice of Duesenberry's demonstration effect. According to this hypothesis, an individual's consumption pattern depends upon the level of consumption of others.

6. Market Behaviour is Ignored

The indifference curve analysis does not shed much light on market changes in the prices of other goods. It deals only with the prices of two goods which is unrealistic.

7. Introspective

The indifference curve analysis requires highly introspective information from the consumer because he is required to order all combinations according to his preference. Hicks himself considered it as most awkward assumption, and removed, it latter in his 'Revision of demand theory.' Prof. Samuelson has developed a theory known as 'revealed preference theory' with a behaviourist model.

In the words of Prof. Robertson "Indifference jumps from the frying pan of difficulty on measuring the utility into the fire of unreality of assuming consumer's complete knowledge of all his scales of preferences."

8. Fewer Assumptions have no Justification

The superiority claimed on the basis of fewer assumptions is not justified by economists. As Georgescu Roegan asks, "could we refuse to take into account of animals with more than two feet on the ground that only two feet are needed for walking."

9. Continuity

Indifference curve is supposed to be smooth and continuous. This is a highly unrealistic assumption.

10. Relation of Transitivity is Objected

Prof. Armstrong criticises the relation of transitivity involved in the indifference curve technique.

According to Prof. Armstrong, the consumer is indifferent between A and B not because the total utility of combination A is equal to the total utility of combination B, but because the difference between the total utilities is so small as to be imperceptible to the consumer. However, if we compare A with C the difference between the total utilities becomes large enough to become perceptible. Thus the consumer will not remain indifferent between A and C; he will either prefer A to C or C to A. Thus if we remove the assumption of transitivity, indifference curve will be discontinuous as shown in Fig. 9.27 (*b*).

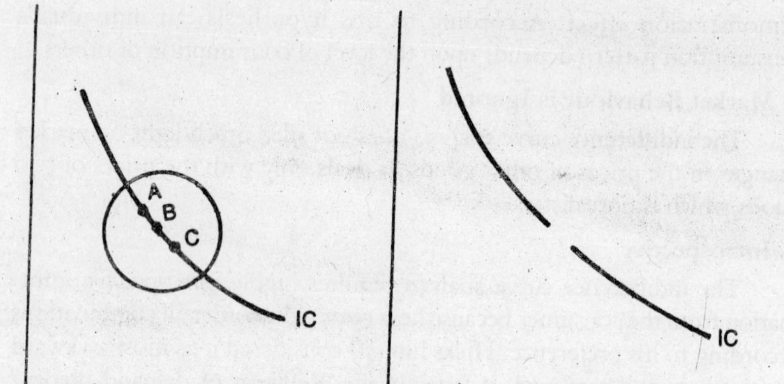

Fig. 9.27

11. Absurd Combination

Indifference curve analysis may look absurd in the case of bulky goods which are not divisible. It is ridiculous to say that a student is indifferent between 1 shirt and 10 pants and 5 shirts and 2 pants, as he derives the same satisfaction from the two combinations. Moreover it is nonsense to say that 2¼ shirts are combined with 6½ pants to get the same indifference curve.

12. Limited Empirical Nature

The indifference curve technique is not very much amenable to empirical research.

13. Constancy of Tastes

The assumption of constancy of tastes is not correct. Moreover, it could not analyse the effect of advertising on consumption behaviour.

14. Group Choices

The indifference curve analysis deals with the equilibrium position of an individual consumer. It throws little light on the analysis of group choices or group equilibrium.

Despite these shortcomings, it makes a considerable improvement on the orthodox cardinal utility analysis.

QUESTIONS

1. Bring out the main assumptions of ordinal utility analysis
2. State and discuss the properties of indifference curves.
3. Write a note on Marginal Rate of Substitution.
4. Explain that price effect consists of income effect and substitution effect.
5. Explain Consumer equilibrium through the technique of indifference curve

◆ ◆ ◆

10

CONSUMER'S SURPLUS

If you don't appreciate what you've got, get what you appreciate.

— *G.B. Shaw*

The concept of consumer's surplus stems from the demand curve. The doctrine was originally stated by the French engineer-economist, J.A. Dupuit in 1844. He tried to measure the consumer's surplus that would accrue to people as a result of the construction of a bridge across a river. Jenkin (1833-85), an English economist used the idea of consumer's surplus in discussing the problem of taxation.

But Alfred Marshall refined the concept in logical details in his epoch-making book 'Principles of Economics.' Recently Prof. Boulding[1] named it "Buyer's surplus." Consumer's surplus is felt in commodities which are highly useful but relatively cheap. Newspaper, salt, match box, postage stamps etc. are some classic examples. For these commodities we are ready to pay more than what we pay, if the alternative is to go without them. The extra satisfaction that we derive is called consumer's surplus.

According to Prof. Marshall,[2] "The excess of the price which he (consumer) would be willing to pay rather than go without the thing, over that which he actually does pay, is the economic measure of this surplus satisfaction. It may be called consumer's surplus."

Prof. Samuelson[3] defines it thus: "The gap between the total utility of a good and its total market value is called consumer's surplus."

1. K.E. Boulding, *Economic Analysis,* Fourth edition, Harper & Row, New York, 1969, p. 640.
2. A. Marshall, *Principles of Economics,* Macmillan, London 1982, p. 103.
3. P.A. Samuelson, *Economics,* McGraw-Hill International Book Co., 1983, p. 413.

To use Hicks',[4] words "It (consumers surplus) is the difference between the marginal valuation of a unit and the price which is actually paid for it."

CONSUMER'S SURPLUS AND THE LAW OF DIMINISHING MARGINAL UTILITY

The concept is based on the law of diminishing marginal utility. According to the law of diminishing marginal utility, utility will diminish for every additional increment of a good. In a market, there will be only one price for a commodity. Suppose a consumer buys 'n' units of a commodity, he will pay the same price for all the 'n' units, eventhough he may get higher satisfaction from the intra marginal units or earlier units.

Although the concept of consumer's surplus has been subject to numerous sophisticated measurements, Alfred Marshall's simple and original presentation is still useful.

Consumer's surplus = Total utility – (Price × Quantity)

Symbolically,

$$\text{C.S.} = \text{TU} - (\text{P} \times \text{Q})$$
$$= \Sigma\,\text{MU} - \text{P} \times \text{Q}$$

where TU = Total Utility

P = Price

Q = Quantity

Σ (Sigma) indicates the sum total.

Table 10.1 illustrates the measurement of consumer's surplus for an individual consumer:

Table 10.1

Units of Commodity	*Marginal Utility (Imaginary price)*	*Market Price (paise)*	*Consumer's Surplus*
1	50	10	40
2	40	10	30
3	30	10	20
4	20	10	10
5	10	10	0
Total 5 units	T.U. 150	50	100

Thus C.S. = TU – (P × Q)

4. J.R. Hicks, *A Revision of Demand Theory,* Clarendon Press Oxford, 1959, p. 95.

$= 150 - (10 \times 5)$
$= 150 - 50 = 100$

The following diagram makes the idea clear.

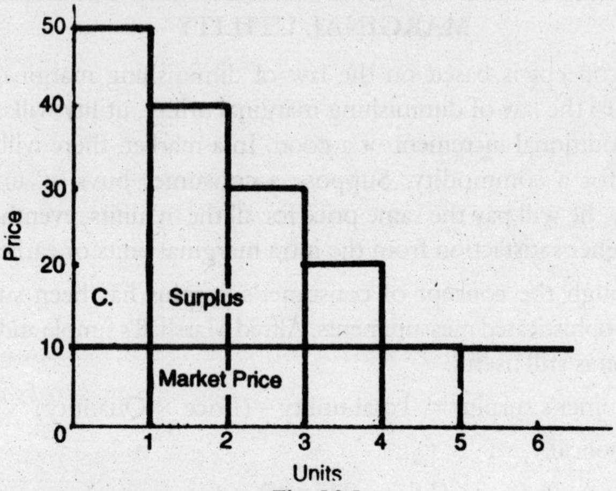

Fig. 10.1

In Fig. 10.1 units of commodity are given along the x-axis, and y-axis represents price. Market price is the same for all units. Therefore, C.S. is 100 (40 + 30 + 20 + 10).

Consumer's Surplus for a Market

Consumer's surplus for the market as a whole can be easily measured by calculating the area below the market demand curve and above the price line.

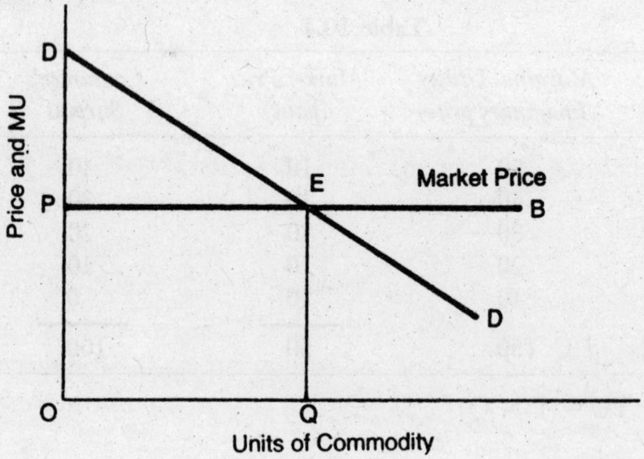

Fig. 10.2

In Fig. 10.2 the demand curve reflects the price a consumer is willing to pay for the successive units of a commodity. The demand curve is based on the law of diminishing marginal utility. The horizontal straight line PB indicates market price and is based on the assumption that market price is the same for all units. OQ is the number of units purchased by the consumer.

ODEQ = The amount of money the consumer is prepared to spend to get OQ units.

OPEQ = The actual amount of money spent by the consumer to get OQ units.

DPE = Consumer's surplus.

From Consumer's Surplus to Consumers' Surplus

The idea of consumer's surplus can be extended to the society as a whole. According to Marshall, if we assume that inter personal differences in income, taste, fashion, etc. are cancelled out, we can measure the total surplus satisfaction enjoyed by the society as a whole. This can be calculated by adding together the consumer's surplus enjoyed by all the consumers individually.[5] Consumers' surplus refers to the surplus of a single consumer; consumers' surplus refers to the sum of the surpluses of a number of consumers.

Market Price and Consumer's Surplus

The relationship between market price and consumer's surplus is inverse. A fall in price will cause an increase in consumer's surplus and vice versa.

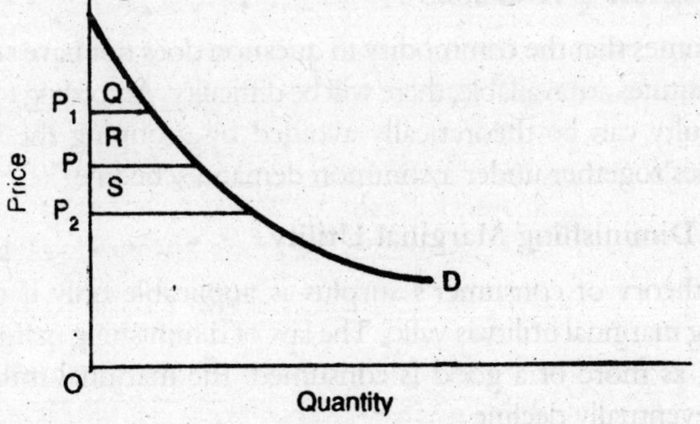

Fig. 10.3

5. H.S. Agarwal — *Micro Economics,* Shiva Lal Agarwala & Company, Agra 1983, p. 152.

When price is OP, consumer's surplus is the area Q plus R. If the price rises to OP_1, the loss of consumer's surplus is area R. Area S is the gain in consumer's surplus when there is a fall in price from OP to OP_2.

ASSUMPTIONS OF THE THEORY

The theory of consumer's surplus rests on the following assumptions.

1. Utility can be Measured

According to Marshall, utility can be measured in cardinal numbers, e.g., the utility from an apple is 1 util, the utility from an orange is 15 utils, and so on. (A util is an imaginary unit with which cardinal utility is measured).

2. Constant Marginal Utility of Money

It assumes that the quantum of money stock with a consumer does not affect the marginal utility of money to him. If this assumption is violated, money cannot perform the function of a measuring rod.

3. Ceteris Paribus

Marshall assumes that the income, taste and the fashion of the consumer remains constant.

4. Independent Marginal Utility

The theory assumes that the utility of a commodity depends upon the quantity of that commodity alone. For example, utility derived from Thums up depends only on its quantity. The quantity of Pepsi does not affect it.

5. No Substitute is Available

It assumes that the commodity in question does not have substitutes. In case substitutes are available, there will be difficulty. According to Marshall, "this difficulty can be theoretically avoided by grouping the two 'rival' commodities together under a common demand schedule."

6. Law of Diminishing Marginal Utility

The theory of consumer's surplus is applicable only if the law of diminishing marginal utility is valid. The law of diminishing marginal utility states that, as more of a good is consumed, the marginal utility of that good will eventually decline.

CRITICISM OF MARSHALLIAN APPROACH TO CONSUMER'S SURPLUS

The doctrine of consumer's surplus has got a mixed blessing among economists. While economists like Taussig, Hicks, Ulisse Gobbi, Cannan, Nicholson etc., have vehemently fired ariel attacks by calling it imaginary, vague and immeasurable, there are others who have hailed it as revolutionary.

To use Prof. Samuelson's words, "The subject is of historical and doctrinal interest, with a limited amount of appeal as a purely mathematical puzzle."[6]

1. Too Many Assumptions

Firstly, Marshall's approach is based on the assumption of cardinal utility. But utility is a subjective entity which cannot be measured.

Economists like Knight criticise the illicit use of "dinner-table illustration" by Marshall and declare the conception to be "a mere shadowy and elusive thing."

Secondly, consumer goods are mostly either competitive or complementary and therefore utilities are not independent as Marshall assumed them to be. Moreover, to assume that the commodities have no substitutes is not correct.

Thirdly, it is not possible to know the whole demand schedule of the consumer. The consumer is not a computer to tell us exactly what prices he would be willing to pay from the 1st to the 100th unit. Thus, we cannot calculate the precise quantity of consumer's surplus.

2. Necessaries of Life

In the case of necessaries, consumer's surplus has no application. In such cases, the consumer will be willing to pay any amount rather than go without them.

Patten divides the economy into 'pain' economy and 'pleasure' economy. In the pain economy there is only removal of pain rather than attainment of pleasure. Only when the necessaries of life have been satisfied, there can be any idea of consumer's surplus.[7]

---

6. Paul A. Samuelson — *Foundations of Economic Analysis,* Harvard University Press, Cambridge — Eighth edition, 1983, p. 195.
7. Quoted in K.K. Dewett's *Price Theory,* 1989, p. 94.

3. Constant Marginal Utility of Money

Prof. Nicholson has criticized the assumption that while purchasing different units of a commodity, the marginal utility of money remains constant.

Marshall has, however, countered this argument by saying that in purchasing different units of a commodity a man spends only a very small portion of his income and accordingly the marginal utility of money is approximately constant. Besides, even if there is a change in the marginal utility of money, the consumer's surplus can still be found as indicated in Fig. 10.4.

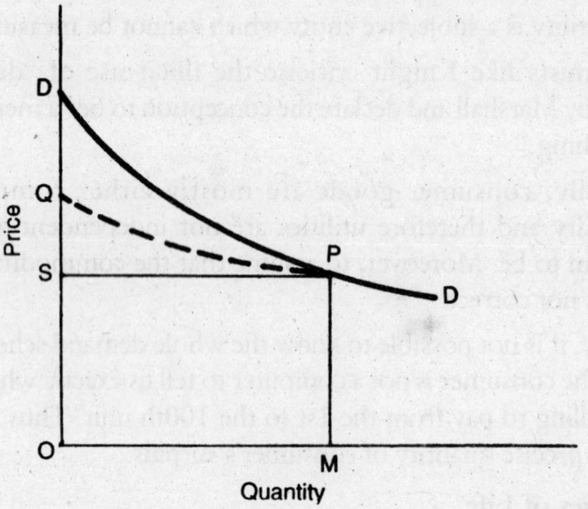

Fig. 10.4

The original consumer's surplus is SPD. But, if the marginal utility of money increases, the consumer's surplus would be reduced to QPD. Thus an increase in the marginal utility of money reduces the consumer's surplus by SPQ.

4. Imaginary

According to the critics, the concept is imaginary and illusory without much theoretical validity.

In the words of Prof. I.M.D. Little "the doctrine of consumer's surplus is a useless theoretical toy."[8]

8. I.M.D. Little — *A Critique of Welfare Economics,* Clarendon Press, Oxford, 1973, p. 180.

5. Neglects the Income Effect

According to Prof. Hicks, Marshall failed to measure the income effect of a price change of a commodity on its quantity demanded. Moreover it does not include the Giffen goods and articles of distinction such as jewellery and diamonds — 'Veblen goods.'

6. Hypothetical

Prof. Nicholson says that the whole doctrine of consumer's surplus is hypothetical and unreal. Quoting an illustration, he says, "Suppose a person is hungry and wants food to eat. He is willing to spend 100. But if he gets it at £ 10, he gains a surplus of £ 90. Similarly he gets a surplus of £ 200 from his house, £ 80 from his clothings and so on." He says, "Of what avail is it to say that the utility of an income of (say) £ 100 a year is worth (say) £ 1000 a year."

THEORETICAL AND PRACTICAL IMPORTANCE OF THE CONCEPT

The concept of consumer's surplus has both theoretical and practical importance.

In the words of Prof. Thomas, "Consumer's surplus seems concrete enough, in fact, we can see it in every day world, though the method of measuring it is purely hypothetical."

Theoretical Importance

1. Choice of Taxes

The doctrine of consumer's surplus pleads a case for direct tax in the place of indirect taxes. In the case of indirect taxes, the burden falls wholly on the community so that the consumer sacrifices not only the marginal unit but also some intra marginal units.

2. Finance Minister

The concept provides a helping hand to the Finance Minister in the determination of a fair-tax policy. While proposing fresh taxation, he has to impose only such taxes which might yield substantial revenue with as little harm as possible to the people.

According to Marshall, imposition of a tax or granting of a subsidy is bound to affect consumer's surplus. So the government should impose taxes on increasing cost industries and provide subsidies to decreasing cost industries.

3. Distinction Between Value-in-Use and Value-in-Exchange

The doctrine of consumer's surplus clearly brings out the distinction between value-in-use and value-in-exchange. Some commodities may possess a higher value-in-use but little value-in-exchange. Water, salt, match box and newspaper are examples of such commodities. The satisfaction derived from these commodities is in excess of the utility suffered by way of price payments. This leads us to the conclusion that the price of a commodity does not necessarily indicate the amount of utility derived from it.

Practical Importance

1. Conjunctural Benefits

The concept enables us to compare the advantages of environment or conjunctural benefits. A person getting Rs. 1,000 in Madras can enjoy better amenities of life than a person getting Rs. 2,000 in a remote Indian village. The simple reason is that many good things of life which one can enjoy in the city are not available in a remote village. Moreover, it can be used as a better index of economic development in different regions at different periods of time.

2. Monopoly Value

The tool of consumer's surplus is useful to the monopolist in fixing the price of his product. The aim of a monopolist is to secure maximum profits.

If the monopolist's product has substitutes, he will allow a margin of consumer's surplus. On the other hand, if there is no need to be afraid of competition, public intervention, or retaliation from consumers he may raise the price so high as to siphon-off the entire consumer's surplus. This is called Dupit-Hottelling theorem.

3. Gains from International Trade

Marshall points out that the exports and imports of a country must be arranged in such a way that the inhabitants get the maximum surplus from international trade.

Heckscher-Ohlin theory of international trade points out that to maximize consumer's surplus we should import those commodities whose costs of production are higher in our country, and should export those commodities which are produced cheaper in the home country.

4. Welfare Economics

This concept is a powerful tool in welfare economics. By calculating the change in consumer's surplus due to a change in price, we can know the impact of a change in the price of any commodity on the different sections of the society. Therefore, consumer's surplus is considered as the "spiritual father" of welfare economics.

5. Cost-Benefit Analysis

The idea of consumer's surplus is useful in the cost-benefit analysis of an investment such as on river bridges, railway connections, dams, parks, etc. The extent of expected consumer's surplus is a crucial factor in decision-making in such projects.

Commenting on the usefulness of the concept, Prof. D.H. Robertson writes, "The theory of consumer's surplus is both intellectually respectable and useful as a guide to practical action, provided you do not expect too much." Prof. Samuelson admits that "The privilege of being able to buy a vast array of goods at low prices cannot be over estimated." Interlinked with many intricate problems of economic theory, the doctrine of consumer's surplus remains a very servicable engine for the discovery of concrete truth.[9] We may conclude in the words of A.C. Pigou "the engine which he (Marshall) has devised, though limited in range, can therefore, often serve us."[10]

MEASUREMENT OF CONSUMER'S SURPLUS: INDIFFERENCE CURVE APPROACH

Prof. J.R. Hicks has rehabilitated the concept of consumer's surplus with the help of his revolutionary tool, namely, indifference curve.

Prof. J.R. Hicks and R.G.D. Allen considered that the assumptions of consumer's surplus is impracticable and unrealistic. According to these economists, utility is a subjective entity which cannot be measured in cardinal numbers. Further, marginal utility of money increases when the stock of money decreases. Utility of a unit of a commodity is not independent but is related to previous units consumed. The Hicksian method of measuring consumer's surplus is superior to that of Marshall's as it achieves the same goals without Marshallian dubious assumptions.

Money is measured along the vertical axis and commodity A is measured along the horizontal axis. Let us suppose that the consumer does not know the price of A. Now he chooses the combination S on indifference curve IC_1, i.e., ON of commodity A + SN of money. To put it in other words, he is prepared to give ON of A for FS of money. Now let us suppose

---

9. Sampat Mukerji — *Modern Micro Economics*, Wiley Eastern, New Delhi, 1990, p. 379.
10. A.C. Pigou: *Some Remarks on Utility*, in Economic Journal 1903.

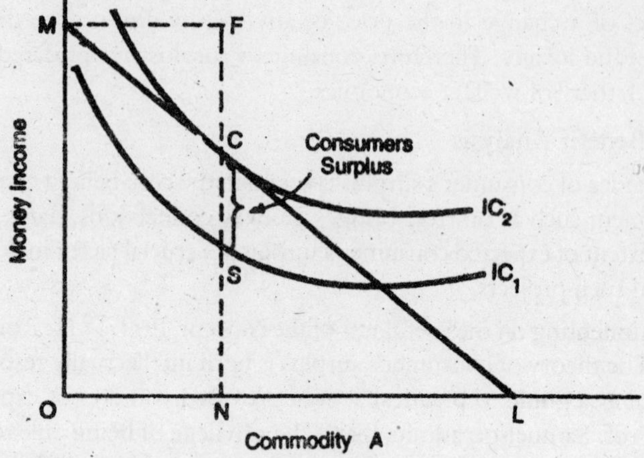

Fig. 10.5

that he knows the price of A which is shown by the price line ML. The consumer finds that he can move on to a higher indifference curve with the same income. The new consumer's equilibrium is C, the point of tangency between price line ML and the indifference curve IC_2. In other words, the consumer has to spend only FC instead of FS to purchase ON quantity of A. Thus the consumer's surplus is CS.

QUESTIONS

1. Define consumer's surplus.
2. Examine the concept of consumer's surplus. How can it be measured in cardinal utility and ordinal utility analysis.
3. "The Hicksian version of consumer's surplus is superior to Marshall's." Comment.
4. What are the uses of the concept of consumer's surplus?
5. What are the practical uses of the concept of consumer's surplus?
6. Explain the use of consumer's surplus.
7. What is consumer's surplus? Explain its practical utility.
8. Compare Marshallian consumer's surplus with its Hicksian treatment.

◆ ◆ ◆

11

ELASTICITY OF DEMAND

"The theory of economics must begin with a correct theory of consumption."
—W. Stanley Jevons, 1871

Prof. Alfred Marshall developed the popular concept of elasticity of demand in his book "Principles of Economics." Before him, the elasticity concept was used by Say (1832) Whewell (1829) and Moffat (1878).

Elasticity is a word which means responsiveness. A rubber band responds to a pull and springs back when it is released. It is elastic. In economics, elasticity expresses the responses of a dependent variable to a change in an independent variable.[1] Demand and supply extend and contract under the influence of such forces as price changes.

Law of Demand and Elasticity of Demand

The law of demand simply states "other things remaining the same, when the price falls demand expands and vice versa." But it does not explain by how much the quantity demanded increases or decreases, as a result of a certain fall or rise in the price of the commodity. To put it in other words, the law of demand simply states the direction of change and not the rate of change.

Elasticity of demand expresses the degree of correlation between the demand and price. It measures the ratio of the relative change in the dependent variable (quantity) to the relative change in an independent

1. W.P. Albrecht — *Micro Economic Principles*, Prentice Hall, New Jersey, 1979, p.87.

variable (price). Price elasticity of demand is therefore a technical term used by economists to describe the degree of responsiveness in demand for a commodity to a change in its price.

Definition of Price Easticity

Price elasticity of demand is commonly known as elasticity of demand. This is because price is the most influential factor affecting demand. "Elasticity of demand measures the responsiveness of the quantity demanded to changes in the price."

— K.E. Boulding

$$e_p = \frac{\text{Percentage change in quantity demanded}}{\text{Percentage change in price}}$$

Suppose, the percentage increase in the quantity demanded is 50%, while the percentage decrease in the price of the commodity is 25%,

$$e_p = \frac{50\%}{-25\%} = -2$$

The numerical value of price elasticity may range between zero and infinity. The price elasticity is always negative because of the inverse relationship between Q and P implied by the law of demand. However, traditionally the negative sign is omitted when writing the formula of the elasticity.[2]

In the place of percentage change we can use the term proportionate change also i.e.,

$$e_p = \frac{\text{Proportionate change in quantity demanded}}{\text{Proportionate change in price}}$$

Symbolically

$$e_p = \frac{\frac{\Delta Q}{Q}}{\frac{\Delta P}{P}}; \text{ Alternatively } e_p = \frac{\Delta Q}{Q} \times \frac{\Delta P}{P}$$

By rearranging

2. A. Koutsoyiannis —*Modern Micro Economics,* The Macmillan Press Ltd. London, 1983, p. 48.

$$e_p = \frac{\Delta Q}{\Delta P} \cdot \frac{P}{Q}$$

An illustration

Price of Mangoes (Rs)	Quantity demanded (Kgs)
5	20
4	24

Thus,

$P = 5, Q = 20\ \Delta P = 1\ \Delta Q = 4$

$$e_p = \frac{\Delta Q}{\Delta P} \times \frac{P}{Q} = \frac{4}{1} \times \frac{5}{20} = 1$$

This means, the elasticity of demand is unity.

Degrees of price Elasticity of Demand

The price elasticity of demand can take on any value between zero and infinity. There are three ranges of price elasticity and two limiting cases. They are

1. $e_p = \infty$ A horizontal demand curve illustrates perfectly elastic demand, in which case quantity demanded is most responsive to price. In other words, a consumer will buy all the quantity of the commodity at this price and nothing else at some other price. Elasticity is infinite.

2. $e_p = 0$. A vertical demand curve illustrates perfectly inelastic demand, in which case quantity demanded is least responsive to price. Elasticity is infinitely inelastic.

3. $e_p = 1$ It implies proportionate change in price and quantity demanded. The demand curve is a rectangular hyperbola.

Limiting Cases

4. $O < e_p < 1$. The case of inelastic demand α a reduction in price will result in a less than proportionate increase in quantity demanded. The demand cruve will be quite steep.

5. $\infty > e_p > 1$ The case of elastic demand, a reduction in price will result in a more than proportionate increase in quantity demanded. The demand curve will be flatter.

Range of Variation of Price Elasticity of Demand

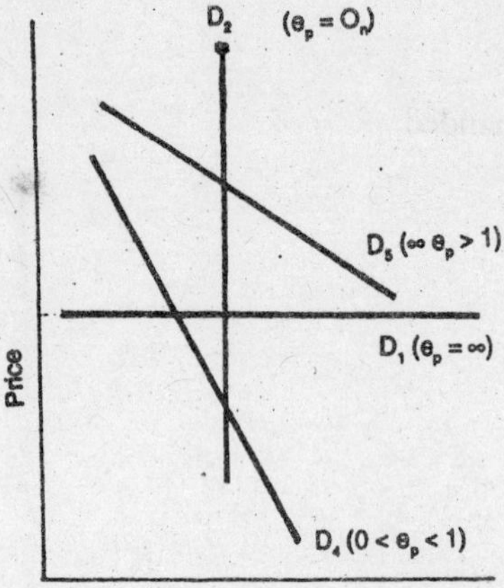

Fig. 11.1

Quantity Demanded

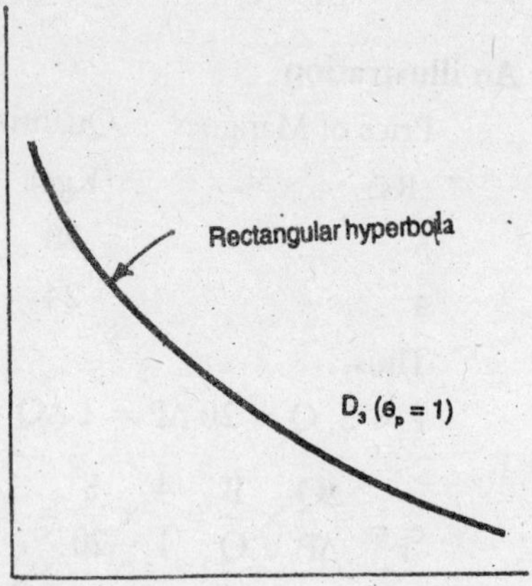

Fig. 11.2

The different kinds of price elasticity can be summarized in Table

Table 11.1

Numerical Value	*Terminology*	*Description*	*Shape of the DemandCurve*	*Examples*
1. $e_p = \infty$	Perfectly elastic	A consumer will buy all the quantity of the commodity at this price and nothing else at some other price.	Horizontal	—
2. $e_p = 0$	Perfectly inelastic	Demand remains unchanged whatever be the change in price	Vertical	Medicines Demand for heroin by and addict
3. $e_p = 1$	Unitary elastic	$\% \Delta Q = \% \Delta P$	Rectangular hyperbola	—
4. $0 < e_p < 1$	Inelastic	$\% \Delta Q < \% \Delta P$	Flatter	Essential goods
5. $\infty > e_p > 1$	Elastic	$\% \Delta Q > \% \Delta P$	Steeper	Luxuries and comforts

MEASUREMENT OF ELASTICITY

For practical purposes, it is not enough to know whether the demand for a good is more elastic or less elastic. It is rather more useful to find out the precise way of measuring utility.

There are four methods of measuring price elasticity

1. The Percentage Method

$$e_p = \frac{\Delta Q}{\Delta P} \times \frac{P}{Q}$$

It is also known as ratio method, when we measure the ratio as:

$$e_p = \frac{\% \Delta Q}{\% \Delta P} \text{ where}$$

$\% \Delta Q$ = percentage change in demand

$\% \Delta P$ = percentage change in price

2. Total Outlay Method

Marshall suggested that the simplest way to decide whether demand is elastic or inelastic is to examine the change in total outlay of the consumer or total revenue of the firm.

Total Revenue = (Price × quantity sold)

TR = (P × Q)

Marshall has laid down the following propositions.

1. Elastic Demand

If $e_p > 1$, the percentage rise in quantity demanded is greater than the percentage fall in price. Revenue increases because the increase in quantity demanded more than offsets the decrease in price. Price and revenue move in opposite directions.

2. Inelastic Elemand

If $e_p < 1$, the percentage rise in quantity demanded is less than the percentage fall in price. Revenue falls because the decline in price is not offset by the relatively small rise in quantity. Price and revenue move in the same direction.

3. Unitary Elastic Demand

If $e_p = 1$, the percentage rise in quantity demanded equals the percentage fall in price. Revenue is unchanged because the decline in price is just offset by the rise in quantity.

Numerical Illustration

Table 11.2

Total Outlay Method

Price		*Quantity (in units)*	*Total outlay (or revenue)*	*Elasticity of demand*
Original	3	10	30	Unitary elasticity
Change	2	15	30	($e_p = 1$)
Original	3	10	30	Elastic demand
Change	2	17	34	($e_p > 1$)
Original	3	10	30	Inelastic demand
Change	2	11	22	($e_p < 1$)

Table 11.3

Changes in Price, Outlay and Elasticities of Demand

Demand	*If price increases, Expenditures*	*If prices decreases, Expenditures*
Inelastic demand	Increase	Decrease
Elastic demand	Decrease	Increase
Unitary demand	Remain unchanged	Remain unchanged

The relationship between the total outlay and price elasticity of demand can also be explained with the help of the following Figure 11.13.

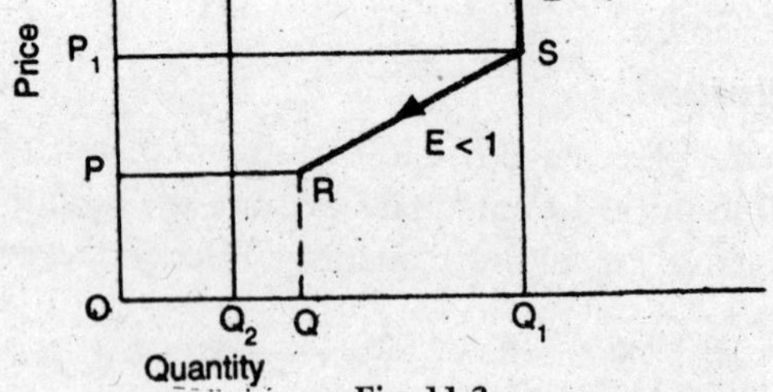

Fig. 11.3

As the price falls from OP_3 to OP_2, the total outlay increases from OQ_2 to OQ_1. This portion (UT) of the total outlay curve indicates $e_p > 1$. If price rises from OP_2 to OP_3, the total outlay diminishes.

Between OP_2 and OP_1 prices, total outlay remains constant. This portion (ST) of the total outlay curve indicates $e_p = 1$. If price rises from OP_1 to OP_2, the total outlay remains constant.

Between P_1 and any price less than P_1 total outlay diminishes. For example if the price falls from OP_1 to OP, total outlay also falls from OQ_1 to OQ. If price increases from OP to OP_1, total expenditure increases. This portion (RS) of the total outlay curve indicates $e_p < 1$.

3. Point or Geometrical Elasticity

Under the total outlay method, the terms 'elastic' and 'inelastic' have been applied to the whole demand for a commodity. This is accurate enough for some purposes, but not for others, because the demand for a commodity can be elastic in one price range and inelastic in another.[3]

When the demand curve is a straight line, it is said to be linear. Graphically, the point elasticity of a linear demand curve is shown by the ratio of the segments of the line to the right and to the left of the particular point.[4]

When a point is taken on the demand curve (like mid point P in Fig. 11.4) it divides the curve into two parts.

$$\text{Point Elasticity} = \frac{\text{Lower segment of the demand curve below the given point}}{\text{Upper segment of the demand curve above the given point}}$$

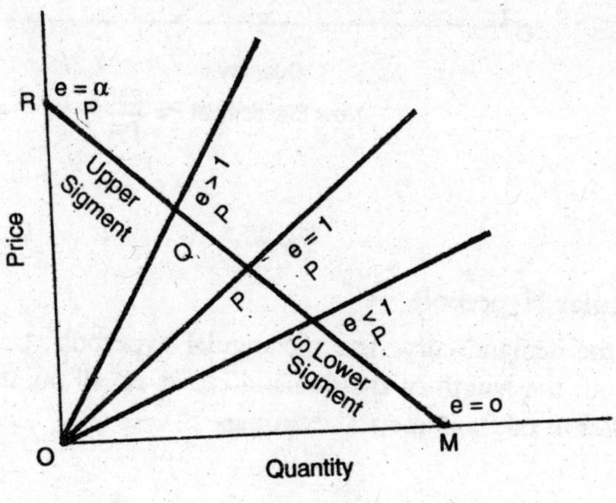

Fig. 11.4

3. D.S. Watson, *Price Theory and its Uses*, Kholsa Publishing House, New Delhi, 1986, p. 42
4. A. Koutsoyiannis, *Op. cit.*, p. 46

or $e_p = \frac{L}{U}$

Where 'e_p' stands for point elasticity, 'L' stands for the lower segment and 'U' for the upper segment.

Therefore, it is obvious that at the mid-point of the linear demand curve, $e_p = 1$. At any point to the right of P, the point elasticity is less than unity ($e_p < 1$); at any point to the left of P, $e_p > 1$; At point R the $e_p = \alpha$ while at M, the $e_p = 0$.

Non-linear Demand Curve

If the demand curve is non-linear, then draw a tangent at the given point extending it to touch both the axises.

Now elasticity at P $= \frac{PM}{PR}$

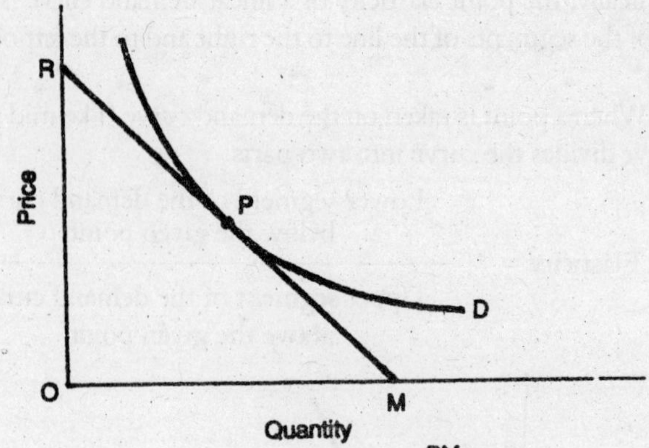

Now Elasticity at P= $\frac{PM}{PR}$

Fig. 11.5

Rectangular Hyperbola

If the demand curve is a rectangular hyperbola, elasticity is unity throughout the length of the demand curve. At all points on the curve $e_p = 1$. Let us take a numerical example.

Table 11.4

Px	*Qx*	*Px×Qx*
9	1	9
6	1.5	9
3	3	9
2	4.5	9
1	9	9

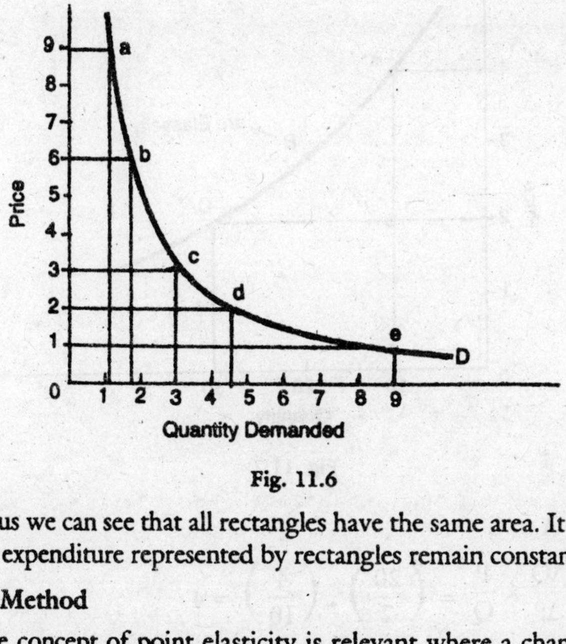

Fig. 11.6

Thus we can see that all rectangles have the same area. It means that the total expenditure represented by rectangles remain constant.

4. Arc Method

The concept of point elasticity is relevant where a change in price and the resulting change in quantity is infinitesimally small. But where the change in price and the consequent change in demand are substantial, the concept of arc elasticity is a more relevant concept.

An arc is a portion or a segment of a demand curve. The question now is to get at the appropriate formula for arc elasticity. The percentage formula,

$$\frac{\Delta Q}{\Delta P} \times \frac{P}{Q}$$

gives different results depending on whether the price is raised or lowered.

Now, let us look at the market demand schedule and the market demand curve (11.7).

Table 11.5

Point	*Px*	*Qx*
A	4	10
B	3	20
C	2	30

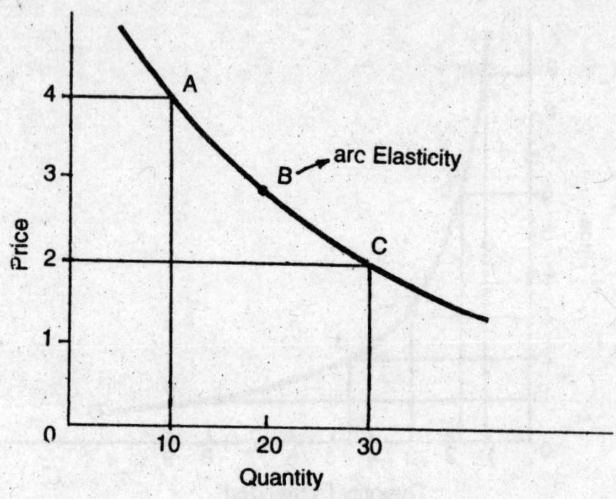

Fig. 11.7

From A to C

$$e_p = \frac{\Delta Q}{\Delta P} \times \frac{P}{Q} = \left(\frac{20}{2}\right) \cdot \left(\frac{4}{10}\right) = 4$$

From C to A

$$e_p = \frac{\Delta Q}{\Delta P} \times \frac{P}{Q} = \left(\frac{20}{2}\right) \cdot \left(\frac{2}{30}\right) = 0.66$$

We thus get different values for e_p: one when the price falls and another, when the price rises.

The way out of this difficulty is to take an average of prices and quantities and then to measure elasticity at the mid-point of the arc. The formula becomes.

$$\frac{\Delta Q}{\frac{1}{2}(Q_1 + Q_2)} \div \frac{\Delta P}{\frac{1}{2}(P_1 + P_2)}$$

Applying this modified formula to find e_p for a movement from A to C or for a movement from C to A, we get.

$$e_p = \frac{20}{\frac{1}{2}(10 + 30)} \div \frac{2}{\frac{1}{2}(4 + 2)} = \frac{20}{20} \times \frac{3}{2} = 1.5$$

This is equivalent to the elasticity at the mid point, i.e., at point B.

FACTORS DETERMINING ELASTICITY OF DEMAND

The elasticity of demand depends upon the following factors.

1. The existence of substitutes

The more substitutes there are for a product, the greater the price elasticity of demand; for example tea, coffee, cold drinks etc.

2. Alternative uses of the commodity

More numerous the uses, higher the elasticity.

3. The importance of the commodity in the consumers' total budget.

Goods that represent a small fraction of the consumers' budget are more inelastic in demand. Examples are salt, match box, pepper etc.

4. The time period under consideration

Demand elasticities tend to be greater in the long run because persons find more substitutes for a good as time goes by.

5. Nature of the commodity

In general, luxury goods are price elastic, while necessities are price inelastic. Foreign travel is an example of a luxury good.

6. Habitual necessaries·

Tobacco and alcohol are price inelastic. The prices of these goods are rising periodically but their demand has not diminished.

7. Joint demand

In the case of joint demand, the demand of the good varies along with the demand of the other good. For example, the elasticity of demand for petrol will depend considerably on the elasticity of demand for cars.

8. Consumer's income

Generally the demand for the poor man is more elastic than the rich man.

9. Possibility of postponement

The demand for goods which can be deferred for sometime is relatively elastic., examples., Woollen clothes, shoes etc.

10. Recurrence of demand

If the demand for a commodity is of a recurring nature, its price elasticity will be higher. Example: Demand for cassettes.

IMPORTANCE OF PRICE ELASTICITY OF DEMAND

Prof. P.A. Samuelson[5] condemns the concept of elasticity as essentially arbitrary and a more or less useless concept. To use his own words "Not only are elasticity expressions more or less useless, but in more complicated systems they become an actual nuisance." But it has both theoretical and practical importance in the spheres of finance, trade and commerce.

In the words of Keynes, "In provision of terminology and apparatus to aid thought, I think Marshall did greater service by the explicit introduction of the idea of elasticity."

1. Paradox of Poverty

The concept of elasticity of demand explains the paradox of poverty in the midst of plenty. Bumper crop, instead of bringing prosperity, may spell disaster if the demand for the commodity is inelastic. The simple reason is that a bumper crop, by lowering prices, may bring in less revenue to the farmers.

2. Price Decisions

While fixing the price of a commodity, sellers, always take the help of the price elasticity of demand for their products. If the demand is less elastic, price will tend to be higher. If the demand is elastic, a lower price is fixed.

3. Monopoly Price

If the monopolist fails to know the elasticity of demand for his product, he would not be able to optimize his profits in the market. Elasticity of demand is used in measuring the degree of monopoly power.

---

5. P.A. Samuelson, *Foundations of Economic Analysis*, Harvard University Press, Cambridge, Mass. 1983, p. 126

Price discrimination is profitable when elasticities are different in different markets. The monopolist will fix a higher price in the inelastic market and a lower price in the elastic market. If the demand curves are iso-elastic in all markets, it is not profitable to practise price discrimination. Similarly, for practising dumping, the concept of elasticity is of great help.

4. Pricing of Joint Products

Some products like wheat and straw, mutton and wool, cotton and cotton seed are jointly produced. It is difficult to calculate their cost of production separately. The producer in such a case fixes a higher price for the product whose demand is inelastic and a lower price for the product having an inelastic demand.

5. Policy of Devaluation

The policy of devaluation will be successful only when the country possesses a perfect knowledge of the elasticities of its exports and imports. Devaluation makes export of goods cheaper in terms of foreign currency. Exports can bring more revenue only when the foreign demand for our product is elastic.

6. Trade Unions and Wages

Trade unions can raise wages for its members only if the demand for their products is inelastic. Likewise, if the demand for a particular type of labour is relatively inelastic, it is easy to raise wages.

7. Pricing in Public Utilities

Public utilities such as supply of water, electricity, transport, postal services etc. are provided by public enterprises. The demand for the goods and services of these institutions is relatively inelastic, since they are vital necessities for daily life. In a welfare state, therefore, the government should nationalise and control these services.

Moreover, the government charge different rates for different uses on the basis of elasticity of demand and try to cover the losses from one group of users by the gains reaped from the other group.

8.Taxation

The Finance Minister has to consider the elasticity of demand while selecting commodities for taxation. If the demand for a commodity is fairly elastic, an increase in tax rate will, reduce the quantity consumed drastically, and as a result the revenue will decrease. That is why generally taxes are levied on commodities like sugar, cigarettes etc. which have an inelastic demand.

9. Incidence of Taxes

The concept of elasticity is of much help in explaining the incidence of indirect taxes like sales tax and excise duty. In the case of inelastic demand, the consumers have to buy the product and must pay the tax.

10. There are many other real world examples emphasising the importance of the concept[6]

The oil producing nations, for example, have been able to increase their total revenue by cutting down the production of oil, because of an inelastic demand for oil.

OTHER TYPES OF ELASTICITY

Income Elasticity of Demand

One of the important determinants of demand for a commodity is consumer's income. The relationship between consumer's income and quantity demanded is positive. Unlike the negative price-demand relationship, positive relationship implies that, as consumer's income increases, demand also increases and *vice versa*.

Income Elasticity of demand for a commodity shows the extent to which a consumer's demand for the good changes as a result of a change in his income.

Symbolically,

$$e_y = \frac{\text{Percentage change in the quantity demanded of x}}{\text{Percentage change in the income of the consumer}}$$

$$= \frac{\Delta x}{x} \div \frac{\Delta x}{y} \quad \text{where x = commodity and y = income}$$

$$= \frac{\Delta x}{\Delta y} \cdot \frac{y}{x}$$

Suppose a consumer's demand for a commodity increases from 10 units per week to 20 units per week when his income rises from Rs. 200 to Rs. 300.

$$e_y = \frac{\Delta x}{\Delta y} \cdot \frac{y}{x}$$

6. Sampat Mukherji —*Modern Economic Theory,* Wiley Eastern Limited, New Delhi 1990, p. 343.

$$= \frac{10}{100} \cdot \frac{200}{10} = 2$$

e_y may be positive or negative. A positive income elasticity implies that an increase in income is associated with an increase in the quantity of goods purchased. Normal goods always have a positive income elasticity of demand.

A negative income elasticity implies an inverse relationship between income and the amounts of a good purchased. An inferior good has an income elasticity that is negative. An example for inferior good is ragi. When the consumer's income increases, he may buy more of rice which is a superior commodity and less of ragi which is an inferior commodity. The positive income elasticity of different commodities is shown in Table 11.6.

Table 11.6

Commodities	*Coefficient of income elasticity*	*Impact on expenditure*
Necessities	Less than unity ($e_y < 1$)	Less than proportionate change in expenditure
Comforts	Almost equal to one ($e_y = 1$)	Almost proportionate change in expenditure
Luxuries	Greater than unity ($e_y >$)	More than proportionate change in expenditure

Types of Income elasticity

There are five types of Income elasticity

1. High Income Elasticity ($e_y > 1$)

In the case of a high income elasticity of demand, the change in quantity demanded is greater than the change in price.

2. Unitary Income Elasticity ($e_y = 1$)

Unitary income elasticity indicates a situation in which the change in quantity demanded is equal to the change in income.

3. Low Income Elasticity ($e_y < 1$)

It refers to a situation in which the change in quantity demanded is less than the relative change in income.

4. Zero Income Elasticity ($e_y = 0$)

It shows a situation in which a change in income will have no effect on the quantity demanded.

5. Negative Income Elasticity ($e_y < 0$)

It refers to a situation in which an increase in income is accompanied by a fall in the amount of goods purchased.

Cross Elasticity of Demand

Cross elasticity of demand measures the percentage change in the quantity of x consumed in response to a given change in the price of some other good y.

Symbolically,

$$Ec = \frac{\text{Percentage change in the quantity demanded of commodity x}}{\text{Percentage change in the price of commodity y}}$$

$$= \frac{\Delta Qx}{Qx} \div \frac{\Delta Py}{Py}$$

$$= \frac{\Delta Qx}{Py} \cdot \frac{Py}{Qx} \text{ where}$$

ΔQx = change in the quantity of x

ΔPy = change in the price of y

Py = price of y

Qx = Quantity of x

If a rise of 5% in the price of coffee results in a 10% increase in the quantity demanded of tea, then the cross elasticity of demand can be numerically calculated as

$$\frac{100}{5} \times \frac{10}{100} = 2$$

The cross elasticity of demand for commodity x may be **positive or** negative depending upon the nature of relationship between x and y commodities.

QUESTIONS

1. What is cross elasticity of demand?
2. Explain with examples the price elasticity demand for a product.
3. What is elasticity of demand? What are its major determinants?
4. What are the determinants of price elasticity of demand?
5. Distinguish between cross elasticity of demand and Income elasticity of demand giving suitable examples.

6. Distinguish between income elasticity of demand and price elasticity of demand.
7. Define elasticity of demand and explain the methods of its estimation.
8. "The concept of elasticity is a versatile tool of economic analysis." — Discuss.
9. Define elasticity of demand. Bring out its uses.
10. Distinguish between point elasticity and arc elasticity.

◆ ◆ ◆

PART III

THEORY OF PRODUCTION

12

MEANING OF FACTORS OF PRODUCTION

"Productive power is the foundation of a country's economic strength."

— Stafford Cripps 1948

In economic terminology 'production' implies creation of utility for sales. The act of utility creation is possible by transforming inputs into output. The output will be having a greater utility than the inputs put together. According to Prof. Hicks, "Production is any activity directed to the satisfaction of other people's wants through exchange." Thus production is an outcome of an economic activity.

Production, in economics, does not mean creation of matter, as man cannot produce matter. It is a well-known fact that "Matter can neither be created nor destroyed." Man can only add utilities to the existing matter by changing its size, shape, form etc.

The creation of utility or production of wealth requires the co-operation of land, labour, capital and organisation. These four factors are called factors of production. They are provided respectively by landlord, labourer, capitalist and entrepreneur. They get rent, wages, interest and profits respectively as the payments for their co-operation in production.

MEANING OF LAND

In ordinary usage, by land we mean soil, or the surface of the earth or ground which we see. But in economics, the term 'land' has a special meaning. It refers to all gifts of nature which yield an income and which are under human control and ownership. It also includes mineral deposits, seas, rivers, natural forests, vegetation, fisheries etc.

Marshall[1] defines 'land' as follows: "By land is meant the material and forces which nature gives freely for man's aid, in land and water, in air, and light and heat." Therefore to economists, "Niagara falls is land, a stream of water in an irrigated territory is a land and a flock of wild geese is land." But air, sunshine, rain or climate etc. should be excluded from land, because they are not under anybody's control and ownership and hence possess no exchange value.

CHARACTERISTICS OF LAND

As a factor of production, land possesses certain characteristics as follows:

1. Free Gift of Nature: Land is a free gift of nature. Man can improve the quality of land by his efforts though he cannot create land. It existed even long before the evolution of mankind.

2. The Supply of Land is fixed: The supply of land is fixed in quantity. Land has no supply price. The price prevailing in the market cannot increase or decrease the supply of land. Thus the total land area available to mankind as a whole is fixed in quantity although the total amount in use may vary from time to time.

3. Land is Permanent: Land cannot be destroyed. The fertility of the soil can be exhausted by continuous cultivation, but its form will remain the same. According to Ricardo, land possesses "original and indestructible powers."

4. Land is Immobile: Land is immobile in the geographical sense. However depending upon the season different varieties of crops can be cultivated or its ownership may be changed. In this sense land possesses mobility.

5. Land is Heterogeneous: Land differs in fertility. Some plots are more fertile, and some plots possess situational advantage. When different grades of land are cultivated, the superior lands or lands which are located nearer the market yield surplus than the inferior or marginal lands.

6. Land is a Passive Factor of Production: Land cannot produce by itself. To grow a crop or extract minerals from the earth man has to apply labour and capital.

---

1. A. Marshall, *Principles of Economics,* 8th edn., Macmillan, London, 1982, p. 115.

7. Land has Many Uses: Land can be used in a variety of ways. It can be cultivated, playgrounds can be formed, factories can be constructed and shipping is possible in the sea and big rivers.

8. No Cost of Production: Land has no cost of production.

9. Primary Factor: Land is a primary factor of production. To start any business or production process, we need the help of land.

10. Law of Diminishing Returns: The yield from land is subject to the law of diminishing returns.

MEANING OF LABOUR

The term 'labour' is used in various senses. Broadly speaking, any work, whether manual or mental, which is undertaken for a monetary consideration is called 'labour' in economics.

Marshall[2] defines labour as "any exertion of mind or body undergone partly or wholly with a view to some good other than the pleasure derived directly from the work."

PECULIARITIES OF LABOUR

Labour is different from other factors of production. It is a living thing, and that makes all the difference. Labour is not only a means of production, but also the beneficiary of production. There are certain characteristics of labour which distinguish it from the rest of the factors of production. Such characteristics are often labelled as peculiarities of labour. These characteristics are given below.

1. Labour is Perishable: Labour is a perishable commodity. Therefore it cannot be stored for the future. Eric Roll remarks, "it has no reserve price." If a labourer, is idle for a day, that day is lost forever and cannot be recovered anymore. The time during which he remains idle is irrevocably lost. Hence, labourers are forced to accept even low wages.

2. Labour is Inseparable from the Labourer: Land and capital can be separated from their owner, but labour cannot be separated from the labourer. A teacher by staying in a cinema theatre cannot teach economics to the students in the class. "The worker sells his work but he himself remains his own property." Labourer has to go to the specified spot to deliver his labour. Therefore the environment and the working conditions in which the worker has to work is of utmost importance in the supply of labour.

---

2. *Op. cit.*, p. 54.

3. Weak Bargaining Power of Labour: Labour has a very weak bargaining power. Labourers are generally poor and have no reserve fund. Moreover in certain occupations like agriculture, they are unorganised. Hence they are exploited by the employers and are paid lower wages than what they ought to get.

4. Less Mobility of Labour: Labour is not as mobile as capital. Adam Smith said "Of all sorts of luggage, the human being is the most difficult to transport." The differences in customs, languages, environments etc., at different places are obstacles to the movement of the workers from one place to another.

5. Inelastic Supply of Labour: The supply of labour can neither be increased nor decreased easily and quickly at will. In other words, there is no rapid adjustment of the supply of labour to its demand. For example, during depression times, when the demand for labour shrinks, the supply of labour cannot be reduced easily. During war when the demand for labour increases, its supply cannot be increased quickly and the wages must rise.

6. Labour is a Means as well as an End: Labour is the cause of production and when production is made the labourer also consumes the product. In other words, he is the means as well as the end of production. Just like the two faces of the same coin, on the one side he is a producer and on the other side he is a consumer.

7. Differences in the Efficiency of Labour: Labour differs in efficiency. Some labourers are more efficient due to their qualities, education, training etc. whereas others are less efficient on account of their ignorance, illiteracy etc.

8. Indirect Demand for Labour: The demand for labour is not direct but indirect. The demand for labour depends upon the final goods which they help to produce. The demand for carpenters and doctors depend upon the demand for housing and health.

9. Increase in Wages may reduce the Supply of Labour: Changes in the price of labour react rather curiously on its supply. In case of ordinary commodities, the relation between price and quantity is direct. More of a commodity will be supplied at a higher price. But in the case of labour when wage rate increases, the supply of labour may decrease. For example, when wages are low, all the members of a family may have to work to earn their livelihood. But when wage rates are increased, the labourer alone may work and his wife and children may stop working. Likewise, workers may prefer more leisure and work for lesser hours when wage rate is increased beyond a certain level. This explains the phenomenon of the backward sloping curve of labour.

10. Cost of Production of Labour: While it is easy to estimate the cost of production of a crop or machine, it is not so in the case of the cost of production of a labourer. Suppose a person becomes a scientist at the age of twenty eight, but, it is difficult to calculate the cost of his education, food, clothing, recreation etc.

11. Capital can be Invested on Labour: In order to make the labourer more efficient, capital can be invested on labour. This process of investment of capital on labour is known as human capital investment. Moreover labour creates capital.

12. Labourer is a Human Being: Machines are passive. The labourer may be very happy and much attached towards his work. In certain cases he may be indifferent towards his work. The employer has to give due recognition to the habits, customs and sentiments of his workers. This aspects of labour has an important bearing on the quantity and quality of work, turned out by the labourer.

13. Labour is an Active Factor of Production: Land and capital are passive factors of production. They cannot yield anything without the participation of man in the production process.

EFFICIENCY OF LABOUR

Efficiency is the productive capacity of labour. It refers to the various qualities of labourers which enable them to do work in a better or more competent way and within a shorter time. Efficiency of labour depends upon a number of factors which are discussed below.

(a) Personal Qualities

1. Racial Qualities: Some races are strong and stout and hence possess more physical efficiency than others. The Punjabis are physically strong and hard working than the Bengalise who have a comparatively weak physique and health. Naturally the efficiency of the former is greater than that of the latter.

2. Hereditary Qualities: A child inherits the skill of his father by birth. The Swiss are considered as the best watch-makers in the world since they have been doing this work from generation to generation.

3. Individual Qualities: A worker's efficiency also depends upon his personal qualities, such as good physique, mental alertness, honesty, resourcefulness, sobriety, initiative etc.

4. Education and Training: Efficiency also depends upon education, both formal and technical. An educated and well trained person is likely to be more efficient as he can do his duties intelligently than an uneducated and untrained person.

5. Standard of Living: A high standard of living is a precondition for a high level of efficiency. A good nourishing food, adequate clothing and a comfortable home are the ingredients of high standard of living. If the workers have a high standard of living the efficiency of the workers is greater.

6. Mobility of Labour: Frequent absentee[illegible] h[illegible]gh rates of turnover which involve greater work and indebtedness of [illegible] [illegible]kers are additive causes for inefficiency.

7. Trade Union: The trade union can also increase the efficiency of labour by way of getting more wages and making arrangements for higher training to their members.

(b) Working Conditions

The labour efficiency also depends upon the conditions under which a worker performs his task.

1. Factory Environment: Lack of proper lighting, ventilation and sanitary arrangements will adversely affect the productive capacity of labour. A pleasant and cheerful surrounding will induce the labourer to put forth his best efforts.

2. Working Hours: Long and continuous hours of work will hamper labour efficiency. There should be a reasonable interval for relaxation and recreation which has an important bearing on the efficiency of the worker.

3. Fair and Regular Payment: A well paid worker is in a better position to put forth his best effort. The wages should not only reasonable but also be paid at the proper time without undue delay.

4. Nature of Machines: The standard of machinery and tools supplied to the workers also determine their efficiency. For instance, a man with computer assistance can perform more work than one without a computer.

5. Prospects of Promotion: If a worker is guaranteed that he will be promoted to a higher position if he performs more work, he will work diligently, and his efficiency will increase.

(c) Social, Political and Economic Conditions

Labour efficiency also depends upon the social, political and economic conditions of the country, where he works.

1. Climate: A cool bracing climate induces people to work more, whereas the extreme climate of the tropical or the Arctic regions make workers become tired soon both physically and mentally. As a result, their efficiency declines in too hot or too cold climatic conditions.

2. Social Conditions: Caste system also adversely affects the efficiency of labour. In many of the villages in rural India, the occupation of a person is determined not by his talents and abilities but by the caste to which he belongs.

3. Religious Factors: Religious preaching also shapes the character of Indian workers. The workers are mostly fatalists and give too much importance to their position and not to their own efforts.

4. Social Security: A properly developed social security system will enhance labour productivity. Job security will promote labour efficiency. The constant fear of a pay cut or dismissal or compulsory retirement at any stage without sufficient reason, may affect efficiency adversely.

5. Political Stability: The efficiency of labour is high in those countries where workers are free from the fear of foreign aggression or internal disturbances. On the contrary if the life of the people is subject to serious threats from military aggression, efficiency will be less.

6. Employer-Employee Syndrome: If the employer-employee relationship is cordial and smooth efficiency of labour will be high. But the relationship between the two parties depends upon the behaviour of the employer towards the employees, and that of the trade union towards the employer. If the employer follows a sympathetic attitude towards the workers, the workers will work more. On the contrary if the trade union follows a militant attitude towards the employer, efficiency will be less.

CAPITAL

Capital is that part of the wealth of individuals and communities, other than land, which is used to assist in the production of goods. According to Marshall, "Capital consists of all kinds of wealth, other than free gifts of nature, which yield income."

Wealth can be looked from two angles, as to whether it is used for immediate consumption or to assist further production. In other words, wealth connotes two forms of economic goods. A car, books, a house etc., are good examples of consumer's goods. These goods are used directly to satisfy human wants. Producer's goods on the other hand are those which do not yield any direct satisfaction, but can be used for further production of wealth. Examples of producer goods are factories, raw materials, canals and bridges, roads and railways etc. These producer's goods are termed as capital in economics. But it is to be noted that capital is a produced means of production. In the words of Prof. Fisher "Capital is that property which is the product of past labour, but which is used as a means to further production."

Capital and Income

Capital is different from income. Suppose a school teacher earns Rs. 2,000 per month. He also has Rs. 20,000 in the savings bank yielding Rs. 200 per month as interest. Now his total income is Rs. 2,200, and his capital assets are Rs. 20,000. Therefore income is a flow of wealth over a period of time, whereas capital is a stock of wealth existing at any given moment of time. Thus capital has only one characteristic, viz., amount; whereas income has two characteristics, viz., time and amount.

Capital and Wealth

We have classified wealth into consumer goods and capital goods. Consumer goods are excluded from wealth. Only capital goods which assist in further production are termed as capital. All capital goods possess the features of utility, scarcity, and marketability. Therefore "All wealth is not capital, but all capital is wealth."

Capital and Money

Money and capital are not similar. Money denotes coins and currency notes which are in circulation. Money by itself has no value unless it is converted into capital goods, such as machines, tools, implements etc. Therefore capital is only that part of money which is used to earn more income. In other words, all money is not capital.

Capital and Land

Land is wealth. It cannot be consumed directly. Land is used for the production of agricultural commodities. So some economists are of the view that land is similar to capital. But this approach is not correct, because there exists some basic differences between the two.

Land	*Capital*
1. Supply of land is inelastic	Supply of capital may be inelastic in the short-run but in the long-run it is elastic.
2. Land is a free gift of nature	Capital is a produced means of production.
3. Land involves no cost of production	Capital involves human efforts and sacrifices. Therefore capital has a cost of production.
4. Land is immobile in the geographical sense	Capital is mobile.
5. Land is permanent	Capital is not permanent; it may be destroyed by continuous use.
6. Land differs in fertility	Income from capital is generally uniform.

Therefore land and capital are not identical in several aspects, which necessitates their separate treatment.

CHARACTERISTICS OF CAPITAL

Capital as a factor of production possesses certain peculiarities.

1. Capital is Man-made: Capital is not a free gift of nature. It is a produced means of production, Knut Wicksell therefore defines capital as "single coherent means of saved-up labour which is accumulated in the course of years."

2. Capital Grows out of Savings: Capital is the result of saving. Saving involves postponement of present consumption. People save for various motives. When saving is high capital will also be high.

3. Capital Depreciates: The wear and tear in a capital asset is known as depreciation. When machines are used continuously beyond a certain limit, it cannot be used for further production.

4. Capital is Variable: Capital is variable in the sense that it can be increased or decreased at will. In other words capital is elastic in nature.

5. Capital is Mobile: Among the four factors of production capital is the most mobile factor. Land lacks mobility in the geographical sense. Labour mobility is not perfect due to economic, social, political, religious and cultural reasons. Entrepreneur also lacks mobility. Capital can be easily sent to any part of the world.

6. Capital is a Passive Factor: Capital by itself cannot produce anything. Capital has to be combined with land and labour in the process of production. For example, even the costly computer may not be of any use unless it is operated by a person.

7. Capital is Productive: Capital is demanded because it increases the productivity of land and labour. A farmer with the help of a tractor or a fisherman with the help of a boat can produce much more than without them.

8. Capital Yields Income: The owner of capital derives income by properly utilising it. As Champman writes "Capital is wealth which yields income."

FUNCTIONS OF CAPITAL

Capital performs the following functions:

Firstly, capital provides subsistence to workers.

Secondly, capital helps to increase the productivity of land and labour.

Thirdly, purchase of raw materials and equipments is made easy with capital.

Fourthly, provision of transport and communication is possible with capital.

Fifthly, capital facilitates effective marketing.

Sixthly, capital formation which is the king-pin of progress is feasible only with the help of capital.

CLASSIFICATION OF CAPITAL

Capital is classified in different ways, depending upon its uses in different types of industries.

1. Private Capital and Community Capital

Private capital refers to capital owned by individuals, e.g., cinema theatre, school, hospital etc. Community capital means the capital owned by the community, e.g., roads and dams.

2. Sunk Capital and Floating Capital

Sunk capital refers to those capital goods which have a specific purpose. It is also known as 'specific' or 'specialized' capital, e.g., road roller and rail engine.

Floating capital refers to those capital items which have a variety of uses. It is also known as 'non-specific' or 'non-specialized' capital, e.g., coal, electricity, machines etc.

3. Fixed Capital and Circulating Capital

Fixed capital consists of durable goods like plant, machinery and buildings. They can be put to use for a number of years. They are fixed capital not because they are fixed in position or place, but because their form does not change much in the process of production.

Circulating capital refers to those items of capital which can be used only once, e.g., seeds, manure, and fertilizers. But the value of circulating capital can be recovered after selling the produced products.

4. Productive Capital and Consumptive Capital

Productive capital refers to those items of capital which are directly used in production, e.g., plant, raw materials etc.

Consumptive capital refers to those capital items which are not directly used in production, but are necessary for labourers to continue production efficiently and continuously, e.g., food, clothing shelter etc.

5. Real Capital and Financial Capital

Real capital refers to various tangible physical assets like machines, tools etc. Financial capital refers to claims of people over real assets, like shares and bonds.

6. Material Capital and Personal Capital

Material assets are tangible assets which can be transferred from one person to another. Personal capital refers to such extraordinary talents and skills such as the melodious voice of a singer or the efficiency of a surgeon. Personal capital cannot be transferred from one person to another.

7. Remunerative and Auxiliary Capital

Remunerative capital refers to capital which is used to pay wages and salaries to labourers. Auxiliary capital refers to all those capital goods that assist the workers to enhance productivity, e.g., machines, raw materials etc.

8. Working Capital and Loanable Capital

Working capital refers to capital used as raw materials, and semi-finished goods which a producer always keeps at hand to continue production without any disturbance. Loanable capital refers to capital which is available in the market for interest (in the form of rent).

9. Lucrative Capital and Human Capital

Lucrative capital means capital which yields a regular income to the owner. Human capital refers to investment on education, health and training etc. The notable contributors to the development of the concepts of human capital are professors Simon Kuznets and Kenneth Galbraith.

10. National Capital and International Capital

The capital assets owned by a nation is known as national capital. The railways and post and telegraph in India are examples of national capital. International capital refers to the capital owned by a group of nations. The capital of I.M.F. and I.B.R.D. are examples of international capital.

CAPITAL FORMATION

The amount which a country adds to its stock of capital during a year is called capital formation in that year.

The method of capital formation as a result of saving will be clearly explained from the following illustration:

Let us assume that a man earns his bread by gathering grass on a pasture land. Every day, he brings a load of grass to the market and sells it for money. If he spends the entire income, savings will be zero. Now suppose he wants to have a sickle for cutting grass. Suppose the price of sickle is Rs. 20, and he saves one rupee per day and buys a sickle after 20 days. Now he can cut more grass with this sickle and his income doubles. In order to bring more grass to the market he wants to purchase a pony. Once again he starts savings, and after a certain period buys a pony. As a result, he raises his income considerably. In this example, the sickle and the pony are capital to the grass cutter. Thus capital grows out of savings.

FACTORS GOVERNING CAPITAL FORMATION

Capital accumulation involves three distinct stages:

1. Creation of savings
2. Mobilization of savings
3. Investment

Creation of Savings: In a country accumulation of capital depends on the level of savings. The volume of savings depends on two sets of factors.

1. The ability to save.
2. The willingness to save.

The ability to save depends on the following factors:

1. Surplus of Income over Expenditure: Saving is the difference between income and expenditure. Saving depends upon the level of income. If a vast majority of people live a hand to mouth existence, more savings may not be forthcoming. Generally the relation between income and saving is positive. That is, when income is high, savings will also be high and vice versa.

2. Pattern of Income Distribution: It is generally believed that the more unequal the distribution of income in a country, higher will be the savings because rich save more than the poor.

The willingness to save depends upon the following factors:

(a) Prudence and foresight: A man with foresight will always try to save a part of his income for the rainy day to meet contingencies like unemployment, accident, sickness, old age etc. It is said that, "If you save money, money will save you."

(b) Habit: Some people are miserly in nature. Misers normally save more by postponing their present consumption. Sometimes they can also save more by tightening their belt.

(c) Family Affection: Love towards one's children and family members is a strong force which induces people to save more. In times of unexpected death, the family is exposed to hardships. This is the rationale behind insurance.

(d) Desire for Social Prestige: In modern times, the status of a person is linked with the resources he commands. Rich people enjoy a lot of social and political influence through their money power. Some people prefer to save more to achieve their ambitions of social prestige.

(e) Business Motive: The success of a business largely depends upon the quantity of money and the quality of capital goods like machinery used in a business. To achieve success in business may also be a strong inducement for saving.

(f) Peace and Security: The prevalence of peace and security is also necessary for savings. If there is no guarantee for life and property, there will be no incentive for saving. A calm and peaceful political climate is congenial for capital formation. Likewise fear of nationalization may also have an adverse effect on saving.

(g) Value of Money: The movement in the currency value of a country also affects savings. If inflation is too high, people would prefer to keep their savings in the form of land or jewelery instead of keeping them as money.

(h) Taxation: The taxation policy should be framed in such a way that it would not fritter away savings. If heavy direct taxes are imposed, it is bound to affect the desire to save. Likewise, a heavy indirect tax may affect the capacity to save.

(*i*) *Education:* If the people in a country are aware of the virtue of saving, savings will be higher. On the other hand, illiterate people may squander away their money on wasteful expenditure and savings will be lesser.

(*j*) *Rate of Interest:* Accumulation of savings is stimulated if the rate of return from investment is higher.

FACTORS AFFECTING THE MOBILIZATION OF SAVING

The next step in the process of capital formation is the mobilization of savings of the households. The following factors are favourable for the mobilisation of savings.

1. Development of Banking: The development of banking and other financial institutions is of utmost importance in mobilising savings. In the absence of proper and adequate saving facilities, people may recklessly waste on superfluous consumption. Banks not only ensure safety to peoples' money but also pay interest. The development of banking facilities in rural India, after the nationalization of commercial banks has enhanced savings to a considerable extent.

2. Development of the Money Market: The development of the various institutions in the money market also offer enormous opportunities for people to save. A well developed money market mobilises the scattered and dormant resources of the economy.

Factors Affecting Investment: Investment may be of two types: (*i*) public investment and (*ii*) private investment. Public investment depends upon the industrial policy of the government. Private investment depends upon a host of factors which are discussed below.

1. Entrepreneurial Ability: Savings do not automatically lead to capital formation. For savings to be invested, there must exist a class of efficient, dynamic and performing entrepreneurs capable of facing boldly the risk and uncertainty in business. In the absence of dynamic entrepreneurs, money may be diverted for speculative dealings. Some of the western countries achieved tremendous progress because of entrepreneurial ability.

2. Expected Rate of Profit: Investment depends upon the expected rate of return on investment. In other words, it is known as the marginal efficiency of capital. During the period of boom, optimism prevails everywhere in the economy which will stimulate investment.

3. Rate of Interest: The cost of money also affects investment. The adoption of cheap money policy encourages investment.

4. Demand for Goods: If the demand for goods is high, the prospect of earning profits will also be high. This also encourages investment.

5. Backward Agriculture: In underdeveloped countries, due to sub-division and fragmentation of holdings, scientific method of cultivation may not be practised. This may affect investment in agriculture.

CAPITAL FORMATION IN INDIA

In India, saving accounts for nearly 25 per cent of the national income which is not low by any standards. But this savings is not properly channelized into investment. Capital formation is low due to the following reasons:

1. Low income
2. Lack of entrepreneurial ability
3. Lack of skilled labour
4. Small size of the market
5. Lack of basic facilities
6. Demonstration effect
7. Heavy taxation
8. Excess labour force
9. Economic backwardness
10. Technological backwardness etc.

ORGANIZATION

Organization as a factor of production came into prominence only in recent years. The Industrial Revolution has completely changed the mode of production. Production in recent times, is carried on in a massive scale with big machines and minute division of labour. In fact the production system has become extremely complicated.

The organizer or entrepreneur performs complex and complicated tasks of combining different factors of production like land, labour and capital together, organizing production, undertaking risks and uncertainties that are involved in modern methods of production. No wonder in these days, an entrepreneur is described as the captain of industry. Henry Ford, Austin and Tata are some of the world famous entrepreneurs.

FUNCTIONS OF AN ENTREPRENEUR

The following are the important functions of an entrepreneur.

1. Planning Production

The first important function of an entrepreneur is to prepare a plan. He decides what to produce, how to produce and how much to produce. The entrepreneur makes decision as to where the factory is to be installed. The location should be better placed in terms of transport and communication facilities. Moreover, he has to decide on the scale of production.

2. Organizing Production

After deciding the quality and quantity of products to be produced, the entrepreneur purchases raw materials and machinery and hires labourers needed for his industry. Then he combines the various factors in appropriate proportions so as to obtain maximum output. Thus co-ordination of the factors of production is one of the most important functions of an entrepreneur.

3. Supervision

The entrepreneur makes arrangements for proper division of labour. Right type of men are placed at the right place. He also provides the workers with suitable machines and tools. In order to achieve maximum output at the lowest possible cost he often supervises the activities of the different departments.

4. Control of Business

The entrepreneur exercises proper and effective control over business with the help of paid managers, accountants etc.

5. Search for Markets

After the product is produced, the entrepreneur has to explore markets for his produce. He has to foresee the trends in the market and ascertain the nature of demand for his product. He has to appoint efficient salesmen, and arrange for proper advertisements for his goods through news papers, magazines, radio, TV etc.

6. Distribution of Income

The entrepreneur determines the reward for the various factors of production in the production process. He makes payment to the landlord, labourer and capitalist in the form of rent, wage and interest. While making payment the entrepreneur is governed by the principle of marginal productivity.

7. Risk-taking and Uncertainty-bearing

According to Prof. Knight "An entrepreneur is a person who performs the dual functions of risk-taking and control." The modern system of production is a round about one where production takes place in anticipation of demand. If he miscalculates, he will incur losses. Thus there may be positive profits or negative losses. Moreover profit is the residue after other factors have been suitably rewarded. Thus production involves greater risks. Risk-taking and uncertainty-bearing, constitute one of the basic functions of the entrepreneur.

8. Innovation

According to J.A. Schumpeter, innovation is an important function of an entrepreneur. Innovations may be in the form of introduction of new methods in the production process, embarking upon new sources of raw materials or improvement in the existing methods and discovery of new markets etc. Thus innovation is a very difficult function.

9. Liaison with the Government

The entrepreneur has to follow the rules and regulations prescribed by the government and the changes in industrial policy effected from time to time. Moreover he has to see whether taxes are paid regularly without delay.

DIVISION OF LABOUR

Adam Smith, the father of political economy, gave importance to the concept of division of labour in his book 'Wealth of Nations'. According to him, the greatest improvements in productive powers are due to division of labour. It was in a pin-making workshop that this wonderful phenomenon of division of labour attracted the attention of Adam Smith. The pin-making was divided into a number of operations. One man draws out the wire, another straightens it, a third cuts it, a fourth points it, a fifth grinds at the top for receiving the head on so on. Thus pin-making was divided into 18 distinct processes.

The term, "the division of labour", describes a method of production in which a complex process is broken-down into a number of small tasks[2].

For example, while making a table, one man will be sawing the wood, another planning it, a a third cutting the joints, a fourth gluing together the various parts, and the last polishing the finished article.

Kinds of Division of Labour

Division of labour may take the following forms.

---

2. J.V. Van Sickle and B.A. Rogge - *Introduction to Economics*, Affiliated East - West Pvt. Ltd., New Delhi, 1968. p. 36.

(1) Simple division of labour : Simple division of labour means that each man is specialised in a certain type of work. e.g., carpenters, blacksmiths, painters, weavers, teachers etc.

(2) *Complex division of labour:* In modern times, the division of labour is very complex in nature. The work in a modern factory is divided and sub divided in to a number of processes and each person is entrusted only with a small part of finishing the ultimate product. For example, in a textile mill, there are various processes like ginning, spinning, weaving, dyeing, bleaching and printing designs. Each process is specialised by a separate set of workers. This is division of labour in the proper modern sense of the term.

(3) *Territorial division of labour:* This form of division of labour refers to certain localities, cities or towns specialising in the production of some commodity or commodities. For example match industries are concentrated in Sivakasi. It is also known as localisation of industries.

ADVANTAGES OF DIVISION OF LABOUR

The following are some of the advantages of division of labour.

1. *Increase in production:* To illustrate the increased productivity of specialisation, Adam Smith provided the classic example of pin-making. One worker could at best make a few dozens of imperfect pins per day. After pin making was divided into 18 distinct operations, ten men could produce 48,000 perfect pins per day.

2. *Increase in Dexterity and Skill:* "Practice makes a man perfect" is an old proverb. After repetitive performances of the same work, a labourer becomes an expert. For example, in the beginning, a typist makes many mistakes. Then, with continuous practice, he improves considerably. In course of time, he may become an expert to type a hundred or more words every minute.

3. *Invention are made possible:* When a worker performs the same task again and again, he becomes an expert capable of inventing new processes in production. Specialisation is the mother of inventions.

4. *Introduction of machinery:* Division of labour is the result of modern large scale production, which implies use of more and more machines. Increased use of machines will help to produce more goods at lesser costs.

5. *Saving in time:* Time is saved as a person need not switch over from one operation to another, while engaged in doing his work.

6. *Saving in tools:* When a worker has to perform a part of the job only, such as sawing the wood, he need not be supplied with a complete set of tools. One set of tools can serve many workers at the same time.

7. *Right man in the Right use :* Under division of labour each man is employed in the job in which his superiority is established most. There will be no round pegs in square holes.

8. *Saving time and Expenses in training:* Less time is taken in learning a particular job. This makes it easier to move from one industry to another. Thus division of labour increases diversity of employment.

9. *Reduction in production costs:* Since division of labour leads to large scale production, the producer can reap external and internal economies of scale. Therefore cheaper goods can be produced.

10. *Work for the disabled:* Under division of labour, even the disabled persons also can find work in jobs which they are most suited.

Disadvantages of Division of Labour

Division of labour is not an unmixed blessing. It has the following drawbacks.

1. *Monotony:* Under division of labour, a worker has to do the same work again and again. Routine work leads to monotony. Sooner the worker finds the work boring and tiresome.

2. *No pride or pleasure:* Specialisation is responsible for the loss of interest of workers in their jobs. On the other hand, a worker in a modern textile mill cannot take pride for the cloth that comes out of the firm.

3. *No sense of Responsibility:* When the product is the collective effort of numerous workers, nobody takes responsibility for the bad work. The proverb "Everybody's business is nobody's business" is very much applicable here.

4. *Retard human development:* When the labourer is assigned only a part of the work, The does not possess a complete knowledge of the work. Repetitive movement cramps a person's mind sand narrows his outlook.

5. *Unemployment:* Under division of labour the worker knows only a particular part of the work. So he is exposed to the risks of unemployment. It he loses his present job, he may find it very difficult to find employment elsewhere.

6. *Loss of skill:* Since the worker is given only one type of work which he has to perform several times, he is denied the opportunity to prove his technical skill.

7. *Exploitation of labour:* The modern factory system employs women and children on a very large scale. The influx of women to the factories disturbs family life. Likewise, the employment of children results in a national loss.

8. *Evils of factory system:* The modern factory system is the result of division of labour. All the evils like gambling, drinking, prostitution etc are attributed to division of labour.

9. *Industrial disputes:* The division of labour divides the society into two classes, workers and employers. The employer always tries to increase his profits by exploiting the workers. The trade unions on the other hand try to put a check on exploitation through collective bargaining. The diverging interests of both the parties gives rise to a severe conflict of view between the employers and the workers which takes the form of strikes, lock-outs etc.

10. *Danger of over-production:* With the help of division of labour, production is carried out on a large scale. Over production occurs when the supply of the product exceeds the demand. This phenomenon is known as market-glut. This is harmful both to the employers and workers.

Conclusion

Inspite of the disadvantages, division of labour is beneficial to the workers, to the producers and to the society as a whole.

LIMITATIONS OF DIVISION OF LABOUR

The application of the principle of division of labour depends on certain essential conditions.

1. *Extent of the market:* Adam Smith remarked that "Division of labour is limited by the extent of the market." If the market for a product is wide, it is easy to sell a large quantity of the product. A village cobbler cannot appoint many persons to make shoes if he is not able to sell not more than two pairs of shoes in a day. It is for the same reason that in a village there are no shops specialising in selling particular goods, instead, there are one or two general shops only.

2. *Nature of Industry:* Division of labour can be applied only in such industries where the work can be split into several processes. In agriculture such a division is not feasible so division of labour cannot be applied.

3. *Availability of labour and capital:* Modern factories employ thousands of workers and expensive machinery. If sufficient technically trained labour and capital are not available, division of labour cannot be extended.

THEORIES OF POPULATION

Historical Background

The rapidly increasing population, encouraged by a misguided poor law in England distressed Malthus the father of population studies deeply.

It was the time when England was passing through Industrial Revolution. The dawn of the Industrial Revolution was accompanied by unemployment, poverty slums, squalor and exploitation of workers.

He feared that England was neading for a disaster, and he considered it his solemn duty to warn his countrymen. He travelled widely and read extensively and concluded that population tends to double itself in every twenty five years.

Malthusian theory is very simple. He begins his theory from two postulates.[3]

1. Population.
2. Food supply.

To use his own words,

"By nature, human food increases in a slow arithmetical ratio; men himself increases in a quick geometrical ratio unless want and vice stop him."

"The increase in numbers is necessarily limited by the means of subsistence. Population invariably increased when the means of subsistence increased, unless prevented by powerful and obvious checks."

Malthus developed his theory on the basis of some biological observations. For instance, according to Huxley, the greenfly in one summer multiplies in number equal to the population of China. Cantillan says "Men multiply like mice in a barn." Human beings are supposed to double every 25 years and a couple can increase to the size of the present population in 1,750 years. What a dreadful prospect for humanity!

Food is necessary for human existence. But its supply is subject to the law of diminishing returns. On the basis of these premises, Malthus concluded that population tends to outstrip the food supply.

Passion between the sexes is natural and it will continue to be the same for ever. According to Malthus, population growth is the stumbling block in the way of mankind's progress towards prosperity." He says "If God gives food, people will bring child also."

THE MAIN POINTS OF MALTHUSIAN THEORY ARE AS FOLLOWS:

1. The population of a country increases in a geometrical progression for and doubles every 25 years. Human beings have an unlimited power of reproduction which they exercise under the impulse of sexual desire. The

3. T.R. Malthus, *First Essay on Population*, Macmillion, London, 1966, p.11

ratio shall be 1:2:4:8:16:32.... and so on. This underlines the need to check the growth of population. As Malthus pointed out "Prosperity was not to depend on population, but population was to depend on prosperity."

2. On the other hand, food supply increases in every 25 years in a slow arithmetical progression. Due to the operation of the law of diminishing returns in agriculture, the ratio shall be 1, 2, 3, 4... and so on.

3. Since population increases in geometrical progression and the food supply in arithmetical progression, population tend to over-run food supply. This over-population leads to starvation, under-nourishment, famines, floods, earthquakes etc.

4. To correct the imbalance between the two, Malthus suggested two kinds of checks known as positive checks and preventive checks.

PREVENTIVE CHECKS

Preventive checks are those checks which can be imposed by men himself in the form of "moral constraint" to control population.

To put it in the words of Malthus "the preventive checks include late marriages, chastity and other similar measures aimed to progress towards happiness."

Malthus was against the modern methods of family planning. He considered promiscuous intercourse, unnatural passions, violations of marriage bed, and improper arts to conceal the consequence of irregular connections i.e., contraceptives as vices.

POSITIVE CHECKS

Positive checks are those which are imposed by nature in the form of wars, famines, misery and starvation, leading to a large number of human deaths and hence bringing a balance between population and food supply.

To use the words of Malthus,

"The Table of Nature is laid for a limited number of guests and those who come univited must starve."

According to Malthus, preventive checks are always in operation in a civilized society and positive checks are crude. Malthus therefore recommended the use of preventive checks for his countrymen in order to avoid this pernicious event.

This is the nut-shell of the Malthusian theory. Malthusian theory in fact, gives a dark and pessimistic future about mankind. It is because of the nature of the theory that some writers like Carlyle dubbed Economics as a "dismal science."

According to Malthus, the poor are responsible for their misery and poverty. Malthus strongly recommended the gradual abolition of 'poor laws' in England. The aid which is given to the poor acts as an inducement to have more children, which aggravates the problem of hunger and misery. The ideas of Malthus were incorporated in the poor law Amendment Act of 1834.

MALTHUSIAN THEORY OF POPULATION

Population increases in geometrical progression 1, 2, 4, 8, 16, 32, 64, 128, 256 in 200 years

Food supply increases in arithmetical Progression 1, 2, 3, 4, 5. 6, 7, 8, 9 in 200 years

Results in imbalance between population and food supply

Correction of Imbalance

Preventive checks late marriage chastity, moral restraint etc.

Positive or natural checks — Famines, epidemics, wars etc.

Of the two preventive checks is the best.

CRITICISM OF MALTHUSIAN THEORY

The Malthusian theory of population has raised a storm of controversy which is not yet over. Both the logical and preventive parts of the theory have been a subject of sharp criticism. According to J.A. Schumpeter the general performance of Malthus is "deplorable in technique and little short of foolish in substance."

1. Malthus has been proved to be a false prophet

The gloomy and pessimistic picture depicted by Malthus about the future generation of mankind has been disproved in the western countries. As a result of the invention and introduction of new techniques in production, output increased tremendously. As a result, the standard of living in these countries has gone up instead of falling as was predicted by Malthus.

Moreover, a country with scarcity of foodgrains can exchange it for its industrial goods. The best example is England, where foodgrain is being imported from other countries. Thus the importance of foreign trade was not visualised by Malthus.

2. Excessive importance to Numerical ratios

His assertion that population increases in geometrical progression and food supply in arithmetical progression has been proved to be wrong by critics. There is no historical proof for this. France some years ago, faced a negative growth rate in population.

3. Law of Diminishing Returns

According to Malthus, the operation of the law of diminishing returns is a limiting factor for food supply. But the application of this law can be postponed. By making use of improved seeds, chemical fertilisers and pesticides etc, the western countries have increased production manifold. The standard of living has made much headway in these countries.

4. Manpower aspect in population

Malthus thought that every increment in population is bad and undesirable. So he was very pessimistic in his approach towards population. In some Gulf countries, the dearth of adequate labour power is a hindrance for speedy development. Cannan is right when he says "a baby comes to the world not only with a mouth and a stomach, but also with a pair of hands."

Moreover Malthus over-emphasised the relationship between population and food supply. As rightly pointed out by Seligman "The problem of population is not merely one of mere size but of efficient production and equitable distribution."

5. Distinction between desire for sex and desire for children

Since Malthus was basically a Christian and a religious man, he attached much importance to moral restraint which is not enough to control population. Moreover he could not demarcate the distinction between the desire for sex and the desire for children. Nowadays people can have sexual desire without the desire for child. In modern days, if a person is given the option to choose a Maruti car and a child he will certainly choose the former. Malthus could not visualise the invention of modern contraceptives which is a hallmark of family planning.

6. Positive checks not a symptom of over population

According to Malthus, population growth is the cause and natural calamities like famine, earthquake and war are the consequences. But natural calamities are not only peculiar to over populated countries. Even developed countries like France and Japan are victims of natural calamities. Hence a water-tight compartmental classification cannot be done on this basis.

7. Biological aspect

The biological argument also runs against Malthus. The biological aspect shows that with the advancement of civilization, the fertility of human beings diminishes. Therefore the fear of excess population is baseless and unscientific.

8. Modern outlook

This theory neglects the influence of standard of living on population. Moreover Malthus failed to give much weightage to the various economic and social tendencies which operate against big families.

9. Socialist's view on Malthusian Theory

Socialists took strong exception to the Malthusian view that the poor are responsible for their poverty. By saying this Malthus had preached the poor to live without the enjoyment of marriage which too was injustice to the poor. Population is not the only reason for poverty. Marx used harsh words against Malthus. "Malthus was altogether a plagiarist by progression. He borrowed non-sense from earlier writers (Theory of population) from Rev. Townsend. His geometrical and arithmetical progression were purely chimerical hypotheses. He copied and paraphraised Rev. Townsend like a slavish plagiarist."

IMPORTANCE OF THE MALTHUSIAN THEORY

The Malthusian theory is not altogether devoid of truth. It has successfully overcome various criticisms and is relevant even today. In all living organisms, there is on the one hand, a desire to propagate their species. On the other, nature places a limit to their expansion by amount of their subsistence. The theory is very much applicable to the third world countries of Asia and Africa. The Malthusian theory is applicable to all communities without any consideration of colour and place.

Malthusian Theory and India

Malthusian theory is fully applicable to India. In the words of Joan Robinson "of all economic doctrines the one most relevant to the under developed countries is that associated with Malthus."

Inspite of the vigorous family planning propaganda, population is increasing at a high rate of 2 per cent per annum.

High death rate may be taken as an indicator of overpopulation. The average life expectancy has not shown considerable improvement over the years. The per capita income and standard of living is one of the lowest in the world. There is complete absence of preventive checks except in socially educated families. The increase in population is controlled by frequent droughts, famines, floods and epidemics which demand a heavy price in the form of human lives.

OPTIMUM THEORY OF POPULATION

The outcome of optimum theory of population is a sharp reaction to the Malthusian theory of population. This theory was mooted first by Prof. Sidgwick in his reputed book, "Principles of Political Economy". But it was popularised by Carr, Saunders "World Population". The other notable contributors to this theory are Dalton, West, Cannan and Robbins.

In a narrow sense, this theory is not a theory of population because it does not explain why population grows or what determines the birth and death rates. This theory is in the form of a normative statement which attempts to define an economically ideal size of population for a country.

According to Malthus, every increase in population is harmful to the society. But the optimum theory states that population growth may be harmful or beneficial for an economy depending upon whether the increase is pulling the economy towards optimum or pushing it away from it.

The optimum means the best and the most desirable size of a country's population. Given the natural resources, capital and technical knowledge, the size of population which maximises the per capita income is called the optimum population.

To use Dalton's words,

"Optimum population is that which gives the maximum income per head".

The optimum theory of population is based on three important concepts.

(i) Under population,
(ii) Over population,
(iii) Optimum population

Under Population and its Disadvantages

If the population of a country is not sufficient to utilise its natural resources efficiently, then the country is said to be under-populated. In this case, an increase in the growth of population will bring into the operation of the Law of increasing returns. Under population has at least two bad effects. Firstly, more quantity cannot be produced, and so production will suffer. Secondly, due to the shortage of labour force, specialisation is not feasible. In the absence of specialisation, economies of large scale production cannot be reaped. But beyond a certain limit, the increase in population is a liability, rather than an asset.

OVER POPULATION AND ITS DISADVANTAGES

If the population of a country is too big in relation to its natural resources, then the country is said to be over-populatied. Over population means that the existing capital and natural resources are shared by more men. The dangers of over population are three. Firstly, the existing resources are not sufficient to provide gainful employment to all. Secondly, due to excessive population, the average productivity will fall. The possibility of disguised unemployment is inevitable. Thirdly, the standard of living will be affected. Famine, war and diseases are the intimate companions of the people.

But this problem can be solved also by supply of capital simultaneously with an increase in population. Thus a confrontation is created between population and productivity. If productivity wins the race, the danger is averted.

OPTIMUM POPULATION

The position of optimum population can be clearly explained with the following illustration.

The total population, national income and per capita income are shown in the Table 12.1 and Fig. 12.1

Table 12.1

Population and per capita Income

Total Population (Million)	*National Income (Million rupees)*	*Per capita income (Rs.)*
100	50,000	500
150	82,500	550
200	1,20,000	600
250	1,62,500	650
300	2,10,000	700
350	2,38,000	680
400	2,64,000	660
450	2,74,500	610
500	2,75,000	550

In the table given above national income of the society increases with an increase in population, but the per capita income first increases, reaches maximum and then declines. The per capita income is maximum at Rs. 700 when population is 300 million. Therefore the optimum level of population for the country is 300 million. Any deviation from this optimum represents less per capita income. This is shown in the following figure 12.1

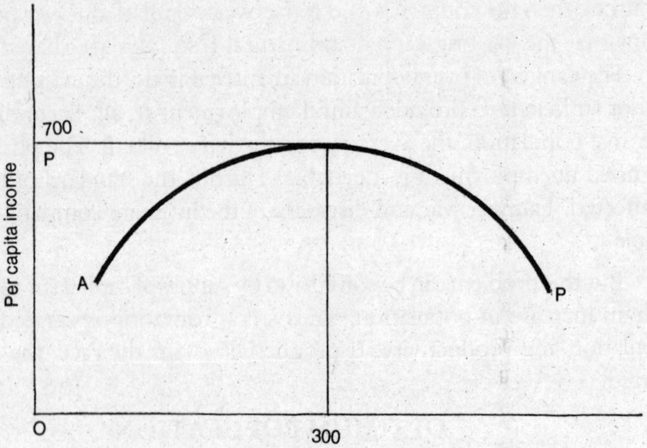

Fig. 12.1

The size of population is measured on the horizontal axis and per capita income on the vertical axis. AP is the per capita income curve. OP is the optimum level of population.

The theory rests on two important assumptions. Firstly, as population increases, the percentage of working population to total population remains constant.

Secondly, as population increases there will be no change in capital, natural resources and technology.

OPTIMUM IS NOT FIXED

Optimum is not a fixed and rigid number, but a moving one. Given the amount of natural and capital resources and the state of technology, there will be a definite size of population at which per capita real income is maximum. But the amount of capital, natural resources and the state of technology are subject to changes. When the technology improves or the new resources are discovered, the optimum level of population will also change. This is shown in Fig. 12.2

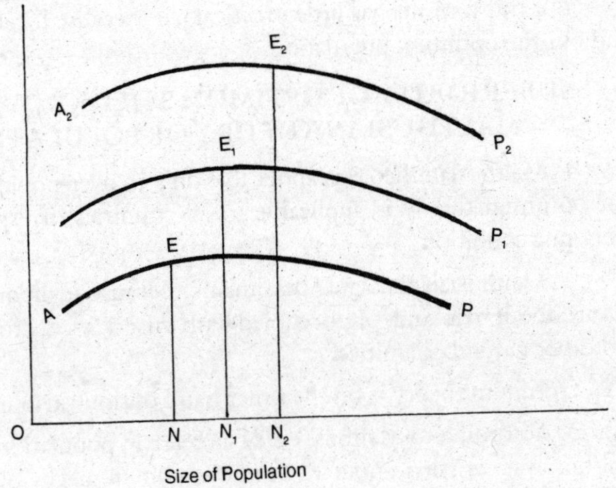

Fig 12.2

In Fig. 12.2 AP is the original per capita income curve with ON population and EN per capita income. With a change in natural resources and technology, the per capita income curve shifts to A_1P_1 and then further to A_2P_2. As a result, the corresponding levels of optimum population are ON_1 and ON_2 respectively.

Dr. Dalton has devised a formula to measure the extent to which the actual population of a country deviates from the optimum. The extent of the deviation is called maladjustment. The degree of maladjustment can be measured with the help of the formula given below.

$$M = \frac{A - O}{O}$$

where

M = Degree of Maladjustment,

A = Actual Population,

O = Optimum Population,

If M>O, it is a case of over-population, If M<O, it is a case of under population. If M = O the population is an optimum size.

For example, if the actual population of a country is 100 crores, whereas its optimum is 50 crores, Then

$$M = \frac{100-50}{50} = \frac{50}{50} = 1$$

this means that the country is over-populated by 100 per cent.

But this formula has little practical use, because it cannot be used to find out the optimum population.

SUPERIORITY OF OPTIMUM THEORY OVER THE MALTHUSIAN THEORY OF POPULATION

1. Malthusian theory is applicable only to over-populated countries. But optimum theory is applicable to all countries, irrespective of their economic condition.

2. Malthusian theory is pessimistic, because it predicted a gloomy picture about mankind, pre-occupied with misery, vice, droughts, diseases and other natural calamities.

Optimum theory is on the other hand optimistic in its approach.

3. According to Malthus, every increase in population is bad. In fact Malthus was worried about the mouths and stomachs of babies as the considered them as 'sterile'.

But optimum theory considers that every increase is good or bad depending upon the natural resources of the economy.

4. Malthus was worried about securing a minimum subsistence level for the individual whereas the exponents of the optimum theory are concerned with securing a maximum per capita income for the country's population.

5. Malthus believed in the operation of the law of dimishing returns. But the exponents of optimum theory consider the possibility of increasing returns up to the point of optimum and decreasing returns only after the point of optimum is reached.

6. Malthusian theory is static because it applies to a period of time. But optimum theory is relatively dynamic since it admits the possibility of changes in per capita income with change in capital, natural resources and technology.

7. Malthusian theory is narrow in outlook because it relates population with food supply. Optimum theory, on the other hand is wider in its outlook because it links population with the wealth of a country.

8. The Malthusian theory of population views man as a consumer and ignores his role as a producer. But the optimum theory recognises both these roles of man. It is a question of reconciling the two roles of man.

CRITICISM OF THE OPTIMUM THEORY OF POPULATION

In spite of its supremacy over Malthusian theory, the optimum theory has its own share of drawbacks.

1. The assumption that the proportion of working population to the total population remains constant as population increases is not correct.

2. The theory is silent over the distributional aspects of income which is more important.

3. The theory gives too much importance to economic aspects at the cost of social and political aspects. A country like Israel cannot reduce its population on economic grounds. Adam Smith rightly says, "Defence is better then Opulence."

4. The concept is merely intuitive. Even if optimum population is desirable, it can be achieved only through changes in social, economic religious, political and cultural backgrounds.

5. The theory ignores the eugenic aspect of the people. Countries like Israel have developed much in spite of their low resources, due to the quality of their labour force.

6. It is difficult to determine the optimum size of population.

7. Difficulty in the measurement of per capita income, poses serious practical difficulties. The per capita income based on national income may not be accurate and precise.

8. The theory is not useful in framing state policies to stabilise the level of employment, income and output in a country.

9. The theory fails to explain why population growth is high in some countries and low in other countries.

10. Dalton's formula of maladjustment is not useful to determine the optimum size of population.

THE THEORY OF DEMOGRAPHIC TRANSITION

The theory of demographic transition is the latest and the widely acclaimed theory among economists. The theory is basically scientific in its outlook and more convincing than other theories of population. The theory postulates three distinct stages in population growth and economic development.

1. The stage of high birth and death rates and a consequent stable population level.

2. The stage of a high birth rate and a declining death rate and a consequent high growth rate of population which may be aptly termed as 'population explosion'.

3. The stage of low birth and death rates and a consequent low growth rate of population.

We shall explain each of these three stages in brief.

FIRST STAGE OF DEMOGRAPHIC TRANSITION

In the first stage of economic development, the economy is basically an agrarian one. People mostly live in rural areas and their only basic source of livelihood is agriculture which is also backward. There are a few consumer goods industries. The tertiary sectors like banking, transport and commerce are under-developed. Birth and death rates are very high. The death rate is very high on account of poor diet, primitive sanitation and the absence of effective medical facilities. On the other hand, the birth rate is high due to early marriages, illiteracy, absence of knowledge about family planning, deep-rooted social beliefs and customs about the size of the family, attitude towards children etc.

The economic reasons also impel the families to have more children. More children supplement the family income. They are considered to be assets rather than liabilities for the family. All these factors create a situation of "baby boom".

Thus in the first stage of demographic transition the high birth rate is counterbalanced or neutralised by the high death rate, and so the actual growth rate of population is not high. In short, it is a stage of high growth potential but of low actual growth.

The population statistics in India indicate the year, 1921 as the "year of Great Divide" Before 1921 the birth rate and death rate were almost equal and the size of population was almost stagnant.

SECOND STAGE OF DEMOGRAPHIC TRANSITION

In the second stage, the economy enters the door step of growth. Primary, secondary and tertiary sectors develop simultaneously. Regular employment enhances family income and so people get regular and sufficient quantities of food. Medical and health facilities expand. Modern life saving drugs and medicines are used. All these factors have an appreciable effect in reducing the death rate. But the birth rate continues to be high or remains almost stable.

Various factors are responsible for the birth rate to be stable. Firstly, children, add more income to the family. Secondly, the life expectancy increases due to an improvement in the standard of living and the dietary habits of the people. Thirdly, the inclination towards family planning is not attractive due to religious dogmas and social taboos. All these factors are responsible for a state of "population explosion". Therefore the high birth and the falling death rates lead to an increase in the average size of the family. India is now in this crucial and critical stage of demographic transition. Though we have achieved tremendous progress in food supply and other related fields, the ever increasing torrent of babies eats up the fruits of economic growth. The standard of living of the people has not improved considerably. Moreover famines and droughts are frequent visitors in various parts of the country.

THIRD STAGE OF DEMOGRAPHIC TRANSITION

The continuous eonomic growth over a span of time enables the population to cross the subsistence level of income and consequently the standard of living improves. During this stage the character of the economy and people changes vastly. Firstly, the economy shifts its importance from agriculture to industry. Secondly, it facilitates the mobility of labour force from rural to urban centres. Thirdly, the role of women changes. The mobility of labour force can be achieved even with he small size of family. Fourthly, women and men prefer late marriage. Fifthly, education expands knowledge and so people discard old customs, dogmas and beliefs and develop individualistic attitudes.

The joint family system breaks down altogether. Sixthly, people will feel the pinch of having more babies. Child-rearing becomes a costly affair. People readily adopt various family planning devices. Lastly, since the death rate is already low, the small size family norm can be achieved only when birth rate falls.

The western countries of the world are passing through this stage of population transition. Thus the birth and death rates are balanced to each other at a lower level. Population in these countries grow only at a slow and normal rate.

QUESTIONS

1. State the features of land.
2. What are the factors of production?
3. Why labour is considered as a unique factor of production?
4. State the peculiar features of labour.

5. What are entrepreneurial functions?
6. How does capital formation take place?
7. Discuss the factors determining efficiency of labour?
8. What are the merits and demerits of division of labour?
9. Examine the Mathusian Theory if population.
10. Discuss the Optimum Theory of population.
11. Explain the Theory of Demographic Transition.

❖ ❖ ❖

13

SCALE OF PRODUCTION

"Sooner or later every war of trade becomes a war of blood."

— Eugene V. Debs, 1916

The scale of production has an important bearing on the cost of production. It is a common experience of every producer that costs can be reduced by increased production. That is why the producers are more keen on expanding the size or scale of production. In the process of expansion, the producer may benefit from the emergence of economies of scale. These economies are broadly classified into two types:

1. Internal Economies and
2. External Economies.

INTERNAL ECONOMIES

When a firm expands its scale of production, the economies which accrue to this firm are known as internal economies.

According to Cairncross, "Internal economies are those which are open to a single factory or a single firm independently of the action of other firms. They result from an increase in the scale of output of the firm, and cannot be achieved unless output increases. They are not the result of inventions of any kind, but are due to the use of known methods of production which a small firm does not find worth while."

Internal economies may be of the following types:

(a) Technical Economies

Technical economies are those which accrue to a firm from the use of better machines and techniques of production. As a result, production increases and cost per unit of production decreases.

Following Prof. Cairncross,[1] we may classify the various kinds of technical economies as follows:

1. Economies of Increased Dimensions

Certain technical economies may arise on account of increased dimensions. For example, a double decker bus is more economical than a single decker. One driver and one conductor may be needed, whether it is a double decker or a single decker bus.

2. Economies of Linked Processes

As a firm increases its scale of operations, it can properly be linked to various production processes more efficiently. For example, in order to obtain the advantage in a linkage process, both editing and printing of newspapers are generally carried out in the same premises.

In the words of Prof. Cairncross, "There is generally a saving in time and a saving in transport costs, when the two departments of the same factory are brought closer together than two separate factories."

3. Economies of the Use of By-products

A large firm is in a better position to utilise the by-products efficiently and attempt to produce another new product. For example, in a large sugar factory, the molasses left over after the manufacture of sugar from out of the sugarcane can be used for producing power alcohol by installing a small plant.

4. Economies in Power

Large sized machines without continuous running are often more economical than small sized machines running continuously in respect of power consumption. For example, a big boiler consumes more or less the same power as that of a small boiler but gives more heat.

5. Economies of Increased Specialisation

A large firm can divide the work into various sub-processes. Therefore division of labour and specialisation become possible. At one stroke, all the advantages of division of labour can be achieved. For example, only a well established big school can have specialised teachers.

---

1. A. Cairncross — ***Introduction to Economics*** — fourth edition, Butterworths, London 1966, pp. 106-122.

(a) Economies of Continuation

Technical economy is also realised due to a long-run continuation of the production process. For example, composing and printing of 1000 copies may cost Rs. 200; but if we increase the number of copies to 2000 it may cost only Rs. 250, because the same sheet plate which has been composed previously can be utilised for the increased number of copies also.

(b) Labour Economies

A large firm employs a large number of labourers. Therefore each person can be employed in the job to which he is most suited. Moreover a large firm is in a better position to attract specialised experts into the industry. Likewise specialisation saves time and encourages new inventions. All these advantages result in lower costs of production.

(c) Marketing Economies

Economies are achieved by a large firm both in buying raw materials as also in selling its finished products. Since the large firm purchases its requirements in bulk it can bargain on its purchases on favourable terms. It can ensure continuous supply of raw materials. It is eligible for preferential treatment. The special treatment may be in the form of freight concessions from transport companies, adequate credit from banks and other financial treatments etc. In terms of advertisements also it is better placed than the smaller firms. Better trained and efficient sales persons can be appointed for promoting sales.

(d) Financial Economies

The credit requirements of the big firms can be met from banks and other financial institutions easily. A large firm is able to mobilise much credit at cheaper rates. Firstly, investors have more confidence in investing money in the well established large firms. Secondly, the shares and debentures of a large firm can be disbursed or sold easily and quickly in the share market.

(e) Managerial Economies

On the managerial side also economies can be achieved; when output increases, specialists can be more fully employed. A large firm can divide its big departments into various sub-departments and each department may be placed under the control of an expert. A brilliant organiser can devote himself wholly to the work of organising while the routine jobs can be left to relatively low paid workers.

(f) Risk-bearing Economies

The larger the size of a firm, the more likely are its losses to be spread among its various activities according to the law of averages.

A big firm produces a large number of items and of different varieties so that the loss in one can be counter balanced by the gain in another. For example, a branch bank can spread its risk by diversification of its investment portfolio rather than a unit bank. Suppose a bank in a particular locality is facing a run on the bank, it can recall its resources from other branches, and can easily overcome the critical situation. Thus diversification avoids "putting all its eggs in one basket."

(g) Economies of Research

A large sized firm can spend more money on its research activities. It can spend huge sums of money in order to innovate new varieties of products or improve the quality of the existing products. In cases of innovation it will become an asset of the firm. New innovations or new methods of producing a product may help to reduce its average cost.

(h) Economies of Welfare

A large firm can provide welfare facilities to its employees such as subsidised housing, subsidised canteens, creches for the infants of women workers, recreation facilities etc.; all these measures have an indirect effect on increasing production and at reducing the costs.

EXTERNAL ECONOMIES

External economies refer to gains accruing to all the firms in an industry due to the growth of that industry. External economies can be enjoyed by all the firms in the industry irrespective of their size. The emergence of external economies is due to localisation.

The main types of external economies are as follows:

1. Economies of Concentration

When a number of firms are located in one place, all the member firms reap some common economies. Firstly, skilled and trained labour become available to all the firms.

Secondly, banks and other financial institutions may set up their branches, so that all the firms in the area can obtain liberal credit facilities easily. Thirdly, the transport and communication facilities may get improved considerably. Further, the power requirements can be easily met by the electricity boards. Lastly, supplementary industries may emerge to assist the main industry.

2. Economies of Information

The economies of information may arise as a result of the collective efforts of the various firms. Firstly, an individual firm may not be in a position to spend enormous amounts on research. But by pooling all their resources new inventions may become possible. The fruits of the invention can be shared by all the member firms. Secondly, publication of statistical, technical and marketing information will be of vital importance to increase output at lower costs.

3. Economies of Disintegration

When the industry grows, it becomes possible to split up production into several processes and leave some of the processes to be carried out more efficiently by specialised firms. This makes specialisation possible and profitable. For example, in the cotton textile industry, some firms may specialise in manufacturing thread, some others in producing dhoties, some in knitting banians, some in weaving sarees etc. The disintegration may be horizontal or vertical. Both will help the industry in avoiding duplication, and in saving time materials.

RELATIONSHIP BETWEEN INTERNAL AND EXTERNAL ECONOMIES

No watertight compartmental division can be made between internal and external economies. When a number of firms are combined into one, external economies will become internal economies. Internal economies are due to the expansion of individual firm while external economies arise due to the growth of the entire industry. External economies are a pre-requisite for the growth of backward regions.

Diseconomies as Limits to Large-scale Production

A firm cannot reap economies of scale indefinitely. There is a limit to production beyond which it is counter-active in the sense that internal and external economies may turn out to be diseconomies. These counteractive forces may become responsible for increased costs of production. These factors are known as internal and external diseconomies.

The following factors limit the size of a firm.

1. Difficulties of Management

If production continues, beyond a particular stage, a chain of complex problems may arise giving rise to increased costs. Supervision becomes lax, complex and intractable, red tapism, and wastages arise, workers may become indifferent, and the rapport between workers and management may disappear. All these activities result in raising average costs.

2. Marketing Diseconomies

The expansion of a firm beyond a certain limit may also lead to marketing problems. Raw materials may not become available at the right time and in sufficient quantities. Moreover, since the firms are operating in a monopolistic world, they have to face stiff and cut-throat competition from their rivals. Therefore, extensive advertising and sales promotion measures may have to be undertaken and it may ultimately lead to higher costs.

3. Financial Diseconomies

Finance is the life-blood of any organisation. For expanding business, the entrepreneur needs enormous amounts of fresh capital. But finance in the required amount and at the appropriate time may not easily be forthcoming. This may retard the development of the firm's growth.

4. Technical Diseconomies

There is a limit to the division of labour and splitting down of the production processes. Beyond a range, further technical economies may not be beneficial and a disproportionate expansion may result in technical diseconomies.

5. Increased Risks

As the size of a firm expands, risks also may increase by leaps and bounds. If the production manager or sales manager miscalculates market trends, sales will suffer which may lead to heavy losses.

6. External Diseconomies

The growth and localisation of industries ultimately lead to increased demand for labour, finance, raw materials, power, transport etc. Thus competition among the various firms tend to increase the cost per unit.

ADVANTAGES AND DISADVANTAGES OF LARGE-SCALE PRODUCTION

Advantages of Large-scale Production

The following are the merits of large-scale production:

1. Internal Economies

When the size of a firm expands, the economies which accrue with the firm are known as internal economies.

2. External Economies

External economies arise due to the growth of the industry. It is shared by all the firms in the industry irrespective of their size.

3. Division of Labour

Large-scale production expands the scope for division of labour. It helps to increase the per capita output and decrease the per unit cost.

4. Utilisation of By-products

A large-scale industry is better placed for producing more, by avoiding wastages. If the wastages or by-products are effectively utilised, it has its own impact in reducing the average cost. For example, a big sugar factory can convert molasses into power alcohol. But a small firm has to throw away the molasses, as waste products.

5. Greater Specialisation in Management

In a big concern, the manager can use his full time and ability in the expansion of the business. He can appoint certain assistants to look after supervisory jobs.

6. Machinery

A large business firm can install expensive and technically up-to-date machines. Therefore all the advantages of machinery can be reaped. But keeping an expensive machinery in a small concern might become uneconomical and a waste.

7. Economies of Buying and Selling

A large firm enjoys a preferential treatment in terms of buying raw materials and selling finished products.

8. Economies of Indivisibility

Some factors of production are not perfectly divisible. When the output is in smaller quantities, the average fixed cost is likely to be higher. On the contrary if output increases, the fixed cost is spread over a larger number of units of output; and naturally the average fixed cost per unit of output declines.

9. Financial Economies

Banks and other financial institutions in the money market may provide financial assistance to large firms at concessional rates. Lower costs of credit may reduce the costs of production.

10. Meeting Adversity

During financial paucity, marketing stress and competition and other stringent times a big firm can face boldly and manage the crisis. But a small firm is most likely to collapse under such pressures.

11. Research

A large business concern can afford to spend huge amounts on research activities. Successful research programmes not only increase the profit of the firm, but also reduce the cost of production considerably.

12. Advertisement

In the modern cut throat competitive world, advertisements through newspaper, radio and T.V. will be a great boon to big producers. People link the quality of a product with its advertisement. As sales increases, the per unit advertisement expenditure decreases.

13. Ancillary Industries

When an industry develops, ancillary industries may be set up profitably. For example, the setting up of a big automobile industry may help the establishment of ancillary industries to supply ancillary parts to the big concern.

Disadvantages of Large-scale Production

Large-scale industries are not free from defects. It has its share of weak spots which are described below.

1. Cut-throat Competition

Modern large-scale industries invite price war. Cut-throat competition involves huge amounts of expenditure on advertisement. The wasteful advertisement expenditure has to be borne by the consumers.

2. Individual Tastes are Ignored

Large-scale industries produce goods of uniform quality, irrespective of individual tastes and preferences. This results in the loss of customers to other competitors.

3. Danger of Overproduction

Large-scale production involves output in large quantities. If supply outstrips demand, there is a possibility of market-glut depression. Depression is bad to all the parties involved in production.

4. No Cordial Relationship

A large business firm is generally managed by paid managers. Therefore the personal touch and sympathy which is supposed to exist between the master and his servants are missed. The hostile attitudes of the managers and labourers may very well end in strikes and lockouts.

5. Dependence on Foreign Markets

A large producer has to depend upon foreign markets for his products. But dependence on a foreign market is extremely dangerous during political upheavals and when the importing country, becomes hostile towards the exporting country. For example the U.S.A. threatens to use Super 301 Act against India, if India fails to protect American patent rights and give preferential treatment to its exports. In such cases too much dependence on foreign markets makes the business risky and uncertain.

6. Possibility of War

In a competitive world due to large-scale production, every country tries to capture a very wide market. Many modern wars are basically due to a scramble for raw materials. The recent Gulf war is a case in point.

7. Lack of Adaptability

Small firms possess the advantage of adaptability. In times of business recession they can easily switch over from low profit yielding to high return yielding businesses. But this is not possible in the case of large business firms because of huge investments on certain lines of production.

8. Management Problem

It is not feasible for a big producer to keep a close watch or personal supervision on various departments. This situation may be exploited by the dishonest workers. Thus inefficient supervision becomes the cause of for high costs of production.

9. Unequal Distribution of Wealth

Large-scale production is one of the basic reasons for the concentration of wealth in the hands of a few. The heavy concentration may result in political upheavals.

10. Formation of Cartels

Pure competition is no doubt good. In order to reap enormous profits, the big industrialists may form themselves into cartels. Formation of cartels is bad to the consumers.

ADVANTAGES AND DISADVANTAGES OF SMALL-SCALE PRODUCTION

Small-scale industries occupy a pride of place in the development of developing countries. Prof. E.F. Schumacher in his book "Small is beautiful" rightly brings out the importance of intermediate technology which is aptly suited to small-scale industries. Small-scale production enjoys the following advantages.

1. Close Supervision

A small-scale producer is better placed in respect of perfect supervision. Firstly, supervision becomes easy as an elaborate system of supervision is not required. Secondly wastages can be avoided to a considerable extent. As Prof. Marshall rightly says, "the master's eye is everywhere." Close supervision ensures effective functioning.

2. Nature of Demand

Small-scale production is better suited to those products whose demand is limited and unstable.

3. Employment Potential

Small-scale industries are labour intensive. In countries like India unemployment is a burning problem. It can be solved through the development of cottage, agro-based and small-scale industries.

4. Capital Light

The finance required to start a small-scale industry is limited. In capital scarce countries like India, the small-scale industries are of vital importance for the country's development.

5. Personal Attachment

In a small-scale industry, the personal attachment between the employer and employees will be strong. This sentimental attachment has the power of averting strikes. The prevalence of peace naturally brings prosperity also.

6. No Evils of Large-scale Production

Small-scale production can avoid the evils of the factory system like over crowding, population-density, water pollution, noise pollution, air pollution, prostitution, theft, murder etc.

1. Lack of Economies

The economies which are available to large-scale production such as labour economies, marketing economies, financial economies, risk bearing economies, technical economies, etc., are not available to small firms. Naturally, the per unit cost of production will be higher.

2. Lack of Research

A small firm cannot devote much of its precious resources on research programmes.

3. Wastages of By-products

Small firms may find it difficult to convert wastages or by-products into another new product.

4. Less use of Machines

Small-scale firms cannot install modern machinery on a large-scale. Therefore the economies available through machinery may not be become available to the small firm.

5. Competition from Large-scale Industries

Large-scale industries and multi-national corporations are stronger in terms of technology and resources. In times of competition small-scale industries will be the first casualty.

QUESTIONS

1. Distinguish clearly between internal and external economies.
2. What are external economies?
3. What are the economies and diseconomies of scale?

❖ ❖ ❖

14

THE THEORY OF PRODUCTION FUNCTION

"Knowledge is the only instrument of production that is not subject to diminishing returns."

—J.M. Clark, 1957

MEANING

The production function is a highly abstract concept that has been developed to deal with the technological aspects of the theory of production.

A production function is an equation, table or graph which specifies the maximum quantity of output which can be obtained with each set of inputs. An input is any good or service that goes into production, and an output is any good or service that comes out of the production process. According to Prof. Richard H. Leftwich.[1]

"The term production function refers to the physical relationships, between a firm's inputs or resources and its output of goods or services per unit of time leaving prices aside."

Suppose we want to produce apples. We need land, water, fertilizers, workers and some machinery. These are called inputs or factors of production. The output is apples.

---

1. *The Price System and Resource Allocation,* 9th edn., The Dryden Press Japan, 1985, p.218.

In abstract terms, it is written as $Q = F (X_1, X_2... X_n)$. Where Q is the maximum quantity of output and $X_1, X_2,... X_n$ are the quantities of the various inputs. If there are only two inputs, labour L and capital K, we write the equation as $Q = F (L,K)$.

The production function shows only the physical relationship between input and output, but says nothing about the optimal combination of inputs.

Two things must be noted when we discuss the production function.

(*i*) It must be considered with reference to a particular period of time.

(*ii*) It is determined by the state of technology. Any change in technology may alter output, even when the quantities of inputs remain fixed.

THE LAW OF RETURNS TO SCALE

In the long run the dichotomy between fixed factor and variable factor ceases. In other words, in the long run all factors are variable. The law of returns to scale examines the relationship between output and the scale of inputs in the long-run when all the inputs are increased in the same proportion.

Assumptions

This law is based on the following assumptions:

1. All factors are variable but enterprise is fixed
2. There is no change in technology
3. Perfect competition prevails in the market
4. Returns are measured in physical terms.

Three Phases of Returns to Scale

There are three phases of returns in the long run which may be separately described as (1) the law of increasing returns (2) the law of constant returns; and (3) the law of decreasing returns.

Depending on whether the proportionate change in output equals, exceeds, or falls short of the proportionate change in both the inputs, a production function is classified as showing constant, increasing or decreasing returns to scale.

Let us take a numerical example to explain the behaviour of the law of returns to scale.

Table 14.1
Table Showing Returns to Scale

Unit	*Scale of Production Returns*	*Total Returns*	*Marginal*	
1	1 Labour + 02 acres of land	4	4	
2	2 Labour + 04 acres of land	10	6	**Stage I**
3	3 Labour + 06 acres of land	18	8	Increasing
4	4 Labour + 08 acres of land	28	10	Returns
5	5 Labour + 10 acres of land	38	10	**Stage II**
6	6 Labour + 12 acres of land	48	10	Constant Returns
7	7 Labour + 14 acres of land	56	8	**Stage III**
8	8 Labour + 16 acres of land	62	6	Decreasing returns

The data of Table 14.1 can be represented in the form of Figure 14.1 given below:

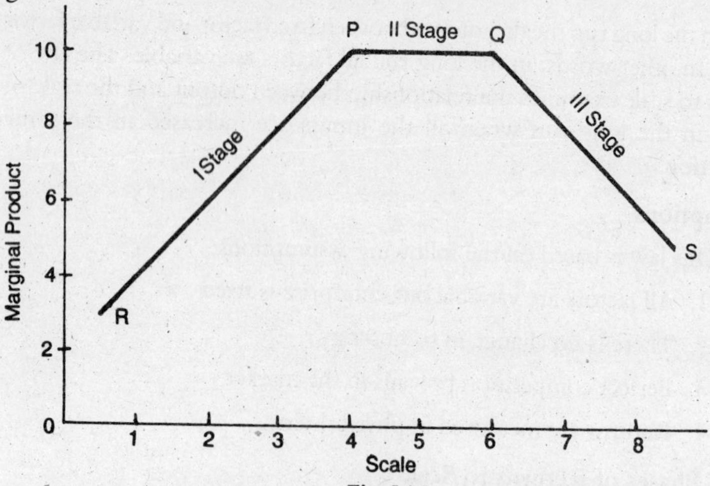

Fig. 14.1

RS = Returns to scale curve

RP = Segment; increasing returns to scale

PQ = Segment; constant returns to scale

QS = Segment; decreasing returns to scale

INCREASING RETURNS TO SCALE

Increasing returns to scale arises due to the following reasons:

(1) Dimensional economies, (2) Economies flowing from indivisibility, (3) Economies of specialisation, (4) Technical economies, (5) Managerial economies, (6) Marketing economies.

Marshall explains increasing returns in terms of "increased efficiency" of labour and capital in the improved organisation with the expanding scale of output and employment of factor unit. It is referred to as the economy of organisation in the earlier stages of production.

CONSTANT RETURNS TO SCALE

As a firm continues to expand, it gradually exhausts the economies, internal and external, which enabled the operation of increasing returns to scale. In this stage, the economies and diseconomies of scale are exactly in balance over a particular range of output. In the case of constant returns to scale increases in all the inputs cause proportionate increases in output.

A production function showing constant returns to scale is often called 'Linear and homogeneous' or 'homogeneous of the first degree.' The Cobb-Douglas production function evolved by the American economists Cobb and Douglas is a linear and homogeneous production function.

DIMINISHING RETURNS TO SCALE

When a business firm continues to expand even beyond the point of constant returns, a stage comes when diminishing returns to scale set in. There are decreasing returns to scale when the percentage increase in output is less than the percentage increase in input. As the size of the firm expands, managerial efficiency decreases. Another factor responsible for diminishing returns to scale is the limitation of exhaustibility of the natural resources. For example, doubling of coal-mining plants may not double the coal output, because of limited availability of coal deposits or due to difficult accessibility to coal deposits.

THE LAW OF VARIABLE PROPORTIONS (OR) LAW OF DIMINISHING RETURNS

The law of variable proportions is one of the basic laws in economics. The law of variable proportions is the modern version of the law of diminishing returns. This law states a technical physical relationship between the fixed and variable factors of production in the short run. Here it is assumed that only one factor of production is a variable factor while other factors are assumed to remain fixed. As we increase the quantity of the variable factor while keeping other factors constant, the output of the variable factor may increase more than proportionately in the initial stages of production, but eventually it will not increase even proportionately. That is why Prof. Ryan calls this law as the law of non-proportional returns.

The 19th century classical economists like Tugot, Ricardo, West and Malthus visualised the operation of this law in agriculture. Alfred Marshall, a neo-classical economist too considered the law of diminishing returns in relation to agriculture only. He thought that in industry increasing returns would prevail.

The law of variable proportions has been defined by economists in the following way: "As the proportion of one factor in a combination of factors is increased, after a point, first the marginal and then the average product of that factor will diminish."[2]

Assumptions of the Law

The law of variable proportions is valid when the following conditions are fulfilled.

1. The state of technology is given.
2. Only one factor is varied and all other factors remain fixed.
3. The fixed factor and the variable factor are combined together in variable proportions in the process of production.
4. The units of the variable factor are homogeneous.
5. The law operates in the short run.

Illustration of the Law

Let us take the case of a farmer who is cultivating one acre of land. Land is a fixed factor. The farmer tries to increase output by varying the variable factor, i.e., labour. The change in, total product, average product and marginal product of labour are depicted in the following table.

Table 14.2

Units of input L	*Total product (TP)*	*Marginal product (MP)*	*Average product (AP)*	*Stage*
1	100	100	100	
2	220	120	110	I
3	360	140	120	
4	460	100	115	
5	530	70	106	
6	570	40	95	II
7	595	25	85	
8	600	5	75	
9	594	–6	66	III
10	560	–34	56	

2. Benhams Economics, 7th Edn., The English Language Book Society, London, 1967, p. 109.

Total Product (TP)

Total product is the amount of output produced from land with the given number of labourers employed.

Average Product (AP_L)

The average product of labour (AP_L) is total product (TP) divided by the number of labourers employed $AP_L = \frac{TP_L}{L}$

Marginal Product (MP_L)

The marginal product of labour (MP_L) is the change in the total product due to a change in labour. $MP_L = \frac{\Delta TP}{\Delta L}$

In our example in Table (14.2) there are increasing returns to labour for the first three units of labour employed. The law of diminishing returns sets in with addition of the fourth worker. Both the average and the marginal products increase at first and then decline. The marginal product declines faster than the average product. When 8 men are employed, total product is at a maximum. The marginal product of the 9th labourer is negative.

Thus,

1. If MP > 0, TP will be increasing as L increases
2. If MP = 0, TP will be constant as L increases
3. If MP < 0, TP will be falling as L increases.

Graphical presentation of the law of variable proportions

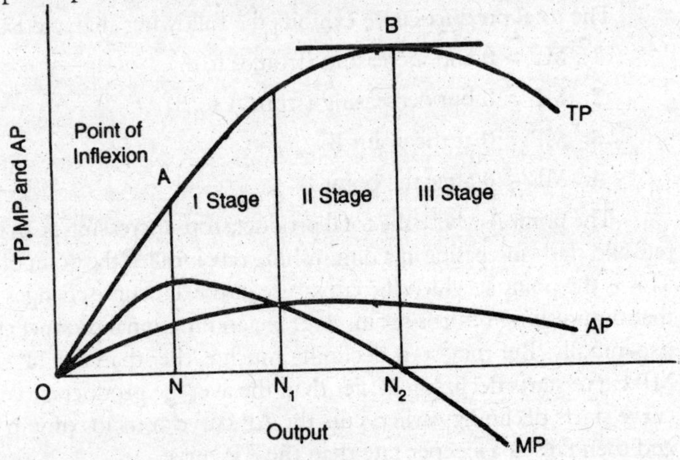

Fig. 14.2

Table 14.3

Properties of Total Product, Marginal Product and Average Product Curves During the Three Stages of Production

Total Product	*Marginal Product*	*Average Product*
Stage I First increases at an increasing rate	increases	increases
then increases at a diminishing rate	reaches a maximum and begins to diminish	continues to increase
Stage II Continues to increase at a diminishing rate	continues to diminish	reaches maximum and begins to diminish
reaches maximum	becomes zero	continues to diminish
Stage III diminishes	becomes negative	continues to diminish but must always be greater than zero

The implications of the law of eventually diminishing returns is shown in Fig. 14.2 OX axis measures the variable input, labour. Average product, marginal product and total product is shown along the vertical axis.

The total product has increased up to the point B. In other words the total product curve reaches a maximum when MP = 0 and then starts declining when MP < 0.

The total product curve exhibits the following characteristics:

1. MP > 0 and increasing (from 0 to A)
2. MP > 0 but decreasing (from A to B)
3. MP = 0 at the point B
4. MP < 0 after the point B

The point A where the total product stops increasing at an increasing rate and starts increasing at a diminishing rate is called the point of inflexion. This is the point at which the curvature of the TP curve changes. It is here that diminishing returns set in. Average and marginal product curves also rise initially. But they start declining much earlier than the TP curve. The MP curve starts declining earlier than the average product curve. The MP curve starts declining earlier, cuts the AP curve at its maximum point (P) and then falls at a steeper rate than the AP curve.

THREE STAGES OF PRODUCTION IN THE SHORT RUN

Production in the short run can be divided into three stages:

Stage I —From the origin to N_1

Stage II — From N_1 to N_2

Stage III — To the right of N_2.

These three stages are illustrated in Fig. 14.2. No profit maximising production would take place in stage I or III. In stage I, the proportion of variable factor to fixed factor is low. Therefore, by adding one more unit of labour, the producer can increase the average productivity for all the units. A restaurant with 100 tables and only two waiters would be operating in a stage I of the short-run production function.[3] By increasing the amount of labour in Stage I the average product of labour increases. As for stage III, it does not pay the producer to be in this region because by reducing the labour input he can increase total output and save in the cost of a unit of labour. In this stage there is too much of the variable factor relation to the fixed factor. A restaurant with too many waiters in relation to the number of tables is an example of stage III. Therefore stage III is considered as an irrational phase of production. Nevertheless, it is quite likely that a firm lacking perfect knowledge may be operating in this stage. In agriculture, this may be found to be very common. For instance, evidence of overcrowding of broilers and layers in poultry houses have been explained by some economists.[4]

Stage II is the only stage in which there is neither a redundancy of the variable factor nor a redundancy of the fixed factor. Throughout this range the average product of labour declines, but the marginal product is positive. Thus, the economically meaningful range is the II stage.

DIMINISHING AND INCREASING RETURNS

The classical economists confined their discussion of the law of diminishing returns to that of agriculture only. Marshall held the view that if the role of nature is more predominant than man, diminishing returns occur and where man occupies a primary role compared to nature increasing returns may occur. In short, he visualised diminishing returns in agriculture and increasing returns in industry.

---

3. David N. Hyman, *Modern Micro Economics, Analysis and Applications,* 1986, p.196.
4. C.E. Bishop, and W.D. Toussaint, *Introduction to Agricultural Economic Analysis,* John Wiley & Sons, p. 41.

The operation of the law of diminishing returns is quicker in agriculture than in industry. The simple reason is that in agriculture nature does the business and man is merely a manager. There is little scope for the application of division of labour. In addition, agriculture is seasonal in character. Further, the overall supply of land is inelastic. Therefore the alternative to increase output is to apply more of labour and capital. But after a point, the increase in the variable factor results in diseconomies of scale. The next option left is to increase output by the extension of plough in less fertile lands also. Since output and fertility are correlated, less fertile lands will yield only lesser returns. Thus the law operates both under intensive and under extensive cultivation.

Increasing returns is a major possibility in industry. In industry the role of man is supreme and nature plays a negligible role. A manufacturing firm benefits from division of labour and specialisation. The emergence of various forms of economies will tend to raise the output more than proportionately. But in industry also there is a limit beyond which diminishing returns will occur.

QUESTIONS

1. What is production function?
2. Explain the laws of returns.
3. State and explain the law of variable proportions.
4. Explain the law of diminishing returns and indicate its significance in economic theory.
5. Elucidate the law of variable proportions.

❖ ❖ ❖

15

ISO-QUANTS AND THE THEORY OF PRODUCTION

"Production is the goose that lays the golden egg."

— George Humphrey, 1954

Meaning

An iso-quant is a firm's counterpart of the consumer's indifference curve. An iso-quant is a curve that shows all the combinations of inputs that yield the same level of output. 'iso' means equal and 'quant' means quantity. So an iso-quant represents a constant quantity of output. The iso-quant curve is also known as an "Equal Product Curve" or "Production Indifference Curve." or "Iso-Product Curve."

The concept of iso-quants can be easily explained with the help of the table given below:

Table 15.1
An Iso-Quant Schedule

Combinations of labour and capital	*Units of labour (L)*	*Units of capital (K)*	*Output of cloth (metres)*
A	5	9	100
B	10	6	100
C	15	4	100
D	20	3	100

The above table is based on the assumption that only two factors of production, namely, Labour and Capital are used for producing 100 metres of cloth.

Combination	A = 5L + 9K = 100 metres of cloth
"	B = 10L + 6K = "
"	C = 15L + 4K = "
"	D = 20L + 3K = "

The combinations A, B, C and D show the possibility of producing 100 metres of cloth by applying various combinations of labour and capital. Thus an iso-quant schedule is a schedule of different combinations of factors of production yielding the same quantity of output.

An iso-product curve is the graphic representation of an iso-product schedule.

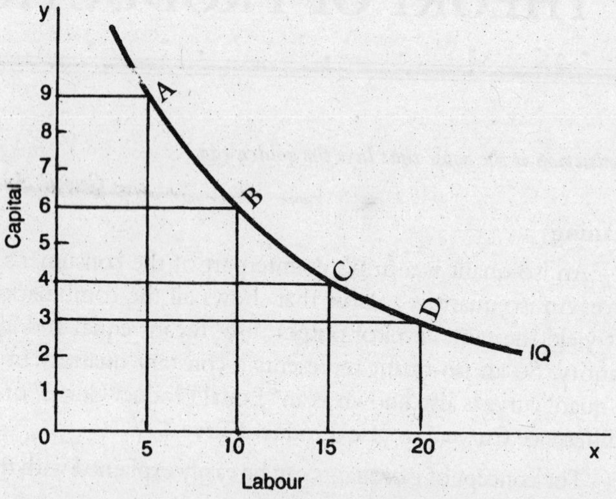

Fig. 15.1

Thus an iso-quant is a curve showing all combinations of labour and capital that can be used to produce a given quantity of output.

ISO-QUANT MAP

An iso-quant map is a set of iso-quants that shows the maximum attainable output from any given combination of inputs.

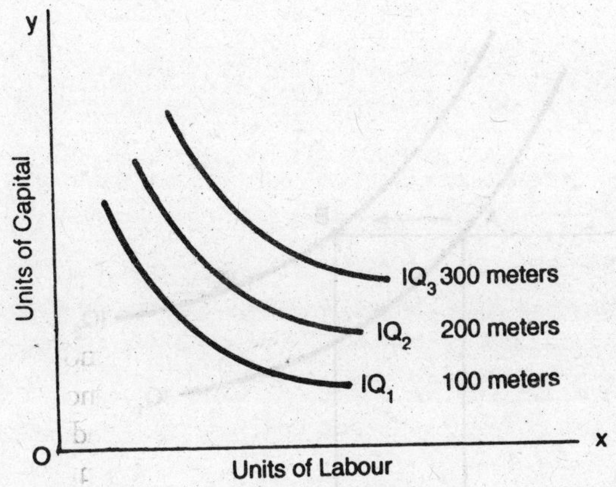

Fig. 15.2

Iso-quants Vs Indifference Curves

An iso-quant is 'analogous to an indifference curve in more than one way. The properties of iso-quants are similar to the properties of indifference curves. But some of the differences may also be noted. Firstly, in the indifference curve technique, utility cannot be measured. In the case of an iso-quant the product can be precisely measured in physical units. Secondly, in the case of indifference curves, we can talk only about higher or lower levels of utility. In the case of iso-quants we can say by how much IQ_2 actually exceeds IQ_1 (in Fig. 15.2).

Properties of Iso-quants

1. An isoquant lying above and to the right of another iso-quant represents a higher level of output.

This is because of the fact that on the higher iso-product curve, we have either more units of one factor of production or more units of both the factors. This has been illustrated in Fig. 15.3.

In Fig. 15.3 points A and B lie on the iso-product curves IQ_1 and IQ_2 respectively.

At point A we have = OX_1 units of Labour and OY_1 units of capital.

At point B we have = OX_2 units of Labour and OY_1 units of capital.

Though the amount of capital (OY_1) is the same at both the points, point B is having X_1X_2 units of labour more. So it will yield a higher output.

Hence it is proved that a higher iso-product curve shows a higher level of output.

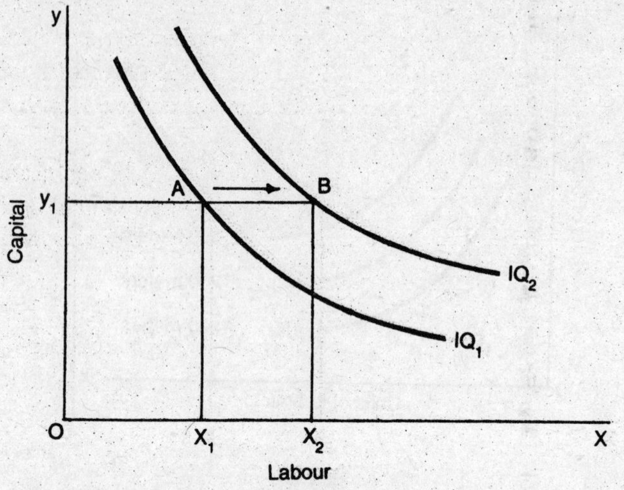

Fig. 15.3

2. Two Iso-product Curves cannot cut each other

Just as two indifference curves cannot cut each other, two iso-product curves also cannot cut each other. If they intersect each other, there would be a contradiction and we will get inconsistent results. This can be illustrated with the help of a diagram as in Fig. 15.4.

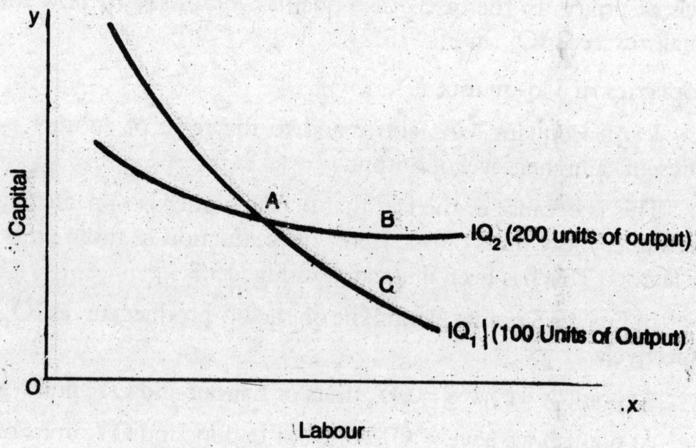

Fig. 15.4

If Fig. 15.4 the iso-product curve IQ_1 shows 100 units of output produced by various combinations of labour and capital and the curve IQ_2 shows 200 units of output,

On IQ_1 we have A = C, because they are on the same isoquant.

On IQ_2 we have A = B

therefore B = C

This is however inconsistent since C = 100 and B = 200. So, iso-quants cannot intersect.

3. Iso-product Curves are Convex to the Origin

An iso-product curve must always be convex to the origin. This is because of the operation of the principle of diminishing marginal rate of technical substitution. MRTS is the rate at which marginal unit of an input can be substituted for another input making the level of output remain the same.

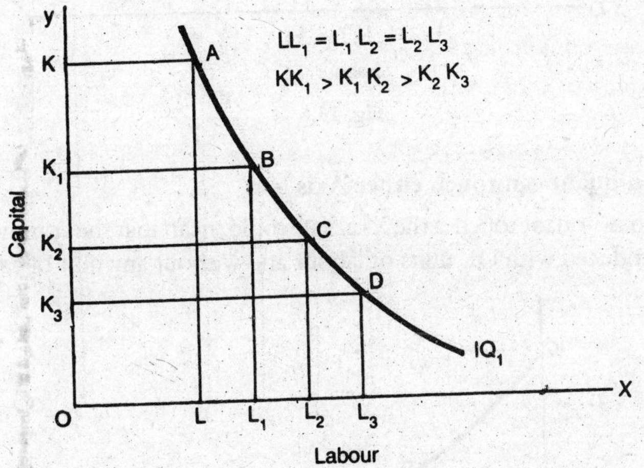

Fig. 15.5

In Fig. 15.5, as the producer moves from point A to B, from B to C and C to D along an iso-product curve, the marginal rate of technical substitution (MRTS) of labour for capital diminishes. The MRTS diminishes because the two factors are not perfect substitutes. In Fig. 15.5, for every increase in labour units by (ΔL) there is a corresponding decrease in the units of capital (ΔK).

It cannot be concave as shown in 15.6 figure.

If they are concave MRTS of labour for capital increases. But this is not true of iso-product curves.

Since MRTS must diminish, the iso-product curves must be convex to the origin.

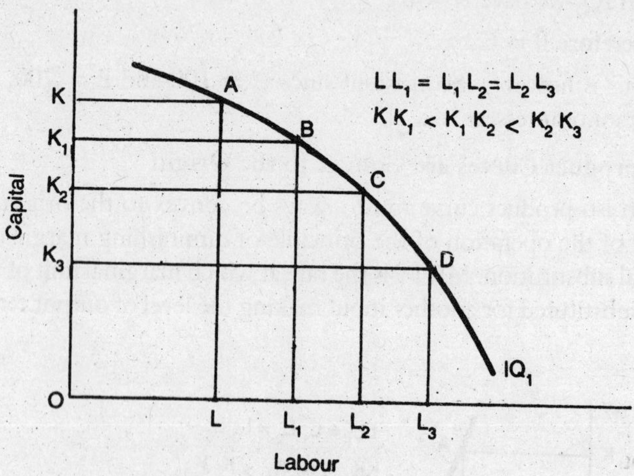

Fig. 15.6

4. No Iso-quant can touch either Axis

If an iso-quant touches the X-axis it would mean that the commodity can be produced with OL units of labour and without any unit of capital.

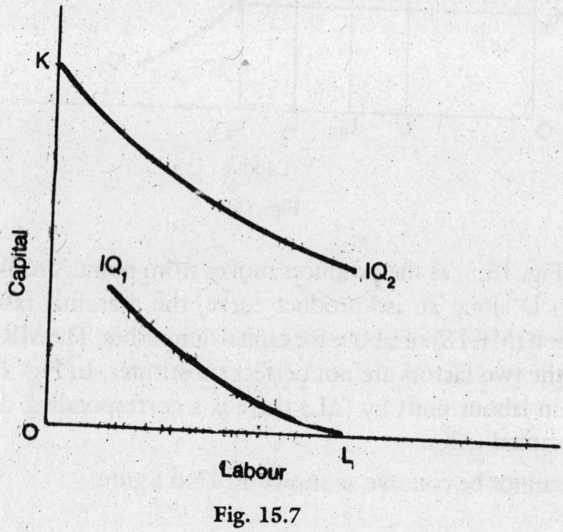

Fig. 15.7

Point K on the Y-axis implies that the commodity can be produced with OK units of capital and without any unit of labour. But this is wrong because the firm cannot produce a commodity with one factor alone.

5. Iso-quants are Negatively Sloped

An iso-product curve slopes downwards from left to right. The logic behind this is the principle of diminishing marginal rate of technical substitution. In order to maintain a given output, a reduction in the use of one input must be offset by an increase in the use of another input.

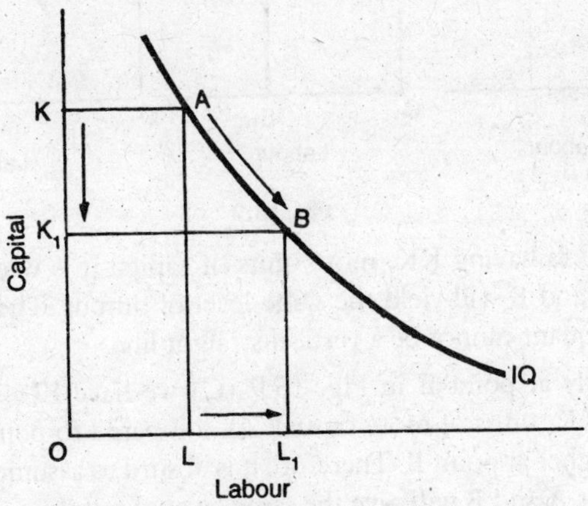

Fig. 15.8

Fig. 15.8 shows that when the producer moves from point A to B, the amount of labour increases from OL to OL_1, but the units of capital decreases from OK to OK_1, to maintain the same level of output.

The impossibility of horizontal, vertical or upward sloping iso-product curves can be shown with the help of the following diagrams.

Consider Fig. 15.9(*A*).

At point A we have OL units of labour and OK units of capital and at B we have OL_1 units of labour and OK units of capital.

$OL_1 + OK > OL + OK$, and so combination B will yield a higher output than A. Therefore, points A and B on the IQ curve cannot represent an equal level of the product. Hence the iso-quant cannot be a horizontal straight line like AB.

Consider Fig. 15.9(*B*).

At point A we have OL units of labour and OK units of capital. At point B we have OL units of labour and OK_1 units of capital.

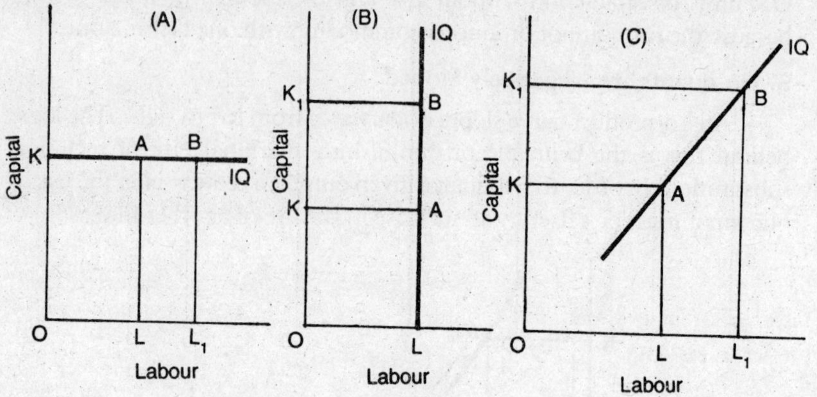

Fig. 15.9

Since B is having KK_1 more units of capital it is wrong to assume that both A and B will yield the same level of output. The conclusion is that the iso-quant cannot be a vertical straight line.

Similarly at point B in Fig. 15.9 (*C*) we have LL_1 units of more labour and KK_1 units of more capital. As compared to point A, both the inputs are higher at point B. Therefore it is absurd to assume that both the combinations A and B will give the same level of output.

6. Iso-quants need not be Parallel

The shape of an iso-quant depends upon the marginal rate of technical substitution. Since the rate of substitution between two factors need not necessarily be the same in all the iso-quant schedules, they need not be parallel.

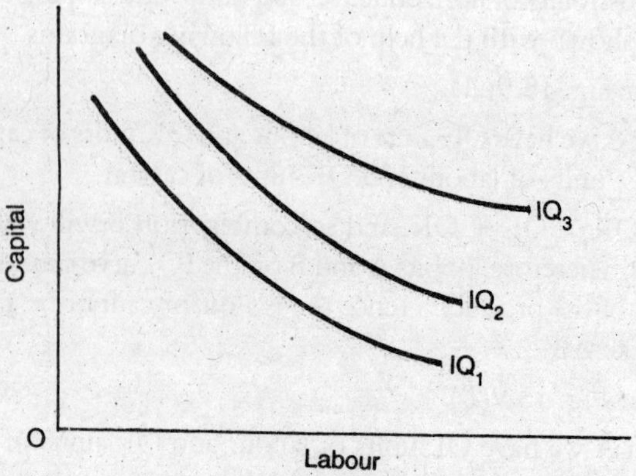

Fig. 15.10

7. Each iso-quant is Oval-shaped

An important feature of an iso-product curve is that it enables the firm to identify the efficient range of production.

Consider Fig. 15.11.

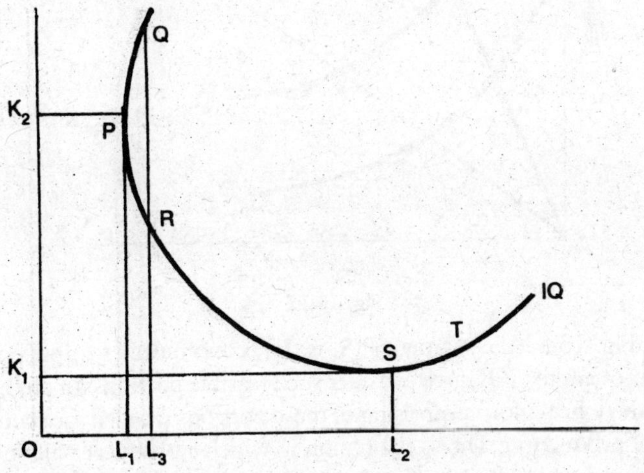

Fig. 15.11

Both the combinations Q and P produce the same level of total output. But the combination Q represents more of capital and labour than P. Combinations Q must therefore be expensive and would not be chosen. The same argument can be made to rule out combination T or any other combination lying on a portion of the iso-quant where the slope is positive. Positively sloped iso-quants imply that an increase in the use of labour would require an increase in the use of capital to keep production constant.

In general, for any input combination on the positively sloped portion of an iso-quant, it is possible to find another input combination with less of both the inputs on the negatively convex portion that will produce the same level of output. Therefore only the negatively sloped segment of iso-quant is economically feasible.

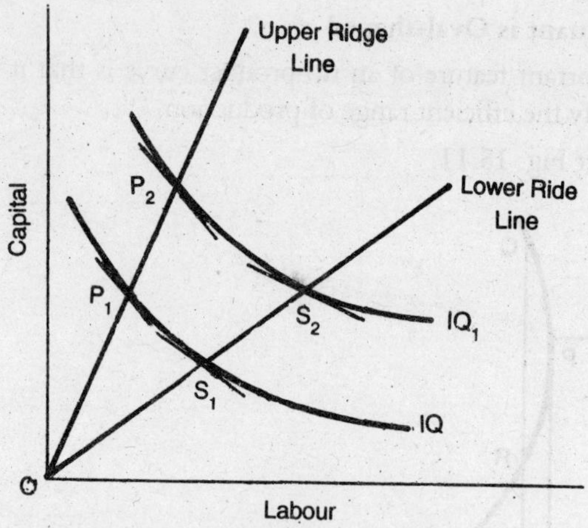

Fig. 15.12

In Fig. 15.12 the segment P_1S_1 is the economically feasible portion of the iso-quant for IQ. If we consider such feasible portions for all the iso-quants, then the region comprising of these portions is called the economic region of production. This is the region in which a producer will operate. It is shown in Fig. 15.12. The lines OP_1P_2 and OS_1S_2 are called ridge lines.[1] Ridge lines may be defined as lines separating the downward sloping portions of a series of iso-quants from the upward sloping portions. They give the boundary of the economic region of production.

MARGINAL RATE OF TECHNICAL SUBSTITUTION

The Marginal Rate of Technical Substitution (MRTS) is the rate at which one input can be substituted for another input without changing the level of output. In other words the marginal rate of technical substitution of Labour (L) for Capital (K) is the slope of an iso-quant multiplied by – 1.

Since the slope of an iso-quant is moving down, the iso-quant is given by – ΔK/ΔL.

$$\text{MRTS} = \frac{-\Delta K}{\Delta L} = \text{Slope of the iso-quant.}$$

1. Ridge lines need not be straight lines always.

Table 15.2

The following table will make the concept clear.

Combinations	*Iso-quant Schedule*		$MRTS_{LK}$	*Output*
	Labour (L)	*Capital (K)*		
A	5	9	—	100
B	10	6	3:5	100
C	15	4	2:5	100
D	20	3	1:5	100

In the above table all the four factor combinations A, B, C and D produce the same level of 100 units of output. They are all iso-product combinations. As we move from combination A to combination B, it is clear that 3 units of capital can be replaced by 5 units of labour. Hence $MRTS_{LK}$ is 3:5. In the third combination, 2 units of capital are substituted by 5 more units of labour. Therefore $MRTS_{LK}$ is 2:5.

In Fig. 15.13

$$MRTS_{LK} \text{ at point B} = \frac{AE}{EB}$$

$$MRTS_{LK} \text{ at point C} = \frac{BF}{FC}$$

$$MRTS_{LK} \text{ at point D} = \frac{CG}{GD}$$

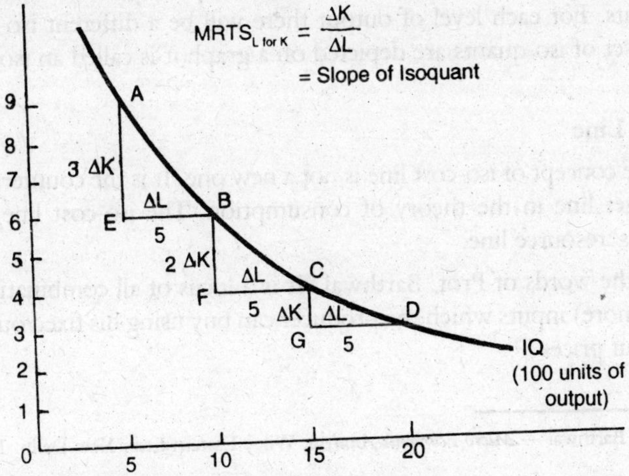

Fig. 15.13

PRODUCER'S EQUILIBRIUM
(Least Cost Combination)

A rational firm seeks maximisation of its profit. Maximisation of profit implies minimisation of cost. The cost is minimum, when the input combination is optimal. In the theory of consumer behaviour we have analysed the equilibrium of a consumer with the help of the indifference curve analysis. Similarly, the producer's equilibrium can be examined with the help of iso-quants. It should be remembered that the iso-quants in the theory of production are, in fact, the counterpart of the indifference curves in the theory of consumption.

Assumptions

The principle of least-cost combination rests on the following assumptions:

1. Capital and labour are the two factors involved in production.
2. All the units of both the factors are homogeneous.
3. The prices of the factor units are given.
4. The total money outlay is also given.
5. There is perfect competition in the factor-market.

In order to analyse producer's equilibrium, the firm under consideration should know its iso-quant map and its iso-cost line.

Iso-quant Map

The iso-quant or equal product map has already been explained in the preceding pages. Iso-quants indicate various possibilities of combining two inputs. For each level of output there will be a different iso-quant. When a set of iso-quants are depicted on a graph it is called an iso-quant map.

Iso-cost Line

The concept of iso-cost line is not a new one. It is the counterpart of the budget line in the theory of consumption. The iso-cost line is the producers' resource line.

In the words of Prof. Barthwal "It is a locus of all combinations of two (or more) inputs which the producer can buy using his fixed outlay at fixed input prices."[2]

---

2. R.R. Barthwal — *Micro Economic Analysis,* Wiley Eastern Ltd., New Delhi, 1992, p. 152.

We shall now draw the iso-cost line on the basis of an imaginary example.

Let us assume that a firm has a sum of Rs. 500 to spend on two factors, labour and capital. Further, let us assume that a unit of labour costs Rs. 10 and a unit of capital (machine) costs Rs. 100. With a total outlay of Rs. 500 the firm could hire 50 units of labour and no capital, or it could hire 5 units of capital and no labour; or some combination of labour and capital in between. OM in the diagram represents 50 workers and ON represent 5 machines.

If we connect the two points N and M, we get the iso-cost line. Thus an iso-cost line gives all combinations of labour and capital at equal cost. The iso-cost line will shift when the prices of factors change, the outlay remaining the same. Likewise, the iso-cost line will shift to the right if the outlay of the firm increases. Hiring more of both inputs will cost more. When the total outlay is Rs. 600, the iso-cost line is N_1M_1. N_2M_2 is the iso-cost line when the outlay is Rs. 700.

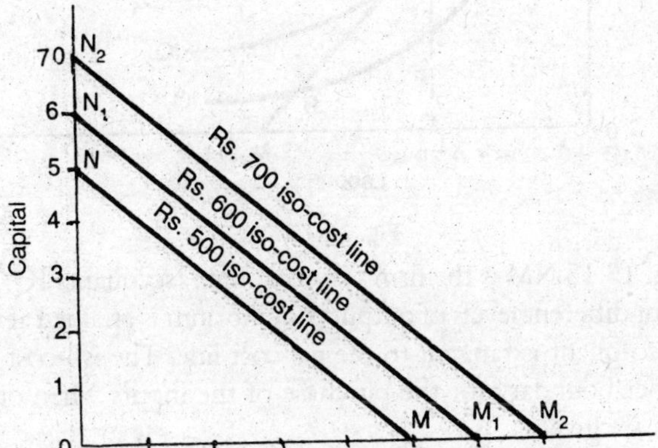

Fig. 15.14

Thus, the iso-cost line depends upon two things: (1) The prices of the factors of production and, (2) the total outlay which the firm wants to make on the two factors of production.

The slope of an iso-cost line is $\frac{P_L}{P_K}$, which is the ratio of the price of labour to the price of capital, when labour is shown on the x-axis and capital is shown on the y-axis.

The Optimum Combination of Inputs

Let us consider the geometry of the producer's equilibrium.

Now the problem confronting the firm is to reach the highest possible iso-quant with its given iso-cost line. In other words, it is the problem of getting the highest amount of output from the given outlay. Towards this end, the equal product map has been super imposed on the iso-cost line NM.

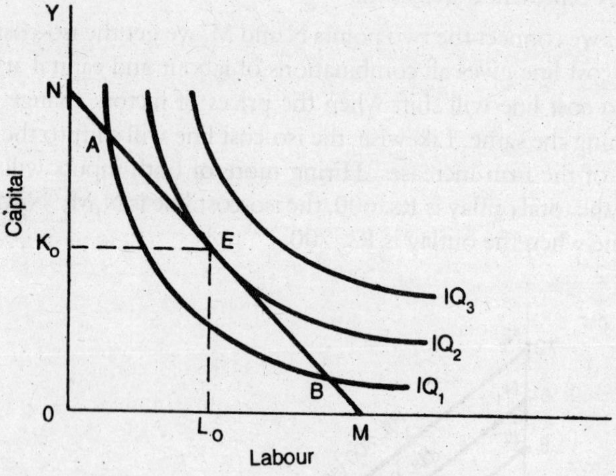

Fig. 15.15

In Fig. 15.15 NM is the firm's iso-cost line. Iso-quants IQ_1, IQ_2 and IQ_3 represent different levels of output. Equilibrium is attained at the point where the iso-quant is tangent to the iso-cost line. The iso-cost line NM sets the upper boundary for the purchase of the inputs when outlay and input prices are given.

Outlay is not sufficient to move to IQ_3. Likewise the segments of iso-quants falling below the iso-cost line indicate under-utilisation of his outlay fully. Rationality on the part of the producer requires full utilisation of resources for optimisation of output.

Points A and B also satisfy the tangency condition and moreover they lie within the reach of the producer. But at these points the firm remains at a lower iso-quant IQ_1, which yields a lesser level of output than that on IQ_2. Thus E is the point of equilibrium from where there is no tendency on the part of the producer to move away. The firm will get its maximum output when it employs OL_0 units of labour and OK_0 units of capital. The equilibrium position of the firm can also be explained in terms of the equality between MRTS and the factor price ratio. The slope of the iso-quant is the marginal rate of technical substitution (MRTS) and the slope of the iso-cost line indicates the factor price ratio. It follows that while in equilibrium,

$$MRTS_{LK} = \frac{P_L}{P_K}$$

Thus the marginal rate of technical substitution can also be written as the ratio of the marginal product of labour to that of the marginal product of capital.

$$\frac{MP_L}{MP_K} = \frac{P_L}{P_K} \text{ or}$$

$$\frac{MP_L}{P_L} = \frac{MP_K}{P_K}$$

ISO-QUANTS AND RETURNS TO SCALE

Let us now examine the responses in output when all inputs are varied in equal proportions.

Returns to scale refer to output responses to an equi-proportionate, change in all inputs. Suppose labour and capital are doubled, then if output doubles, we have constant returns to scale. If output is less than double, we have decreasing returns to scale, and if output is more than double, we have increasing returns to scale.

Depending on whether the proportionate change in output equals, exceeds or falls short of the proportionate change in both inputs, a production function is classified as showing constant, increasing or decreasing returns to scale.

For computing the returns to scale in a production function, we calculate the function co-efficient represented by the symbol 'ε'. The ratio of the proportionate change in output to a proportionate change in all inputs is called the function co-efficient ε. That is $\varepsilon = \frac{\Delta q / q}{\Delta \lambda / \lambda}$ where the proportionate changes in output and all inputs are shown by $\Delta q/q$ and $\Delta\lambda/\lambda$. Then the returns to scale is classified as follows:

$\varepsilon < 1 =$ Increasing returns to scale

$\varepsilon = 1 =$ Constant returns to scale

$\varepsilon > 1 =$ Decreasing returns to scale

Increasing Returns to Scale

When output increases by a proportion that exceeds the proportion by which inputs increase, increasing returns to scale prevail.

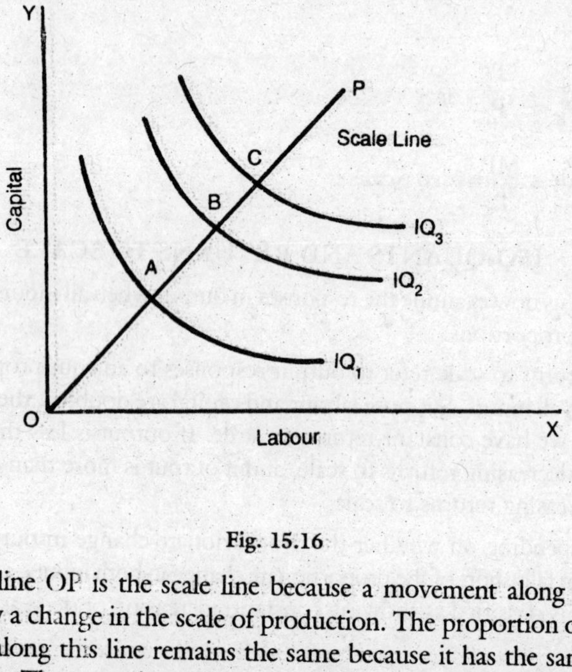

Fig. 15.16

The line OP is the scale line because a movement along this line shows only a change in the scale of production. The proportion of labour to capital along this line remains the same because it has the same slope throughout. The operation of increasing returns to scale is shown by the gradual decrease in the distance between the iso-quant. For example, OA>AB>BC.

Causes of Increasing Returns to Scale

There are several technical and/or managerial factors that contribute to the operation of increasing returns to scale.

1. Increasing Specialisation of Labour

Increasing returns to scale can be the result of increase in the productivity of inputs caused by increased specialisation and division of labour as the scale of operations increase.

2. Indivisibilities

In general, indivisibility implies that an equipment is available only in minimum sizes or in definite ranges of size. Specialised machines are generally far more productive than less specialised machines. In large-scale operations the possibility of using specialised machines are higher, so productivity will also be higher.

3. Geometric Necessity

For some production processes, it is a matter of geometric necessity. A larger scale of operation makes it more efficient. For example, to double the grazing area, a farmer need not have to double the length of fencing. Similarly, doubling the cylindrical equipment (like pipes and smoke stacks) and spherical equipment (like storage tanks) requires less than twice the quantity of metal.

Decreasing Returns to Scale

Decreasing returns to scale prevail when the distance between consecutive iso-quants increase. For example, OA<AB<BC.

Decreasing returns arise when diseconomies are greater than economies. Difficulties in co-ordinating the operations of many factories and communication problems with employees may contribute to decreasing returns to scale. More than proportionate increases in managerial inputs may be required to expand output when an organization becomes very large. (See Fig. 15.17)

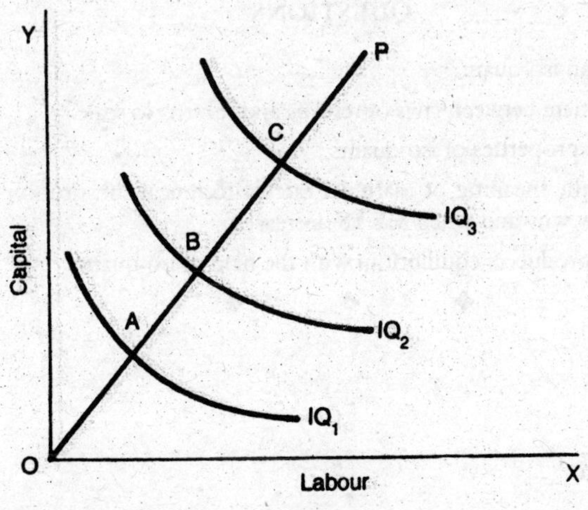

Fig. 15.17

Constant Returns to Scale

Constant returns to scale prevail when output also increases by the same proportion in which input increases. In the case of constant returns to scale the distance between successive iso-quants remains constant. For example, OA = AB = BC. (See Fig. 15.18)

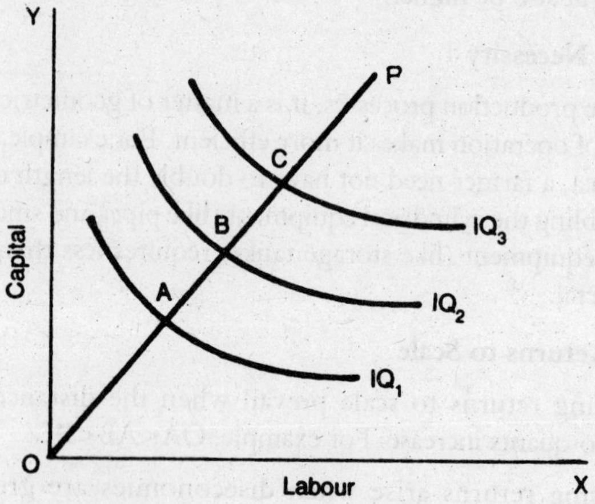

Fig. 15.18

Constant returns arise when economies exactly balance with diseconomies. As economies of scale are exhausted, a phase of constant returns to scale may set in operation.

QUESTIONS

1. Explain an iso-quant.
2. Differentiate between laws of returns and returns to scale.
3. State the properties of iso-quants.
4. Explain the meaning of marginal rate of technical substitution (MRTS) and show why and when MRTS decreases.
5. Explain producers equilibrium with the help of iso-quants

❖ ❖ ❖

*** PART FOUR ***

THEORY OF PRODUCT PRICING

16

COST AND COST CURVES

"A class in economics would be a real success if the students gained from it a real understanding of the meaning of cost in all its many aspects."

—*J.M. Clark*

INTRODUCTION

The relationship between cost and output is known as the cost function. Cost functions are derived from production functions. The production function expresses the functional relationship between input and output. In simple terms, the production function states that output depends upon various quantities of inputs. If prices of inputs are known we can calculate the costs of production. The cost of production of a commodity is the aggregate of prices paid for the factors of production used in producing that commodity.

Money Cost and Real Cost

Money cost or nominal cost is the total money expenses incurred by a firm in producing a commodity. It includes the following elements:

1. Cost of raw materials
2. Wages and salaries of labour
3. Expenditure on machinery and equipment
4. Depreciation on machines, buildings and such other capital goods

5. Interest on capital
6. Other expenses like advertisement, insurance premium and taxes.
7. Normal profits of the entrepreneur.

Real Cost

Real cost is a subjective concept. It expresses the pains and sacrifices involved in producing a commodity.

Marshall defined real cost as follows, "The exertions of all the different kinds of labour that are directly or indirectly involved in making it; together with the abstinences or rather the waitings required for saving the capital used in making it."

But real costs are not amenable to precise measurement. Modern economists therefore prefer the concept of opportunity cost.

Private, External and Social Costs

Sometimes, there is a discrepancy between the cost incurred by a firm and the cost incurred by the society. For example, Mathura Oil Refinery discharges its wastes in the Yamuna river causing water pollution. Likewise, various types of air pollution and noise pollution are caused by various agencies engaged in production activities. Such pollutions result in tremendous health hazards which involve cost to the society as a whole. A cost that is not borne by the firm, but is incurred by others in the society is called an external cost.[1]

The true cost to the society must include all costs, regardless of the persons on whom its impact falls and its incidence as to who bear them.

Thus, social cost = private cost + external cost

or external cost = social cost – private cost

Implicit Cost and Explicit Cost

Explicit costs are those costs which are actually paid by the firm. To put it in other words, explicit costs are paid out costs. Explicit costs include wages and salaries, prices of raw materials, amounts paid on fuel, power, advertisement, transportation, taxes and depreciation charges. Explicit costs are recorded in the firm's books of account.

Implicit costs are the imputed value of the entrepreneur's own resources and services. In other words, implicit costs are costs which self-owned and self-employed resources could have earned in their best alternative uses. It refers to the highest income which might have been received by him if he

---

1. Robert Y. Ahw, *Micro Economics Theory and Applications,* John Wiley & Sons, New York, 1976, p. 210.

has let his labour, building and money to someone else. These costs are frequently ignored in calculating the expenses of production.

Historical and Replacement Cost

Historical cost refers to the cost of an asset, acquired in the past whereas replacement cost refers to the cost which has to be incurred for replacing the same asset.

Increment and Sunk Costs

The increment costs are the additions to costs resulting from a change in product lines, introduction of a new product, replacement of obsolete plant and machinery etc.

Sunk costs are those which cannot be altered, increased or decreased by changing the rate of output and the level of business activity. All the past costs are considered as sunk costs because they are known and given and cannot be revised as a result of changes in market conditions.

OPPORTUNITY COST

Modern economists have rejected the labour and sacrifices nexus to represent real cost. Rather, in its place they have substituted opportunity or alternative cost.

The concept of opportunity cost occupies an important place in economic theory. The concept was first developed by an Austrian economist, Wieser. The other notable contributors are Daven Port, Knight, Wicksteed and Robbins. The concept is based on the fundamental fact that factors of production are scarce and versatile.

Our wants are unlimited. The means to satisfy these wants are limited, but, they are capable of alternative uses. Therefore the problem of choice arises. This is the essence of Robbins' definition of economics.

The opportunity cost of anything is the alternative that has been foregone. This implies that one commodity can be produced only at the cost of foregoing the production of another commodity. As Adam Smith observed, if a hunter can bag a deer or a beaver in the course of a single day, the cost of a deer is a beaver and the cost of a beaver is a deer. A man who marries a girl is foregoing the opportunity of marrying another girl. A film actress can either act in films or do modelling work. She cannot do both the jobs at the same time. Her acting in film results in the loss of an opportunity of doing modelling work.

In the words of Professors Byrns and Stone "opportunity cost is the value of the best alternative surrendered when a choice is made."[2]

In the words of John A. Perrow "Opportunity cost is the amount of the next best produce that must be given up (using the same resources) in order to produce a commodity."[3]

Importance of the Concept of Opportunity Cost

1. Determination of Relative Prices of Goods

The concept is useful in the determination of the relative prices of different goods. For example, if a given amount of factors can produce one table or three chairs, then the price of one table will tend to be three times equal to that of one chair.

2. Fixation of Remuneration to a Factor

The concept is also useful in fixing the price of a factor. For example, let us assume that the alternative employment of a college professor is work as an officer in an insurance company at a salary of Rs. 4000 per month. In such a case he has to be paid at least Rs. 4,000 to continue to retain him in the college.

3. Efficient Allocation of Resources

The concept is also useful in allocating the resources efficiently. Suppose, opportunity cost of 1 table is 3 chairs and the price of a chair is Rs. 100, while the price of a table is Rs. 400. Under such circumstances it is beneficial to produce one table rather than 3 chairs. Because, if he produces 3 chairs, he will get only Rs. 300, whereas a table fetches him Rs.400, that is, Rs. 100 more.

Limitations: The concept has the following drawbacks:

1. Specific

If a factor's service is specific, it cannot be put to alternative uses. The transfer cost or alternative cost in such a case is zero. This is pure rent, according to Mrs. Joan Robinson.

2. Inertia

Sometimes, factors may be reluctant to move to alternative occupations. In such a case, a payment exceeding the pure transfer cost will have to be made to induce it to take to an alternative occupation.

---

2. Byrns and Stone, *Micro Economics,* Scott, Foresman and Company, London, 4th Edn., 1989, p. 6.
3. John A. Perrow — *Economics,* 1971, p. 36.

3. Perfect Competition

The concept rests on the assumption of perfect competition. But perfect competition is a myth which seldom prevails.

4. Private and Social Costs

A discrepancy is likely to arise between private and social costs. For example let us assume that a chemical factory discharges industrial refuse into a river. This causes serious health hazards which cannot be measured in money terms.

5. Alternatives are not clearly known

The foregone opportunities are often not ascertainable. This also poses a serious limitation on the concept.

SHORT-RUN AND LONG-RUN COST CURVES

A study of different cost concepts is helpful in understanding the behaviour of costs over time.

Meaning of Short-run and Long-run

In the short-run, some factors are fixed while others are variable. The fixed factors are plant, equipment and a unique kind of skilled labour.

Short-run is defined as that period of time in which the firm can expand or contract its output only by varying the amounts of variables factors such as labour and raw materials. In the short period the size of the plant cannot be altered. More production is possible only by over working the existing plant or by hiring more workers and by purchasing and using more raw materials.

Long-run is defined as that period of time in which both fixed and variable factors are variable and both the factors can be adjusted. Over a long period of time, the firm can expand its output by enlarging the size of the existing plant or by building a new plant of a greater productive capacity.

Short-run Fixed and Variable Costs

Fixed costs are those costs that are invariant to the rate of production. They are the costs of indivisible factors such as building, machinery, vehicles etc. Once these costs are incurred they can be used over a period of time at no further cost. Even if production is nil, fixed cost will have to remain the same.

Fixed costs usually include the following:

1. Rent for building
2. Interest for capital
3. Insurance premium
4. Property, business taxes etc.
5. Depreciation charges.
6. Salaries of permanent staff

Variable costs vary with the level of output. It rises when output expands and falls when output contracts. When output is nil, variable cost becomes zero.

Variable costs usually include the following:

1. Payments for raw materials
2. Wages for labour
3. Fuel and power charges
4. Excise duties, sales tax etc.
5. Interest on short term loans
6. Transport costs.

Table 16.1

Cost Schedule

(Amount in Rupees)

Total output units	*Total Fixed Cost*	*Total Variable Cost*	*Total Cost (2+3)*	*Average Fixed Cost (2 ÷ 1)*	*Average Variable Cost (3 ÷ 1)*	*Average Cost (4 ÷ 1)*	*Marginal Cost*
1	*2*	*3*	*4*	*5*	*6*	*7*	*8*
0	50	0	50	—	—	—	—
1	50	50	100	50	50	100	50
2	50	78	128	25	39	64	28
3	50	98	148	16.7	32.7	49.3	20
4	50	112	162	12.5	28	40.5	14
5	50	130	180	10	26	36	18
6	50	150	200	8.3	25	33.5	20
7	50	175	225	7.1	25	32.1	25
8	50	204	254	6.3	25.5	31.8	29
9	50	242	292	5.6	26.9	32.4	38
10	50	300	350	5	30	35	58
11	50	385	435	4.5	35	39.5	85

Total Fixed Cost

The total obligations of the firm per time period for all fixed inputs are called total fixed cost. Total fixed cost remains 'constant' or 'fixed' irrespective of the size of the output. Suppose Mr. Marcel has borrowed a certain sum of money from Tino to produce knifes. Every month he has to pay Rs. 200 towards interest charges. For some reason or other the business unit is temporarily closed for a few months. Now production is zero, yet he has to pay the interest at the fixed stipulated rate.

Again as production starts and goes on increasing the total fixed cost remains the same. Diagrammatically the total fixed cost curve is a straight line parallel to the OX-axis.

Total Variable Cost

Total variable cost varies with output. In the above example of Marcel, when the production was temporarily shut down, the variable cost was zero. As output increases, the total variable cost also increases. But the variation in variable cost is not in proportion to the variation in output. Production is subject to the laws of increasing, constant and diminishing returns. Up to 4 units, the total variable cost increases, but at a diminishing rate. During the intermediary stage of 5 and 6 units variable cost increases but at a diminishing rate. After 6 units of output, total variable cost increases at an increasing rate. Diagrammatically the total variable cost curve is an upward sloping curve.

Total Cost

Total cost is the sum of total fixed cost and total variable cost.

TC =TFC + TVC Where,

TC = Total Cost

TFC = Total Fixed Cost

TVC = Total Variable Cost

But it should be noted that total fixed cost is the same irrespective of the level of output. Therefore a change in total cost is influenced by the change in variable cost only.

The relationship between total fixed cost, total variable cost and total cost will be clear from the following diagram. (Fig. 16.1)

Average Fixed Cost

The average fixed cost is the fixed cost per unit of output. It is obtained by dividing the total fixed cost by the number of units of the commodity produced.

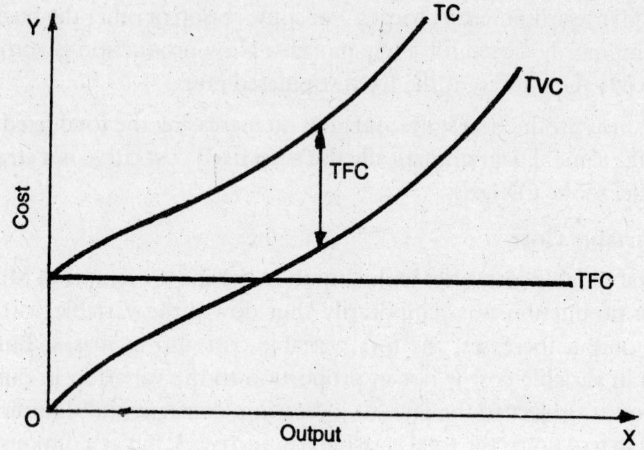

Fig. 16.1

$$\text{Symbolically AFC} = \frac{\text{TFC}}{\text{Q}}$$

$$\text{or AFC} = \text{AC} - \text{AVC}$$

The average fixed cost (AFC) is a rectangular hyperbola which never meets the horizontal or vertical axis. Since the total fixed cost is constant, as total output becomes larger and larger, the entire AFC must become smaller and smaller. This continuous falling of AFC, as output expands, is what business people commonly call 'spreading the overhead.'

Average Variable Cost

The average variable cost is the variable cost per unit of output. It is obtained by dividing the total variable cost by the number of units of the commodity produced.

$$\text{Symbolically AVC} = \frac{\text{TVC}}{\text{Q}}$$

$$\text{or AVC} = \text{AC} - \text{AFC}$$

Diagrammatically, the AVC is 'U' shaped. The law of variable proportions provides the fundamental explanation for the shape of this curve. It means that the AVC curve first falls, reaches a minimum and then begins to increase.

Average Total Cost or Average Cost

Average total cost or average cost is the cost per unit of output. It is obtained by dividing the total cost by the total number of units of the commodity produced.

$$\text{Symbolically, ATC} = \frac{TC}{Q}$$

$$TC = TFC + TVC$$

$$\text{Therefore ATC} = \frac{TFC + TVC}{Q}$$

$$= \frac{TFC}{Q} + \frac{TVC}{Q}$$

$$ATC = AFC + AVC$$

The AC curve is 'U' shaped in nature.

WHY THE SHORT-RUN AVERAGE COST CURVE IS 'U' SHAPED?

Professors Stonier and Hague have given a simple and advanced explanation for the 'U' shaped average cost curve.

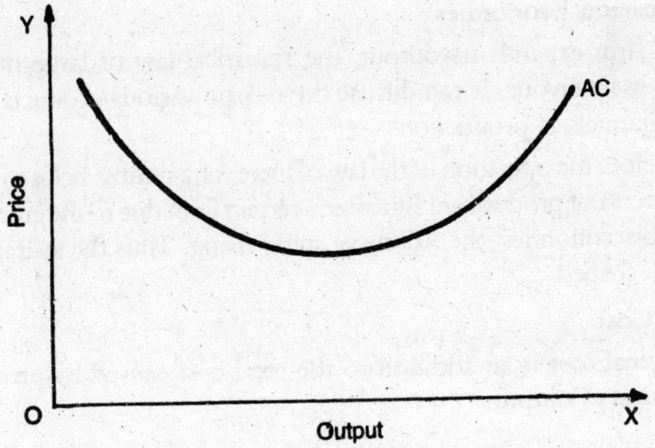

Fig. 16.2

Simple Explanation

The average cost is the sum of AFC and AVC. In the initial stages both the AFC and AVC go on falling. Consequently the AC also goes on falling. After a certain stage the AVC starts rising. The AFC falls no doubt but the rise in AVC is greater than the fall in the AFC. So the AC goes on rising after reaching a minimum point.

Advanced Explanation

When the size of a firm expands, there emerges certain economies of scale. The economies of scale reduces the average cost of production. The important economies are:

1. Technical Economies

Technical economies arise as a result of the adoption of new and scientifically developed machinery.

2. Managerial Economies

The unit cost of administration falls as production expands.

3. Marketing Economies

The average cost of marketing tends to be lower when a larger output is involved.

4. Financial Economies

As the size of the firm expands, it can borrow funds at lower rates of interest.

5. Risk-bearing Economies

As a firm expands its output, the statistical law of large numbers works out in its favour. It can diffuse the risk on various products and in different channels of production.

Therefore the operation of the law of increasing returns helps to reduce the average cost of production. But after a certain limit due to the emergence of certain diseconomies, the AC curve starts rising. Thus the average cost curve is 'U' shaped.

Marginal Cost

Marginal cost is an addition to the total cost caused by producing one more unit of output.

$$\text{Marginal Cost} = \frac{\text{Change in Total cost}}{\text{Change in output}}$$

or

$$MC = \frac{\Delta TC}{\Delta Q}$$ where ΔTC is change in total cost,

ΔQ is change in output.

It is worth noting that MC is independent of output. It is only the variable cost that varies with a variation in output in the short-run. Therefore the marginal costs are in fact due to the changes in variable costs. This can be proved algebraically as:

$$\begin{aligned} MC &= TC_n - TC_{n-1} \\ &= (TVC_n + TFC) - (TVC_{n-1} + TFC) \\ &= TVC_n - TVC_{n-1} + TFC - TFC \\ &= TVC_n - TVC_{n-1} \end{aligned}$$

The various cost curves can be shown as shown in the following diagram.

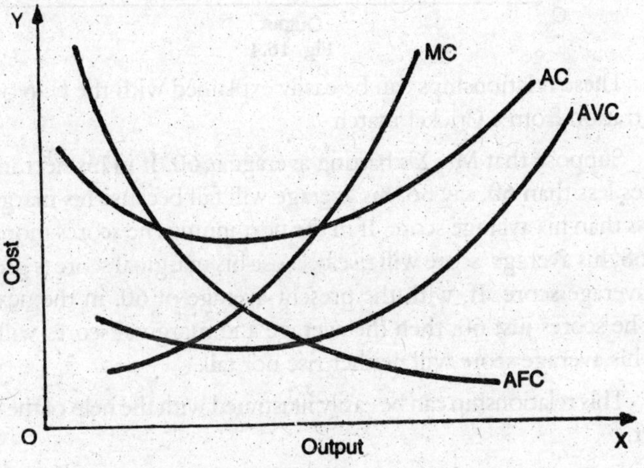

Fig. 16.3

RELATIONSHIP BETWEEN AVERAGE AND MARGINAL COST CURVES

According to Professor Richard Lipsey[4] the relationship between the marginal and the average cost is more a mathematical one rather than economics. The relationship can be briefly stated as follows:

4. R.G. Lipsey, *An Introduction to Positive Economics,* ELBS, 1969, p. 277.

1. When marginal cost is less than average cost, average cost is falling.
2. When marginal cost is greater than average cost, average cost is rising.
3. The MC curve must cut the AC curve at AC's minimum point and from below.

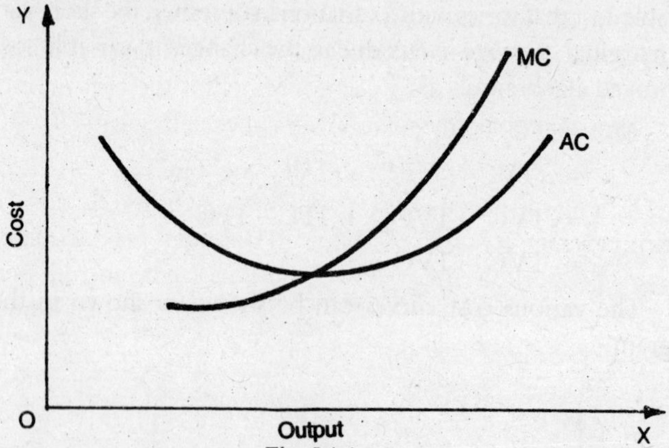

Fig. 16.4

These relationships can be easily explained with the help of a simple illustration from a Cricket match.

Suppose that Mr. X's batting average is 60. If in his next innings, he scores less than 60, say 56, his average will fall because his marginal score is less than his average score. If in the next innings he scores more than 60, say 68, his average score will rise because his marginal score is greater than his average score. If, with the present average of 60, in the next innings also he scores just 60, then the average and marginal scores will be equal and his average score will neither rise nor fall.

This relationship can be easily illustrated with the help of the following chart.

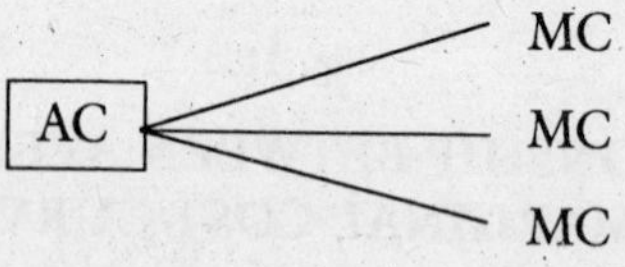

When marginal cost is above the average cost, the AC rises because the MC pulls AC upwards. When marginal cost is below the average cost, the AC falls because the MC pulls AC downwards and when MC is the same as the AC, the average cost remains the same.

Long-run Cost Analysis

Long-run is a period long enough to enable all costs to vary. The firm can expand its plant to meet the long term increase in demand or reduce its plant capacity to adjust itself to a drop in demand. Likewise there is sufficient time for installing new plants. Unwanted buildings can be sold and administrative and marketing staff can be altered. Therefore the dichotomy between fixed and variable costs disappear in the long run. In the short-run the firm must be content with the best utilisation of the given plant, but in the long-run it can choose any plant size from among the many feasible plant sizes.

The long run average cost curve (LAC) is the envelopes of the various short-run average cost curves. When all factors of production can be used in varying proportions the scale of operations can be altered. Each time the scale of operation changes, a new average cost curve will have to be drawn for the firm. Look at the figure given below.

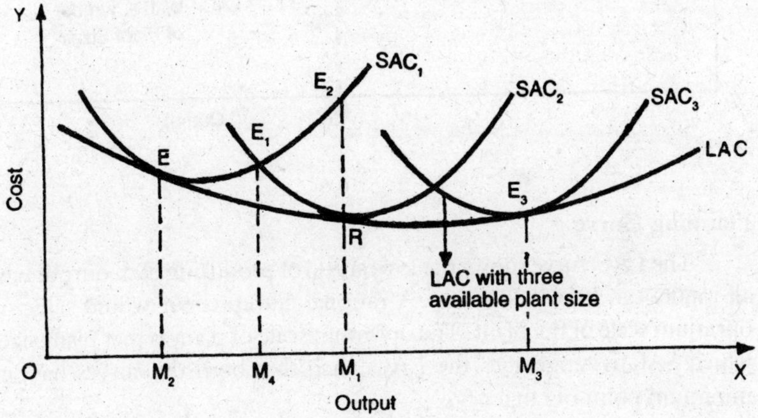

Fig. 16.5

Let there be three plants represented by their average cost curves SAC_1, SAC_2 and SAC_3. Each curve represents the scale of the firm. Originally the firm has a plant size relating to SAC_1. Now the firm produces OM_4 output with M_4E_1 as the average cost.

Suppose the demand for the product increases, so that the firm wants to expand its output from OM_4 to OM_1. OM_1 output can be produced by using the same plant. The average cost will rise from M_4E_1 to M_1E_2 in the long run. But OM_1 output can be produced by installing a new plant shown by SAC_2 with a higher capacity. If the firm operates on a plant relating to SAC_2, the average cost of OM_1 output will be M_1R. SAC_3 relates to the plant of a much higher capacity. The above analysis is a simple model based on three possible plant sizes. In reality a firm can make a choice from a variety of plants. This is shown in the following figure 16.6.

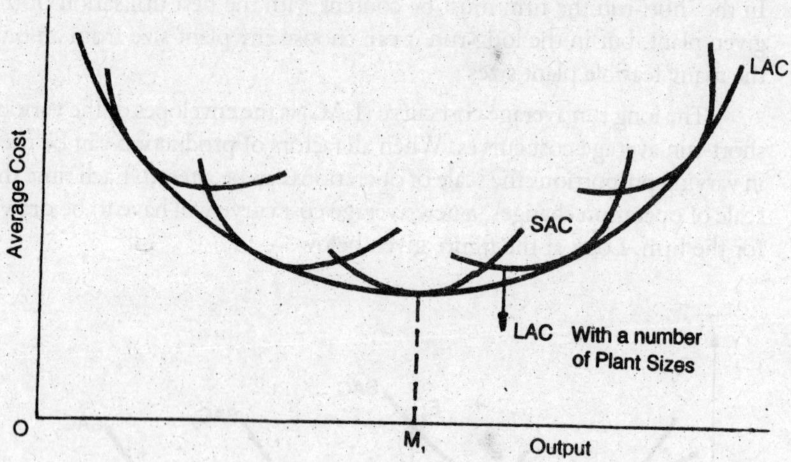

Fig. 16.6

Planning Curve

The LAC curve shows the lowest AC of producing each output when all inputs can be varied freely. A rational entrepreneur would select the optimum scale of the plant. The optimum scale of plant is that plant size at which SAC is tangent to the LAC, such that both the curves have the minimum point of tangency.

In Fig. 16.7 at OM_1 level of output, SAC is tangent to LAC at both the minimum points. Thus OM_1 is the optimum scale of output, as it has the minimum per unit cost. Since the LAC curve envelopes all SAC curves, it is called as the envelope curve. LAC is also known as the planning curve, since it guides the entrepreneur in his decision to plan for the future expansion of his output.

The LAC will be a horizontal line if the factors are perfectly divisible and the prices of inputs remain constant. The reason for a horizontal line is due to neither economies nor diseconomies in production. Such an LAC curve is shown in Fig. 16.7 where it is tangent to the curves SAC_1, SAC_2 and SAC_3 at their minimum points. The implication of a horizontal LAC is that all plants can be operated at their minimum cost. But for different levels of output, separate plants will be used. For instance, plants relating to SAC_1, SAC_2 and SAC_3 will be used for OM_1, OM_2 and OM_3 levels of output respectively. Since the minimum costs of all the plants are identical, the optimum scale of a plant will be indeterminate as every level of output is an optimum one.

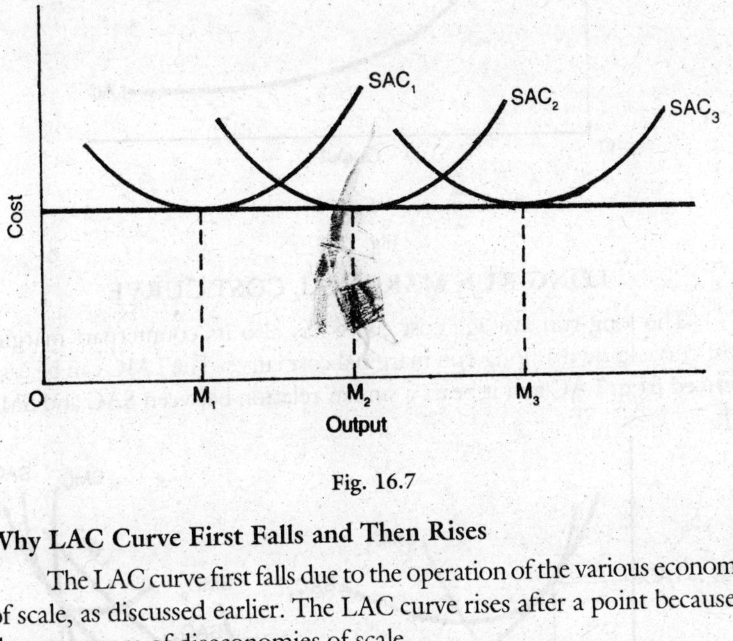

Fig. 16.7

Why LAC Curve First Falls and Then Rises

The LAC curve first falls due to the operation of the various economies of scale, as discussed earlier. The LAC curve rises after a point because of the emergence of diseconomies of scale.

L-Shaped Long-run Average Cost Curve

Various questionnaires and engineering studies suggest the possibility of an L shaped long-run average cost curve. Long-run costs may be divided into production costs and managerial costs. Production costs fall continuously with increases in output. But the managerial costs may rise at a higher level of output. Since the fall in production cost is more powerful than the rise in managerial costs, the LAC falls with an increase in the scale of production. Technical progress is the most important contributory factor for the 'L' shaped curve.

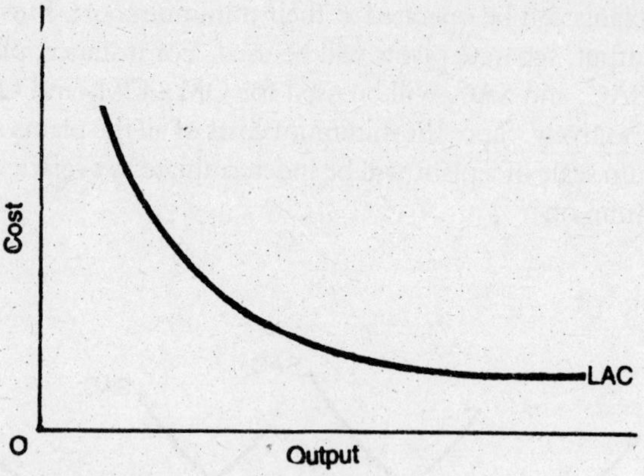

Fig. 16.8

LONG-RUN MARGINAL COST CURVE

The long-run average cost curve has also its counterpart marginal cost curve known as long-run marginal cost curve. The LMC can be easily derived from LAC and it bears a similar relation between SAC and SMC.

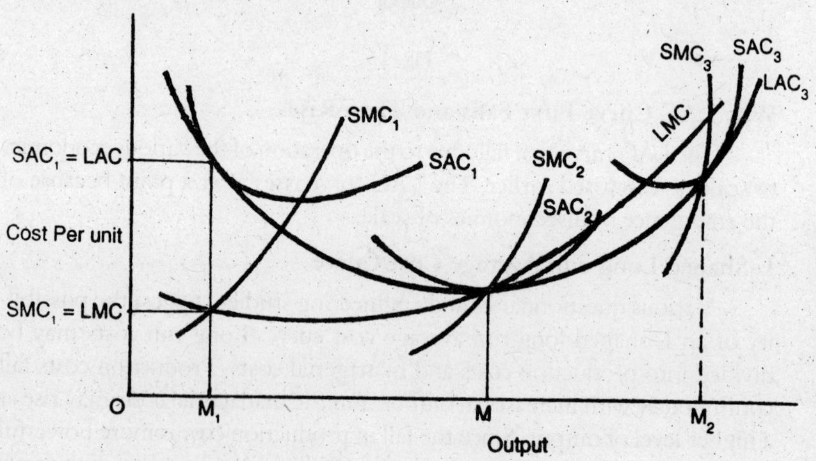

Fig. 16.9

The following relationships may be observed between LMC and SMC. (1) At output OM_1 SMC_1 = LMC. At SMC_2, LMC = SAC_2 = LAC. (2) SAC_1 = LAC (at tangency) and SMC_1 = LMC (an intersection). Similarly for output levels OM and OM_2, the relationship can be traced.

QUESTIONS

1. Why do the cost curves generally assume 'U' shape?
2. How will you divide total cost? Explain the shape of the long-run average cost curve.
3. Explain with diagrams short run cost curves.
4. Distinguish between fixed and variable costs. What is the importance of this distinction in the theory of value?
5. What is meant by opportunity cost? What is its economic significance?
6. Why is short-run average cost curve 'U' shaped?
7. Why is the long-run average cost curve known as planning curve?
8. Explain the relationship between average and marginal cost curves?
9. Why long-run average cost curve is likely to be 'L' shaped?
10. Explain the relationship among fixed cost, variable cost, average cost and marginal cost with illustrations.
11. What is an envelope curve?
12. What are costs of production? How are the long-run costs different from short-run costs.
13. Graphically examine the relationship between ATC and AVC. Is long-run average cost curve necessarily 'U' shaped?
14. Discuss the shape of the short-run and long-run cost curves of a firm.

❖ ❖ ❖

17

REVENUE AND REVENUE CURVES

"It is relatively easy to fix prices that are already fixed."

—J.K. Galbraith, 1952

INTRODUCTION

Cost and revenue are just like two different faces of the same coin. The costs and revenues of a firm determine its nature and the levels of profit. Cost refers to the expenses incurred by a producer for the production of a commodity. Revenue denotes the amount of income which a firm receives by the sale of its output. The revenue concepts commonly used in economics are total revenue, average revenue and marginal revenue.

Total Revenue

Total revenue refers to the total sale proceeds of a firm by selling its total output at a given price. Mathematically TR = PQ where TR = Total Revenue, P = Price, Q = Quantity sold. Suppose a firm sells 100 units of a product at the price of Rs. 5 each, the total revenue will be 100 × Rs. 5 = Rs. 500/-.

Average Revenue

Average revenue is the revenue per unit of the commodity sold. It is obtained by dividing the total revenue by the number of units sold.

Mathematically $AR = \frac{TR}{Q}$

Where AR = Average revenue

TR = Total revenue

Q = Quantity sold.

In our example, average revenue is $= \frac{500}{100}$ = Rs. 5. Thus, average revenue means price.

Marginal Revenue

Marginal revenue is the addition to total revenue by selling one more unit of the commodity.

Algebraically it is the total revenue earned by selling 'n' units of the commodity instead of n–1. Thus,

$MR_n = TR_n - TR_{n-1}$ where MR_n = Marginal revenue of the nth unit

TR_n = Total revenue of n units

TR_{n-1} = Total revenue of n–1 units

n = Any given number of units sold.

Suppose 5 units of a product are sold at a revenue of Rs. 50 and 6 units are sold at a total revenue of Rs. 60. The marginal revenue will be Rs. 60 - Rs. 50 = Rs. 10. It implies that the 6th unit earns an additional income of Rs. 10.

RELATIONSHIP BETWEEN AR AND MR CURVE

Let us consider the relationship between marginal, average and total revenue under pure competition and under imperfect competition.

1. Under Pure Competition

Under pure (or perfect) competition, a very large number of firms are assumed to be present. The supply of each seller is just like a drop of water in a mighty ocean so that any increase or decrease in production by any one firm exerts no perceptible influence on the total supply and on the price in the market. The price in the market is determined by the collective forces of demand and supply so that only one price tends to prevail for the whole industry. Each firm has to take the market price as given and sell its quantity at the ruling market price. In simple terms, the firm is a 'price-taker' and the firm's demand curve is infinitely elastic. As the firm sells more and more at the given price, its total revenue will increase but the rate of increase in the total revenue will be constant, since AR = MR.

Table 17.1
Pure Competition

Q	*AR* (*P*)	*TR*	*MR*
1	10	10	10
2	10	20	10
3	10	30	10
4	10	40	10
5	10	50	10
6	10	60	10
7	10	70	10

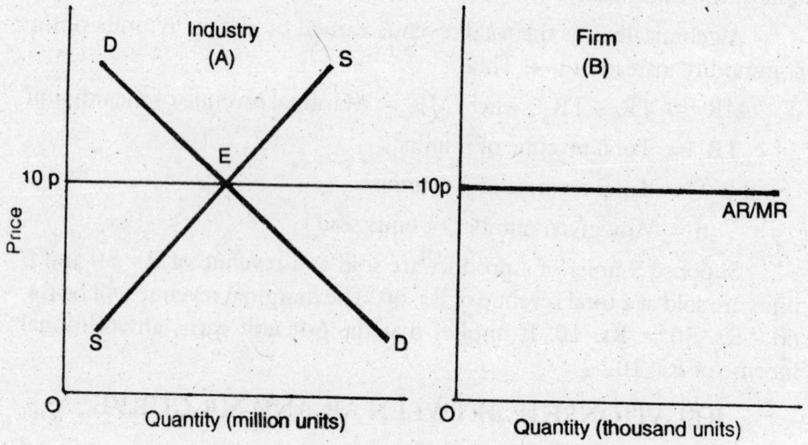

Fig. 17.1

In Fig. 17.1 OX-axis represents the number of units sold and OY axis represents the price per unit. The price of the unit remains constant at P^{10}. Consequently AR and MR curves coincide with each other.

Under Imperfect Competition (Monopoly)

Unlike under perfect competition, a firm under imperfect competition such as under monopoly can sell more only by lowering its price. Therefore the average revenue curve is downward sloping and its corresponding marginal revenue curve lies below it.

Table 17.2
Monopoly

Q	AR(P)	TR	MR
1	10	10	10
2	9	18	8
3	8	24	6
4	7	28	4
5	6	30	2
6	5	30	0

In Table 17.2 AR falls by Re.1 at a time whereas MR falls by Rs.2/- at each stage.

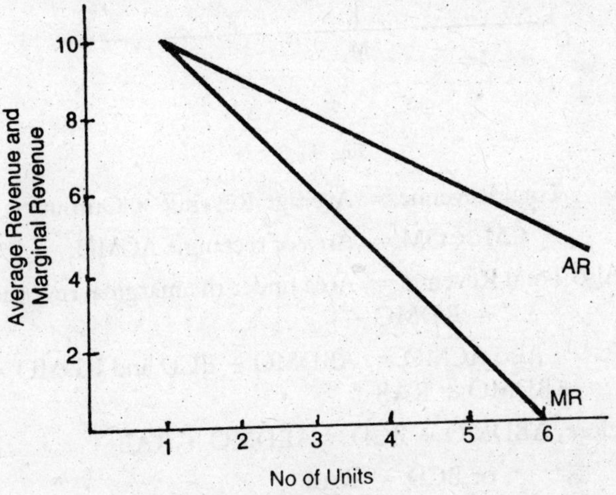

Fig. 17.2

In Fig. 17.2, OX-axis represents the number of units of the commodity sold. OY represents the price. The AR curve as well as the MR curve slope downwards. But the rate of fall in marginal revenue is double that of the fall of the average revenue.

How much is MR below AR?

(i) When MR and AR are straight lines and slope downwards

When AR and MR are straight lines, sloping downwards, the marginal revenue falls twice as much as the fall in the average revenue. In other words, the marginal revenue will cut any line perpendicular to the Y-axis at half-way to the average revenue curve. This can be proved mathematically. In Fig. 17.3, AB = BC.

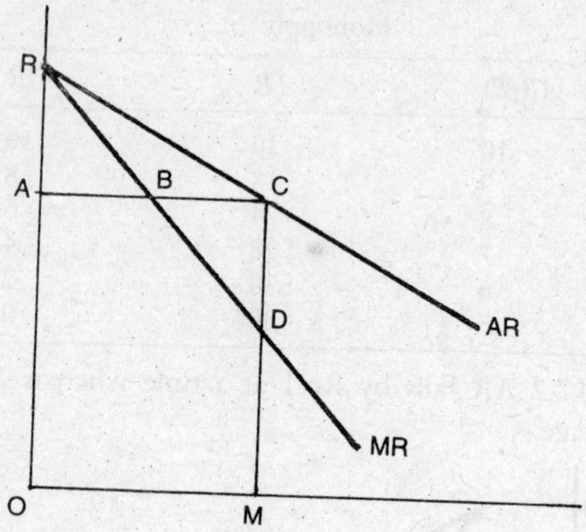

Fig. 17.3

Total Revenue = Average Revenue × Output

CM × OM = Area of rectangle ACMO

Also Total Revenue = Area under the marginal revenue curve = RDMO

Also ACMO = ABDMO + BCD and RDMO = ABDMO + RAB

Therefore, ABDMO + BCD = ABDMO + RAB

or BCD = RAB

But RAB = BCD, being right angles

and RBA = CBD, being vertically opposite angles

Thus the two triangles are equal in area and BCD = RAB

Therefore, AB = BC

Hence it is proved that the marginal revenue curve will cut any line perpendicular to the Y-axis at half-way to the average revenue curve.

(ii) When the Average Revenue Curve is Convex to the Origin

When the average revenue curve is convex to the origin, the marginal revenue curve cuts any perpendicular line to the Y-axis at more than half-way from the average revenue curve. This is shown in Fig. 17.4.

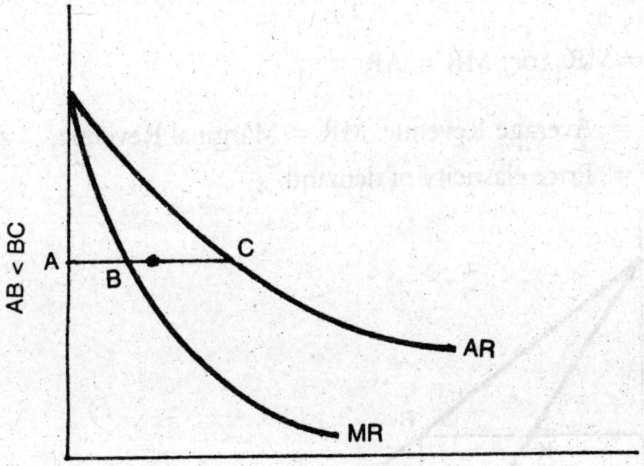

Fig. 17.4

(iii) When the Average Revenue Curve is Concave to the Origin

When the average revenue curve is concave to the origin, the marginal revenue curve cuts any perpendicular line to the Y-axis at less than half-way from the average revenue curve. This is shown in Fig. 17.5.

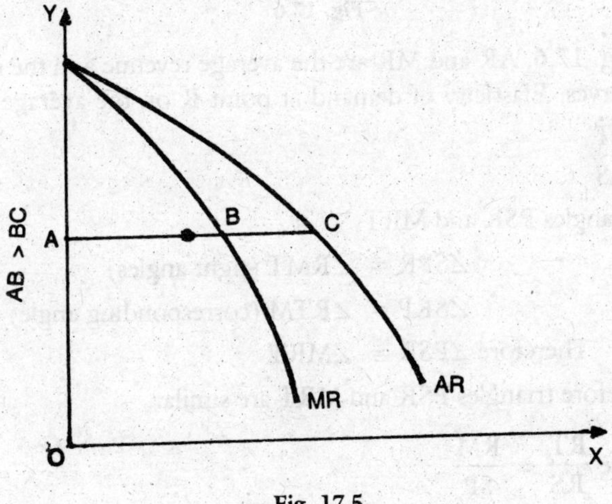

Fig. 17.5

Price Elasticity, Average Revenue and Marginal Curve

Mrs. Joan Robinson in her book 'The Economics of Imperfect Competition' has shown the empirical relationship between Price elasticity, Average revenue and Marginal revenue.

The relationship is expressed in the formula.

$$AR = MR \text{ (or) } MR = AR \frac{e}{e-1}$$

where AR = Average Revenue, MR = Marginal Revenue,

e = Price elasticity of demand.

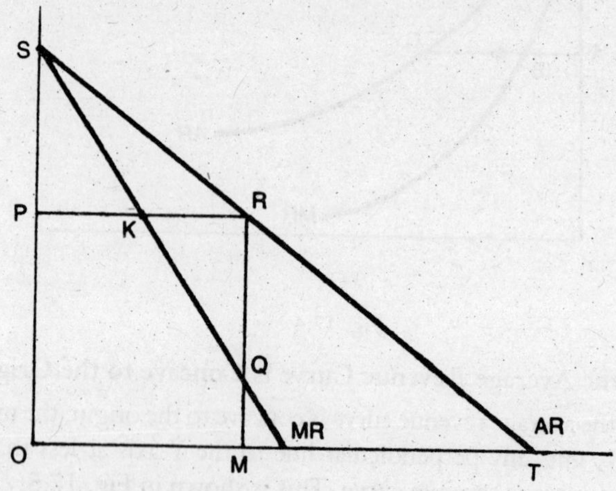

Fig. 17.6

In Fig. 17.6, AR and MR are the average revenue and the marginal revenue curves. Elasticity of demand at point R on the average revenue curve $= \frac{RT}{RS}$

In triangles PSR and MRT

$$\angle SPR = \angle RMT \text{ (right angles)}$$

$$\angle SRP = \angle RTM \text{ (corresponding angle)}$$

$$\text{Therefore } \angle PSR = \angle MRT$$

Therefore triangles PSR and MRT are similar.

$$\text{Hence } \frac{RT}{RS} = \frac{RM}{SP} \qquad \text{... (1)}$$

Now in triangle PSK and KRQ

$$PK = KR$$

$$\angle PKS = \angle RKQ \text{ (vertically opposite angles)}$$

$$\angle SPK = \angle KRQ \text{ (right angles)}$$

Therefore triangles PSK and RQK are congruent.

Hence PS = RQ ... (2)

From (*i*) and (*ii*) we get

$$\text{Elasticity at R} = \frac{RT}{RS} = \frac{RM}{SP} = \frac{RM}{RQ}$$

$$\text{But } \frac{RM}{RQ} = \frac{RM}{RM - RQ}$$

But RM = Average revenue = price

QM = Marginal revenue

$$\text{Elasticity at R} = \frac{\text{Average revenue}}{\text{Average revenue} - \text{Marginal revenue}}$$

$$= \frac{AR}{AR - MR}$$

If A stands for Average revenue

M stands for Marginal revenue

e stands for elasticity on the average revenue curve

$$\text{Then } e = \frac{A}{A - M}$$

Therefore

$$e\,(AR) - e\,(MR) = AR$$

$$e\,(AR) - AR = e\,(MR)$$

$$AR = \frac{e(MR)}{e - 1}$$

$$AR = MR\,\frac{e}{e - 1}$$

$$MR = AR\,\frac{e - 1}{e}$$

A Few examples:

(1) Suppose the price of a product is Rs. 6 and the elasticity of demand is 2. Marginal revenue will be?

$$MR = AR\,\frac{e - 1}{e}$$

$$= \text{Rs. } 6 \times \frac{2-1}{2} = \text{Rs. } 6 \times 1/2 = \text{Rs. } 3$$

$$MR = \text{Rs. } 3$$

(2) When the price of the product is Rs. 6 and price elasticity of demand is 1, marginal revenue will be:

$$MR = AR \frac{e-1}{e}$$

$$= \text{Rs. } 6 \frac{1-1}{1} \text{ Rs. } 6 \times 0 = 0$$

If MR = 0, it is a case in which the MR curve coincides with the x-axis.

SOME SPECIAL CASES OF REVENUE CURVES

Mrs. Joan Robinson has also pointed out many special cases of Marginal and average revenue curves.*

Rectangular Hyperbola: If the demand for the firm's product is unitary elastic (e=1), then the average revenue will assume the form of a rectangular hyperbola. This limiting case is possible under pure monopoly where the monopoly product has no substitutes at all.

According to the formula $MR = AR \frac{e-1}{e}$

putting e = 1, we have $MR = AR \frac{1-1}{1}$

$$= AR \times 0 = 0$$

Thus when the elasticity of demand is equal to one or unity, though not the average revenue curve, the marginal revenue curve will be zero. Therefore the marginal revenue curve coincides with the X-axis.

Under Oligopoly: Oligopoly is a market where there are only few sellers. The demand curve of a firm under oligopoly is not supposed to be smooth. The demand curve has a kink at point P on the demand curve indicating the price policy of the firm. If the firm raises the price above this price (kink P), his rivals will not follow suit. Consequently his sales and profit will suffer. On the contrary, if it lowers the price, the rival firms will retaliate by following the same action. So the firm cannot gain more by

* Mrs. Joan Robinson: *The Economies of Imperfect Competition,* Macmillan & Co. Ltd., London, 1965, Chapter 2.

lowering the price. When there is a kink in the average revenue curve, the marginal revenue is discontinuous at the point of the kink. The gap in the marginal revenue depends upon the nature of the elasticity on the upper and lower portions of the kinked demand curve. This is shown in Fig. 17.7.

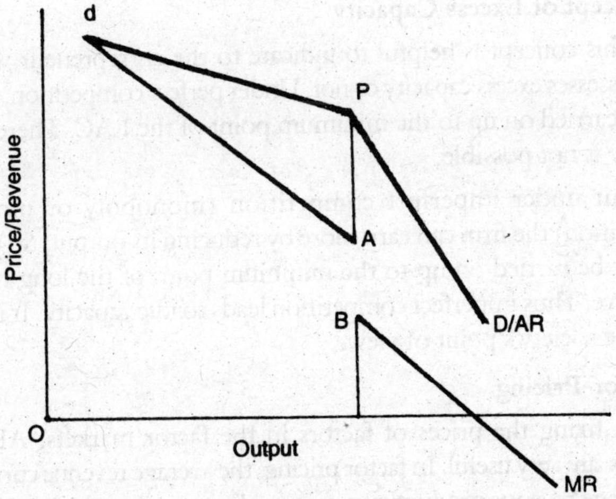

Fig. 17.7

SIGNIFICANCE OF THE CONCEPT OF REVENUE

1. In Determining the Nature of Profit

The concepts of MR and AR both together constitute a powerful analytical tool in economic analysis. Average revenue is the price per unit of output. To find out whether the firm earns supernormal profits or only normal profits or losses the following rule is followed. At the point of equilibrium —

1. If AR is tangent to AC there will be normal profit
2. If AR is above AC there will be supernormal profits
3. If AR is below AC there will be loss

2. Helpful in Decision-making

The concept is also vital in determining the equilibrium of a firm. The aim of every firm is to obtain maximum profits. The rule for profit maximisation is MC = MR.

If MR > MC expansion in output will be profitable

If MR < MC expansion incurs loss

If MC = MR equilibrium output is attained

The intersection of MC = MR determines price, output, and the profit or loss of a firm.

3. Concept of Excess Capacity

This concept is helpful to indicate to the entrepreneur whether the firm possesses excess capacity or not. Under perfect competition, production will be carried on up to the minimum point of the LAC. Therefore excess capacity is not possible.

But under imperfect competition (monopoly or monopolistic competition) the firm can earn more by reducing its output. So production will not be carried on up to the minimum point of the long run average cost curve. Thus imperfect competition leads to idle capacity. It is a wastage from the society's point of view.

4. Factor-Pricing

In fixing the prices of factors in the factor markets, AR and MR concepts are very useful. In factor pricing, the average revenue curve becomes the average revenue productivity curve and marginal revenue curve becomes the marginal revenue productivity curve, ARP and MRP are inverted 'U' (bell shaped) curves. The point of intersection of MFP and MFC (Marginal Factor Cost) determines the equilibrium level of price, output and profit for a firm under various cost conditions.

QUESTIONS

1. Trace the relationship between price, total average and marginal revenue of a competitive firm.
2. Explain the geometrical relationship between the linear AR and MR curves.
3. Explain the relationship between AR and MR curves under perfect competition and imperfect competition.
4. Prove: Elasticity of Demand = $\frac{\text{Average Revenue}}{\text{Average Revenue} - \text{Marginal Revenue}}$

❖ ❖ ❖

18

SUPPLY

"You can make even a parrot into a learned political economist all he must learn are the two words "Supply" and "Demand."

— Anonymous

INTRODUCTION

The word "Supply" implies the amount offered for sale at a given price. Like demand, supply is always at a price and it relates to a point of time. The relationship between price and quantity is inverse in the case of demand. But in the case of supply the relationship between the two variables price and quantity is direct.

STOCK AND SUPPLY

Supply is different from stock. The term "stock" implies a fixed quantity while the term "supply" implies that the amount offered can be increased or decreased. Stock is the actual quantity of a commodity which can be brought into the market for sale at short notice. Supply refers to that part of the stock which is actually offered for sale at a given price in the market. In the case of perishable commodities like flowers, fish and vegetables, supply and stock are the same because all the stock must be disposed off at the current market price and cannot be held back. But in the case of durables, if the current market price is not profitable, then it can be held back. In short, stock is potential supply.

THE LAW OF SUPPLY

The law of supply states the functional relationship between price and the quantity offered for sale. The law of supply is a hypothesis that states that, other things being equal, the higher the price the greater will be the willingness of sellers to make a product available. At higher prices, more sellers are interested in producing the product, and each existing seller wants to sell more. The opposite holds good when prices decline.

The law of supply can be explained with the help of a schedule and a curve.

Supply Schedule

Supply schedule represents the relationship between prices and the quantities that the firms are willing to produce and supply.

Suppose the following is an individual's supply schedule of oranges.

Table 18.1

Price per dozen Rs.	*Quantity supplied (in dozens)*
4	3
6	6
8	9
10	12
12	13

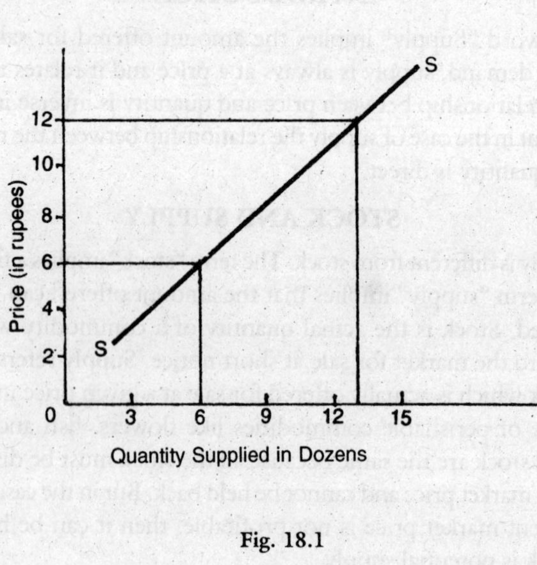

Fig. 18.1

The supply curve is a graphical representation of the law of supply. The supply curve has a positive slope, and it moves upwards to the right. This curve shows that at the price of Rs. 6/- six dozens will be supplied and at the higher price Rs. 12/- a larger quantity of 13 dozens will be supplied.

Market Supply Curve

The summation of supply curves of all the firms in the industry gives us the market supply curve.

Table 18.2

Supply Schedule for Two Suppliers and the Market Supply Schedule

	Quantity Supplied		
Price	*Supplier A*	*Supplier B*	*Market Supply*
4	5	6	5 + 6 = 11
6	7	7	7 + 7 = 14
8	9	8	9 + 8 = 17
10	11	9	11 + 9 = 20
12	13	10	13 + 10 = 23

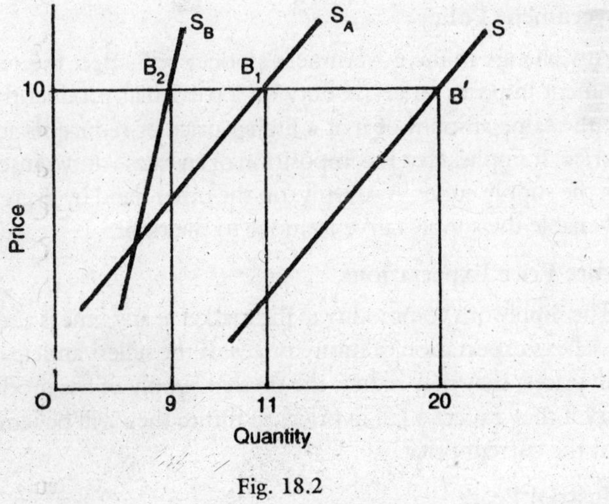

Fig. 18.2

In the Figure 18.2 given above there are three supply curves. It is assumed that there are two sellers in the industry A and B. S_A is the supply curve for A and S_B is the supply curve for B. By the lateral summation of these curves we get the market supply curve.

FACTORS DETERMINING THE SUPPLY OF A COMMODITY

The supply of a commodity depends upon the following factors.

1. Objectives of the Firm

Different firms may follow different objectives. Some firms may be interested in maximising profits, while others may be interested in sales or revenue maximisation or satisficing etc. The amount of commodity supplied is often influenced by the objectives of the firm. Normally, sales maximisation firm's output will be greater than the profit maximisation firm's output.

2. State of Technology

Technical improvements reduce the costs of production enabling a shifting of the supply curve to the right. Similarly, obstacles in the existing technology increases costs of production, forcing a shift in the supply curve to the left. A constant state of technology keeps the supply curve at the existing level.

3. Political Disturbances

Political disturbances may destabilise trade and thus create a scarcity for certain kinds of goods.

4. Government Policy

Any change in the government's policy will affect the supply. If the government imposes an excise duty on a particular product the firm may supply the same amount of it at a higher price or reduce its supply at the same price. It implies that the imposition of an excise duty causes a leftward shift in the supply curve. A subsidy, on the other hand by decreasing costs, would enable the supply curve to move to the right.

5. Future Price Expectations

The supply of a commodity in the market at any time is also influenced by the seller's expectation of future prices. If the sellers anticipate in future a rise in prices, they may reduce the present supply of the product. On the contrary if they expect a fall in prices in future they will be tempted to sell more at the current price.

6. Industrial Peace

The existence of industrial peace is a precondition for regular supply. If the industry is subject to strikes or lockouts, it will have its impact on the supply of the commodity.

7. Natural Factors

Natural factors like changes in weather conditions, floods, drought, pest attack etc. affect supply. This is more pronounced in agricultural production. Moreover the occurrence of abnormal or extraordinary situations like war, fire etc. also affect the supply of products.

8. Prices of Factors of Production

The cost of production is an important item affecting the supply. A fall in input prices will reduce the cost of output. As a result, more quantity could be supplied at the old price or, the original quantity could be produced at a lower price. A rise in the prices of inputs will have the opposite effect.

9. Price of the Good which is to be Supplied

Ceteris paribus, the higher the price of a commodity, the larger will be its supply.

10. Prices of Other Goods

The supply of a commodity depends upon the prices of other goods also. For example, if the price of good X rises, the producer of good Y may switch over his production to good X as it has become relatively more attractive than the price of Y.

11. Number of Firms or Sellers

Supply of a commodity in a market depends upon the number of firms involved in the production and distribution of the product in the market. When the sellers are few, the supply will be limited. On the contrary, if the producers and sellers are large, the supply will also be large.

12. The Entry of New Firms

The entry of new firms into the industry will also affect the supply. In the short run, the existing firms may earn abnormal profits. This will induce other firms to enter into the industry. On the contrary, if some of the existing firms are incurring losses, some firms will leave the industry. So the supply will decrease.

13. Discovery of New Raw Materials

The discovery of new raw materials will reduce the cost of production but will increase the supply. But the exhaustion of old supplies of raw materials will affect the supply.

14. Development of Transport

Development of efficient and quick means of transport will also increase the supply because it facilitates the movement of goods from one place to another.

15. Business Combinations

The existing firms may follow a policy of collusion in the form of cartels. In order to raise the price and profit, supply may be reduced by them.

EXCEPTIONS TO THE LAW OF SUPPLY

The Law of supply states "Other things being equal, the supply of a commodity extends with a rise in price and contracts with a fall in price." There are however a few exceptions to the law of supply.

1. Exceptions of a Fall in Price

If the firms anticipate that the price of the product will fall further in future, in order to clear their stocks they may dispose it off at a price that is even lower than the current market price.

2. Sellers who are in Need of Cash

If the seller is in need of hard cash, he may sell his product at a price which may even be below the market price.

3. When Leaving the Industry

If the firms want to shut down or close down their business, they may sell their products at a price below their average cost of production.

4. Agricultural Output

In agricultural production, natural and seasonal factors play a dominant role. Due to the influence of these constraints supply may not be responsive to price changes.

5. Backward Sloping Supply Curve of Labour

The rise in the price of a good or service sometimes leads to a fall in its supply. The best example is the supply of labour. A higher wage rate enables the worker to maintain his existing material standard of living with less work, and he may prefer extra leisure to more wages. The supply curve in such a situation will be 'backward sloping' SS_1 as illustrated in Figure 18.3.

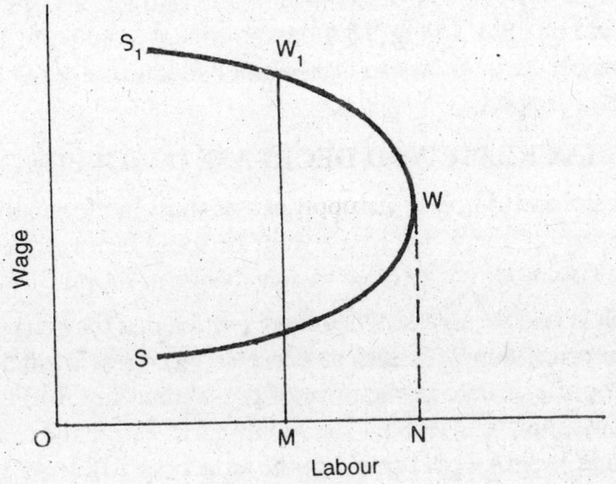

Fig. 18.3

At WN wage rate, the supply of labour is ON. But beyond NW wage rate the worker will reduce rather than increase his working hours. At MW_1 wage rate the supply of labour is reduced to OM.

EXTENSION AND CONTRACTION OF SUPPLY

'Extension' and 'contraction' of supply refer to movements on the same supply curve. If with a rise in price, the supply rises, it is called an extension of supply; if, with a fall in price, the supply declines, it is called a

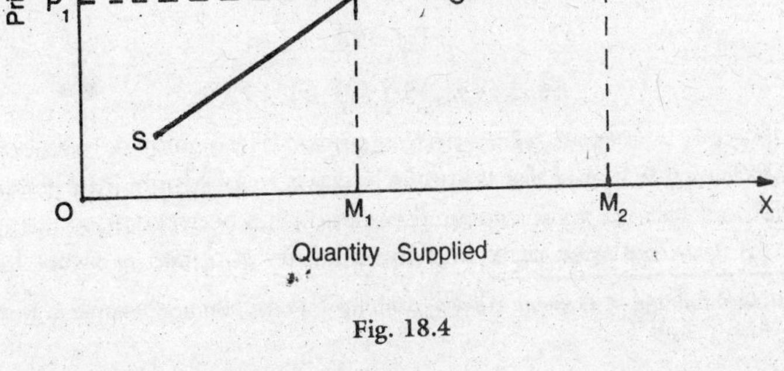

Fig. 18.4

contraction of supply. The 'extension' and 'contraction' of supply are illustrated in Fig. 18.4. In Fig. 18.4 the movement from point E to E_1 on the same supply curve shows an extension of supply and E_1 to E shows a contraction of supply.

INCREASE AND DECREASE IN SUPPLY

'Increase' and 'decrease' in supply causes shifts in the supply curve. A shift in the supply curve due to a change in some factor other than the price of the commodity is referred to as a change in supply.

Supply is said to increase when more is offered in the market without a change in price. Supply is said to decrease when less is offered in the market without a change in the price of the commodity. In Fig. 18.5 at price EM the supply is OM. SS is the supply curve before the change. S_1S_1 shows an increase in supply because at the same price ME = M_1E_1 more is offered for sale, i.e., OM_1 instead of OM. S_2S_2 shows the decrease in supply because at the same price ME = M_2E_2 less is offered for sale, i.e., OM_2 instead of OM.

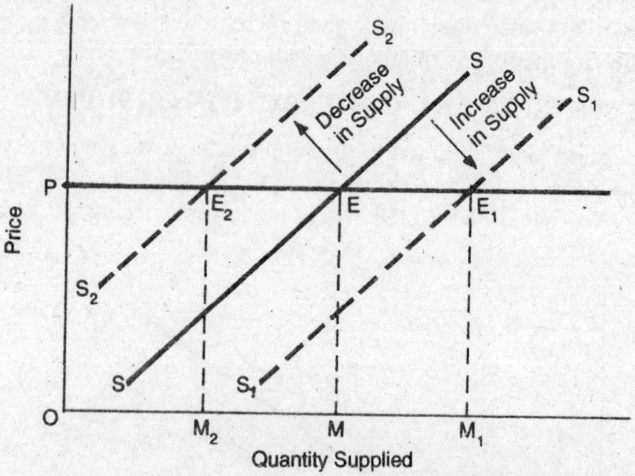

Fig. 18.5

ELASTICITY OF SUPPLY

Supply is responsive to price changes. The extent to which supply extends for a given price rise is known as elasticity of supply. Prof. Boulding[1] uses a beautiful analogy to explain the relationship between price and supply, "The relation between price and the quantity supplied is rather like the

1. K.E. Boulding — *Economic Analysis*, Volume I, Fourth Edition, Harper & Row, New York, p. 180.

relation between a whistle and a dog — the louder the whistle, the faster comes the dog; raise the price and the quantity supplied increases. If the dog is responsive — in economic terminology, "elastic" — quite a small crescendo in the whistle will send him bounding along. If the dog is unresponsive or "inelastic", we may have to whistle very loudly before he comes along at all."

Elasticity of supply may also be defined as the ratio of the percentage change or the proportionate change in quantity supplied to the percentage or proportionate change in price.

$$E_s = \frac{\text{Proportionate change in supply}}{\text{Proportionate change in price}}$$

$$= \frac{\text{Change in quantity supplied}}{\text{Original quantity supplied}} \times \frac{\text{Change in Price}}{\text{Original Price}}$$

Let Q = Original supply

ΔQ = Change of supply

P = Original price and

ΔP = Change of price, then

$$E_s = \frac{\Delta Q}{Q} \div \frac{\Delta P}{P} = \frac{\Delta Q}{Q} \times \frac{P}{\Delta P}$$

$$= \frac{\Delta Q}{\Delta P} \times \frac{P}{Q}$$

Example:

Suppose that the price of an article rises from Rs. 4 to Rs. 5 and as a result supply rises from 200 to 300. Then

$$E_s = \frac{100}{1} \times \frac{4}{200} = 2.$$

Since both price and quantity move in the same direction, E_s has a positive sign.

KINDS OF SUPPLY ELASTICITY

There are two limiting cases of elasticity of supply which are of economic significance.

(*i*) Elasticity of supply equal to infinity

(*ii*) Absolutely inelastic supply

Another way of expressing the range of elasticity is that elasticity of supply is greater than one, less than one or equal to one.

Table 18.3
Kinds of Elasticity of supply

Co-efficient	*Elasticity*
$E_s = \alpha$	Perfectly elastic
$E_s = 0$	Perfectly inelastic
$E_s = 1$	Unit are elastic
$E_s > 1$	Relatively elastic
$E_s < 1$	Relatively inelastic

The following Figure 18.6 illustrates the various types of elasticity clearly.

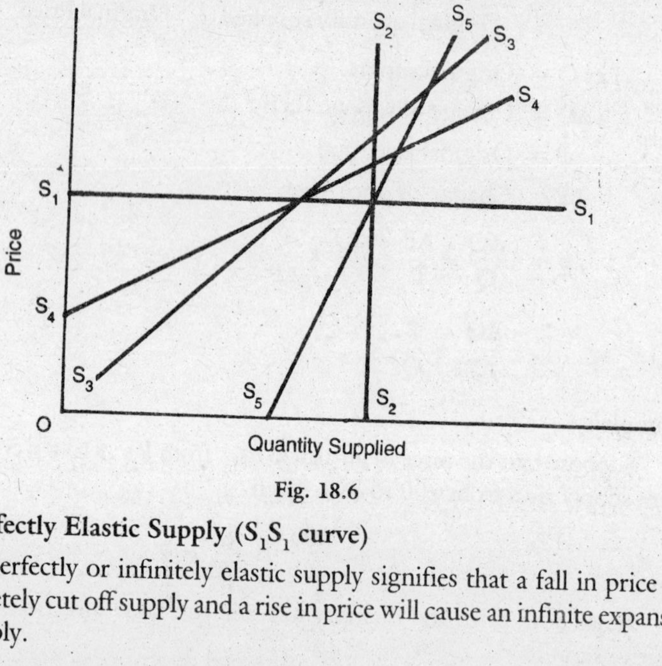

Fig. 18.6

1. Perfectly Elastic Supply (S_1S_1 curve)

Perfectly or infinitely elastic supply signifies that a fall in price will completely cut off supply and a rise in price will cause an infinite expansion of supply.

2. Perfectly Inelastic Supply (S_2S_2)

Perfectly inelastic supply means that changes in price will not bring about any change in supply.

3. Unitary Elastic Supply (S_3S_3)

When elasticity of supply is unitary, a change in price will cause a proportionate change in quantity supplied. Any straight line supply curve passing through the origin has a unitary elasticity throughout its length regardless of its slope.

4. Relatively Elastic Supply (S_4S_4)

When the proportionate change in quantity is greater than the proportionate change in price the supply is relatively elastic. Any straight line supply curve that intersects the vertical axis has an elasticity greater than one throughout its length.

5. Relatively Inelastic Supply (S_5S_5)

When the proportionate change in quantity is less than the proportionate change in price, the supply is relatively inelastic. Any straight line that cuts the horizontal axis has an elasticity less than one.

Generally elasticity of supply can vary from one price range to another.

At a low price and for small quantities, supply is perfectly elastic. But as quantity continues to increase, supply becomes less and less elastic. At higher supply prices, supply is perfectly inelastic. This is shown in Fig. 18.7.

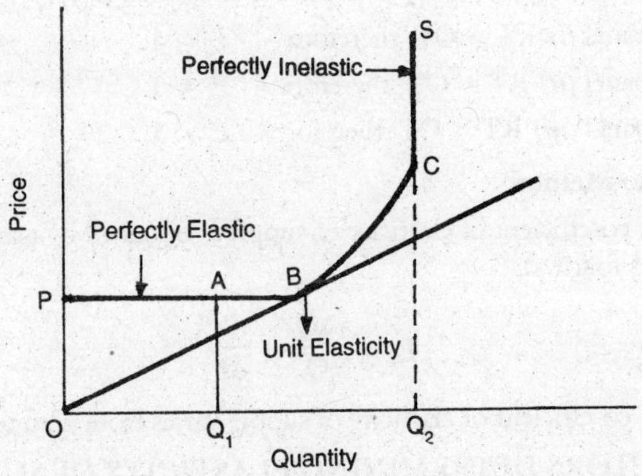

Fig. 18.7

MEASUREMENT OF ELASTICITY OF SUPPLY

Elasticity of supply can be measured by using two methods:

(i) The Point Method and

(ii) The Ratio Method.

The Point Method

On the given supply curve the price elasticity at a point is measured by the distance along a tangent to the horizontal axis divided by the distance along it to the vertical axis.

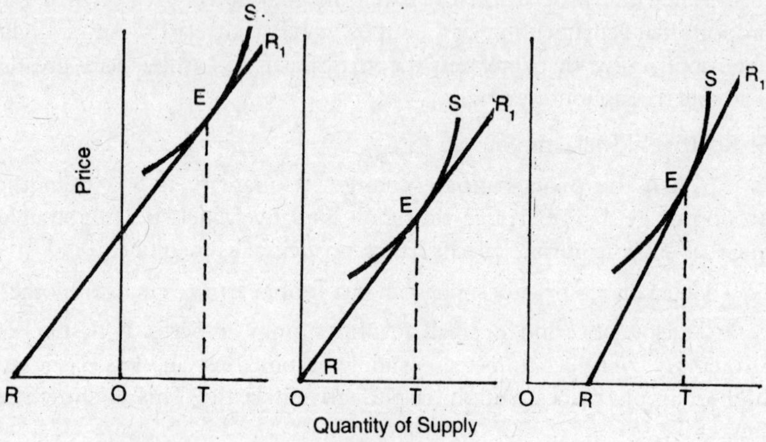

Fig. 18.8

The elasticity of supply at point T is measured as RT/OT

In panel *(i)* RT > OT, therefore $E_s > 1$

In panel *(ii)* RT = OT, therefore $E_s = 1$

In panel *(iii)* RT < OT, therefore $E_s < 1$

The Ratio Method

The co-efficient of elasticity of supply is obtained by using the ratio method as follows:

$$E_s = \frac{\Delta Q}{Q} \times \frac{P}{\Delta P}$$

The co-efficient of elasticity of supply varies from zero to infinity.

FACTORS DETERMINING ELASTICITY OF SUPPLY

Elasticity of supply is determined by the following factors:

1. The Nature of Commodities

On the basis of nature, commodities are divided into perishable goods and durable goods. In the case of perishable goods like fish, vegetables etc., the supply is less elastic, whereas in the case of durable goods the supply tends to be more elastic.

2. Time Period

The element of time exercises an important influence on the elasticity of supply. In almost every industry, supply will be more elastic in the long-run than in the short-run.

3. Mobility of Factors

Availability of factors of production and mobility of factors of production also affect the elasticity of supply. Mobility of factors causes elasticity of supply and vice versa.

4. Technique of Production

The adoption of advanced technology or replacement of capital intensive techniques, in the place of traditional or labour intensive techniques makes the supply more elastic.

5. Number of Markets and the Number of Products Produced

If a firm sells its product in different markets, then its supply will be elastic. This is because of the fact that a fall in price in any one market will induce the firm to sell in other markets. Again, when it produces a variety of products, it can easily transfer resources from production of one product to the others, so that each of his products will be elastic in supply.

6. Scale of Production

Goods can be produced either on a large-scale or on a small-scale. Goods produced on a large-scale are elastic while goods produced on a small-scale are inelastic.

7. Natural Factors

The supply of agricultural goods are inelastic by nature. The influence of nature is more pronounced in agricultural production. That is why it is said that 'Nature does the business and man is merely a manager.' The presence of external factors beyond man's control tends to make the supply of agricultural products inelastic.

PRACTICAL USES OF ELASTICITY OF SUPPLY

1. The elasticity of supply of a good is a major factor in determining as to how much of its price will alter when there is a change in the conditions of demand.[2]

---

2. J. Harvey, *Modern Economics*, Third edition, The Macmillan Press Ltd., London 1983, p. 191.

Let us explain this with the help of supply and demand of sugarcane as shown in Fig. 18.9.

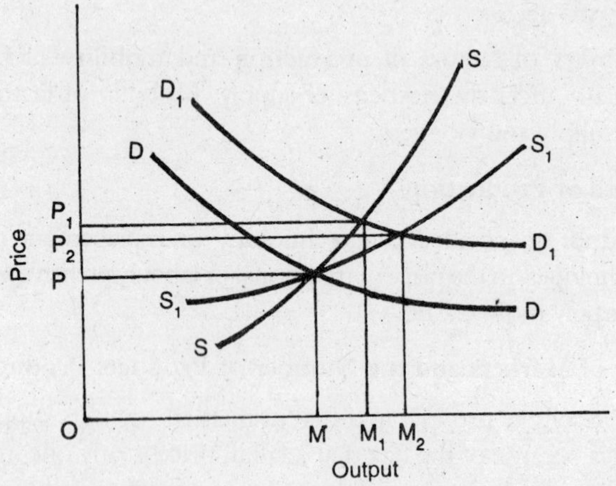

Fig. 18.9

In Fig. 18.9, DD is the demand curve and SS is the supply curve. OP is the price. If demand for sugar increases to D_1D_1 in the short-run it is inelastic, for its supply can be expanded only by adding labour, fertilisers etc. Therefore the supply increases only by a small amount (MM_1). But in the long period more land can be put under sugarcane. Supply is, therefore more elastic and is represented by the curve S_1S_1. The long-run price falls to OP_2 and quantity increases to OM_2.

2. The elasticity of supply is significant in determining the extent of taxation.

Where the supply of a good is inelastic the government can impose a tax on the producer without having a great effect on the amount of the goods offered for sale. For example, a man owns a mineral well for which a maximum rent of Rs. 100 can be got. The owner gives it on rent for Rs. 1000 per month. Suppose the government levies a tax of Rs. 500 a year on this mineral well. This means that the owner will have to pay the tax from out of his own pocket, since he cannot get it from the user. If the tax amount is increased to Rs. 1000, the owner of the mineral well will stop letting it on rent because the net income from the mineral well becomes zero.

DERIVATION OF SUPPLY CURVES

Supply curves are derived from cost curves because supply depends on cost of production. The concept of supply curve is relevant only under perfect competition. In a competitive market price is determined by the two forces of demand and supply. Since in a perfectly competitive market the supply of each seller is only a negligible portion of the market supply he has no control over the price. Like an individual consumer, he is a price-taker; as an optimistic seller, he believes that he can sell any quantity he is able to produce at the prevailing price. If the price rises, he supplies more. In the case of monopoly or imperfect competition the producer can fix the price. The producer will choose that price-output combination which maximises his profit. But a competitive producer has to adjust his supply as per the change in price.

INDUSTRIES SUPPLY CURVE IN THE SHORT-RUN

A competitive industry is a collection of firms producing a homogeneous product. Thus, firms in a perfectly competitive market all taken together form an industry. The industry's supply curve is obtained by summing up the individual firm's supply curves. The industry supply curve portrays the functional relationship between the price of a good, and various quantities of the goods offered for sale by all the firms in the market.

A competitive firm always adjusts its output until the price is equal to its marginal cost so that it can maximise its profits. The marginal cost curve therefore gives the relationship between price and the quantity supplied

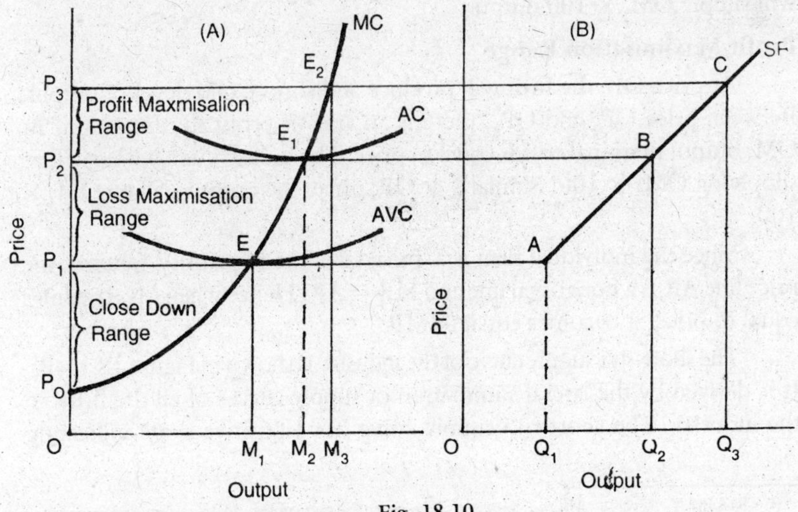

Fig. 18.10

by the competitive firm. Price must exceed AVC, otherwise the firm will cease its operations. Quantity supplied by the firm at any price below AVC will be zero. The competitive firm's short-run supply curve is therefore that portion of its Marginal Cost curve which is above the minimum point of the AVC curve.

Close Down Range

If the price is lower than the minimum AVC, the firm should shutdown its operations. Since price cannot cover even AVC, continuing the operations of the firm will invite the shutdown of the firm.

Loss Minimisation Range

If the price is equal to AVC, then the firm has to decide whether to run the firm or close it down. But the firm will continue its operations due to various reasons.[3]

1. A higher valuation is given to a going concern than to a closed firm.
2. More prestige is attached to the owner or manager of a going concern than to that of a firm that has ceased to operate.
3. By keeping the operation going, the firm will not lose its competent personnel.

Thus if the price is above AVC and below AC, the firm is in the range of loss minimisation. AT OP_1 price, the firm will produce and supply OM_1 output. If there are 100 firms in the industry, the industry as a whole will supply $OM_1 \times 100$ output.

Profit Maximisation Range

At price OP_2 the firm will produce and supply OM_2 level of output. Between price OP_2 and OP_3, there is an area of profit maximisation. At OM_2 output marginal cost is equal to price. The industry as a whole will be supplying $OM_2 \times 100$. Similarly at OP_3 price, the output will be $OM_3 \times 100$.

Since the individual firm is a 'price taker' and 'quantity adjuster' the price line AR is a horizontal line and MR = AR. Hence when MC becomes equal to price, it becomes equal to MR.

The short-run supply curve of the industry is shown in Figure 18.11(B). It is derived by the lateral summation of supply curves of all the firms in the industry. The short-run supply curve has a positive slope indicating

3. Robert Y. Ahw — *Micro Economics, Theory and Applications,* John Wiley & Sons, New York, 1976, p. 263.

that supply increases as price increases. At OP_1 price industry's supply is OQ_1, at OP_2 price it is OQ_2 and at OP_3 price it is OQ_3.

INDUSTRIES SUPPLY CURVE IN THE LONG-RUN

In order to discuss the long-run pricing it is necessary to understand how the entry of new firms into an industry affects the prices of the factors of production.

An industry is a constant cost industry if the prices of the factors of production remain constant as the industry's output expands. An industry is an increasing cost industry, if the prices of the factors of production increase as the industry's output expands. An industry is a decreasing cost industry if the prices of the factors of production decrease as the industry's output expands.

Constant Cost Industry

If external economies and diseconomies exactly balance, the cost of production will become constant. The duration of the supply curve of a constant cost industry is illustrated as follows.

The pencil-making industry is often quoted as an example. This industry uses an insignificant portion of the total demand for wood and lead, which are the main inputs of the pencil making industry — A relatively large increase in the industry's demand for wood and lead will not affect their prices. Similarly, the increased demand for labour as a result of the expansion of the pencil-making industry will not raise the wages of labour employed by it.

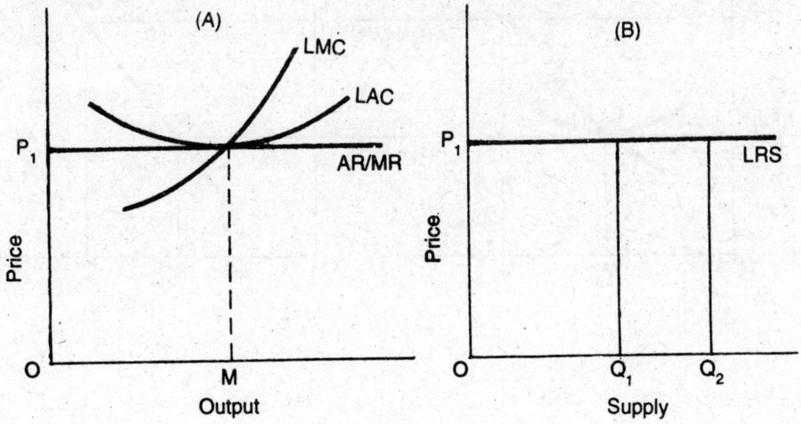

Fig. 18.11

It can be seen from the left hand side diagram that at the price OP_1, the firm is in the long-run producing OM output. The price OP_1 is equal to the long-run average and marginal costs. If we assume that there are 100 firms in the industry and the cost curves of all firms are identical at price OP_1, the whole industry will supply OM × 160 quantity of the product which may be represented by OQ_1.

Now if the demand for the product increases more firms will enter into the industry in the long-run to meet the increased demand. Since constant costs are assumed to prevail, the price will remain at OP_1. If the number of firms becomes 160, the quantity supplied by the industry will increase to OM × 160 which is represented by OQ_2.

Increasing Cost Industry

An industry is said to be an increasing cost industry if its long-run supply curve has a positive slope, indicating that the prices of factors increase as the industry's output expands. In the case of an increasing cost industry the external diseconomies will overweigh the external economies.

Suppose the industry is operating under the law of increasing cost or diminishing returns. The entry of new firms increases the demand for factors. In case the supply of the factors is inelastic to the industry, the increased demand for the factors will result in higher prices of the factors, thus shifting the cost curve upwards.

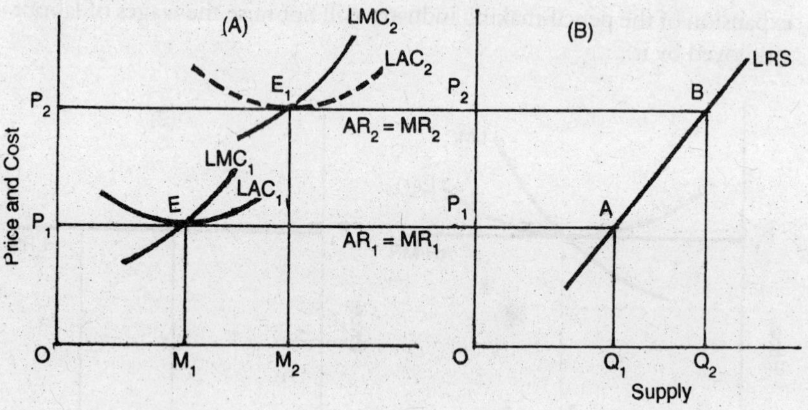

Fig. 18.12

Initially the firms are in equilibrium at E. The price is OP_1 and output is OM_1. The price OP_1 becomes equal to LAC_1 and LMC_1. Suppose we assume that all the 100 firms in the industry have identical cost curves. The industry's supply will be $OM_1 \times 100$, which is represented by OQ_1.

Suppose the price rises to OP_2. This attracts new firms into the industry and the firms increase to 160. There will be net external diseconomies as a result of an increase in input prices. Given the new cost curve LAC_2 and LMC_2 the firms are in equilibrium at point E_1. At the price OP_2 each firm will be producing an output OM_2. At this output the price OP_2 becomes equal to both LAC_2 and LMC_2. The total output of the industry will be $OM_2 \times 160 = OQ_2$. This is shown in the right hand side of the figure. The supply curve (LRS) slopes upwards to the right indicating that supply extends with a rise in price.

Decreasing Cost Industry

An industry is said to be a decreasing cost industry if its long run supply curve has a negative slope indicating that the prices of factors fall as the industry's output expands.

In the case of a decreasing cost industry the entry of new firms may provide a larger pool of trained labour, so that the cost associated with the hiring of workers is reduced. Entry of new firms may also provide the critical mass of industrialisation, which permits the development of a more efficient transportation and communication network. These cost reductions are called external economies which accrue to the industry as well as to the firms.

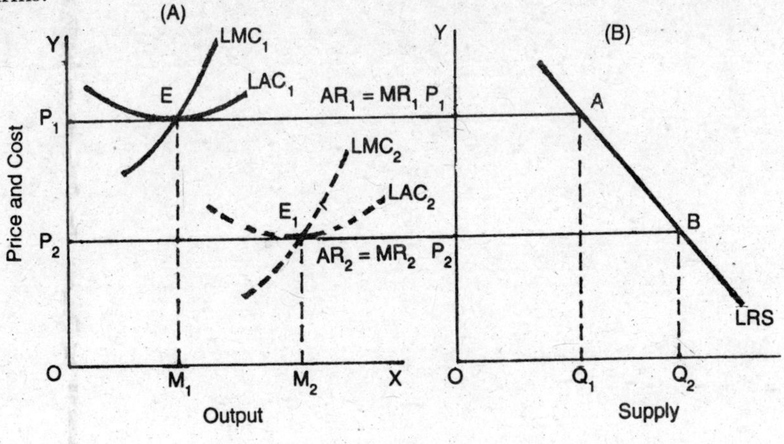

Fig. 18.13

The original equilibrium is at point E when the firms supply OM_1 quantity at OP_1 price. At OP_1 price, if there are 100 firms (with identical cost curves) the total output will be $OM_1 \times 100 = OQ_1$. This is shown on the right hand side of the Figure. (18.13 (B)).

Suppose there is an increase in the demand for the product, new firms enter into the industry. As a result of the emergence of external economies, cost curves shift downwards from LAC_1 to LAC_2 and to LMC_2. The firms will be in equilibrium at point E_1, where OM_2 output is supplied by the firms at OP_2 price. The total output of the industry is $OM_2 \times 160$ (assuming that the number of firms are 160). It is equal to OQ_2 as shown in the right hand side of the figure. The long run supply curve is the line AB which has a negative slope. This implies that if there are strong external economies the industry's supply can expand in the long run at a decreasing price.

QUESTIONS

1. What is meant by Joint-Supply? Give two examples.
2. Explain with suitable diagrams perfectly elastic supply and perfectly inelastic supply.

❖ ❖ ❖

19

MARKET AND MARKET STRUCTURES

"It is pauperism and a glutted market that lie at the root of the economic distress of the time."

— Karl Rodbertus, 1898

INTRODUCTION

Market occupies a unique position in the modern complex monetary organization. Adam Smith in his 'Wealth of Nations', rightly points out, that division of labour is limited by the extent of the market. Market helps the producers to take basic economic decisions on what to produce, and how much to produce. Market significantly affects the producers, consumers, and the various other sections of the society.

Prof. Wicksteed has remarked, "The market is the characteristic phenomenon of economic life. The constitution of markets and market prices are the central problems of economics."

MEANING OF MARKET

In ordinary language, "market" refers to a place where commodities are bought and sold, e.g., Madurai market, Chennai market, Mumbai market etc. But in economics, "market" has no reference to a place but for a particular commodity which is being bought and sold. For example, we speak of a cotton market, tea market, wheat market, gold market, share market and so on.

In economics "market" refers to a group of buyers and sellers taking part in the exchange of a commodity. The buyers and sellers may be scattered within a country or may be abroad. But there must be some contact by means of fairs, meetings, published price lists, or through telephone, telegram or other means of communication.

According to Cairncross, a market is "simply the network of dealing in any factor or product between buyers and sellers."

FEATURES OF A MARKET

The above definitions point out the four basic features of a market.

1. Consumers and Sellers

The existence of buyers and sellers. The number of buyers and sellers may be large or small.

2. Contact

Existence of some contact among the buyers and sellers. The contact may be direct or indirect.

3. A Commodity

There is a commodity to deal with. In the case of different commodities, there will be different markets.

4. A Price

There should be a price for the commodity that is bought and sold in the market.

CLASSIFICATION OF MARKETS

Markets may be classified into various ways.

1. On the Basis of Area

According to the area covered, markets may be classified into local markets, regional markets, national markets, and international markets.

(a) Local Market

Local market refers to a market in a particular village or locality. Generally perishable goods like vegetables, milk, butter etc. have local markets.

(b) Regional Market

Regional market refers to a market which covers a particular region. Generally bulky articles like bricks and stones have regional markets.

(c) National Market

If the demand and supply of a commodity is spread over the entire country, the market is said to be a national market. Generally wheat, rice and cotton etc. have national markets.

(d) International Market

When the demand and supply of a commodity is at the global level, the market is said to be an international market. Generally valuable metals like gold, silver, diamonds etc. have an international market.

2. On the Basis of Time

On the basis of the time element, market is classified into very short period, short period, and long period markets.

(a) Very Short Period Markets

A very short period is one in which supply cannot be increased or decreased to adjust to demand. Examples for very short period markets are vegetables, fruits, milk etc.

(b) Short Period

Short period refers to a period of time in which the rate of production is variable. Increased production is possible by an intensive use of capital or by enlarging the size of the plant.

(c) Long Period

Long period is a period of time in which the supply of the commodity can be varied according to the conditions of demand. Long period involves many years.

3. On the Basis of Commodity

On the basis of the commodity involved, markets may be classified into bullion market, share market, money market or capital market.

(a) Bullion Market

Bullion market is a market for valuable metals like gold, silver, diamonds etc.

(b) Share Market

Share market is a place in which shares are bought and sold, e.g., Mumbai share market.

(c) Money market

Money market is a place in which short term credit instruments are bought and sold, e.g., London money market, New York money market.

***(d)* Capital market**

Capital market is meant for very long period loans of a capital nature.

4. On the Basis of Transactions

On the basis of transactions, market may be classified into the spot market, and the future market. Spot market is one where goods are physically exchanged on the spot. Future market is one where an agreement is made on the spot but exchange of goods take place in future, as agreed upon by the parties.

5. On the Basis of the Volume of Business

Sometimes on the basis of the volume of business, markets are broadly classified into wholesale markets and retail markets. In the wholesale market goods are transacted in large quantities, while in retail market goods are transacted in small quantities.

6. On the Basis of the 'Status of Sellers'

On the basis of the status of sellers, markets are broadly classified into primary markets, secondary markets and terminal markets. A primary market is one where goods are transacted from the producers to the wholesalers. Where the wholesalers act as an intermediate link between the producers and retailers it is known as a secondary market. A terminal market is one where the goods are transferred from the retailers to the ultimate consumers.

7. On the Basis of Government Regulations

On the basis of government regulations, markets may also be classified as regulated markets and unregulated markets. A regulated market is one where transactions are governed by various rules and regulations framed by the government. On the other hand, a market where transactions of goods and services are left to market forces of demand and supply is known as an unregulated market.

8. On the Basis of Competition

According to the degree of competition, markets may also be classified into perfect markets and imperfect markets.

Perfect Market

A perfect market is one where there is perfect competition. Sometimes a distinction is made between pure competition and perfect competition. Perfect competition is a wider concept which includes not only the conditions of pure competition but also a few more.

Features of Perfect Competition

1. Large number of buyers and sellers.
2. Homogeneous product.
3. Free entry or exit.
4. Perfect knowledge about the market on the part of the buyers and sellers.
5. Absence of transport cost.
6. Perfect mobility of the factors of production.

Imperfect Market

A market is imperfectly competitive if the action of one or more buyers or sellers have a perceptible influence on price.[1] An imperfect market may assume the following form.

***(a)* Monopoly**

Monopoly is a market with a single seller of the product. Since there is only one seller, he has a complete control over the price so that he can influence the price. A monopolist may follow a uniform price policy or a discriminatory price policy for his product.

***(b)* Monopolistic Competition**

Monopolistic competition is a market in which there are many sellers producing products which are close but not perfect substitutes. Monopolistic competition is a blend of competition and monopoly. Non-price variation, that is product variation and selling costs are the two important features of monopolistic competition.

***(c)* Oligopoly**

Oligopoly is a market with few sellers. There is mutual inter-dependence between firms and the price and output decisions of one firm will have a considerable effect on other firms.

***(d)* Other Forms of Competition**

Bilateral monopoly	— Single seller vs single buyer
Monopsony	— Single buyer vs many sellers
Duopsony	— Two buyers vs many sellers
Oligopsony	— A few buyers vs many sellers.

1. J.M. Henderson and R.E. Quandt — *Micro Economic Theory* — McGraw Hill, Book Company, New York, 1971, p. 206.

The following table shows at a glance the basic characteristics of four important market models.

Table 19.1

Basic Characteristics of The Four Market Models

Market Model Characteristics	*Pure Competition*	*Monopolistic Competition*	*Oligopoly*	*Pure Monopoly*
1. Number of firms	Many and independent	Many and independent	Generally interdependent	One and independent
2. Size of firms (relative to total market)	Very small	Very small	Generally large	Complete domination
3. Type of product	Homogeneous	Slightly differentiated	Homogeneous or differentiated	Unique
4. Degree of control over price	None	Limited	Considerable collusion; otherwise restrained by interdependence.	Considerable
5. Conditions of entry	Very easy	Easy	Significant obstacles.	Blocked
6. Amount of non price competition	None	Considerable	Considerable	Limited

FACTORS AFFECTING THE SIZE OF A MARKET

The size or extent of a market depends upon various factors. These factors can be broadly divided under two heads.

1. Nature of the commodity and
2. General conditions

NATURE OF THE COMMODITY

1. Wide Demand

A commodity which is in universal demand will have a wide market. The classic example is fuel oil. On the other hand a commodity which is local in character will have a limited market. For example, Tamil films and Malayalam novels have only a regional market.

2. Durability

A commodity which is durable in nature will have a wide market. Goods like gold, silver, etc., have very wide markets since such commodities can be preserved for a long time and can be transported without any damage. On the other hand perishable commodities like vegetables, flowers and milk have only limited markets. But the development of processing facilities, refrigeration and air-lifting have greatly increased the size of the market for perishable goods also.

3. Portability

Another pre-requisite for a wide market is that the commodity should be easily portable. It must be small in size but possess a high value. Goods like machines and cotton textiles are easily portable and so they command wide markets. On the other hand bricks and stones enjoy only a narrow market.

4. Grading and Sampling

Grading means dividing the goods on the basis of quality. Sampling means a part representing the whole. Goods which are amenable to grading and sampling generally command an international market. Grading helps the purchasers to identify the quality of the product without the inspection.

5. Adequate Supply

To have a wider market the commodities should have an adequate supply. But rare pictures and paintings though they could not be supplied in plenty enjoy international markets because of their prestige value.

GENERAL CONDITIONS AFFECTING THE DEMAND FOR A COMMODITY

1. Peace and Security

The existence of political stability, peace and security are of vital importance for smooth trade. If the law and order situation in a country deteriorates due to political unrest and the revolutionary attitudes of certain groups, markets will get hampered.

2. Stable Currency and Efficient Financial Institutions

With the help of well developed banks and other financial institutions, marketing can be profitably and easily carried on over wide and extensive areas. In the modern world, international trade occupies an important place. The extent of international trade depends upon the value of the home currency and the confidence it inspires among foreigners.

3. Government Policy

The import and export policy of the government has also a considerable impact on the size of the market. If the government imposes a lot of restrictions in the form of quotas and duties, trade will be affected. Likewise restrictive policies of the importing country will also have an adverse effect on the exporting country.

4. Transport and Communication

A properly developed transport system in the form of roads, railways, steamships and aeroplanes is highly useful for the widening of both internal and international trade. Likewise, efficient means of communications like posts and telegraphs, telephones etc., help the traders to keep in touch with their distant markets and send information regarding market trends.

5. Degree of Division of Labour

According to Adam Smith the division of labour depends upon the extent of the market. But in a sense, the extent of the market also depends upon division of labour. Division of labour by reducing the average cost of production increases the size of the market.

QUESTIONS

1. Define Market. Enumerate the main features of a market.
2. Discuss the criteria on the basis of which markets can be classified.
3. What determines the size of a market?
4. What is the basis on which market structures are classified?

20

EQUILIBRIUM OF THE FIRM AND INDUSTRY UNDER PERFECT COMPETITION

"*The Competition is like horse manure. It's everywhere.*"

— R. Wayne Oldham, 1984

MEANING

The concept of perfect competition was mentioned in a casual way by Adam Smith in his Wealth of Nations. Edgeworth was the first to attempt (in his book "Mathematical Psychics", 1881) a systematic and rigorous definition of perfect competition. The concept received its complete formulation in Frank Knight's book, *Risk, Uncertainty and Profit* (1921).[1]

Perfect competition in economic theory has a meaning which is diametrically opposite to the every day use of the term. As Prof. Koutsoyiannis[2] remarks, "Perfect competition is a market structure characterised by a complete absence of rivalry among the individual firms."

1. G.S. Maddala, *Micro Economics, Theory and Applications,* McGraw Hill International Editions, 1989, p. 283.
2. A. Koutsoyiannis, *Modern Micro Economics,* Macmillan, London, Second Edition 1983, p. 154.

According to Prof. Bach[3] "perfect competition exists in markets where there are so many sellers that no one is big enough to have any appreciable influence over market price."

THE ASSUMPTIONS OF PERFECT COMPETITION

Perfect competition is characterised by the following assumptions:

1. Large Number of Buyers and Sellers

There are large number of buyers and sellers, each buying or selling only a trivial fraction of the total market transactions. Market price is determined by the two forces of demand and supply. They take the market price as a given parameter beyond their control, and try to sell and buy as much as they wish at that price. In this sense, both buyers and sellers are 'price takers' and quantity adjusters. Price takers are people who make a decision on whether to buy or sell at a given price.[4]

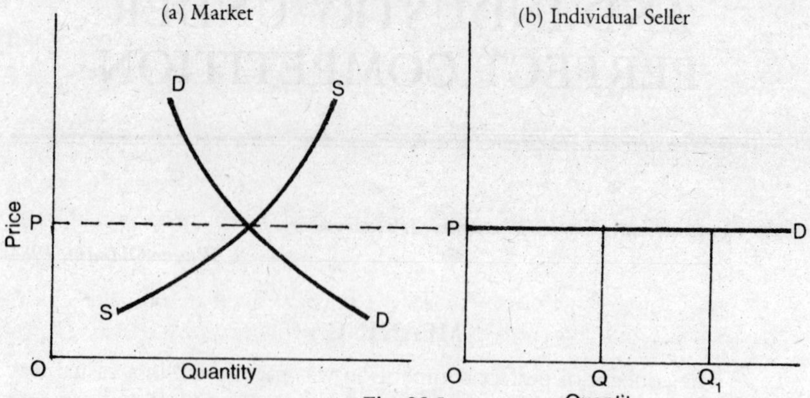

Fig. 20.1

2. Homogeneous Product

Under perfect competition, rival firms sell a standardized good or service. There are no brand names, trade marks, patents in perfectly competitive market. For example, the market for eggs is likely to be competitive. This is also known as the homogeneity condition. The implication of this is that buyers will be indifferent about the choice of the seller from whom they buy the product. If one seller raises his price, all consumers immediately buy from his competitors.

---

3. George Leland Bach, *An Introduction to Analysis and Policy,* 10th edition, Prentice Hall of India Private Ltd., 1982, p. 270.
4. John Craven, *Introduction to Economics,* Basil Black Well, Oxford, Second Edition, 1990, p. 65.

3. Absence of Collusion or Artificial Restraint

Another condition is that there is no collusion among the buyers or sellers or sellers and buyers. Moreover there are no restraints by the government in the form of tariffs, subsidies, rationing of production etc.

4. Perfect Mobility of Factors of Production

Another important characteristic of perfect competition is that the factors of production are free to move from one firm to another throughout the economy. This means that labour can move from one job to another and from one region to another. Capital raw materials and other factors are not monopolised.

5. Profit Maximisation

The goal of all firms in the industry is profit maximisation.

6. Perfect Knowledge

All buyers and sellers in the market possess perfect knowledge regarding the current and potential price and the availability of the commodity.

7. No Transport Costs

This assumption is essential, as the same price will prevail only then in the market. Information regarding market trends is free and costless. Future uncertainty is therefore ruled out.

Perfect Vs Pure Competition

Sometimes, the concept of pure competition is distinguished from that of perfect competition. The difference is a matter of degree. While 'perfect competition' has all the characteristics enumerated above, 'pure competition' relaxes the assumptions of perfect mobility of the factors of production and perfect knowledge.

In short,

Perfect competition – perfect mobility and knowledge = pure competition.

PERFECT COMPETITION IN PRACTICE

Perfect competition is an 'ideal market structure' rather than an actual market reality. The model of perfect competition fits in for agricultural products like rice, wheat, cotton and eggs. It is extremely difficult to satisfy all the conditions simultaneously. Therefore perfect competition is termed as a myth. In spite of this, we study this type of market in economic theory because of the following reasons.[5]

---

5. R.R. Barthwal, *Micro Economic Analysis* — Wiley Eastern Limited, New Delhi, 1st Edition, 1991, p. 223.

1. It provides a simplified model to understand the complex economic system.
2. It provides crude and approximate estimates of economic variables.
3. It provides a strong base for political ideology and welfare maximisation.
4. It helps in developing the norms for desirable performance applicable to an industry.

EQUILIBRIUM OF THE FIRM AND INDUSTRY

Conditions of Equilibrium for the Firm

A firm is in equilibrium when the following conditions are satisfied: (1) MC = MR (2) MC must cut MR from below.

Conditions of Equilibrium for the Industry

An industry is in equilibrium when the following conditions are fulfilled.

1. When there is no tendency for the firms either to enter or leave the industry.
2. When all the firms are in equilibrium

In short at the point of equilibrium

MC = MR ... (1)

AC = AR ... (2)

Since AR = MR, AC = MC.

Short Period Equilibrium of the Firm and Industry

The short-run is a period in which the number and plant size of the firms are fixed. In this period the firm can produce more only with the help of variable inputs along with the given fixed factors.

In the short run market price is determined by the interaction of the market forces of demand and supply. This price is given to the firms. The firm in a perfectly competitive market is a price taker and a quantity adjuster. The firm can sell any amount it wants to sell at that price. The equilibrium position of a firm can be analysed with the help of the marginal analysis as well as with the total cost-total revenue analysis. We shall first discuss the marginal analysis under identical cost conditions and under different cost conditions.

Under Identical Cost Conditions

In this case, it is assumed that all the firms are operating under identical cost conditions. This is possible only when all the factors of production are homogeneous. Under identical cost conditions, MC curves and AC curves of all the firms in the industry are the same. Figure 20.2 shows the short-run equilibrium of the industry on the left hand side and that of the firm on the right hand side.

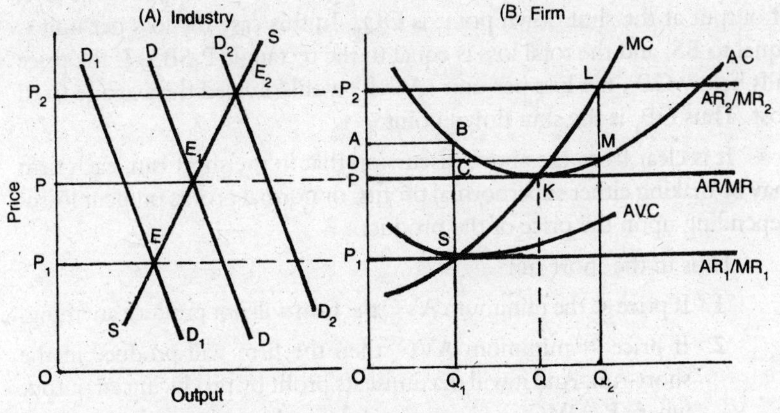

Fig. 20.2 (A) Fig. 20.2 (B)

In Fig. 20.2 (A), the equilibrium market price in the industry OP is determined by the demand curve DD and the supply curve SS. Price OP is given to the firms. As a result, the average revenue curve AR coincides with the marginal revenue curve Fig. 20.2 (B).

K is the point of equilibrium because at this point both the conditions of equilibrium (MC = MR and MC curve cuts the MR curve from below) are satisfied. OQ is the equilibrium level of output. At this level the firms are earning only normal profits. A firm earns normal profit when the MR curve is tangent to the AC curve at its minimum point.

Now suppose that the demand curve for the industry is D_2D_2, E_2 is the equilibrium of the industry. The corresponding firm's equilibrium is attained at the point L. Each firm produces OQ_2 output. Since areas under the respective average revenue and average cost curves measure total revenue and total cost, the difference between the two shows profit. Each firm earns super normal profits equal to the area of the rectangle P_2 LMD.

When price falls below OP, the firm will earn less than normal profit. This means that the firm is not fully covering its cost of production. In the short run, however, producers often find that they lose less by remaining in business than by shutting it down. As long as P = AVC the firm will continue to operate at a loss in the short-run rather than shut it down.

When the price of the product is such that it just allows the firm to cover its minimum average variable cost, the firm is at the shut down point. This point is (Fig. 20.2 (B)) denoted by S. When the price is equal to AVC, the loss per unit is equal to the average fixed cost. Suppose the level of output at the shut down point is OQ_1. In this case the loss per unit is equal to BS, and the total loss is equal to the rectangle P_1SBA. If the price falls below OP_1, the loss per unit (AC–P) would exceed the average fixed cost. Thus OP_1 is the shut down point.

It is clear from the above discussion that in the short run, each firm may be making either supernormal profits, or normal profits or incur losses depending upon the price of the product.

Thus in the short run

1. If price < the minimum AVC the firm will not produce anything.
2. If price = minimum AVC, then the firm will produce in the short-run. And it will maximise its profit by producing an output where P = MC.
3. The firm will make a profit only if P exceeds minimum AC.

The industry as a whole is in equilibrium when all the firms are in equilibrium. This indicates a situation when MC = MR = AR = AC. In such a situation all firms will earn only normal profits. In the words of D.S. Watson[6] "An industry is in equilibrium in the short run when the output of the industry holds steady, there being no force acting to expand output or to contract it. If all firms are in equilibrium, then so is the industry."

2. Different Cost Conditions

Now let us introduce an element of heterogeneity among the factors of production; suppose there is a variation in the efficiency of the entrepreneurs. As a result of this difference in efficiency, the cost conditions of the firm will also differ. Firms with more efficient entrepreneurs will be able to produce at lower costs than others. The price of the product is determined by the industry which is the same for all firms. Therefore depending upon the shapes of cost curves some firms may suffer losses, some may earn super-normal profits, some may earn normal profits, while

6. *Price Theory and its Uses* — Khosla Publishing House, New Delhi 1986, p. 262.

others may continue the business with loss of fixed cost or close down the business.

The following diagrams will illustrate the point more clearly.

Super Normal Profit

Category I

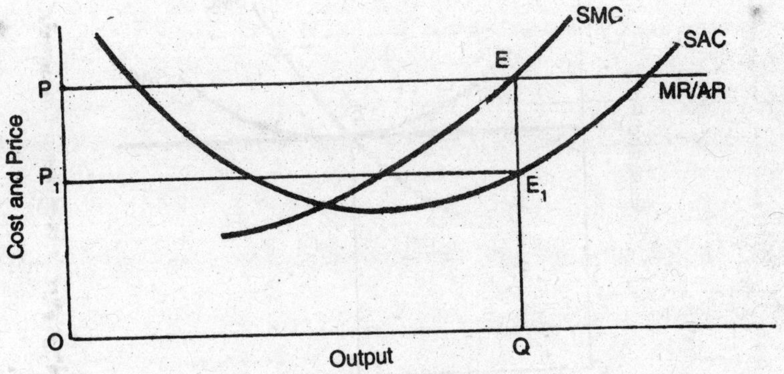

Fig. 20.3

$$\begin{aligned} \text{Profit} &= TR - TC \\ &= AR \times \text{Total output} - AC \times \text{Total output} \\ &= OP \times OQ - OP_1 \times OQ \\ &= OPEQ - OP_1E_1Q \\ &= PP_1E_1E \end{aligned}$$

Thus firms in category (1) will earn super normal profits equal to PP_1E_1E.

Loss

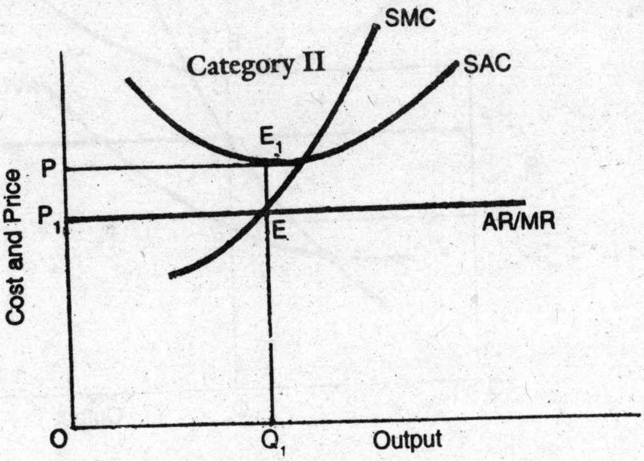

Fig. 20.4

Thus firms in category (II) will incur a loss equal to PP_1EE_1.

Normal Profit

Category III

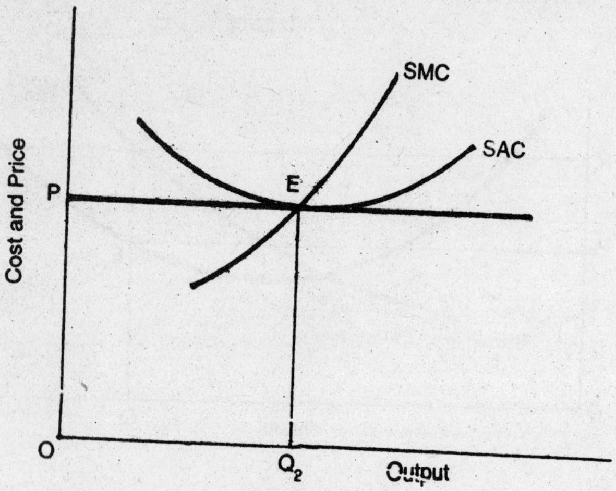

Fig. 20.5

Firms in category (III) cover only their SAC which includes normal profit.

Firm Covering Average Variable Cost

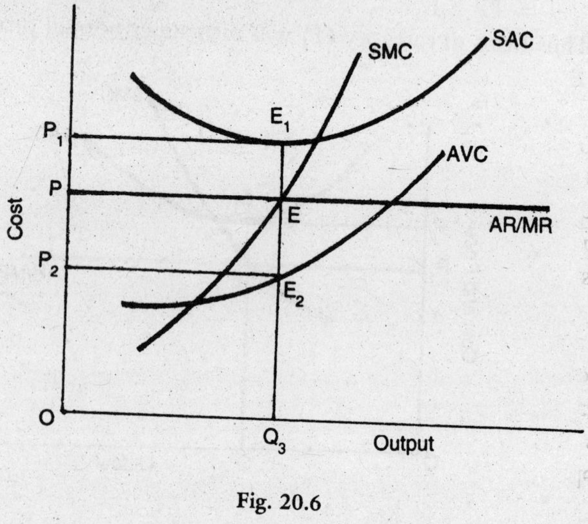

Fig. 20.6

Fig. 20.6 shows that at OQ_3 level of output the firm is able to cover the average variable cost and a part of the average fixed cost. The loss per unit of output is E_1E (AC – P). The total loss is represented by the rectangle $P_1P\ EE_1$. Firms in category (IV) will continue to operate at a loss in the short run rather than shut down their production.

Shut Down Point

Category V

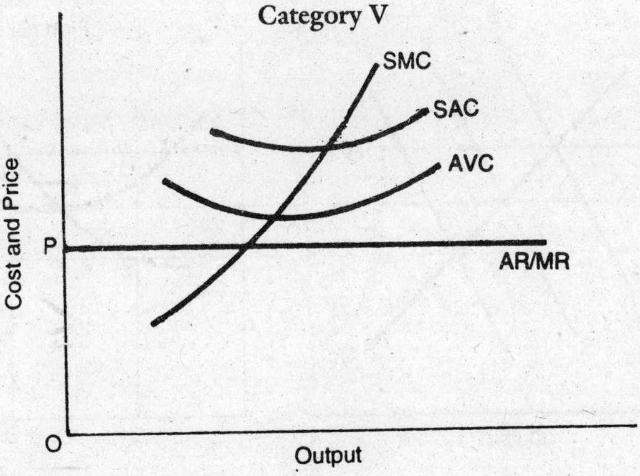

Fig. 20.7

Firms in category (V) are not able to cover even the average variable cost. Thus when the price falls below minimum AVC, the firms will shut down their operation immediately.

Long run Equilibrium of the Firm and Industry

In the long run, the dichotomy between fixed cost and variable cost disappears. All factors are variable. In the long run the firm can pick from the full menu of choices. In the long run existing firms will make adjustments in their output and costs. If after these adjustments a firm is still unable to cover its total costs, it will leave the industry. If existing firms earn economic profits in an industry, these profits will lure additional firms. When economic profits in the industry become zero, there will be no incentive either to enter or leave. The number of firms in the industry will remain stable. As the average cost of production includes the normal profit, this will occur when price is equal to the minimum Long run average cost (LRAC min).

The long-run competitive equilibrium can also be analysed under identical and different cost conditions.

I. Identical Cost Conditions

In the long-run under identical cost conditions, it is assumed that all factor units including entrepreneurs are homogeneous. Since the price of the factors of production is also uniform the cost curves of the firms are identical.

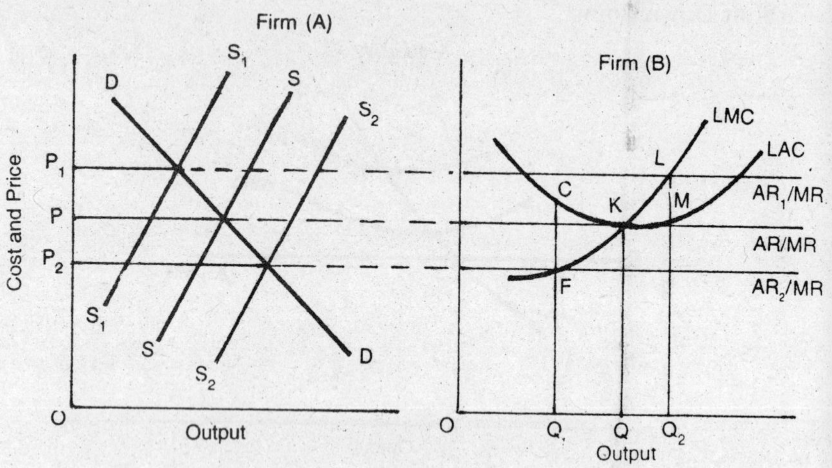

Fig. 20.8

In the long-run, a firm will be in equilibrium when price = LRMC = LRAC = MR = AR. In Fig. 20.8 (A) DD is the demand curve and SS is the supply curve. The market price is OP, which is given to the firms. At OP price, each firm will produce OQ units of output and earn a normal profit. Suppose the price in the market becomes OP_1. In this case the firm will expand its scale beyond the minimum point of the LAC curve until the LMC curve equals the marginal revenue curve at OQ_2 output. The firms are earning abnormal profits equal to LM per unit. But the existence of such a lucrative return will attract new firms into the industry, as there are no barriers to entry. Supply will increase, shifting the short run supply curve to SS and the price of the commodity will drop to OP. Now OQ output will be produced at the equilibrium point K.

If price is OP_2, the firm will curtail its output to OQ_1. The loss per unit is CF. Some firms will leave the industry and shift the industry supply curve to the left, from S_2S_2 to SS. Once again, equilibrium is established at point K where each firm will produce OQ output and earn a normal profit.

1. P > minimum LAC, new firms will enter the industry and reduce the price.

2. P < minimum LAC, some firms will leave the industry and increase the price.
3. P = minimum LAC, there will be no tendency for firms to leave the industry and the industry will be in equilibrium.

Thus in the Long-run Price = LRMC = AR = MR. this is known as the "full equilibrium" position. As Stonier and Hague[7] rightly point out "In perfect competition, with all factors homogeneous, each firm, and the industry as a whole, will be in full equilibrium where marginal revenue = marginal cost = average cost = average revenue (price)."

2. Different Cost Conditions

In case the entrepreneurs are heterogeneous, some firms will be able to produce the same output at lower costs than others. This means that some firms will be able to earn super normal profits. The firms which earn supernormal profits are the "intra-marginal firms" as distinct from the 'marginal firms, which just earns a normal profit. These two cases are shown in Fig. 20.9.

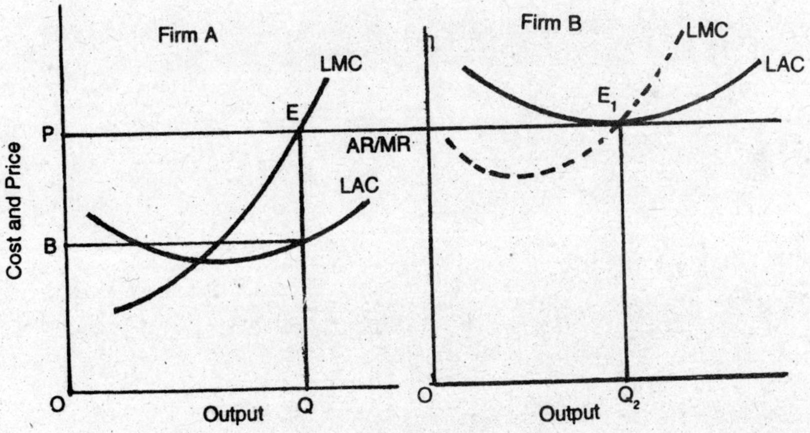

Fig. 20.9

7. A.W. Stonier and D.C. Hague — *A Textbook of Economic Theory*, Longman, London, 1988, p. 156.

Let us assume that there are two firms A and B. Firm A has a more efficient entrepreneur, and therefore enjoys lower costs than firm B. At the price OP, firm A is earning supernormal profits of PBCE even in the long run. But firm B is earning only normal profits. Therefore firm A is the intra-marginal firm and firm B is the marginal firm. Unless the influx of very efficient producers are able to compete more effectively with firm A than with firms like B, firm A will continue to earn supernormal profits even in the long-run.

QUESTIONS

1. State the features of a perfectly competitive market.
2. Perfect competition is an idealistic market situation which does not exist anywhere in the world — substantiate.
3. How does a firm reach equilibrium under perfect competition in the short-run?
4. Distinguish between pure competition and perfect competition.
5. How does an industry achieve equilibrium production in the short-run under perfect competition?

❖ ❖ ❖

21

PRICING UNDER PERFECT COMPETITION

"*Perfect Competition is a market structure characterised by a complete absence of rivalry among the individual firms.*"

— *Koutsoyiannis*

INTRODUCTION

A market in which all the buyers and all the sellers are price takers is called a perfectly competitive market. Price is determined by the industry. An industry is a collection of firms producing identical goods. The equilibrium price is determined at a point where the demand for and the

Table 21.1

Demand, Supply, the Equilibrium Price and the Output

Price (in Rs.)	*Quantity demanded* (Qd)	*Quantity supplied* (Qs)	*Direction of change in price*
1	60	0	↓
2	50	20	↓
3	40	40	↓
Equilibrium price		Equilibrium quantity	Equilibrium
4	30	60	↑
5	20	80	↑

supply of the total industry are equal. To put it in other words, at the equilibrium price, what the buyers are willing to purchase is exactly matched by what the sellers are willing to offer at that price. Quantity demanded and quantity supplied at the equilibrium price is known as the equilibrium quantity.

Table 21.1 shows how price is determined by the forces of demand and supply. When the price is Re.1, 60 units are demanded but no supply is forthcoming. With the rise in price, demand falls and supply increases. When the price is Rs.2, the demand is 50 units but the supply is only 20 units. Demand is more than supply at this price and so, the price of the product rises from Rs. 2 to 3. As a result, demand falls to 40 and supply increases to 40. Both the buyers and sellers are satisfied with this price. Thus Rs. 3 is the equilibrium market price at which the demand for and the supply of the product is 40 units. If price is increased still further, say to Rs. 4, it increases the supply of goods to 60 units, but the demand is reduced to 30. Likewise if the price increases still further, say to Rs. 5 demand will fall to 20 but supply will increase to 80 units. Thus at the equilibrium market price and output, quantity demanded (Qd) equals quantity supplied (Qs). If Qs > Qd, the price tends to fall. If Qs < Qd price tends to rise.

GRAPHIC ILLUSTRATION

Demand and supply curves can be used to analyse the equilibrium market price and the equilibrium output.

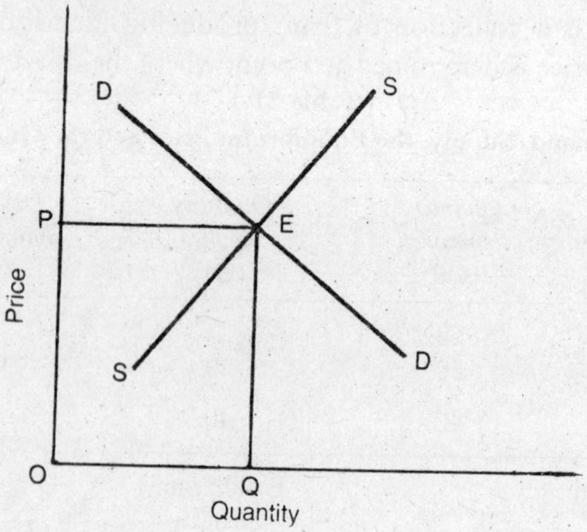

Fig. 21.1

In Fig. 21.1 quantity is shown along the X-axis and price along the Y-axis. The market equilibrium E is established at the point of intersection of the demand and supply curves. By drawing a perpendicular from the equilibrium point to the X-axis we get the equilibrium quantity demanded and supplied, i.e., OQ. Likewise, by drawing a perpendicular to the Y-axis from the point of equilibrium we get the market price (OP).

Table 21.2
Market Equilibrium

Market Condition	*Relationship between quantity demanded and supplied*	*Market Price*
Equilibrium	$Q_D = Q_S$	In Equilibrium
Shortage	$Q_D > Q_S$	Rises
Surplus	$Q_D < Q_S$	Falls

IMPORTANCE OF TIME ELEMENT IN PRICE THEORY

According to Marshall, the price of a commodity is determined by both demand and supply. He stresses the importance of time element in the determination of price. Before Marshall, there was a controversy regarding the relative importance of demand and supply in the determination of price. Marshall resolved this controversy with the introduction of the time element in his theory of value. In his view to the answer to the question as to which one is more important, depends upon the time period under consideration. He quoted the analogy of two blades of a pair of scissors in this connection. Just as both the blades are needed to cut a piece of cloth, both demand and supply are equally essential in the determination of price.

But "as a general rule" Marshall said "the shorter the period which one considers, the greater must be the share of our attention which is given to the influence of demand on value; and the longer the period, the more importance will be the influence of cost of production on value."

Marshall distinguishes four time periods in which the equilibrium between demand and supply are sought to be brought about:

1. the market period,
2. the short period,
3. the long period, and
4. the secular period.

THE MARKET PERIOD PRICE DETERMINATION

The market period is a very short period in which the supply of a commodity is fixed. It is the variations in demand that determine the price in such a market period. The time period is so short that supply is not responsive to demand. This market period may be an hour, a day or a few days, or even a few weeks depending upon the type of the commodity under consideration as to whether it is a perishable or semi-durable one.

The price prevailing in the market period is known as the market price. This price is not fixed. It oscillates with the nature of the commodity many times within a day, week or month.

Marshall explains the market price in the following words: "The market value is often more influenced by passing events and by causes whose action is fitful and short-lived than by those which work persistently."

The determination of market price is explained separately for perishable and durable commodities.

PERISHABLE COMMODITIES

In the case of perishable goods like fish, milk, vegetables, flowers etc., the supply is limited to the existing stocks. The fundamental feature of this period is that the supply of the commodity is absolutely fixed and therefore, the supply curve of each firm will be a vertical straight line. As each firm's supply curve is a vertical line, the market supply curve obtained by aggregating the individual supply curves must also be a vertical straight line. During the market period, demand is more important than supply in determining the price. In other words, utility is more important than cost.

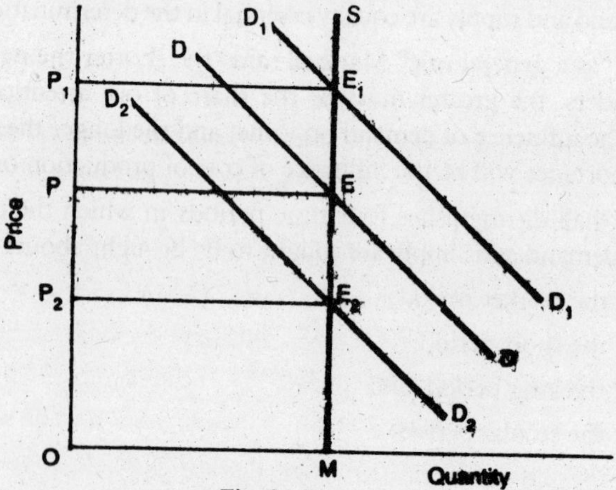

Fig. 21.2

Fig. 21.2 depicts the price determination of a perishable commodity like fish. MS is the supply curve which is a vertical straight line representing perfectly inelastic supply. DD is the initial demand curve which intersects the supply curve MS at E. The equilibrium price is OP and the quantity demanded and supplied is equal to OM. Now due to a sudden rise in the demand for fish from DD to D_1D_1, the new equilibrium is established at E_1 and the price increases to OP_1. If demand decreases, the demand curve becomes D_2D_2, and the new equilibrium price becomes OP_2.

DURABLE COMMODITIES

If the commodity under consideration is a durable commodity the supply curve cannot be a vertical straight line throughout its length, because some of the goods can be preserved or held back from the market and carried over to the next period. Then there will be two critical price levels. At one price, the seller will be prepared to sell the entire stock. If the price is below a particular level, the seller does not sell the entire quantity but holds back the stock for a better time. The price below which a seller refuses to sell is called his reservation price. There are several factors which influence the reserve price of a seller.

1. Durability of the Commodity

The durability of the commodity is the basic factor in influencing the reserve price. The more durable a commodity is, the higher will be its reserve price.

2. Future Price

The reserve price also depends upon the seller's expectations regarding its future price. If the seller anticipates the price to rise in future, he will fix a higher reserve price and vice versa.

3. Liquidity Preference

Liquidity preference implies the desire to keep ready cash. A strong liquidity preference will induce the seller to clear the stock of goods even at a lower price. On the other hand, if the liquidity preference is weak, the reserve price will be higher.

4. Storage Expenses

The longer the time and greater the cost involved in storing the commodity, the lower will be the reserve price and vice versa.

5. Future Demand

If the seller expects a high demand for the product in future, he will fix a high reserve price and vice versa.

6. Future Cost of Production

If the cost of production of the commodity is expected to fall in future, the seller will fix a lower reserve price.

7. Time for New Supply

The time required for new supplies to reach the market will also have a bearing on the reservation price. If the time gap is longer, a higher reserve price will be fixed.

8. Past Cost

Some obstinate sellers attach too much importance to past costs and refuse to sell at a price below that cost. This tendency on the part of the seller may end in greater loss.

TES is the supply curve which indicates that the firm will refuse to sell anything below the price OT, and up to the price OP the quantity offered for sale increases with an increase in price. At price OP the whole stock is offered for sale, but above this price, supply remains the same. From this point E the supply curve becomes a vertical straight line. To put it in other words, even if a higher price is offered by the buyers, the sellers are unable to supply accordingly.

If the demand curve is D_1D_1, and it intersects the supply curve TES at point E_1, the equilibrium price is OP_1. The sellers sell OM_1 quantity. They withhold M_1M quantity. A shift in the demand curve from D_1D_1 to DD shows an increase in demand, and along with it the new equilibrium price rises from OP_1 to OP. The entire stock is sold. If the demand increases

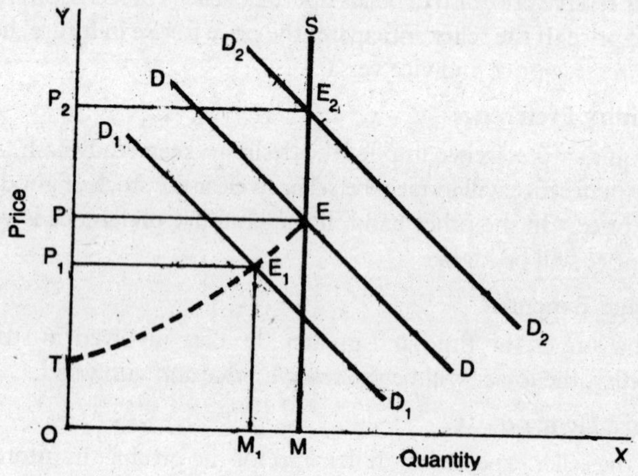

Fig. 21.3

from DD to some higher level such as D_2D_2 the quantity sold remains at OM level. But the price rises to OP_2. Thus the further increase in demand beyond DD will have only the effect of raising the price, and the quantity supplied remains unchanged.

During the market period, on account of the haggling and bargaining of the buyers and the sellers, price is tossed hither and thither like a shuttle-cock according to the relative strength of the two parties.[1]

THE SHORT PERIOD PRICE DETERMINATION

The short period refers to that period in which supply can be adjusted to a limited extent. The short period has been defined by Stigler as "the period in which the rate of production is variable, but in which there exist a fixed plant."[2]

In the short run, the fixed factors like machinery, plant etc. cannot be altered. Variable factors may be increased or decreased according to the changes in demand. As a result, the short period supply curve will be elastic to some extent. The short period price is determined by the interaction of the forces of short-run demand and supply. It can be shown with the help of the following Figure 21.4.

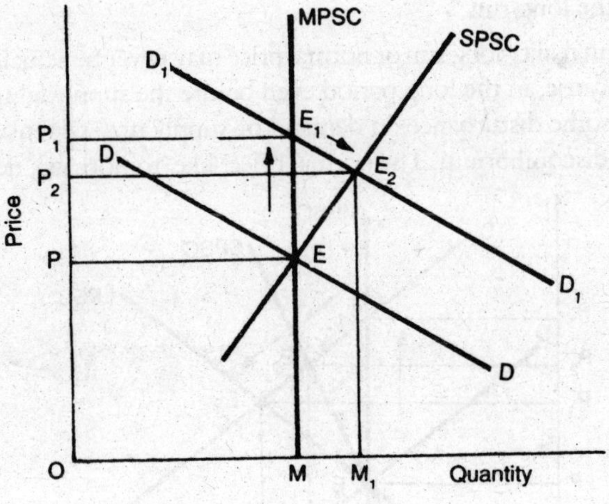

Fig. 21.4

1. K.N. Prasad, *Lecturers on Micro Economic Theory,* Himalaya Publishing House, Mumbai, 1987, p. 204
2. George J. Strigler — *The Theory of Price,* Macmillan, London, 1966, p. 14.

DD is the initial demand curve and MPSC is the market period supply curve. Both intersect at point E. The market price is OP and the quantity supplied is OM. A shift in demand curve from DD to D_1D_1 represents an increase in demand. The market price will also rise from OP to OP_1. The short period supply curve (SPSC) shows that, in the short period, supply is able to adapt itself somewhat to a limited extent to the changed demand conditions. The new demand curve D_1D_1 intersects the SPSC, at OP_2 price. Now the quantity supplied is OM_1. The new short-run equilibrium price becomes OP_2 which is higher than the initial market price OP, but it is not so high as the second market period price OP_1. The short run supply has also increased from OM to OM_1.

THE LONG-RUN PERIOD — PRICE DETERMINATION

"Long-run" period is a period of many years. Long period is the time period during which the supply conditions are fully able to meet the new demand conditions. In the long-run both fixed as well as variable factors are variable. In this period, new plants can be installed and new firms can enter into the market and the old firms can leave the market. Long period price is called by Adam Smith as "natural price" and Marshall called it as 'normal price.' According to Marshall "The normal value or price of a commodity is that which economic forces would tend to bring about in the long run."

But in reality long run or normal price may never be actually achieved. This is because, in the long period even before the supply adjusts itself to demand, some disturbance, in demand or supply may take place, thereby causing a disequilibrium. The normal price, like 'tomorrow', never comes.

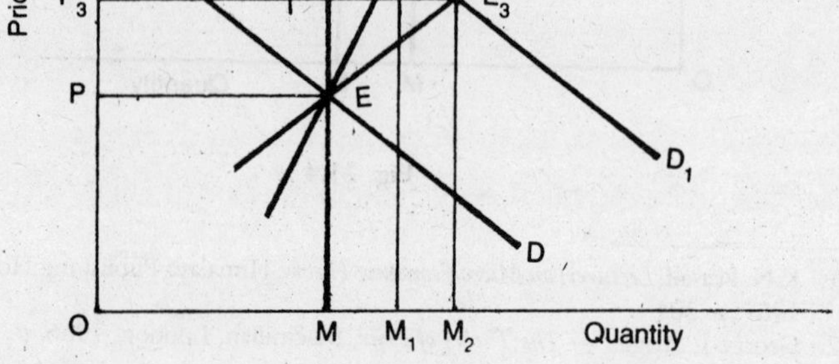

Fig. 21.5

The following diagram illustrates the determination of the price in the long period.

MPSC = Market period supply curve

SPSC = Short period supply curve

LPSC = Long period supply curve

DD = Initial demand curve

D_1D_1 = Increased demand curve

The original market price is OP. As a result of an increase in demand the price has moved from OP to OP_1 in the very short period. The supply curve in the short run normal period is SPSC. In the short period, the price falls from OP to OP_2 because the supply can be increased to some extent. The long run supply curve is LPSC. In the long period price further falls to the level of OP_3 because supply can adjust fully to the demand.

Long-Run Normal Price in Constant Cost Industry

In the case of a constant cost industry, the cost of production remains constant even as the production level is changed. To put it in other words, the emergence of external economies is equally counter balanced by diseconomies as production expands, and so the cost of production remains the same. Since larger quantities of the commodity can be produced at the same cost, the supply curve will be parallel to the X-axis.

In the words of Stigler "...a constant cost industry is usually defined as one whose supply price is the same for all outputs and also is one in which the prices of outputs do not vary with input."

The pricing process is illustrated in Figure 21.6 given below:

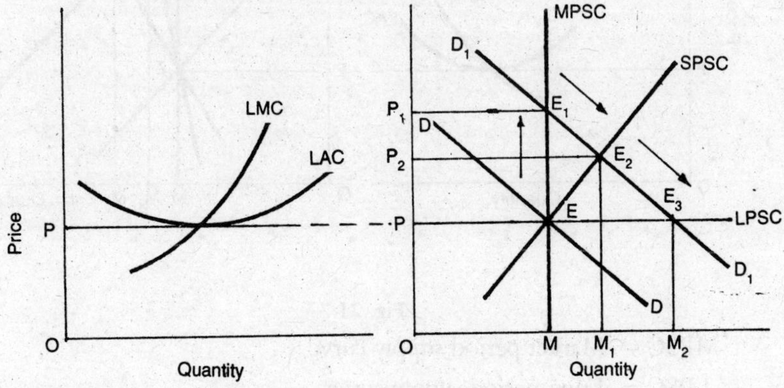

Fig. 21.6

The market period supply curve MPSC intersects the demand curve DD and the price is OP. D_1D_1 is the increased demand curve. Since the supply is inelastic the price moves from OP to OP_1. The price OP_1 is higher than OP and so the existing firms will be making abnormal profits. As a result, new firms will enter into the industry and produce more. Since a constant cost condition is assumed, the long period supply curve will be parallel to the X-axis cutting the new increased demand curve. The long run normal price is OP which is equal to the original price. The output has increased from OM to OM_2.

Long-Run Normal Price in an Increasing Cost Industry

The supply curve of an increasing cost industry will slope upwards from left to right showing that an increased output will be available at an increased cost and, therefore at an increased price. Increasing costs are the most typical of the actual competitive world conditions. In this industry, external diseconomies tend to outweigh external economies. Increase in the costs of production shifts the LAC and LMC upwards for all the firms. In the long-run price is always equal to the minimum average cost. So price increase also will equal to the minimum LAC. This pricing is explained in the following figure.

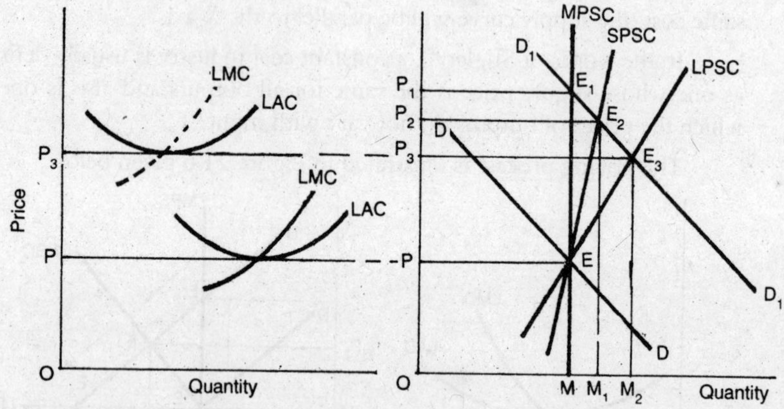

Fig. 21.7

MPSC = Market period supply curve

LPSC = Long period supply curve

SPSC = Short period supply curve

To begin with, DD is the demand curve and MPSC is the short period supply curve. OP is the market price. D_1D_1 is the increased demand curve. The price is OP_1 which is higher than OP.

In the short period, the existing firms will increase the supply, and the increased demand curve D_1D_1 intersects the short period supply curve at E_2. Consequently the market price falls from OP_1 to OP_2. In this situation the existing firms will make extra profits. As a result, new firms will enter the industry and start producing more. The cost curves will go up higher and higher as the industry is working under increased cost conditions. The output of the industry increases from OM to OM_2 as a result of the entry of new firms. Price in the long run will fall to OP_3 at which the demand curve D_1D_1 intersects the LRSC. Thus OP_3 is the long run normal price.

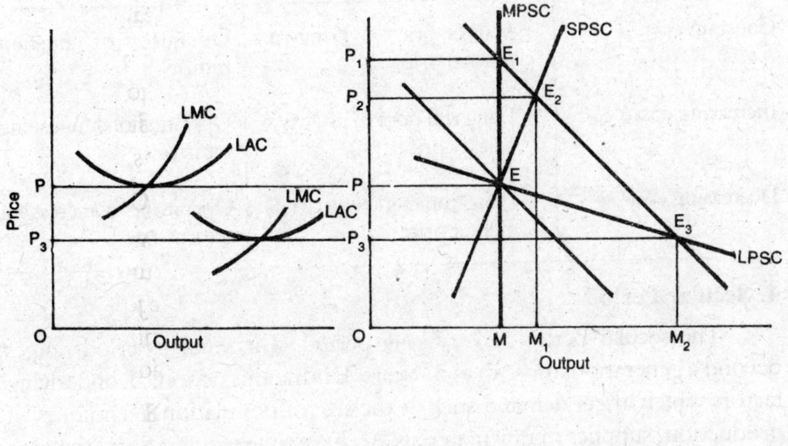

Fig. 21.8

This long run normal price OP_3 must be equal to the minimum long run average cost. New firms will continue entering the industry until all the firms earn only normal profits. But this minimum average cost is higher than the initial minimum cost because costs have risen due to the entry of new firms. The new normal price OP_3 is higher than the original normal price OP.

Long Run Normal Price in a Decreasing Cost Industry

In the case of a decreasing cost industry, the external economies may be more than external diseconomies as a result of which the cost of production tends to decrease. The normal price will be lower than the market price. The LRSC slopes downwards, from left to right, showing that as output increases per unit cost decreases.

The initial equilibrium point is E where the price is OP and the output, OM. With the increase in demand from DD to D_1D_1 the market price rises to OP_1. In the short run, when the supply increases from OM to OM_1 the price falls from OP_1 to OP_2. In the long run new firms will enter the industry and cause a downward shift in the demand curves of all the firms. When the supply increases further to OM_2, in the long run, the price also falls to OP_3. This long run price OP_3 is less than the original market price OP. The above features of an industry can be summarised as follows:

Table 21.3

Nature of Industry	*Price*	*Reason*
Constant cost	Market price = Long-run normal price	Operation of constant returns
Increasing cost	Long run normal price is > market price	Operation of diminishing returns
Decreasing cost	Long-run market price is < market price	Operation of increasing returns

4. Secular Period

The secular period is very long period. The secular period ranges beyond a generation, more than 33 years. During this period, all underlying factors which affect demand such as the size of population, techniques of production, supplies of raw materials etc. have time to alter. Since the time period is too long, Marshall does not analyse pricing under the secular period. He treats secular price as a kind of normal price, and as a historical category.

DISTINCTION BETWEEN NORMAL PRICE AND MARKET PRICE

Market Price	*Normal Price*
1. It is a very short period price.	It is a long period price.
2. Supply curve is vertical.	Supply curve is horizontal.
3. It is influenced more by demand factors.	It is influenced more by supply factors and the cost of production.
4. All goods have a market price.	Only reproduciable goods alone have a normal price.
5. Market price may be higher or lower than the cost of production.	Normal price is equal to the cost of production.
6. A firm with a market price can earn super normal profits or incur losses	A firm with a normal price can earn only normal profits.
7. Market price is a reality.	Normal price is a mirage.
8. There will be a temporary equilibrium between demand and supply.	There will be a permanent equilibrium between demand and supply.
9. Market price fluctuates frequently (even daily).	Normal price is relatively stable.

QUESTIONS

1. How is market price determined under competitive conditions?
2. Explain the role of time in the determination of price.
3. Discuss the importance of Marshall's time element in price theory.

❖ ❖ ❖

22

MONOPOLY

"The holder of a Monopoly is a Sinner and Offender."

— Mohammed

INTRODUCTION

At one end of the market spectrum is perfect competition, with many sellers and at the other end is monopoly, with only one seller. "Monopolist" is a Greek word, Mono means one and Polist means seller.

Monopoly is a market structure in which there is a single seller, there are no close substitutes for the commodity it produces and there are barriers to entry.[1] The key to monopoly power is the ability to control the availability of a product.

When a commodity has distinct physical properties and these are recognised by everybody as distinct, then a firm producing such a commodity can be called a monopoly firm. Joel Dean, an authority on managerial economics calls a monopolis product as "a product of lasting distinctiveness." Such a product has no acceptable substitutes. Its distinctiveness lasts for many years. The best example of monopoly is the Reserve Bank of India which alone has the right to issue currency notes.

1. A. Koutsoyiannis — *Modern Micro Economics,* 2nd Edn., The Macmillan Press Ltd., London, 1983, p. 171.

CHARACTERISTICS OF MONOPOLY

The main features of monopoly are as follows:

1. One seller and a large number of buyers.
2. There is absence of competition.
3. No close substitutes.
4. Cross elasticity of demand for a monopolist's product is zero in case of pure monopoly and very low in the case of simple monopoly.
5. Difficult for new firms to enter.
6. The distinction between firm and industry disappears.
7. Control over the supply of the commodity.

The type of monopoly explained above is simple monopoly. There is also a pure or perfect or absolute monopoly which is described later. But our analysis is based on a detailed discussion of simple monopoly and discriminating monopoly.

TYPES OF MONOPOLY

Monopoly is the anti-thesis of competition. There are various kinds of monopoly.

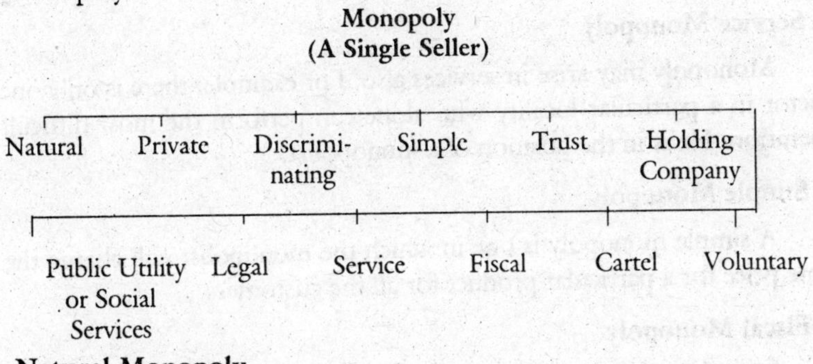

1. Natural Monopoly

A natural monopoly is a special type of monopoly that arises due to economies of scale.

In the words of Baumol,

"A natural monopoly is an industry in which economies of scale and other related forms of saving make it cheaper to produce when there is one firm rather than several."

Natural monopolies arise on account of concentration of raw materials in a particular region. An example of natural monopoly is the nickel supply of Canada (about 90 percent of the world's supply). Likewise, most of the world's diamond mines are owned by the De Beers Company of South Africa. Factors like climate, environment and nearness to market, may also create natural monopolies.

2. Social Monopoly

Social monopolies are owned and managed by the government. The aim of this monopoly is not profit, but to be of service to the people. Therefore, it is sometimes called welfare monopoly.

Example: Railways, electricity, post and telegraphs etc.

3. Private Monopoly

A private monopoly is owned and operated by a private individual or companies for the consideration of profit. Profit maximisation is the sole objective of such monopolies.

4. Legal Monopoly

Legal monopolies are conferred on certain firms and are protected by law for them to enjoy for some given period of time, the fruits of their labour. The special trade marks, copyrights and patents are the best examples of legal monopoly.

5. Service Monopoly

Monopoly may arise in services also. For example, there is only one doctor in a particular locality who alone can perform the most difficult operation. He is in the position of a monopolist.

6. Simple Monopoly

A simple monopoly is one in which the monopolist will charge the same price for a particular product for all the customers.

7. Fiscal Monopoly

Sometimes some activities like minting of coins or printing of currency will be undertaken only by the government for various reasons. Such monopolies are known as fiscal monopolies.

8. Discriminating Monopoly

A discriminating monopoly is one in which different prices are charged for the same product for different customers.

For example, Lawyers charge different rates for different clients.

9. Voluntary Monopolies

Voluntary monopolies are created to eliminate competition and to reap abnormal profits.

(a) **Cartel:** A cartel is a group of firms whose objective is to limit the scope of competitive forces in the market. For example, OPEC (the Organisation of Petroleum Exporting Countries).

(b) **Trust:** When all the firms merge into one association, the monopoly is referred to as a trust. The Associated Cement Companies (ACC) in India is an example of a Trust.

(c) **Holding Company:** A holding company is one which obtains a monopoly position by owning the majority of shares in a company or a group of companies.

CAUSES OF MONOPOLY OR BASES OF MONOPOLY

The main causes that lead to monopoly are the following:

1. Strategic Raw Materials

A monopoly may arise on account of some natural causes. A single firm may control the supply of key raw materials which are needed for the production of a product. Bauxite is a necessary ingredient for the production of aluminium. For many years the Aluminium Company of America (ALCOA) owned almost every source of bauxite in the U.S.

2. Patent's Over Inventions

Patent's copyrights and trademarks are recognised by law because they encourage inventions. A firm which acquires patent rights for the production of a particular commodity gets an absolute monopoly over that product. This leads to legal monopoly.

3. Market Franchise

Sometimes the government may give the exclusive right to sell a certain good or offer a service in a particular area. A particular bus company may be allowed to provide bus service in a specific route. Likewise, a particular firm may be allowed to cable television service in a particular area. These franchises create monopoly profits for the holders of the franchises. Such monopolies are also known as franchise monopolies.

4. Cost of Establishing an Efficient Plant in Relation to the Market

In certain cases, the size of the market may be such as not to support more than one plant of optimal size. The industry may enjoy a so-called natural monopoly — an industry in which the efficient size of a plant is large relative to the size of the market, and the monopolist's LAC declines throughout the relevant range of output.[2]

Competition for supply by more than one firm is a sheer economic and social waste. Consider the case of two railway stations in a particular town or two post offices in a particular village, which may be unnecessary.

5. Fiscal Monopolies

There are certain monopolies like post offices, minting of money, and printing of notes which are owned by the state itself. These are known as fiscal monopolies.

6. Ignorance or Control of a Secret Process

A monopolist may survive and persist as his rival competitors may not be aware of the abnormal profits being reaped by the existing firms or they may not be able to acquire the necessary technical knowledge involved in the production of that particular product.

7. Deliberate Policy to Exclude Competitors

The existing firm may adopt a policy of limit-pricing. It may incur a huge advertisement expenditure or may involve in a process of continuous product differentiation to prevent the entry of new firms.

8. Monopolistic Combinations

Sometimes in order to avoid cut-throat competition and the resultant price-war, various firms may combine among themselves. Their aim is to take a common decision with regard to price, output and the sharing of markets. Monopolistic combinations may take various forms such as pools, cartels, syndicates, trusts, holding companies and mergers.

9. Transport Cost

Sometimes the cost of transporting goods to a potential market may be so great (relative to the price of the good) that most of the firms remain out of the area and give a degree of monopoly power to the local producer there.

10. Reputation

If a firm acquires a very high reputation for the production of a particular commodity, it gains a certain degree of monopoly power whether such a reputation is justified or not.

---

2. Robert Y. Ahw — *Micro Economic Analysis, Theory and Applications*, John Wiley & Sons, New York, 1976, p. 290.

PURE MONOPOLY

The concept of pure monopoly was first enunciated by Prof. E.H. Chamberlin, in his theory of monopolistic competition. Pure monopoly constitutes one end of the market spectrum, the other being perfect competition.

A pure monopoly is defined as a firm that is also an industry. It is the only supplier of some particular commodity for which there exist no close substitutes.[3] The cross elasticity of demand of the monopolist's product is zero. Since he is the only seller he has no actual or prospective rivals.

In the case of 'pure' or 'perfect monopoly', a producer is so powerful that he is always able to take the whole of all consumer's incomes whatever may be the level of his output.

According to Profs. Stonier and Hague "it would occur when the average revenue curve of the firm is a rectangular hyperbola with an elasticity equal to one."

To put it in other words, the total outlay of the firms' product is the same at all prices and therefore the MR is always zero, i.e., the MR curve coincides with the X axis.

According to Prof. Chamberlin, the only perfect monopoly conceivable would be embracing the supply of everything.

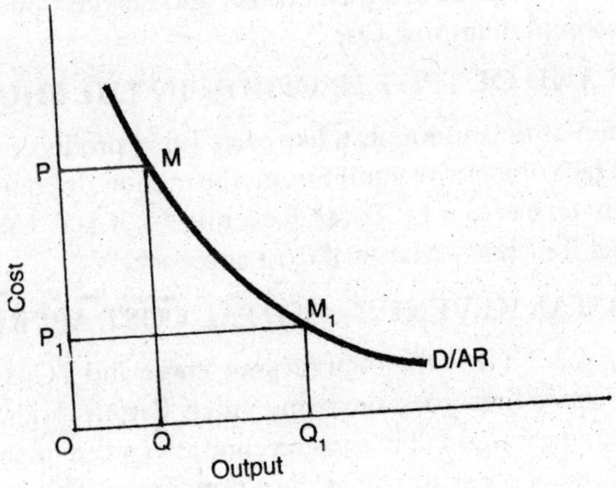

Fig. 22.1

3. William J. Baumol and Alan S. Blinder, *Economic Principles and Policy,* Harcourt Brace, Jovanovich, New York, 1979, p. 191.

A 'pure monopolist' can fix either the price or the output, but not both at the same time.

As in Fig. 22.1, if he fixes the output as OQ_1, his price will be OP_1, if he fixes the price at OP level, he can sell only OQ quantity of his output.

Though in theory, there is no competition for a monopolist, in actual practice, he has to tackle the problem of indirect and potential competition.

Indirect Competition

As pointed out by Prof. Chamberlin, pure monopoly exists when the pure monopolist controls all goods and services consumed by the consumers. Only in such a case he takes all of the consumer's income. This is a highly unrealistic and abstract phenomenon. Moreover, his unlimited power is restricted by the fact that all commodities compete for a place in the consumer's budget — the products of monopolists as well as the products of perfectly competitive firms. Therefore if the price of the monopolist's product is too high, the consumers may avoid purchasing the monopolist's products.

Potential Competition

If the existing monopoly firm is reaping abnormal profits, it will attract potential competitors. This is particularly true when the price-output policy of the existing monopolist is such that potential competitors feel they can readily capture a substantial portion of the market. Whenever entry is possible, the position of an existing monopolist becomes perilous.

Thus, in the words of Profs. Stonier and Hague, "pure monopoly is merely a theoretical limiting case."

PRICE AND OUTPUT DECISION IN THE SHORT-RUN

The aim of the monopolist, like every other producer is to maximise his profit. Like competitive equilibrium, the monopoly equilibrium can be analysed in terms of (1) Total Revenue — Total Cost approach. (2) Marginal Revenue – Marginal Cost approach.

1. TOTAL REVENUE — TOTAL COST APPROACH

In Fig. 22.2 TR is the total revenue curve and TC is the total cost curve. TR curve first goes on rising, then flattens and finally slopes downwards indicating a fall in total revenue after a certain level of output. TC curve shows a constant rise as output increases. The monopolist will maximise his profits at that level of output where the vertical distance between TR and TC will be the highest. In other words, the level of output at which the slopes of TR and TC curves are equal. The monopolist will sell OQ output at AQ price. His profits will be AB. Any other level of output will give only a lesser level profit.

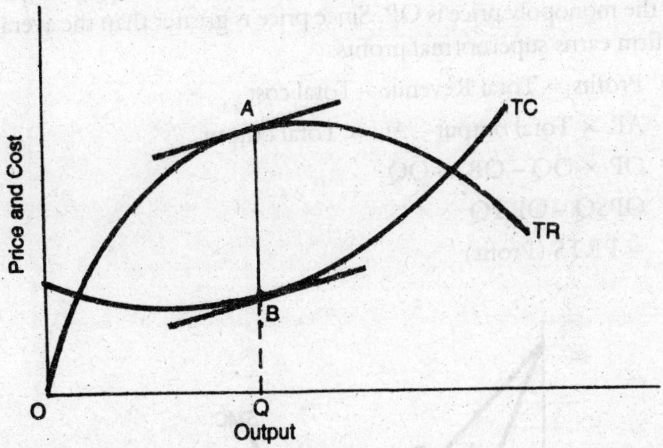

Fig. 22.2

2. MARGINAL REVENUE — MARGINAL COST APPROACH

Since the monopolist is the sole seller of a product for which there are no close substitutes, the monopolist faces the negatively sloped market demand curve for his product. This implies that the monopolist can sell more units of the product only by lowering its price. Because of this, the marginal revenue is smaller than the product price and the marginal revenue curve is below the demand curve. The monopolist's profits are maximum where MR = MC. This equality rule does not imply that the monopolist can earn a profit. This depends on the cost structure of the firm.

The necessary conditions for the monopolist to maximise his profits in the short run are analogous to those under perfect competition.

1. If ATC = P (Break-even)
2. If ATC > P (Loss)
3. If P > AVC (Business will be continued)
4. If P < AVC (shut down point)

Thus in the short run, the aim of the monopolist, like that of a perfect competitor, is to maximise profits or minimise losses.

1. Monopoly equilibrium when price is greater than Average cost (Supernormal profit)

Fig. 22.3 explains short run monopoly equilibrium at point E where SMC curve cuts the MR curve from below. The monopoly output is OQ and the monopoly price is OP. Since price is greater than the average cost, the firm earns supernormal profits.

Profits = Total Revenue – Total cost

AR × Total output – AC × Total output

OP × OQ – OR × OQ

OPSQ – ORTQ

= PRTS (Profit)

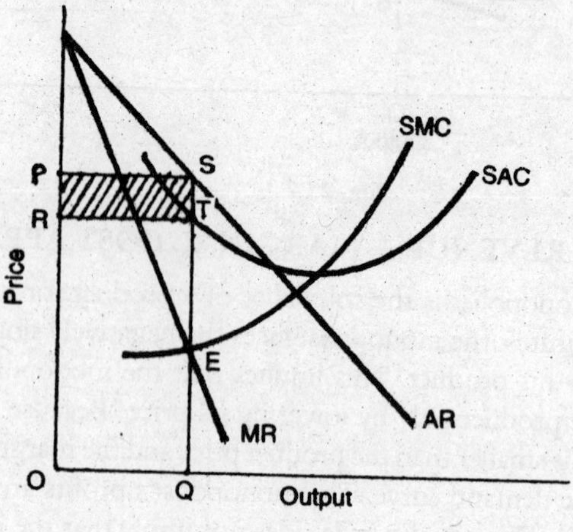

Fig. 22.3

Monopoly Equilibrium when price is equal to Average Cost (Normal Profits)

Fig. 22.4 illustrates a case in which the monopolist's earns only normal profits. When a firm earns only normal profits its price is equal to average cost.

Profits = Total Revenue – Total cost

= AR × Total output – AC × Total output

= OP × OQ – OP × OQ

= OPSQ – OPSQ

= Normal profits

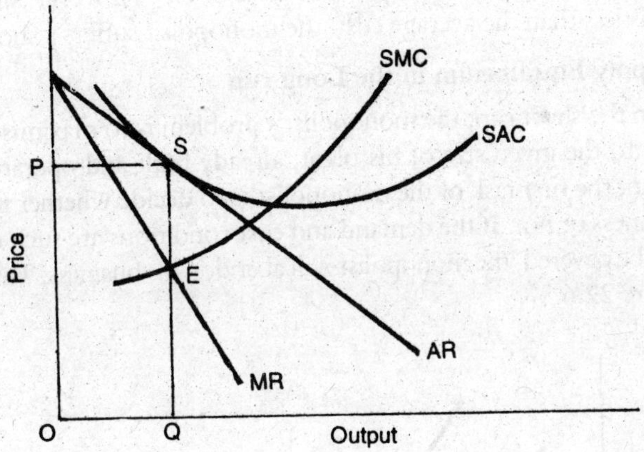

Fig. 22.4

Monopoly Equilibrium when price is less than Average Cost

Profits = Total Cost – Total revenue

= A.C. × Total output – AR × Total output

= OR × OQ – OP × OQ

= ORSQ – OPTQ = PRST (loss)

There is no certainty that the monopolist can always make a profit. In the short run, the monopolist may incur losses and continue to produce if his price covers more than his average variable cost.

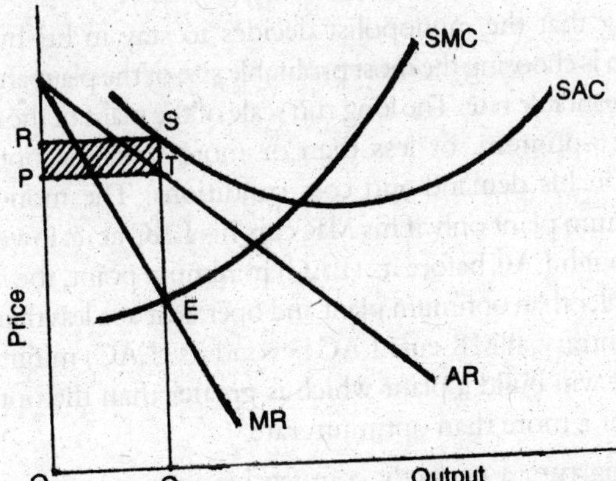

Fig. 22.5

In Fig. 22.5 the monopolist equates MR with MC and produces an output of OQ. He charges a per unit price of OP. However, since AR (or price) is less than the average cost, the monopolist suffers a short run loss.

Monopoly Equilibrium in the Long run

In the short run, the monopolist's problem is to maximise his profit subject to the given size of his plant, already built and operating. In the long run, the first task of the monopolist is to decide whether to continue his business or not. If the demand and cost conditions are such that, LAC, cannot be covered, the monopolist will abandon his business. This is shown in Figure 22.6.

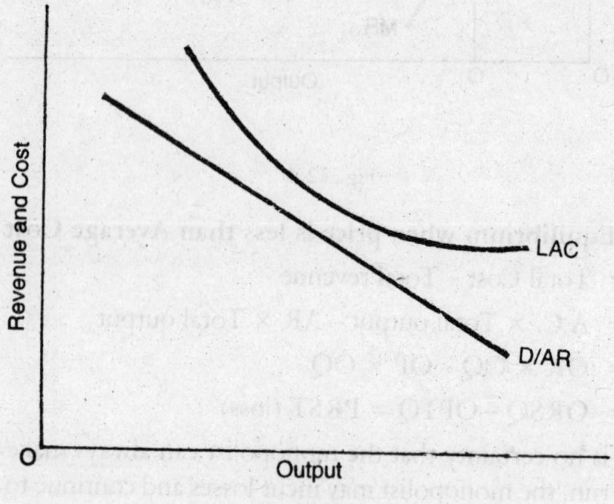

Fig. 22.6

Assuming that the monopolist decides to stay in his business, the second problem is choosing the most profitable size of the plant and operating it at the most profitable rate. The long run scale of the plant of the monopolist may be of the optimum, or less than or more than the optimum size depending upon his demand and cost conditions. The monopolist will build the optimum plant only if his MR cuts his LAC at its lowest point. If MR passes through LAC before its (LAC) minimum point, the monopolist will build a smaller than optimum plant and operate it at a less than optimum rate. On the contrary, if MR cuts LAC beyond its (LAC) minimum point, the monopolist will build a plant which is greater than the optimum size and operate it at a more than optimum rate.

In the long-run, a perfectly competitive firm receives only normal profits, because free entry and exit eliminates any profit or loss in the industry.

A monopolist, on the other hand, by virtue of his monopoly power, may enjoy his profit even in the long run because it is difficult for other firms to enter the market and break up the monopoly.

Table 22.1

Monopolists Criteria for Maximizing Profits

	Marginal Condition			*Average Condition*			
				Short-Run		*Long-Run*	
DECISION	MR>MC	MR=MC	MR<MC	P>SAVC	P<SAVC	$P \geq LAC$	P<LAC
	Raise output	Optimal output	Lower output	Produce	Shut down	Stay in business	Exit industry

1. Price control,
2. Control of monopolies through taxation,
3. A combined method of price control, subsidy and taxation,
4. Anti-monopoly Laws.

1. Price Regulation

Price regulation is a common feature in the case of public utilities like gas, water and telephone service etc. The price fixed by the government is generally lower than the monopoly price. This lower price will compel the monopolist to produce more in order to maximise his profit. Therefore the twin benefits of price regulations are:

1. Consumers obtain the monopoly product at a lower price.
2. The monopolist produces a larger quantity of output.

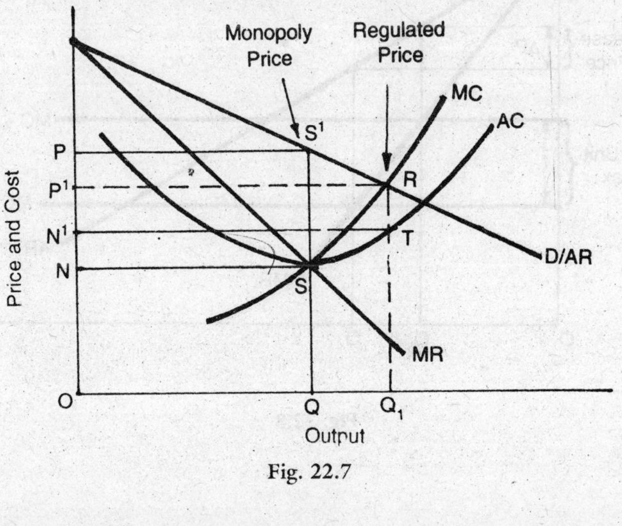

Fig. 22.7

This is explained with the help of Fig. 22.7.

The monopoly pricing is based on the principle of MC = MR. The monopoly output is OQ and the monopoly price is OP. Monopoly profits are equal to the area PS^1SN. The new regulated price is OP^1 ($=Q_1R$). At this price, the new output OQ_1 is greater than the initial output and is produced at a level at which the marginal cost equals the regulated price. Even though the monopoly price has been regulated, his loss in profit is compensated by the increase in output. The new profit is P^1RTN^1 ($P^1N^1 \times OQ_1$)

2. Control of Monopolies Through Taxation

Taxation is considered as a powerful weapon by the government to reduce the monopoly profits. The government may impose the following taxes: (1) A Specific tax. (2) A Lump sum tax. (3) A Profit tax.

(1) A Specific Tax

A specific tax per unit of output will cause an upward shift in the marginal cost by the amount of the tax. The effect is that the quantity produced declines and the price increases, although the increase in price is lesser than the amount of per unit tax.

Constant Marginal Cost Curve

For the sake of simplicity let us assume that the marginal cost is

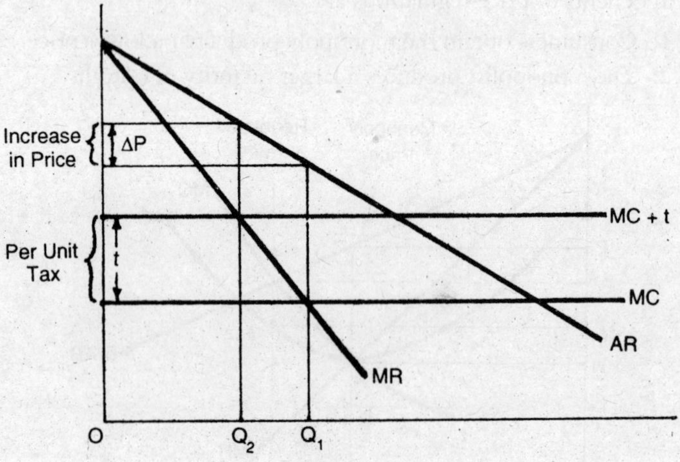

Fig. 22.8

constant. The following Fig. 22.8, will explain the concept more clearly.

MC is the horizontal marginal cost curve. AR is the average revenue curve and MR is the corresponding marginal revenue curve. Now suppose the government imposes a tax 't' per unit of output.

The new marginal cost curve is MC + t. Here the specific tax is treated as a variable cost. In this example, the increase in price is less than the amount of the tax. So the MC curve shifts from MC to MC + t.

(2) A Lump Sum Tax

A lump sum tax, simply taxes the monopolist by a fixed amount, regardless of the quanity of the product sold by him. A licence fee is a tax of this kind. A lump sum tax is like a fixed cost. So it causes an upward shift in the average cost curve. Since the marginal cost is independent of the fixed cost, its shape will not change. The net effect is that the price and output remain the same in both cases, but the per unit profit and the total

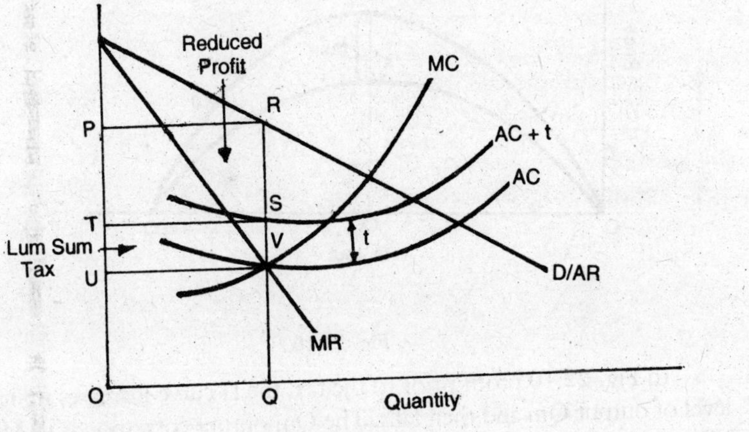

Fig. 22.9

profits of the monopolist's firm declines. This is explained in Fig. 22.9.

Table 22.2

	Per Unit tax	*AC*	*MC*	*Output*	*Price*	*Profit*	*Per Unit profit*
Before the tax	—	AC	MC	OQ	OP	PRVU	RV
After the tax	t	AC+t	MC	OQ	OP	PRST	RS

Thus there is no change in the price and output combinations even after the tax is levied. Therefore the amount TSVU goes to government's kitty. This levy of a lump sum tax helps the government to get some amount of the monopolist's exorbitant profits, which could be spent on welfare activities.

(3) A Profit Tax

Suppose the government imposes a tax of 50 per cent per period on the monopoly profits. How would such a tax affect the monopolist's pricing and output decision. For the sake of simplicity let us assume that the incidence and impact of the tax is entirely on the monopolist.

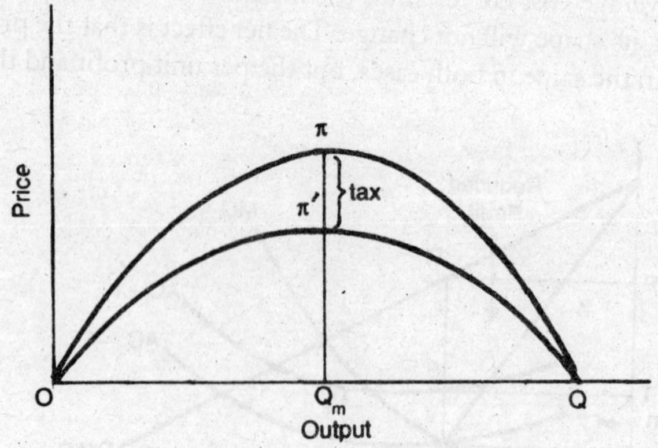

Fig. 22.10

In Fig. 22.10 profit prior to the tax, the Π curve increases up to the level of output Qm and then falls. The Qm output corresponds to MC = MR equality because at this level of output the total profit is maximum. After the imposition of the tax, profit is shown by the Π^1 curve. The curve clearly shows that at each level of output, the profit is one-half of the previous amount (i.e., Π^1Qm is half of ΠQm). Therefore, like the lump sum tax, the price and output decisions remain unchanged. The only thing is that the level of profit has been reduced to the amount of the tax.

3. A Combined Method of Price Control, Subsidy and Taxation

Mrs. Joan Robinson has suggested the tax and subsidy method to eliminate monopoly profits. The government may adopt price control and at the same time impose a condition on the monopolist that he should produce more than a certain fixed quantity of output at the regulated price.

In the above Fig. 22.11, AC_1 and MC_1 are the average and marginal cost curves of the monopolist's firm. The regulated price by the government is OP. But at this price, the marginal cost is greater than the average cost. It implies the existence of losses. In order to avoid this loss, the government now pays a subsidy which is an amount equal to the difference between the marginal cost and average cost, i.e., CE.

After the payment of subsidy the average and marginal cost curves of the monopolist are AC_2 and MC_2 respectively. Now, the new marginal cost curve MC_2 is equal to the regulated price, i.e., OP or QE = MC_2. But the new average cost curve AC_2 is less than the regulated price, i.e., AC_2 < OP. Therefore the monopoly firm earns super-normal profits equal to PE DF. These profits are absorbed by the government in the form of lump sum taxes. In the end the firm will earn only normal profit. It should be noted that the amount of profits PEDF are equal to the amount of subsidy BCEP.

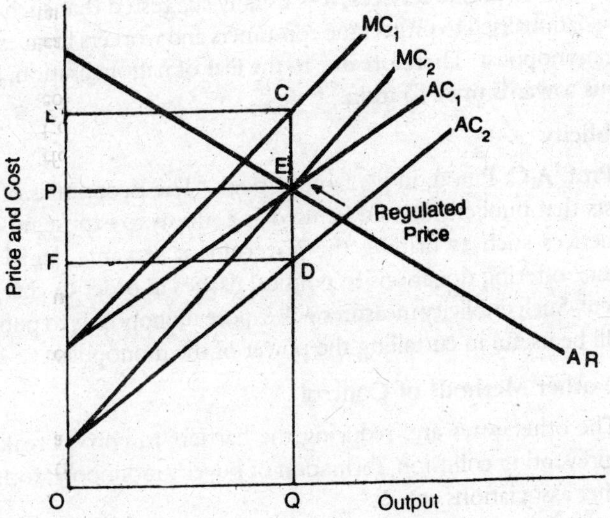

Fig. 22.11

4. Anti-Monopoly Laws

Anti-monopoly laws have been passed in various countries to curtail the power of the monopolists. On the basis of the recommendations made by the Monopolies Inquiry Commission, the Government of India introduced the necessary Bill in December 1969 and passed an Act called Monopolies and Restrictive Trade Practices Act, which came into force from June 1, 1970.

OTHER METHODS OF CONTROL

1. Limitations on Monopoly Power

The monopolist should not charge a price to take away all the consumer's surplus. Patents, copyrights and government monopolies are the possible cases where new entries may be restricted. The monopoly power is not endless. The monopoly power may be curtailed by the power of the suppliers of inputs and trade unions. This is termed as 'countervailing' power. He has to take into account factors like, composition of the commodity in the consumer's budget, availability of substitutes and the possibility of potential entrance. If the price is too high, the people may avoid purchasing monopoly products. Moreover, he has a knowledge of the elasticity of demand also for his product.

2. Nationalisation

When a monopolist produces public utilities such as gas, and electricity or provides telephone services, it is usually suggested that such industries may be nationalised to protect the consumers and workers from exploitation by the monopolist. Therefore due to the fear of nationalisation, he may be cautious towards price fixation.

3. Publicity

Prof. A.C. Pigou, in his famous book "The Economics of Welfare" suggests that publicity should be used as a means to expose monopolists' malpractices such as bribing the government servants, legislators and ministers, offering donations to political parties in order to charge higher prices etc. Such publicity measures will expose monopolists to public wrath, and will be useful in curtailing the power of the monopolist.

4. The other Methods of Control

The other ways are, reducing the barriers to entry, breaking large firms, preventing collusion, formation of buyer's monopoly, formation of consumer associations etc.

MONOPOLY AND PERFECT COMPETITION COMPARED

Since monopoly and perfect competition are polar extremes, a comparison between the two will illuminate their differences.

Perfect Competition	*Monopoly*
1. It is the most perfect form of competition	1. It is the negation of competition
2. Many Sellers	2. Single Seller
3. An individual Seller has no control over the market supply	3. Complete control over the market supply.
4. Product is homogeneous	4. Product has no close substitute
5. Firm is a price-taker	5. The firm (the monopolist) is a price maker
6. A competitive form determines its output at a given price	6. A monopolist can fix both price as well as its output to be sold in the market
7. Entry is free and easy	7. Entry is blocked
8. Prices are uniformly charged to all the buyers	8. Under discriminating monopoly, different prices may be charged to different buyers for the same product
9. Under Perfect competition, industry is composed of all the firms producing homogeneous goods	9. Under monopoly the firm itself is the industry
10. It is an ideal market in which there is no exploitation of buyers	10. A monopolist may exploit the buyers by charging higher prices.
11. A firm earns only normal profit in the long run	11. A monopoly firm may enjoy super normal profits in the long run
12. There is no excess capacity in production	12. Existence of excess capacity is possible

QUESTIONS

1. What are the features of monopoly?
2. What are the major determinants of the monopoly power of a firm? Explain with suitable examples.
3. How would a monopolist fix his price and output? Explain with diagrams.
4. Explain monopoly equilibrium in terms of marginal analysis.

5. What are the methods by which monopoly power can be contained in a developing country like India?
6. Why monopolies are regarded as evils in an economy? What are the conventional ways of regulating monopolies? Examine their potential effectiveness.
7. Write a note on 'Pure Monopoly.'
8. A monopolist can control either price or quantity but not both. Do you agree with this view? Why?
9. Distinguish between "Competitive Equilibrium" and "Monopoly Equilibrium."
10. How does a monopolist reach equilibrium when his fixed costs increase?
11. Explain the determination of price and output under monopoly and the importance of elasticity of demand in price determination.

❖ ❖ ❖

23

PRICE DISCRIMINATION

"In principles there are no value judgements in economics."

— Milton Friedman, 1967

INTRODUCTION

One of the pricing strategies most commonly used by a monopoly firm or a firm with monopoly power is called price discrimination.

A monopolist is a 'price maker' rather than a 'price-taker.' By virtue of his monopoly power, he is able to charge different prices to different customers for the same product. For example, if a radio-manufacturer charges Rs. 1000/- for a radio to one customer and Rs. 900/- for a similar radio to another customer, he practices discrimination in price between two buyers. Thus price discrimination occurs when a good or service is sold at different prices that do not reflect differences in production costs.

In the words of Mrs. Joan Robinson[1] "The act of selling the same article, produced under a single control, at different prices to different buyers is known as price discrimination."[1]

According to Prof. Stigler "sale of technically similar products at prices which are not proportional to their marginal cost is price discrimination."[2]

1. *The Economics of Imperfect Competition,* Macmillan & Co., Ltd., London, 1965, p. 179.
2. *The Theory of Price* — The Macmillan, London, 1966, p. 81.

FORMS OF PRICE DISCRIMINATION

Price discrimination may take several forms. Some important forms are given below:

1. Personal Discrimination

Price discrimination is personal when different prices are charged for different persons.

For example, Lawyers charge different rates of fees to different types of clients, depending on their income and status.

2. Time Discrimination

Time discrimination depends upon the time at which the service is being rendered. For example, telephone rates for STD during night time is less than during day time.

3. Age Discrimination

If discrimination is on the basis of age, it is referred to as age discrimination.

For example, bus transport companies and railways charge half the rates for children below 12 years of age.

4. Sex Discrimination

If different rates are charged for the same product or service on the basis of sex, it is known as sex discrimination.

For example, in certain cinema houses, ladies are admitted to shows at concessional rates.

5. Locational Discrimination

When a monopolist charges different rates for identical products on the basis of location, it is known as locational discrimination. For example, dumping.

6. Size Discrimination

On the basis of quantum of transactions, different rates may be charged, e.g., prices in the retail market is higher than prices in the wholesale market.

7. Quality Variation Discrimination

If the price discrimination is attributed to the quality of the product, it is called quality variation discrimination. For example, paper back is cheaper than the deluxe editions of the same book, meant for libraries.

8. Special Service Discrimination

If price discrimination is resorted to on the basis of comforts or special services, it is known as special service discrimination. For example, Air travel fee differs for first class travel from second class travel.

9. Use Discrimination

If different rates are charged for the same service on the basis of its use it is known as use discrimination. For example, Electricity board may charge less for industrial users and more for domestic users.

10. Product Discrimination

If discrimination is based on products it is known as product discrimination. For example, railways charge different rates for carrying coal and bales of cotton for the same distance.

DEGREES OF PRICE DISCRIMINATION

The renowned British English economist, Prof. A.C. Pigou[3] in his book the 'The Economics of Welfare' has given three degrees of price discrimination, viz.,

(*i*) First degree price discrimination,
(*ii*) Second degree price discrimination,
(*iii*) Third degree price discrimination.

First Degree Price Discrimination

Discrimination of the first degree is a limiting case. It can occur only when there are few buyers and the monopolist is shrewd enough to know the maximum price they will pay.

Price discrimination of the first degree occurs when the monopolist, by virtue of his monopoly power is able to charge the maximum price each consumer is willing to pay leaving for no consumer's surplus. Mrs. Joan Robinson calls this as 'perfect price discrimination.'

According to Prof. Robert Y. Ahw "The discriminatory pricing that attempts to take away the entire consumer's surplus is called first degree or perfect price discrimination."

For example, suppose there is only one neurosurgeon in the world capable of performing a rare brain operation. Anyone who wants to undergo this operation must come to the physician. The surgeon is therefore a monopolist with the power to engage in perfect price discrimination.

3. A.C. Pigou, *The Economics of Welfare,* Macmillan, London, 1952, p. 279.

This is also known as 'take-it-or-leave-it' price discrimination, because in negotiating with each buyer the monopolist charges him the price he is willing to pay under threat of denying the selling of any quantity to him; he offers each buyer a 'take-it-or-leave-it' choice.[4]

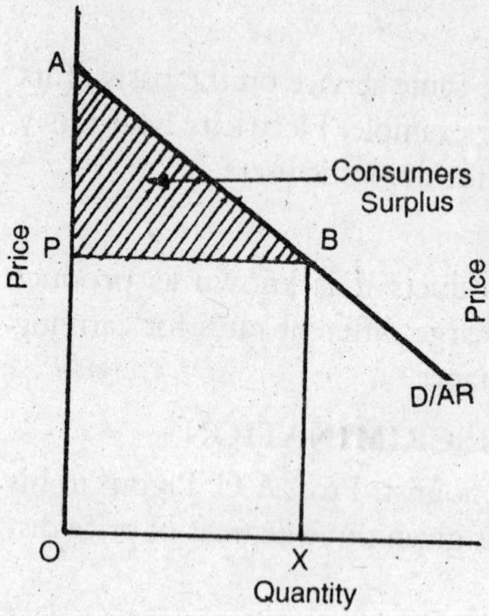

Fig. 23.1

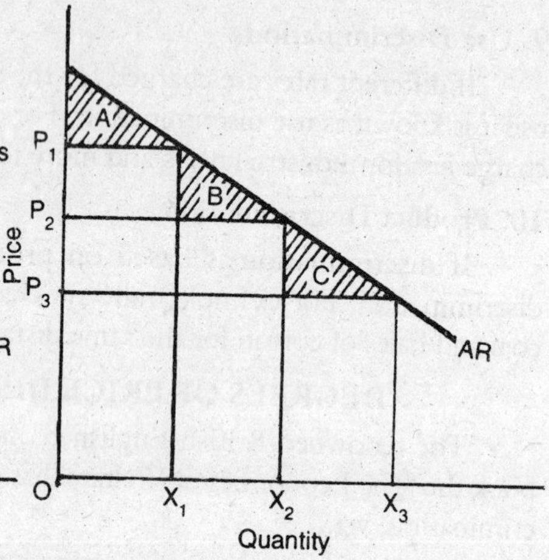

Fig. 23.2

$$C.S. = TU - (P \times Q)$$
$$= OABX - OPBX = APB$$

Second Degree Price Discrimination

The price discrimination of the second degree is practised when there are many customers with different tastes and with varying income levels. In this case, total revenue by charging discrimination is larger than total revenue obtained by charging a uniform price. In price discrimination of the second degree the firm captures parts of consumer's surplus.

In Fig. (23.2) it is assumed that the monopolist charges OP_1 price for OX_1 units, OP_2 for XX_2 units and OP_3 for X_2X_3 units. If the monopolist charges the same price OP_3, the total revenue will be less ($OP_3 \times OX_3$). But with three different prices the firm snatches parts of the consumers surplus. The surplus which is available to the consumer is shown by the triangles A, B and C.

4. A. Koutsoyiannis — *Modern Micro Economics* — Second Edition, The Macmillan Press Ltd., London, 1983, p. 195.

The second degree price discrimination is limited to services sold in blocks of small units, cubic feet of gas, kilowatt, hours of electricity, minutes of telephoning — that can be easily metered, recorded and billed.[5]

Third Degree Price Discrimination

A monopolist under third degree price discrimination divides his buyers into two or more than two sub-markets on the basis of elasticity of demand and charges a different price for consumers in each sub market. In price discrimination of the third degree, the firm does not take away any consumers surplus.

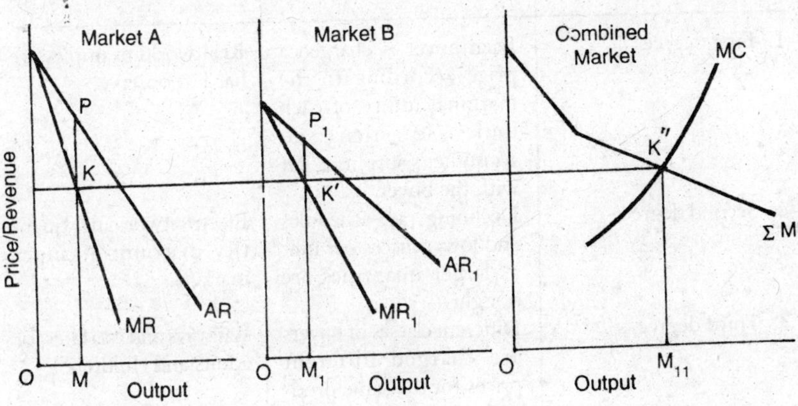

Fig. 23.3

For calculating the equilibrium output of the monopolist, the combined marginal revenue in the two sub-markets is to be traced. The combined marginal revenue (ΣMR) is obtained by the lateral summation of the two marginal revenue curves in the two sub-markets. This is shown in Fig. 23.3 (c). The marginal cost curve of the monopolist output (MC) cuts the ΣMR at output OM_{11}. At this output MR is $M_{11}K^{11}$.

The monopolist has to allocate the total output OM_{11} in the sub-markets in such a way that marginal revenue in each of the two sub-markets is equal to $M_{11}K^{11}$. He will sell output OM and charge price MP in market, 'A' which is less elastic and sell output OM_1 and charge price M_1P^1 in market 'B' which is more elastic.

5. D.S. Watson — *Price Theory and Its Uses,* 1986, Khosla Publishing House, New Delhi, 1986, p. 356.

Conditions for discriminating monopolist's equilibrium:

1. It must be profitable for him to sell his output in more than one market.
2. Marginal revenue in both the sub-markets must be the same.
3. Combined marginal revenue must also be equal to the aggregate marginal cost.

Prof. R.L. Miller[6] has given a very useful chart which provides in a nut shell the idea of the degree of price discrimination, as follows:

Type of Price discrimination	*Attribution*	*Illustrations*
1. First degree	Each buyer is charged a price according to the marginal utility of each unit, so that no consumer's surplus is left with the buyer.	Real world examples are hard to observe.
2. Second degree	Declining rate schedules and lower prices per unit as larger quantities are bought.	Electricity pricing, quantity discount at super markets.
3. Third degree	Different classes of buyers are charged different prices for the same product.	Railways and bus fares for adults and children.

WHEN PRICE DISCRIMINATION IS POSSIBLE

Price discrimination is practicable only when certain conditions are fulfilled.

1. There must be Some Imperfection in the Market

Under perfect competition price discrimination is impossible. The presence of an imperfect market is a prerequisite for price discrimination. When there are different markets, or where parts of the markets are separated by tariffs, consumer's ignorance, or transport costs, the monopolist can exercise some control over each market.

6. D.M. Mithani — *Economic Theory — Micro Analysis* — Himalaya Publishing House, 1987, p. 261 (Quoted).

2. Elasticities of Demand in the Different Markets must be Different

When elasticities are different the demand curves must slope differently. In order to maximise his profit, the monopolist will charge a higher price in the inelastic market and a lower price in the elastic market.

3. No 'Seepage' is possible between Markets or Different parts of the Same Market

Suppose an exporter in a particular country sells his goods at a cheaper rate in a foreign country and at a higher rate in the home country, reimport to the country of origin is not possible due to the presence of transport costs or physical controls.

According to Stonier and Hague[7] price discrimination can occur due to the following reasons:

1. Discrimination owing to Consumer's Preference

(*a*) It can happen when consumers in one part of the market do not know that prices are lower in another part of the same market.

(*b*) It can exist where the consumer has an irrational feeling that a higher price is co-related with a better quality product.

(*c*) Discrimination can occur if price discrimination is so small that the consumer does not think it worthwhile to pay any attention to it.

2. Discrimination based on the Nature of the Product

This type of discrimination occurs when the product in question is a direct service. While it is possible for hairpins to be resold by a customer who is charged a lower price to another who pays a higher price, it is impossible to do this with haircuts or beauty treatments effected in a beauty parlour, and so different prices cannot be charged for different persons for such services.

3. Discrimination because of Distance and Frontier Barriers

A product may be sold in one town for 10 paise and in another town for 20 paise. So long as the cost of transport exceeds the difference in prices, resale will not be profitable. Similarly, a monopolist can charge higher prices in a country levying tariff duty on his commodity and lower prices elsewhere where no such duties are levied. Because of import tariff it is obviously not profitable to import the commodity from countries where it is sold at a cheaper rate.

---

7. *A Textbook of Economic Theory*, Longman, London, 1988, pp. 203-204.

WHEN PRICE DISCRIMINATION IS PROFITABLE?

Price discrimination is profitable when there are variations in elasticity in the different markets. The monopolist will charge a higher price in the inelastic market and lower price in the elastic market. To use Mrs. Joan Robinson's words, "The sub-markets will be arranged in an ascending order of their elasticities, the highest price being charged in the least elastic market, and the lowest price in the most elastic market."[8]

Discrimination is Not Profitable when the Demand Curves are Iso-elastic

When in the two markets elasticity of demand is the same, then, the marginal revenue will also be the same.

The formula for Marginal Revenue = Average Revenue $\times \frac{e-1}{e}$, where 'e' stands for elasticity of demand.

Under discriminating monopoly, the monopolist aims at equating marginal revenue of one market with that of the other (i.e., $MR_A = MR_B$). To put in terms of mathematical equations,

$$MR_A = MR_B$$

$$= AR_A \frac{e_A - 1}{e^A} = AR_B \frac{e_B - 1}{e^B}$$

$$= P_A 1 - \frac{1}{e_A} = P_B 1 - \frac{1}{e_B}$$

Where P_A and P_B are the prices and e_A and e_B are the elasticities of demand in markets A and B respectively. If e_A equals e_B, P_A will be equal to P_B. This means that there will be no price discrimination.

In Fig. 23.4

AR_a = Average revenue in market A

MR_a = Marginal revenue in market A

AR_b = Average revenue in market B

MR_b = Marginal revenue in market B

At price OP, MR is the same in both the markets =

i.e., $M_1 R_1 = M_2 R_2$

8: *The Economics of Imperfect Competition, op. cit.*, p. 187.

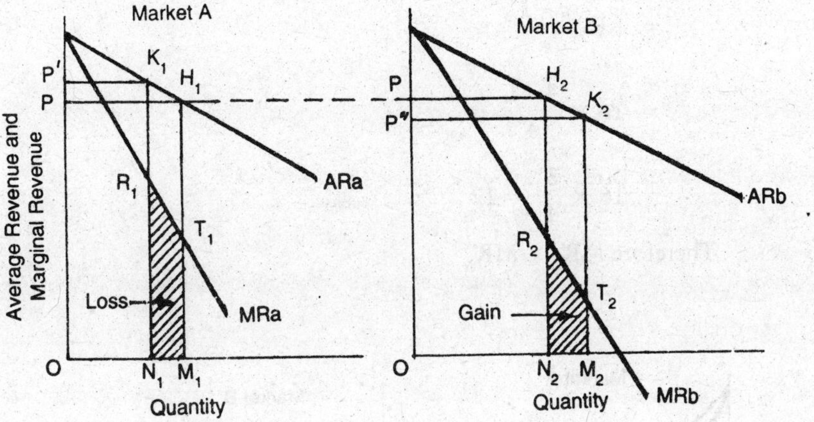

Fig. 23.4

Now let us suppose the monopolist transfers $N_1 M_1$ from market A and adds the same $M_2 N_2$ in market B.

In such a case

$$\text{Gain} = M_2 N_2 T_2 R_2$$

$$\text{Loss} = N_1 M_1 T_1 R_1$$

$$\text{Loss} > \text{Gain}$$

Therefore it is not profitable to shift any unit of the commodity from one market to another.

Price Discrimination is Profitable Only When Elasticities Differ

The monopolist will find it profitable to charge discriminatory prices only when the elasticities of demand in the two markets are different. If the elasticity of demand is different in each market and if the monopolist charges the same price, his profits will not be maximum.

Suppose the monopoly price is Rs. 16, the elasticity of demand in market A and market B are 2 and 4 respectively.

Then, the marginal revenue in market A

$$= AR \frac{e-1}{e}$$

$$= 16 \times \frac{2-1}{2} = 16 \times 1/2 = 8$$

The marginal revenue in market B

$$= AR \frac{e-1}{e}$$

$$= 16 \times \frac{4-1}{4}$$

$$= 16 \times \frac{3}{4} = 12$$

Therefore $MR_B > MR_A$

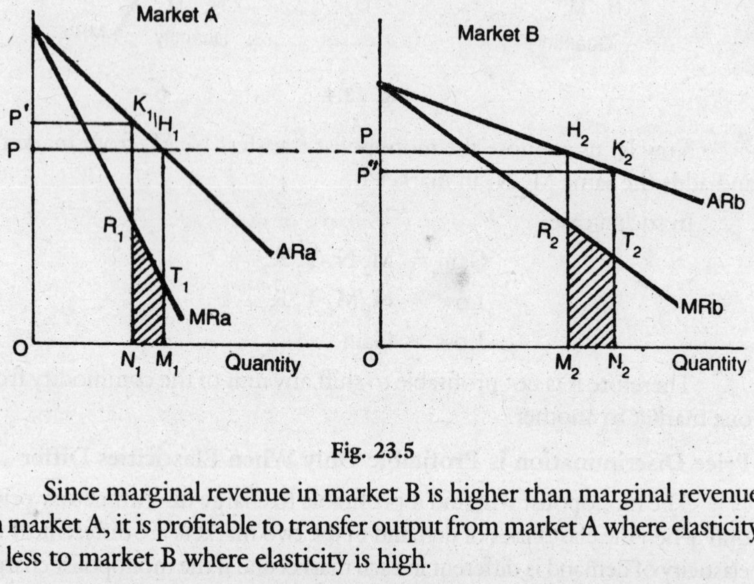

Fig. 23.5

Since marginal revenue in market B is higher than marginal revenue in market A, it is profitable to transfer output from market A where elasticity is less to market B where elasticity is high.

In the above Figure 23.5 elasticity of demand is greater in market B than in market A, which is indicated by the slope of the AR curves.

$$MR_B = M_2R_2$$

$$MR_A = N_1R_1$$

$$M_2R_2 > N_1R_1$$

Now if sale in market A is reduced by M_1N_1, the loss in revenue is $M_1N_1R_1T_1$. But if it is added in market B which is equal to M_2N_2 the gain in revenue is $M_2N_2R_2T_2$

$$M_2N_2R_2T_2 > M_1N_1R_1T_1$$

This process of shifting units from market A to market B will continue till $MR_A = MR_B$.

EFFECTS OF PRICE DISCRIMINATION

At least three effects can be traced out from the price output equilibrium process under discriminating monopoly.

1. It enhances the monopoly power of the producer,
2. Monopolist can reap higher profits,
3. The total output under discriminating monopoly, may be higher than under simple monopoly.

IS PRICE DISCRIMINATION BENEFICIAL TO SOCIETY?

Price discrimination has had a bad reputation. In the past, it has been condemned as illegal and immoral. In the United Kingdom and in the United States, railways were prohibited to charge discriminatory prices.[9]

Whether price discrimination is economically and socially justified will depend upon whether it is advantageous or pernicious to the interest and welfare of the consumers and for the society as a whole. In certain exceptional cases, price discrimination is advantageous to the society; at other times, it is bad.

As Prof. Lipsey rightly remarks, "whether or not an individual judges price discrimination to be an evil is likely to depend upon the details of the case, as well as upon his own personal value judgements...." Certainly there is nothing in economic theory to suggest that price discrimination is always in some sense worse than non-discrimination under conditions of monopoly or oligopoly.

1. Price Discrimination as a Means of Survival

According to Stigler, "Economists are considerably divided on the best pricing policy for an industry whose existence requires discrimination."

George J. Stigler[10] has given an illuminating example to make the point clear.

A community consists of two classes of consumers, with their respective demand curves for a commodity, D_1 and D_2. Adding these demand curves, the total demand curve is RST.

9. R.G. Lipsey — *An Introduction to Positive Economics,* ELBS, London, 1969, p. 332.
10. *The Theory of Price, op. cit.,* pp. 213-214.

We must note that the total demand curve RST lies below the AC curve at all levels of output. If the monopolist must charge a single price in both markets, there is no way by which he can recover his entire cost. By practising discrimination, the monopolist is able to survive and prosper.

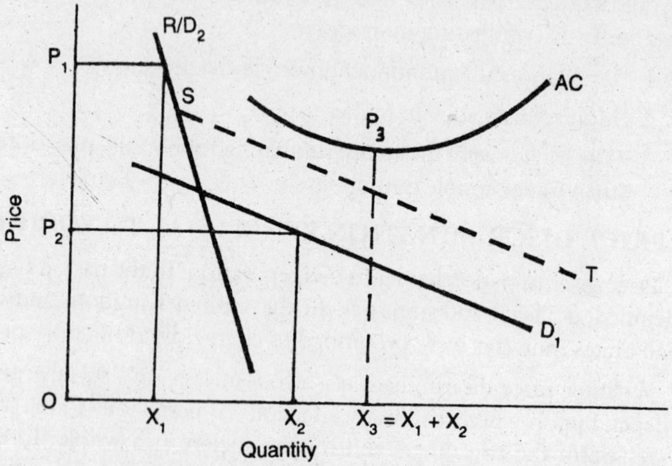

Fig. 23.6

With discrimination X_1 quantity can be sold at price P_1 and another quantity X_2 at price P_2 and the total quantity ($X_1 + X_2 = X_3$) can be sold for an average price P_3, which exceeds its cost.

Numerical Illustration

For example let us assume that at different levels of output the value of AC is as follows:

at X = 100, the AC = 20

at X = 400, the AC = 14

at X = 500, the AC = 9

If the firm can sell to the high income market 100 units of X at P_1 = 15 and the low income market 400 units at P_2 = 8, the firm's total revenue is

$$TR = R_1 + R_2 = X_1P_1 + X_2P_2$$
$$= 100\ (15) + 400\ (8)$$
$$= 4{,}700$$

and its total cost is

$$TR = (AC)(X) = (AC)(X_1 + X_2) = (9)(500) = 4500$$

Thus, with price discrimination the firm not only covers its total cost, but also realises an excess profit of Rs. 200.

2. Price Discrimination may help Weaker Sections of the Society

Many essential services such as services of railways or doctors cannot be provided profitably unless price discrimination is practised. Doctor's service in a rural village is often quoted for the necessity of price discrimination. If the doctor charges a uniform fee for all his patients, his income would be meagre. On the contrary, if he charges the well-to-do patients more than others, he can earn enough to continue to stay in the village. This is true in the case of railways also. In the words of Mrs. Joan Robinson, "It may happen for instance, that a railway would not be built or a country doctor would not set up his practice, if discriminations were forbidden."[11]

3. Egalitarian Society

Price discrimination has an equity value also. Under this principle, the rich pay more than the poor. The poor are more benefited at the cost of the rich people. Therefore from the point of view of reducing inequalities of income and wealth price discrimination is desirable.

4. More Output

One form of price discrimination, known as dumping may also result in increased output. If the monopolist produces only for the home market, production will be less and the average cost will be higher. On the contrary, if he produces both for the home and foreign markets, the average cost can be reduced. Though the price in the home market may be higher than in the foreign market, in the absence of dumping, price would be still higher.

Price Discrimination is Harmful

Price discrimination is harmful under the following circumstances:

1. When Profit Motive is the Only Consideration

Some private monopolists may practise price discrimination simply to increase profits. For example, an ice factory may charge higher prices for retail sale of ice in summer. This type of price discrimination must be controlled.

---

11. *The Economics of Imperfect Competition*, *op. cit.*, p. 203.

2. Misallocation of Resources

According to critics of price discrimination, there is concentration of resources in those industries which practise price discrimination. Moreover one of the paretian optimum condition for maximum satisfaction is

$$MRS_{xy}^{A} = MRS_{xy}^{B}$$

This condition is violated under the policy of price discrimination.

3. International Price Discrimination

In the international sphere, sometimes, dumping is deliberately resorted to eliminate rivals. Once the rival is eliminated higher prices may be charged again.

According to Joan Robinson, "From the point of view of the society as a whole, it is impossible to say whether price discrimination is desirable or not. It is obviously wasteful, from the point of view of the society, if any commodity fails to be produced up to the point where its marginal utility (shown by its demand price) is equal to its marginal cost."

DUMPING

In international trade the policy of price discrimination between two markets is known as dumping.[12]

Dumping is a special case of price discrimination in which a monopolist charges a higher price in the home market and a lower price in the foreign market.

Prof. William Fellner defines dumping as "the sale of goods in other countries below the exporter's total cost of production."[13]

But this definition is not correct because it does not clearly specify whether the cost of production refers to the average or marginal cost of production.

Prof. Haberler[14] defines dumping as "the sale of goods abroad at a price which is lower than the selling price of the same goods in the same circumstances at home taking account of differences in transport cost."

Under dumping, we assume that the monopolist enjoys monopoly power in the home market and faces perfect competition in the foreign

---

12. K.E. Boulding — *Micro Economic Analysis* — Fourth Edition, Harper & Row, New York, 1969, p. 501.
13. William Fellner — *Modern Economic Analysis* — International Student edition, 1960, p. 442.
14. G.V. Haberler, *The Theory of International Trade* — William Hodge and Company Limited, London, 1950, p. 296.

market. In other words, in the foreign market the elasticity of demand for the monopolist's product is elastic but in the home market elasticity of demand for his product is inelastic. Thus the monopolist's demand curve or average revenue curve in the foreign market is a horizontal straight line and coincides with the marginal revenue curve. In the home market the average revenue curve or the demand curve slopes downwards and the marginal revenue curve will lie below it.

MOTIVES OF DUMPING

The monopolist may resort to dumping for a variety of reasons.

1. To Get Rid of Surplus Production

It is possible that, due to a miscalculation of future demand the producer might produce more in relation to demand in the home market. This surplus production, if it is sold in the home market will depress the price of not only the extra output but the price of his entire product. To get rid of this surplus production he may sell the excess output even at a lower price in the foreign market.

2. To Crush Rivals in the Foreign Market

The intention of the monopolist may be to secure monopoly power by driving competitors away in the foreign market. Towards this end, he may charge a price which is lower than his marginal cost of production. Once the foreign rivals are crushed, and the market is cleared he can raise the price again to reap maximum profits even in the foreign market.

3. Economies of Production

If the monopolist sells his product in both the markets, output will be larger. When the size of a firm expands, the firm can obtain economies in various forms. This will lower the cost of production. In the absence of dumping, the output in the home market will be less. So, naturally the cost of production will also be higher. Thus he may adopt dumping to realise economies of production.

4. To Create Demand in Foreign Markets

Initially in order to woo the goodwill of the buyers in a new and as yet untapped market, he may set a lower price. But once the demand for his product is established and his product becomes attractive and popular in the foreign market, he may indulge in a price increase on a later occasion. Thus to develop new trade connections dumping may be practised.

5. To Take Advantage of Differences in Demand Elasticity

The monopolist may also resort to dumping because of the elastic nature of demand for his product. In the foreign market, there will be cut-throat competition among the various rivals, but in the home market there may be virtually no competition at all. Moreover the foreign consumer may possess substitutes for his product whereas consumers in the domestic country may not be in such a favourable position. So he can charge a higher price at home than abroad.

Price-output determination under dumping can be explained by the following Figure 23.7.

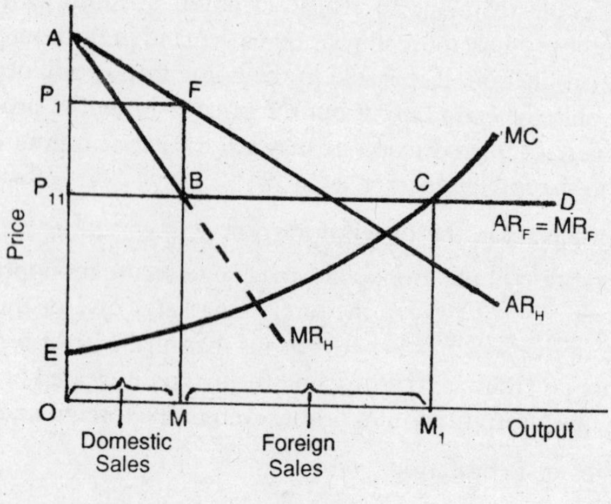

Fig. 23.7

AR_F = Average Revenue in the Foreign market

MR_F = Marginal Revenue in the Foreign market

AR_H = Average Revenue in the Home market

MR_H = Marginal Revenue in the Home market

MC = Marginal Cost

ABCD = Combined Marginal Revenue Curve

For equilibrium, the dumping monopolist must produce an output that equalises his marginal cost to his combined marginal revenue. The intersection of the monopolist's marginal cost curve with the combined marginal revenue curve at C gives a total output of OM_1 which maximises profit.

The total output OM_1 must now be shared between the two markets. The firm has to distribute it in such a way that $MR_H = MR_F = MC$. Accordingly the output sold in the home market is determined at OM and the rest MM_1 is sold in the foreign market. Price in the home market is MF while that in the foreign market is M_1C. The monopolist's total profits are represented by the shaded area ABCE. These profits are at a maximum and are contributed by both the markets.

QUESTIONS

1. What is a discriminating monopoly? Under what conditions is price discrimination possible and profitable?
2. Explain the degrees of price discrimination with suitable diagrams.
3. Explain the principles involved in the success of price discrimination. Do you think that price discrimination is anti-social?
4. Show graphically the price output determination in discriminating monopoly.
5. Price discrimination tends to be more common in the sale of services than in the sale of manufactured goods. Explain.
6. What is Dumping? How are price and output determined under dumping?
7. What are the conditions required for the existence of discriminating monopoly? Describe the pricing process.
8. Explain any two types of price discrimination.
9. What are the effects of monopoly price discrimination on the consumer society of a country?
10. Discuss the conditions under which price discrimination can be successfully practised.
11. Explain the concept of price discrimination under monopoly. Under what conditions it is possible and profitable?

24

MONOPSONY

"Monopolies are sacrifices of the many to the few."

—*James Madison 1788*

Monopsony refers to monopoly on the buyer's side. In the words of Hugh Gravelle[1] "Monopsony is defined as a market in which there is a single buyer of a commodity who confronts many sellers." The essential feature of pure monopsony is that there is only one firm, that is the buyer of an input in a particular market. Pure monopsony is as rare as pure monopoly. A single mining firm that employs all workers in mining jobs in an isolated frontier town would be an example of pure monopsony.

Just as the monopolist is interested in getting maximum profits, the monopsonist is interested in getting maximum surplus. To get maximum surplus he equates marginal cost (that is the cost of buying an additional unit) with marginal utility. This process has been shown in Fig. 24.1.

D is the demand curve. This demand curve shows the marginal utility of the input. So the demand curve is the same as the marginal utility curve. The supply curve of the input is assumed to be constant. Equilibrium is attained at the point where marginal utility is equal to marginal cost. R is the point of equilibrium at which MU = MC. The equilibrium price and quantity are OP and OM respectively.

1. Gravelle H. and Rees R. *Micro Economics,* 7th edn., Longman, Inc., New York, 1988, p. 380.

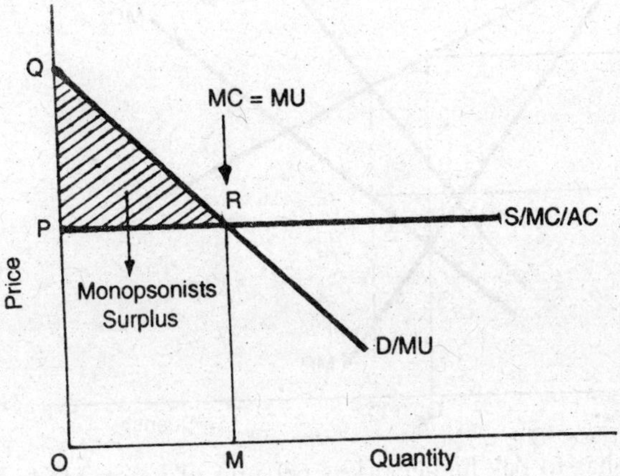

Fig. 24.1

Monopsonist's surplus = Amount, the monopsonist is willing to pay – actual amount, the monopsonist pays.

$$OQRM - OPRM = PQR$$

Thus the shaded portion of the figure PQR represents monopsonist's surplus.

Suppose the supply of an input service to a firm with monopsony power is upward sloping. To obtain larger quantities of the input, the

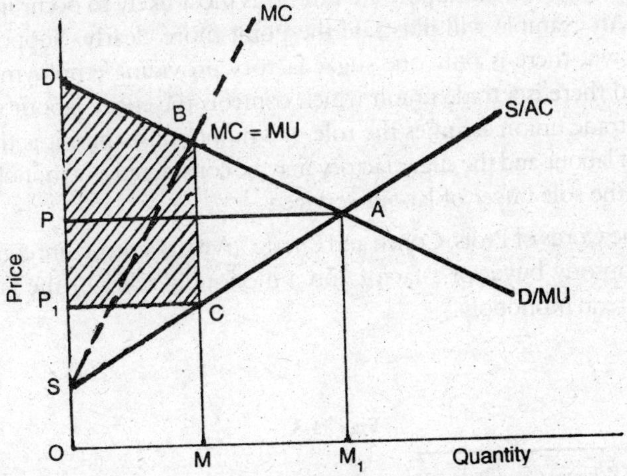

Fig. 24.2

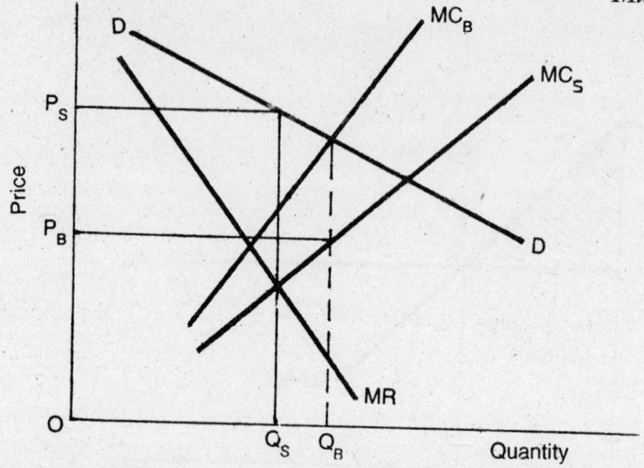

monopsonist has to pay higher prices per unit of input. SS denotes the average cost curve. Correspondingly marginal cost is also shown by the dotted line MC.

In Fig. 24.2 the equilibrium is attained at the point B where MC = MU. The total expenditure of the monopsonist is OM × MC = OP_1CM. But the total amount which he is willing to pay for OM input is ODBM. The monopsonist's surplus is shown by the shaded area P_1DBC.

BILATERAL MONOPOLY

Bilateral monopoly is a special case of a market structure in which a single seller (monopolist) faces a single buyer (monopsonist). Real world examples of bilateral monopoly are rare. It is most likely to occur in factor markets. An example will illustrate the point more clearly. Suppose in a remote town, there is only one sugar factory providing employment for labour and there is a trade union which controls the entire labour supply. Now the trade union assumes the role of a monopolist since it is the only supplier of labour and the sugar factory may be considered as a monopsonist since it is the sole buyer of labour serviced.

In the words of Profs. Cohen and Cyert,[2] "A market structure consisting of a monopsony buyer of a factor and a monopoly seller of the factor is called bilateral monopoly."

Fig. 24.3

2. Cohen K.J. and Cyert R.M., *Theory of the Firm*, 7th Edn., Prentice Hall of India Private Limited, New Delhi, 1981, p. 278.

In Fig. 24.3 DD is the demand curve, MR is the marginal revenue curve, and MC is the marginal cost curve of the single seller. If the monopolist is powerful he will make the buyer behave as though there were many buyers as under perfect competition. He will equate his MC with MR and produce Q_S quantity of output and will charge P_S price.

However if the single buyer (monopsonist) is powerful, he can make the monopolist behave like a perfect competitor. Thus MCs will be the monopolist's supply curve. Corresponding to this supply curve, we can construct the MC_B curve, which shows the marginal cost of buying an additional unit. MC_B exceeds price and to enable it to purchase an additional unit, the buyer must pay a higher price. And that higher price will pertain to all the units purchased. The buyer equates his marginal cost of buying an additional unit with the marginal value of an additional unit (as given by the demand curve) and purchases Q_B units. Since the seller is behaving like a competitor with the supply curve MCs, he will sell Q_B units at a per unit price of OP_B.

Under bilateral monopoly, if one of the parties refuses to accept the conditions of exchange put forth by the other, exchange will not take place. This type of market is also known as the theory of bargaining. The final outcome obviously depends upon the relative strength and bargaining skills of the two parties as also upon so many other factors.

QUESTIONS

1. Discuss how input prices are determined under a monopsonistic market condition.
2. Explain why price is indeterminate under bilateral monopoly.
3. Analyse the characteristics of monopsony.
4. What is monopsony? Explain price determination under bilateral monopoly.

25

MONOPOLISTIC COMPETITION

"Both monopolistic and competitive forces combine in the determination of most prices."

— E. H. Chamberlin

INTRODUCTION

Monopoly and perfect competition are mutually exclusive and many industries fall in between them. While perfect competition is a myth, pure monopoly is a rarity. In actual life it is difficult to find examples of perfect competition and pure monopoly. The theories of perfect competition and monopoly have constituted "classical" micro economic theory from Marshall to Knight.[1]

In the late 1920s and early 1930s economists expressed their disappointment and displeasure with perfect competition and pure monopoly as tools in explaining real world's business behaviour. Some duopoly models like Cournot and Edgeworth were developed before the 1930s. But they were considered as academic intellectual exercises rather than explaining real world situations. In fact, in 1926, Piero Sraffa in his article "The Laws of Returns under Competitive Conditions" pointed out the necessity for abandoning both perfect competition and pure monopoly.

In 1933, the price theory was reformulated by the pioneering works of Prof. Edward H. Chamberlin's "The theory of Monopolistic

1. C.E. Ferguson, *Micro Economic Theory*, 1st edn., AITBS, New Delhi, 1983, p. 299.

Competition:" — A reorientation of the theory of value, and Prof. Joan Robinson's "The Economics of Imperfect Competition." These economists launched a heavy attack on the orthodox neo-classical models of the firm.

Although there are similarities in their books, there are major differences as well.

A market for a product is said to be perfectly competitive if the following conditions are satisfied.

1. A large number of buyers and sellers.
2. Homogeneous product.
3. Free entry and exit of firms.
4. Perfect knowledge on the part of the buyers.
5. Perfect mobility of the factors of production.
6. No transport costs.

The absence of any one or two conditions will make the market an imperfect one. But imperfect competition or market is a loose term, referring to a multitude of market situations.

If we say that the wall of a room is painted white, we can easily visualise a white wall; but if we say that a particular wall is not white we cannot really visualise the colour of the wall. For, it is possible that the wall is painted black or blue, or red, or orange, and so on. Likewise, perfect competition refers to a market situation whereas imperfect competition does not specify the market.[2] The imperfect market may be duopoly, oligopoly, monopsony, oligopsony, etc.

We shall explain the whole matter with the help of a simple chart.

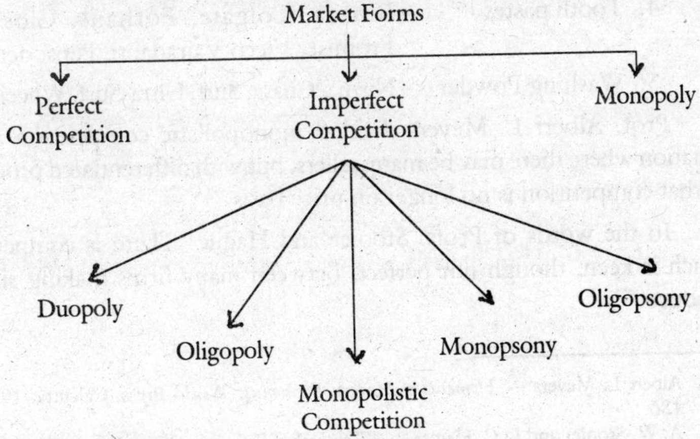

2. K.P.M. Sundharam, *Micro Economics,* Sultan Chand & Sons, New Delhi, 1988, p. 330.

Thus perfect competition and pure monopoly are two extremes and imperfect competition is a middle ground between the two. Monopolistic competition is thus a form of imperfect competition

DEFINITION OF MONOPOLISTIC COMPETITION

If perfect competition is the thesis, monopoly is the anti-thesis, then monopolistic competition is the synthesis between the two.

Monopolistic competition refers to a market situation in which a large number of sellers are offering similar but not identical products. As Chamberlin pointed out, it is a blend of competition and monopoly. Therefore both competitive and monopoly elements exist side by side in such a market. The number required, to refer to monopolistic competitive firms may be 25, 40, 55 or 70. Retail stores in large cities are generally monopolistically competitive in nature; general stores, medical stores, restaurants, barber shops, dry cleaners, bicycle repair shops, shoe making industry, food processing industry and so on are good examples for a monopolistic competitive market.

The following are some examples of monopolistic competition in the Indian context:

1. Shampoo — Sunsilk, Clinic Plus, Ponds, Chik, Velvette, Kadal, Handy, Khushbu.
2. Blades — Swiss, Ashok, 7 'O' clock, Laser, Wilkinson Sword.
3. Tea — Three Roses, Ruby, A.V.T. Premium, Brooke Bond.
4. Tooth pastes — Binaca, Colgate, Forhans, Close-up, Promise, Vicco Vajradanti, Pepsodent.
5. Washing Powder — Nirma, Chase, Surf, Ultra-Surf, Wheel, Rin.

Prof. Albert L. Meyers defined monopolistic competition as "A situation where there may be many sellers, but with differentiated products, so that competition is no longer on price basis."[3]

In the words of Profs. Stonier and Hague "There is competition which is keen, though not perfect, between many firms making similar products."[4]

---

3. Albert L. Meyers — *Elements of Modern Economics,* World Press, Calcutta, 1956, p. 186.
4. A. W. Stonier and D.C. Hague — *A Textbook of Economic Theory,* Longmans, 1988, p. 211.

Features of Monopolistic Competition

The following are the main features of monopolistic competition.

1. Large Number of Sellers

The number of firms under monopolistic competition is relatively large, but it is not as large as under perfect competition. Since there is homogeneity of goods, competition is keen though not perfect.

2. Product Differentiation

Product differentiation is the corner stone of monopolistic competition. Product differentiation is the process of altering goods that serve almost identical purposes so that they differ in minor ways. As Chamberlin pointed out, the products are heterogeneous rather than homogeneous. But the products are only marginally differentiated. Therefore the cross elasticity of demand among the products are high.

Product differentiation like beauty is in the eyes of the beholder — and in economics the beholder is always the buyer.[5]

Product differentiation creates brand loyalty. The products may be differentiated in the following ways.

(1) By Changing the Quality of the Product

Real or physical differences may be created through changes in design, colour, materials used and the style of the product.

(2) By Advertisement

Advertisement and sales promotion measures pave the way to create imaginary or artificial differences. Nowadays there is an irrational taste among consumers for products which are splashed on television, screens, newspapers or voiced through the radio. Product differentiation may also exist with respect to conditions surrounding its sale such as, the convenience or store location, delivery at the door step, credit facility, prompt service, the nice million dollar smile of the sales girl, gifts, etc.

(3) By Patent Rights and Trade Marks

Patent rights and trade marks also play their part to create product differentiation. For example, Coca Cola is a patent right granted by the U.S. Congress to their inventions. Trade marks like Pears, Rexona, Mysore Sandal etc. provide varieties to consumers to prefer as per their choice.

---

5. Milton H. Spencer, *Contemporary Economics,* Worth Publishers New York, 1974, p. 430.

3. Non-Price Competition

Product variations and selling costs are alternative methods adopted by firms to increase sales. Since the products are slightly differentiated, selling cost is an inevitable variable which affects the sales pattern. Therefore, through advertisement the seller seeks to achieve a delicate balance between commodity homogeneity and heterogeneity.

(4) Freedom of Entry and Exit

Like perfect competition, the firms under monopolistic competition are free to enter or leave the industry. When firms in an industry are making super normal profits, new firms with a slight difference in the product will enter and the excess profit will be washed away. Therefore the firms will earn only normal profits in the long-run.

(5) Independent Behaviour

Another noticeable feature of monopolistic competition is that it has an independent price policy. Under perfect competition, the firm is simply a 'price taker' and it has to adjust the output according to the prevailing price which is determined by the two forces of demand and supply. Since the number of firms under monopolistic competition is large, if a firm lowers its price, its impact is thin by its spread over many of its rivals so that the sales damage caused to the rivals will be negligible. Therefore there is no possibility of retaliation in the form of price war as under oligopoly.

EQUILIBRIUM UNDER MONOPOLISTIC COMPETITION

Under perfect competition, the individual seller can sell as much as he pleases at the on going price. Under monopolistic competition, his market is separate from that of his rivals to some extent. The firm's sales are limited by three factors:

1. Price,
2. The nature of the product, and
3. Advertising outlays.

The present analysis is based on Prof. Edward H. Chamberlin's "The theory of Monopolistic Competition."

1. Price Problem

The demand curve facing a firm under perfect competition is horizontal and the firm has no independent price problem. It can produce and sell any level of output as it pleases at the prevailing price. But the demand curve facing a firm under monopolistic competition is sloping downwards to the right.

Since the products are slightly differentiated, from its rivals, consumers can find many close substitutes for the product, so that the monopolistically competitive firm's demand curve is highly price elastic.

By way of product differentiation the firms create 'Brand loyalty' or 'Store loyalty.' The downward sloping demand curve indicates that a seller can raise his price to some extent without losing all of his customers. Likewise it can lower its price to attract new customers to his kingdom but cannot get all the customers of other similar products.

A firm under monopolistic competition will try to get maximum profits. Towards this end, it may increase its profits by raising the price and selling less or by lowering its price and selling more. Thus price-output adjustment becomes necessary for a firm under monopolistic competition.

2. Nature of the Product

The second problem faced by a firm is the adjustment of his product through product variations. The volume of its sales depends upon the manner in which his product differs from those of his competitors. Product variation refers to an alteration in the quality of the product such as technical changes, a new design, better materials, a new and attractive package or container, prompt and courteous service, a different way of doing business or a different location. Where the possibility of differentiation exists, the sales depend upon the skill with which the product is distinguished from others.

3. Advertising Outlay

Selling costs play an important part under monopolistic competition. Every seller tries to influence the volume of his sales by incurring additional expenditure. Additional expenditure implies expenditure over and above his cost of production. Just as he adjusts price and products to maximise his output, he adjusts his advertising outlay and demand for his product in such a way as to ensure that his profits are maximum. Under perfect competition, selling cost is a waste, because the seller can sell any quantity at the existing price. But under monopolistic competition due to keen rivalry among producers, it is inevitable to attract other customers towards his side. Gains from advertising expenditure under monopolistic competition are due to two factors.

(*i*) imperfect knowledge on the part of the buyers as to what type of product would give him the maximum satisfaction.

(*ii*) the possibility of altering wants by advertising or selling appeal.

Monopolistic competition therefore involves a complex problem with respect to all the three variables, viz., (*i*) price, (*ii*) product and (*iii*) selling outlay. It would be a very much complicated affair to discuss their effects simultaneously. We shall therefore, discuss individual equilibrium with reference to prices and output adjustment, with the assumption that product variation is constant and that selling costs are absent. In the end of the chapter, we shall discuss selling costs in detail.

INDIVIDUAL EQUILIBRIUM

Now the question is optimum price output combination for a monopolist. Like every seller, whether a monopolist or perfect competitor, he wants to reap maximum profits. Therefore the seller will go on producing till marginal revenue is equal to marginal cost, where profits will be maximised. If MR > MC, it is beneficial to the producer to produce more and on the contrary if MC > MR, it is necessary to reduce output. The desirable level of output is at the point where MC = MR.

In the short-run a monopolistically competitive firm may reap super normal profits, or incur losses.

Short Run Individual Equilibrium with Super Normal Profits

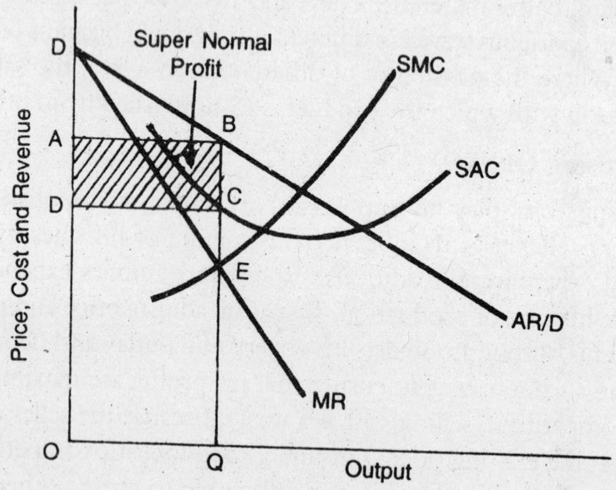

Fig. 25.1

Total Profit: AR × Total output – AC × total output

QB × OQ – QC × OQ

= OQBA – OQCD

= ABCD (Gain)

In Fig. 25.1 SAC and SMC are respective short-run average and marginal cost curves. DD is the demand curve or average revenue curve. At point E, MC = MR. The firm's equilibrium output is OQ. Average revenue BQ is greater than the average cost CQ. The total cost is OQCD and the total revenue is OQBA. The excess revenue between the two (ABCD) is the maximum supernormal profit. The rationale behind this super-normal profit is that other rival firms are not able to produce substitutes with a high cross elasticity of demand. The super normal profits lure new firms to enter, carrying the profits to be competed away.

Short Run Individual Equilibrium with Losses

In Fig. 25.2 the firm incurs losses because its price is less than its short run average cost at the equilibrium level of output. BQ is the average cost and CQ is the average revenue. The total losses are equal to the area ABCD. This loss may cause an exodus of inefficient firms from the industry.

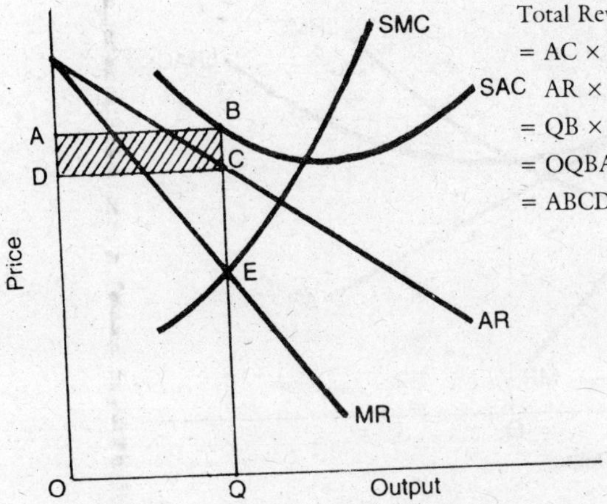

Total profit = Total cost-
Total Revenue
= AC × Total output
AR × Total output
= QB × OC - QC × OQ
= OQBA - OQCD
= ABCD (Loss)

Fig. 25.2

Long Run Individual Equilibrium with Normal Profits

As we have seen above, the firms under monopolistic competition may earn super normal profits in the short-run. Since entry is free, new firms with slightly differentiated products may enter the industry. As new firms enter and start production, supply will increase and the price will fall. In this way, the super normal profits will be competed away and the firms will earn only normal profits. On the other hand, the firms which suffer losses will leave the industry so that the remaining firms will be earning only normal profits. But an important point that has to be noted under long-run, is that the average revenue curve will be more elastic, since a large number of substitutes will be available in the long-run.

In Fig. 25.3 the long-run equilibrium is shown. Here the average revenue curve is tangent to the long-run average cost curve at M. Therefore the long-run equilibrium output is OQ. The average revenue and average cost are equal to QM. Therefore the firms will earn only normal profits which include the cost of production.

In the short-run there is only one condition for equilibrium, i.e., Marginal revenue = Marginal cost.

In the long-run, it has to satisfy both the conditions that,

Marginal revenue = Marginal cost and

Average revenue = Average cost

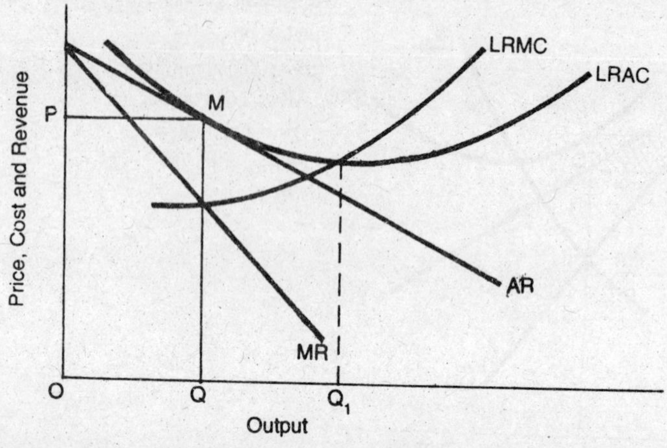

Fig. 25.3

Less than Optimum

The long-run equilibrium of a firm under monopolistic competition is similar to a firm under perfect competition in the sense that both are earning only normal profits. However, one vital difference exists. Under perfect competition, output will be produced up to the minimum point of the long run average cost curve. But under monopolistic competition output is stopped not at the minimum point of LRAC curve, but at the falling portion of the LRAC curve. Therefore the output under monopolistic competition is lesser than the optimum output under perfect competition. Therefore on the basis of the above diagram, we can show that there exists an excess capacity to the extent of QQ_1.

EXCESS CAPACITY

Prof. Edward Chamberlin's "The theory of Monopolistic Competition" and Joan Robinson's "theory of Imperfect Competition" point out the existence of an excess capacity. The concept is not new. Reference to excess capacity was made in the earlier works of Wicksell, Cairnes and Piero Sraffa also. But the credit for the systematic development of the concept goes to Prof. Chamberlin followed by Kaldor, Kahn, Harrod and Cassels.

THE CLASSICAL CONCEPT OF EXCESS CAPACITY

All classical economists including Marshall and Pigou were of the view that the society's welfare will be maximised, if production is carried on up to the minimum point of the long-run average cost curve.

The concept is defined as "the difference between ideal output and the output actually attained in the long-run." Excess capacity results in a higher consumer price. To put it in other words, the difference between the output corresponding to minimum LRAC curve and that produced by the monopolistically competitive firm in the long-run is called excess capacity.

The obvious examples of excess capacity are neighbourhood barber shops, gas stations, drug stores and grocery stores.

The production of ideal output under perfect competition is shown by the following Figure 25.4.

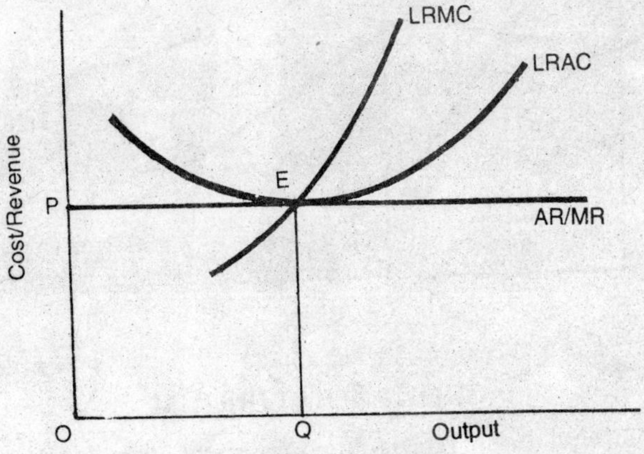

Fig. 25.4

The horizontal axis measures output and the vertical axis measures cost and revenue. The firm is in equilibrium at the level of output OQ where the long-run average cost is minimum. Here the double conditions of equilibrium are fulfilled.

1. LRMC = MR
2. AR (price) = minimum LRAC

Thus the ideal output under perfect competition reveals the absence of excess capacity.

Long Run Equilibrium of a Firm under Monopolistic Competition

In Fig. 25.5 the firm is in long-run equilibrium at the level of output OM at which marginal revenue is equal to marginal cost. Here the equilibrium is attained at the point where the long-run average cost curve is tangent to the average revenue curve. But an important point to be noted is that the average cost curve at this point is falling and continues to fall up to ON level of output. By producing its output up to ON the firm can reduce its average cost, which in turn will be beneficial to the society. This means that this firm is producing MN output less than the ideal output of ON. Thus MN represents the existence of excess capacity under monopolistic competition.

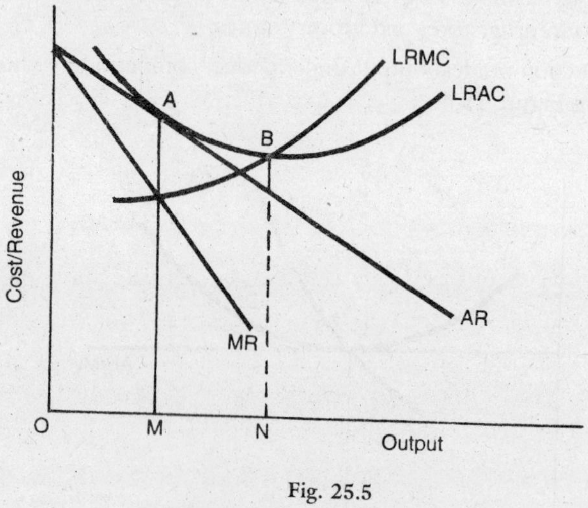

Fig. 25.5

GROUP EQUILIBRIUM

Group equilibrium refers to the adjustment of prices and "products" of a number of producers whose goods are fairly close substitutes. The word industry under perfect competition refers to all the firms producing a homogeneous product. Under monopoly there is no distinction between a firm and an industry. The concept becomes fuzzy under monopolistic competition, because of product differentiation. An industry may be defined as one having two or more groups. A group is a collection of firms producing products which are close substitutes. In other words, a group consists of products with high cross elasticities of demand. Firms can enter the product group and their entry will have important repercussions in the market.

An example may illustrate the difference between industry and 'group' very clearly. In the book industry, there may be several groups. One group may be publishing detective novels, another group may be dealing in religious books, a third group may be publishing textbooks and so on. Competition among the groups are not severe, but competition within a group is keen.

Problems in Group Equilibrium

The qualitative variation of products in the group leads to wide differences in the cost curves of the various firms. Likewise, the difference in the buyer's preferences may result in a variety of demand curves in respect of shape (elasticity) as well as their position (distance from horizontal and vertical axis). All these result in heterogeneity of prices, outputs and profits of the various firms in the group. In these circumstances, an analysis of group equilibrium becomes complex and complicated. Therefore Chamberlin explains the group equilibrium with the following assumptions:

1. There is a large number of firms producing differentiated products, which are close substitutes for each other's products.

2. Each firm has an independent price policy and faces a fairly elastic demand curve.

3. Any adjustment of price or of 'product' by a single producer spreads its influence over so many of his competitors that the impact felt by any one is negligible and does not lead him to any readjustment of his own situation. Prof. Stigler calls this assumption as 'symmetry assumption.'

4. The last is a heroic assumption which states that "both demand and cost curves for all the 'products' are uniform throughout the group. It is required only that consumer preferences be evenly distributed among the different varieties, and that differences between them be not such as to give rise to differences in cost."

If the demand curves of all the firms in a group are same, it would mean that all the firms have an equal share in the market. Suppose there are 50 firms in a group, then each firm has a 2 percent share of the total sales of the group.

Chamberlin develops his theory of group equilibrium by using two types of demand curves DD and dd. DD is the demand curve a firm faces if all firms charge the same price. dd is the demand curve, if the other firms do not charge the same price.

Long-Run Equilibrium: Price Competition: Closed Entry

In Fig. 25.6 DD and dd are the two types of demand curves. LRAC is the long-run average cost curve. The corresponding marginal revenue curve and the long-run marginal cost curve have been omitted to simplify the analysis.

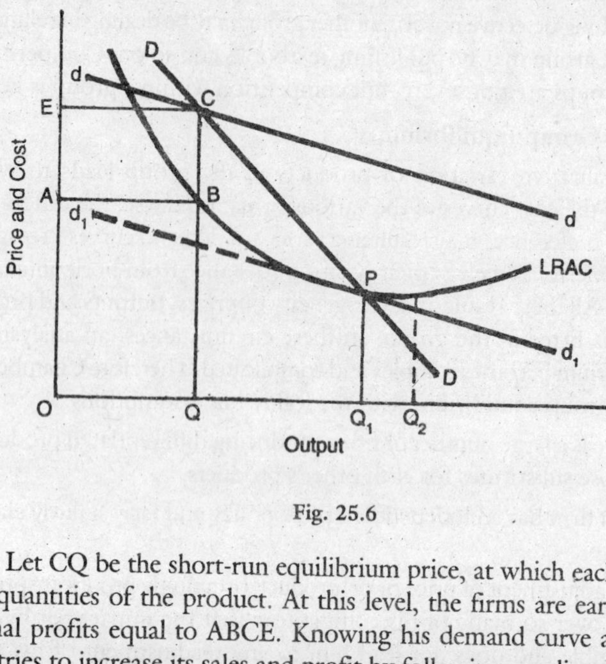

Fig. 25.6

Let CQ be the short-run equilibrium price, at which each firm sells OQ quantities of the product. At this level, the firms are earning super normal profits equal to ABCE. Knowing his demand curve as dd, each firm tries to increase its sales and profit by following a policy of price cut on the assumption that the rivals would not retaliate. As Chamberlin points out, his competitors are so numerous that the market of each one of them is inappreciably affected by his move. The same incentive of larger profits which prompts one seller to reduce his price leads the others to do likewise. In this process the demand curve dd "slides" downwards along DD as prices are lowered, and the movement comes to a stop at the price of Q_1P.

Long-Run Equilibrium: Price Competition: Open Entry

The position of DD depends upon the number of sellers in the market. If there are many sellers, the share of each in the total market is small; then it lies farther to the left. On the contrary if there are fewer sellers, the share of each of them in the total is large, and then it lies farther to the right. Now it is assumed that the entry is open to potential competitors. The flow of resources by the firm conceivably continues until DD is pushed leftwards to a position of tangency with the long-run average cost curve at C.

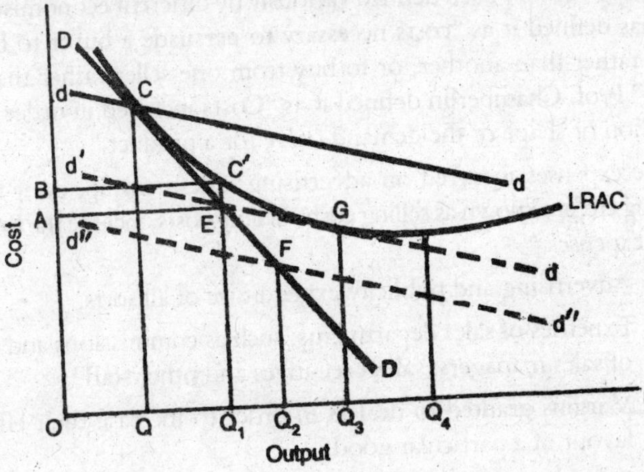

Fig. 25.7

In Fig. 25.7 at price QC, and at the level of output OQ, the cost equals price. This position is not a stable position. In order to increase Their profit and sales, the firms may lower their prices. Now the demand curve dd slides along the DD curve. Now let us assume that the demand curve d_1d_1 passes through point E on the demand curve DD. As a result of a fall in price, the sale of each firm has increased to OQ_1. At this price Q_1E and output OQ_1 each firm suffers an area equal to AEC_1B. If it slides further to point F, the casualty will be much higher. In order to escape from this heavy loss some firms may leave the group. This has its impact on price and output. Finally, the long-run equilibrium will be attained at point G where the demand curve d_1d_1 becomes tangent to the long-run average cost curve.

SELLING COST

Advertising is an important tool in monopolistic competition. While it has no role under perfect competition, it has some place under monopoly. (The role is to inform the consumers about the price and the quality of his product). With the help of advertisement a firm under monopolistic competition balances the delicate problem of homogeneity and heterogeneity. Homogeneity tries to show that its product is a close substitute for the products of others. Heterogeneity tries to prove that its product is superior to that of others.

Selling cost has been defined variously by different economists. Prof. Meyer has defined it as "costs necessary to persuade a buyer to buy one product rather than another, or to buy from one seller rather than from another." Prof. Chamberlin defined it as "Costs incurred in order to alter the position or shape of the demand curve for a product."

The expenses incurred on advertising, salesmanship, door-to-door convassing etc. are known as selling costs. Selling costs, include the following items of expenses:[6]

1. Advertising and publicity expenditure of all sorts.
2. Expenses of sales departments, such as commissions and salaries of sales managers, sales executives and other staff.
3. Margins granted to dealers in order to increase their efforts in favour of a particular good.
4. Expenses for window displays, demonstration of goods, free distribution of samples etc.

Economists are sharply divided over the necessity of selling costs. While some economists are in favour of advertisements others are against. According to Baumol,[7] the decision as to how far one can stretch the advertising cost will depend upon the firm's objective — whether it wants to maximize its sales or to maximize its profits. He says that advertisement is subject to diminishing returns. Therefore, a profit maximising firm should carry on its expenditure up to a point where the differences between total revenue and total costs are maximum.

---

6. D.M. Mithani — *Principles of Economics,* Himalaya Publishing House, Mumbai, 1987, p. 346.
7. W.J. Baumol — *Economic Theory and Operations Analysis*, Prentice Hall, New Delhi, 1982, p. 386.

Differences Between Production Cost and Selling Cost

The following important points of distinction costs may be noted.

1. Cost of production includes all expenses which must be incurred in order to provide the commodity or service, transport it to the buyer, and place it into his hands ready for consumption. Cost of selling, on the other hand includes all outlays made in order to secure a demand, or a market for the product.

2. Production costs are meant for the creation of utilities. Selling costs on the other hand are meant to create and shift the demand for the product.

3. Increase in the costs of production increases the supply of the product. On the other hand, selling costs increases demand for the product.

4. The amount of production cost depends upon the quantity of production. On the other hand, the amount of selling cost depends upon the nature of competition.

5. Production costs contribute to the economic welfare of the country; on the other hand, selling costs do not contribute much to the economic welfare of the community.

The average selling cost is "U" shaped. The analysis of selling cost is similar to that of the average cost. In Fig. 25.8, at OQ level of output the advertising cost per unit is OP. The firm has the lowest selling cost OP_2 at OQ_1 level of output. If the firm wants to sell OQ_2 level of output the

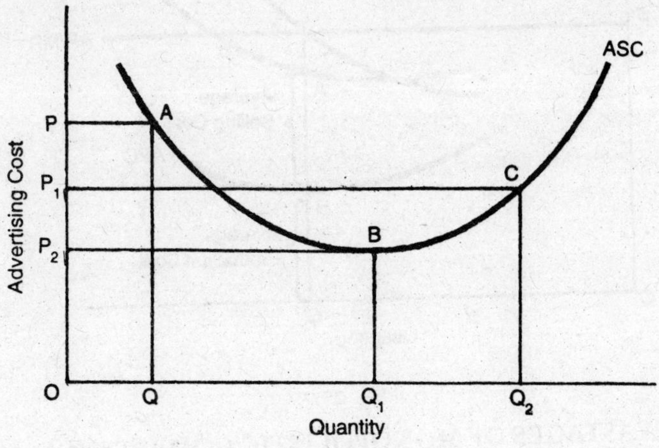

Fig. 25.8

average selling cost rises to OP_1. Therefore the 'U' shape is due to the operations of economies and diseconomies in advertisement. But after reaching the saturation point in sales, the curve becomes vertical indicating the ineffectiveness of certain advertisements.

The shape and the position of the selling cost curve will depend upon a number of factors such as the price of the product, availability of the substitutes, the degree of substitution, the quality of the product, and the qualities of its substitutes, the incomes of the consumer and their tastes and so on.

Combined Cost

Combined cost = Production cost + Selling cost

The cost of a firm includes production costs and advertisement costs. The profit maximising firm spends an amount on advertisement so that the combined marginal cost of production and advertising is equal to the rice. In Fig. 25.9, APC is the average production cost and BA is the average selling cost. ATC = APC + ASC. AR = MR = P, which is a horizontal line based on the assumption that the firm can sell more by advertising while keeping the price constant. The maximum output is fixed on the principle of MC = MR. The total output is OQ. AB is the per unit expenditure and the profits are maximum.

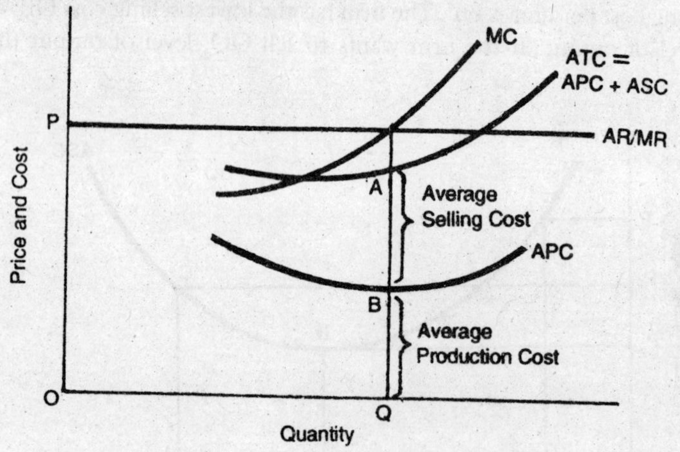

Fig. 25.9

WASTAGES OF MONOPOLISTIC COMPETITION

The evils of monopolistic competition are known as the wastages of monopolistic competition. As pointed out by Prof. Chamberlin, "Many of the so-called wastes of competition are really wastages not of pure competition, but of monopolistic competition." Some of the wastages are as follows:

1. Excess Capacity

Under monopolistic competition a firm's equilibrium output is less than its optimum. In Fig. (25.8) the equilibrium output is OM, which is less than the optimum output ON. There is unused capacity which is regarded as a waste in monopolistic competition. Moreover, eventhough the firm is earning only normal profits, the price paid by the consumer is more than under perfect competition.

2. Cross Transport

The presence of cross-transport is another waste of monopolistic competition. Since the products are differentiated, a firm in Jammu may be selling a commodity to its consumers in Kanyakumari. In this case, the consumer has to pay a higher price which would include transport costs. In the absence of product differentiation, the seller will sell his product in Jammu. The same is the case with the producers in Kanyakumari.

3. Waste of Advertisement

Under monopolistic competition, a huge expenditure is incurred on advertisements to woo the consumers. Advertisements may be classified into informative and competitive advertisements. Informative advertisement educates people, about the quality, price and place of availability. Therefore, this type of advertisement cannot be regarded as a waste.

But the aggressive, cut-throat or do or die competition which result in evil designed practices of salesmen under monopolistic competition leads to sheer wastage of resources. Moreover, it wrongly directs the consumer towards a particular product. Prof. Galbraith in his 'Affluent Society' points out that advertising is one of the violations of consumer's sovereignty.

4. Unemployment

Under monopolistic competition, as we have seen earlier, the resources are not utilitised up to the minimum point of the long run average cost curve. This aggravates the problem of unemployment. Moreover, in order to charge a higher price to reap higher profits, production is curtailed. This also has its impact on unemployment.

5. Inefficient Firms

Under monopolistic competition, there are a large number of inefficient firms. The inefficient firms are not advantageously placed to produce more and reduce their price as compared to their efficient rivals. Such firms continue in their business without leaving room for others.

These firms sustain their production either due to the ignorance of the consumers or due to the presence of transport costs. But the existence of such firms is not desirable from the social point of view.

6. Consumers are Hypnotised

Product differentiation, like beauty is in the eyes of the buyer. By way of different brand names, colour, package, beautiful displays consumers are hypnotised to buy even inferior quality goods at higher prices. Many honest firms which are unable to spend money lavishly on advertisement die prematurely.

Conclusion

Thus under monopolistic competition, the consumers suffer by way of high prices, producers incur losses through cut-throat competition and the valuable resources of the community are wasted.

QUESTIONS

1. Explain the characteristic features of monopolistic competition.
2. Define non-price competition.
3. Explain the concepts of selling costs and product differentiation.
4. What are selling costs? How do they differ from production costs? Why are selling costs incompatible with perfect competition?
5. Explain with suitable diagrams the wastes of competition.
6. How does Chamberlin explain group equilibrium in the context of product differentiation.
7. What do you understand by monopolistic competition? What are the characteristic features that distinguish it both from pure competition and pure monopoly?
8. How is price determined under monopolistic competition?
9. How is output determined when selling costs are included by a monopolistic competitor?
10. Examine the equilibrium of the firm under monopolistic competition in the long run.
11. Under what market conditions does non-price competition assume importance?

❖ ❖ ❖

26

DUOPOLY MODELS

Seek out your faults and others' merits.

THE COURNOT MODEL

Duopoly is a type of an imperfect market structure in which there are only two sellers. A model of oligopoly, indicating duopoly was first given by a French economist, Augustin Cournot in the year 1838.[1] This model was criticised by Betrand, a French mathematician, who developed his own model of duopoly in 1883. English economist Edgeworth developed his model of duopoly in 1897.

Assumptions

The Cournot model is based on the following assumptions:

1. There are two profit maximising duopolists say A and B, each owing an artesian mineral water well.
2. Both the duopolists produce an identical product.
3. The cost of production is assumed to be zero.
4. Both the duopolists sell at an identical price.
5. Both face a downward sloping linear demand curve.
6. There is no collusion among the duopolists.
7. Each duopolist assumes the supply of his rival to be constant.

1. Augustin Cournot, *Researches into the Mathematical Principles of the Theory of Wealth*, New York, Macmillan, 1897.

On the basis of this model, Cournot concluded that each seller ultimately supplies one-third of the market and charges the same price, leaving a third of the market without any supply.

Cournot's model can be illustrated with the help of Fig. 26.1. DD is the market demand curve for mineral water and the corresponding marginal revenue curve is MR. OD is the maximum quantity which can be produced and supplied by the two duopolists. But if the two producers produce the maximum quantity of OD the market price will have to come to zero.

Suppose initially A is the only seller. A behaves like a monopolist and produces output $OX_1 = 1/2\ OD$ (because at this point MC = MR = O) and sells at a price OP_1 and makes a profit OP_1AX_1.

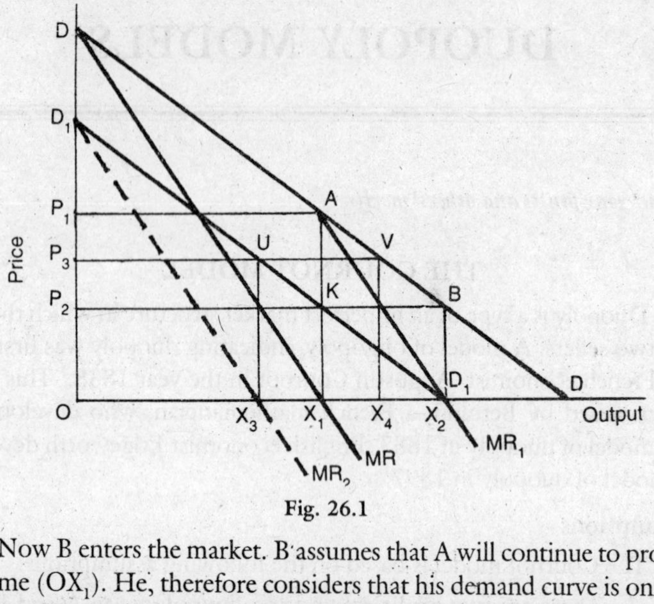

Fig. 26.1

Now B enters the market. B assumes that A will continue to produce the same (OX_1). He, therefore considers that his demand curve is only the segment AD (and not DD). The corresponding marginal revenue curve for B becomes MR_1. Given this demand curve and marginal revenue curve for B, he would like to sell X_1X_2 quantity of water as at this level his MR = MC = O. For this level of output, B charges a price OP_2 (= X_2B) and reaps a profit equivalent to the area X_1X_2BK. Total output has increased with B's entry and hence, the product price falls. Since the product is homogeneous A has to accept the price OP_2 set by B. Therefore the profit has to come down from OP_1AX_1 to OP_2KX_1.

Duopolist A's new demand curve is D_1D_1 which is obtained by horizontally subtracting B's output from the market curve, i.e., (1–1/4)

3/4 of the market demand. To maximise his profit A will therefore supply 1/2 (3/4) = 3/8 of the market. Now A's market share has fallen from 1/2 to 3/8.

Now it is B's turn to react. Firm B reacts on Cournot's assumption, and will produce one-half of the unsupplied quantity of the market, i.e., 1/2 (1 – 3/8) = 5/16. Now the turn is in favour of A who will produce one-half of the remainder of the market, i.e., 1/2(1 – 5/16) = 11/32.

This action-reaction pattern will be continued in successive periods. In the process, A continues to lose his market share and B continues to gain. Eventually an equilibrium will be reached in which each firm produces one-third of the total market. Together they cover two-thirds of the total market. One-third of the market will be left unsupplied as shown in Fig. 26.2.

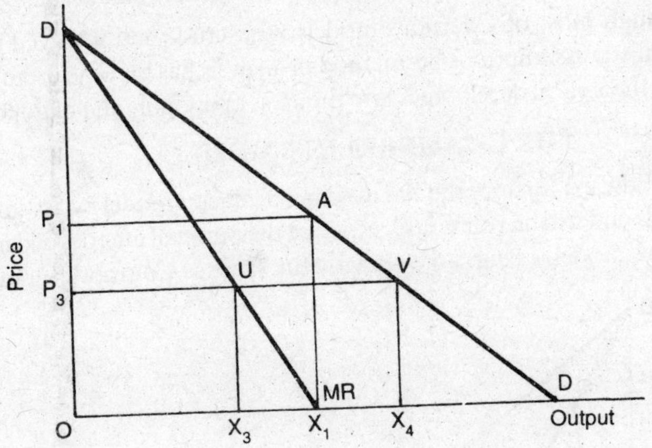

Fig. 26.2

The equilibrium of the duopolists may be obtained as follows:

Table 26.1

Period	*Duopolist A*	*Duopolist B*
I	1/2 (1) = 1/2	1/2 (1/2) = 1/4
II	1/2 (1–1/4) = 3/8	1/2 (1–3/8) = 5/16
III	1/2 (1–5/16) = 11/32	1/2 (1–11/32) = 21/64
IV	1/2 (1–21/64) = 43/128	1/2 (1–43/128) = 85/256
V	1/2 (1–85/256) = 171/512	1/2 (1–171/512) = 341/1024
	⋮	⋮
N	1/2 (1–1/3) = 1/3	1/2 (1–1/3) = 1/3

Cournot's model can be extended to situations of more than two sellers, that is to the case of oligopoly also. The formula is of total output, in which 'n' stands for the number of producers. If there are 100 producers the supply will be 100/101 of OD, if the number of producers is large, it will tend to approach OD, the price being virtually zero.

Cournot's model leads to a stable equilibrium. However, his model is subject to strong criticisms.

The basic defect is that the behavioural pattern in which each seller assumes his rival's supply to be fixed repeatedly by observing the changes made by him. Betrand suggests that the duopoly model should be based on the assumption of a constant price of the rival and not on constant output. Edgeworth has developed a model on this basis.

Secondly the assumption of costless production is unrealistic.

Although most of Cournot's models were crude and involved very many unrealistic assumptions his method of analysis has become useful for subsequent theoretical developments in the areas of duopoly and oligopoly.[2]

THE CHAMBERLINS' MODEL[3]

Prof. Edward Chamberlin has modified Cournot model by assuming that the rivals understand reality and recognise their mutual interdependence. Chamberlin's model is (Fig. 26.3) exactly the same as Cournot's model.

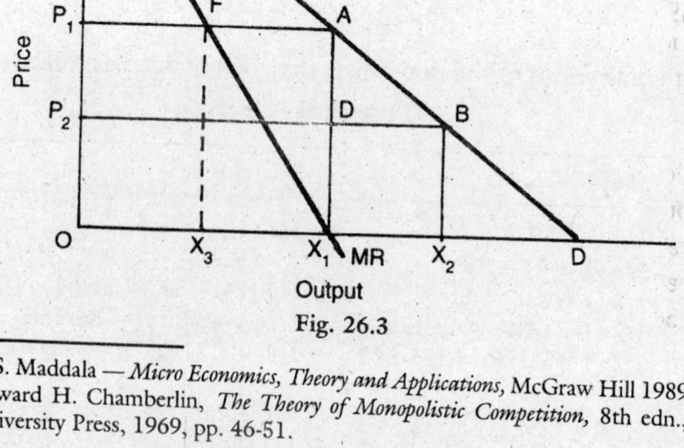

Fig. 26.3

2. G.S. Maddala — *Micro Economics, Theory and Applications,* McGraw Hill 1989, p. 388.
3. Edward H. Chamberlin, *The Theory of Monopolistic Competition,* 8th edn., Oxford University Press, 1969, pp. 46-51.

DD is the market demand curve for mineral water and MR is the corresponding marginal revenue curve. Now the producer A enters the price market, produces an output OX_1 and charges price OP_1 which will give a monopoly of OP_1AX_1. Now B enters the market and produces an output equal to X_1X_2, charges a price OP_2 which will yield a profit of X_1X_2BD. As a result of B's reaction A's profit has come down from OP_1AX_1 to OP_2DX_1, and up to this Chamberlin's analysis is similar to Cournot's treatment of duopoly. Now producer A realises the mutual interdependence of the two producers and the necessity to share monopoly output of OX_1 and monopoly profit of OP_1AX_1. Thus the rivals share the monopoly output OX_1, fix the monopoly price OP_1 and share equally the monopoly profit of OP_1AX_1, i.e., OP_1FX_3 for A and X_3FAX_1 for B. $OP_1FX_3 + X_3FAX_1 = OP_1AX_1$

Thus Chamberlin's analysis involves a kind of understanding for mutual benefit.

THE EDGEWORTH MODEL

F.Y. Edgeworth[4] (1845-1926) an English economist, developed a theory in 1897 similar to Betrand's that each duopolist assumed that the rival's price was constant. The Edgeworth model is depicted in Fig. 26.4.

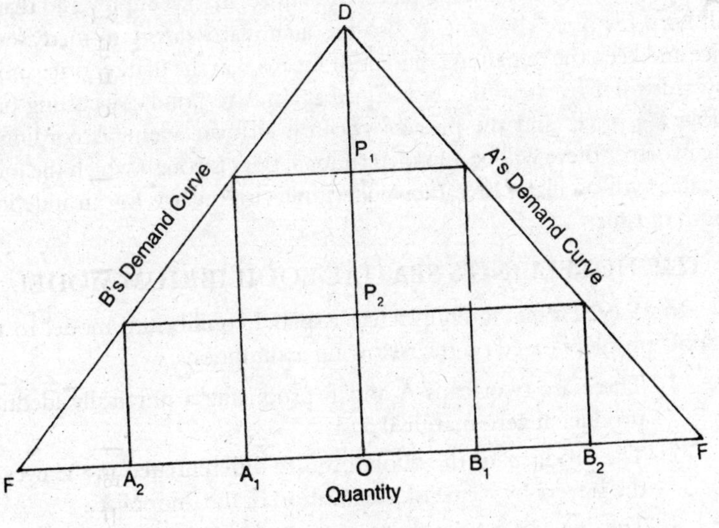

Fig. 26.4

4. F.Y. Edgeworth — *Papers Relating to Political Economy,* London, Macmillan, Vol.I, p. 118.

For the sake of simplicity, let us assume that there are two producers selling homogeneous products and incurring zero marginal cost. The entire market is divided equally between A and B when both the firms charge the same price. DE is the demand curve facing A and DF is the demand curve facing B. Assuming that prices are equal, the total competitive output is EF. The maximum output A can produce is OA_2 and the maximum output B can produce is OB_2. If both the duopolists have formed some sort of a tacit agreement then they will sell OA_1 and OB_1 quantities respectively at OP_1 price. To put it in other words, under collusion, they will act as they would under monopoly.

But suppose there is no collusion, and further suppose that A reduces the price slightly below OP_1, then all of B's customers will go to A. But A can provide only an output of OA_2. Thus B is left with sales equal to A_2E (or B_2F). Instead of accepting a reduction in revenue, B reduces the price slightly below that of A's price and captures A's customers. But B can serve only OB_2 quantity of output. This process of price cut goes on until price falls to OP_2 and each of the duopolists produces the maximum possible output. A sells OA_2 and B sells OB_2.

However, the price OP_2 is not stable, because one firm can raise its price and increase its revenue. Now A begins to raise his price with the assumption that B has already placed his entire, market supply and that he will keep his price constant. B also has a similar strategy to increase the price and keep the remaining market. It means that the market price moves upwards till it reaches OP_1. Now once again A responds by cutting price below B's price, and the process goes on all over again. According to Edgeworth, "there will be an indeterminate tract through which the index of value will oscillate, or rather will vibrate irregularly for an indefinite length of time."

THE HOTELLING'S SPATIAL EQUILIBRIUM MODEL

In 1929, Hotelling enunciated a spatial equilibrium model to the duopoly problem based on the following assumptions:

1. There are two firms A and B producing a physically identical product at zero marginal cost.
2. The products of the duopolists are differentiated in the eyes of the buyers by virtue of the location of the duopolists.
3. The demand is completely inelastic.
4. Buyers are uniformly distributed (one per unit of distance) along a line KL which may be the main street in a town or a transcontinental rail road.

5. No buyer has any preference for either seller except on the ground of price plus transportation costs.
6. Transportation costs vary in proportion to the distances between buyers and sellers.
7. The duopolists A and B locate themselves at X_A and X_B, respectively, on the line KL.

Given these assumptions, the Hotelling's model is illustrated in the following Figure (26.5).

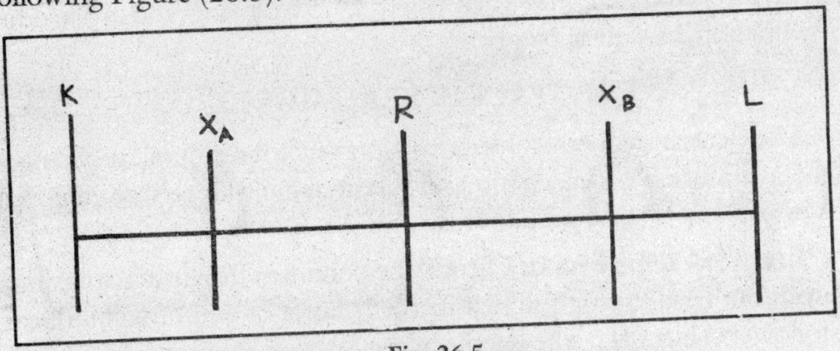

Fig. 26.5

The two sellers have their places of business at X_A and X_B along the length of the market line KL which is divided into a number of regions. To the left of X_A firm A will have its sheltered market and similarly to the right of X_B firm B will have its sheltered market. They both compete for the market in between X_A and X_B.

The market area between X_A and X_B will be shared by the two firms. How can we find the boundary for their markets in the area? For this, let us introduce the concept of delivered price which includes the price charged at the location plus a transportation cost for the product at the rate of say Rs. 'C' per unit product per unit distance.

If the distance of R from X_A is x and the distance of R from X_B is y and P_A and P_B are the prices charged by A and B respectively, then at R

$$P_A + C_X = P_B + C_Y$$

A gets all the customers along KR and B gets all the customers along RL. A's profit is $P_A KR$ and B's profit is $P_B RL$. This is the short-run equilibrium of the duopolist.

In the long-run firm A will have an incentive to move toward X_B and expand its sheltered market. Similarly firm B will have an incentive to move towards X_A and expand its sheltered market. Hence a stable solution is reached when both A and B locate themselves at the midpoint of KL. If this is, so the spatial dimension of the analysis becomes irrelevant in the long run for the duopoly firms.

The Hotelling solution has some practical implications from the point of view of social welfare. A and B should locate at one-quarter and three quarters of the distance from K to L so as to minimise transportation costs. Hotelling's solution also explains the phenomenon that sellers tend to locate themselves in close proximity. Thus, it explains the concentration of firms and business in many cities. Since the firms are located close to each other, they have to compete with each other by advertising and by product differentiation, as well as by price.

THE STACKELBERG MODEL

The German economist Heinrich Von Stackelberg developed a model on the assumption of leadership and followership (see section oligopoly for a discussion of the dominant firm).

In the Stackelberg model, firm I, the dominant firm tries to maximize its profit but it will recognise that its own choice of output will influence the followers (Firm II). The details of the Stackelberg solution cannot be easily arrived without the use of calculus, and it is beyond the scope of this book. The conclusion of the model is that with linear demand functions, the total output is three-fourths of the competitive output, with the dominant firm producing twice as much as that of the follower.

QUESTIONS

1. Give a brief outline of Cournot, Chamberlin and Edgeworth models of duopoly and highlight the essential differences between them.
2. What are the assumptions that underline the Cournot duopoly model? Explain how the Cournot equilibrium is approached. What percentage of the competitive output is produced by a duopoly firm in the Cournot equilibrium?
3. What are the assumptions of Cournot's model of duopoly?

❖ ❖ ❖

27

OLIGOPOLY

"Anybody can cut prices, but it takes brains to make a better article."

—Alice Hubbard, 1899

MEANING

Oligopoly is an umbrella term that describes market forms that fall between the extremes of monopoly and monopolistic competition.

Oligopoly is competition among the few. In Greek 'Oligoi' means 'few'. So, a market (Poly), where there are a few sellers of output is called oligopoly.

In the words of Peter C. Dooley,[1] "An oligopoly is a market of only a few sellers, offering either homogeneous or differentiated products."

Prof. Baumol[2] defines it as follows, "An oligopoly is a market dominated by a few sellers atleast several of which are large enough relative to the total market to be able to influence the market prices."

Prof. Stone defines it as "Oligopolies are industries dominated by a few firms whose decisions are inextricably and consciously linked."

Dominic Salvator[3] points out that the sources of oligopoly are generally the same as for monopoly. That is why oligopoly is also called as partial monopoly. An oligopoly results from innovations, cost conditions, control of an essential resource, legal restrictions, differentiation, large fixed costs,

---

1. *Elementary Price Theory,* 2nd edition. Appleton-Century Craft, New York, 1973, p. 110.
2. *Economics, Principles and Policy,* 4th edition, Harcourt Brace, New York, 1988, p. 617.
3. *Managerial Economics,* McGraw Hill International editions, New York, 1989, p. 476.

or mergers. An extreme case of oligopoly is duopoly where there are only two firms. Good examples of oligopoly are to be found in the industries producing oil, detergents, tyres, motor cars, synthetic fibres and cigarettes.

MAIN FEATURES OF OLIGOPOLY

The following are the salient features of oligopoly.

1. Few Sellers

Oligopoly is a market structure in which a small number of rival firms dominate the industry and many small firms act as price takers. It is under oligopoly that rivalry among firms takes its most direct and active form. The products sold by oligopolistic firms can either be homogeneous or differentiated. In general the number of firms vary from 5 to 10.

2. Lack of Uniformity

Lack of uniformity in the size of firms is also a unique feature of oligopoly. Some firms may be small and others may be large. For example, eight largest firms in the United States account for over 85% of the photographic equipment supplies. The market is of course, dominated by the Kodak corporation.

3. Advertisement

Advertising and selling costs have a strategic importance for oligopoly firms. In this context Prof. Baumol[4] rightly remarks that, "it is only under oligopoly that advertising comes fully into its own." He further writes "...under oligopoly, advertising can become a life and death matter, where a firm which fails to keep up with the advertising budget of its competitors may find its customers drifting off to rival products."

4. Elements of Monopoly

Under oligopoly, there are only few firms in the market. The existence of product differentiation creates 'brand loyalty' on the part of the consumers which is the basic source of monopoly power. Moreover, through collusion, the existing firms can raise the price and earn some monopoly income.

5. Constant Struggle

Competition is of a unique type in the oligopolistic market. Competition here implies struggle of rivals against rivals.

---

4. William J. Baumol — *Economic Theory and Operations Analysis,* 4th Edition, Prentice Hall, New Delhi, 1982, p. 410.

6. Uncertainty

As Prof. Zeuthen points out, it is difficult to calculate the consequence of current economic changes on the basis of facts already in existence. So uncertainty in the behaviour of firms is a special feature of oligopoly.

7. Interdependence

The cross elasticity of demand for the oligopoly product is high. Therefore the sellers are aware of their interdependence with their rivals. Each firm in the industry is presumed to recognize the fact that a change in its price or output will cause a reaction by the competiting firms.

8. Existence of Price Rigidity

In an oligopolistic market each firm sticks to its own price. If a firm tries to reduce the price the rivals will also retaliate by reducing their prices. So it will not produce any advantage. Likewise if a firm tries to raise the price, other firms will not do so. In this situation the firm which intended to raise the price will lose its customers. So there is price rigidity in an oligopolistic market.

CLASSIFICATION OF OLIGOPOLY

1. On the Basics of Product Differentiation

If the products of the rival firms are homogeneous it is known as pure or perfect oligopoly. On the contrary if the products are heterogeneous, it is termed as differentiated or imperfect oligopoly.

2. On the Basis of Entry of Firms

If entry is open to the new firms it denotes open oligopoly. On the other hand, if free entry is restricted, it becomes closed oligopoly.

3. On the Basis of Agreement

A market situation in which rival firms, instead of competing, follow a common price policy is known as collusive oligopoly. The collusion may be in the form of an agreement or an understanding between the firms.

The former is called open collusion while the latter is known as a tacit collusion.

4. On the Basis of Price Leadership

Partial oligopoly refers to a situation in which the dominant firm known as the price leader fixes the price policy and the other firms simply follow the price fixed by the leader. Full oligopoly indicates a situation where no firm is dominant enough to assume the role of a price leader.

EQUILIBRIUM WITHOUT PRODUCT DIFFERENTIATION

Among the various forms of oligopoly perfect oligopoly and differentiated oligopoly are the two major types. Perfect oligopoly implies absence of product differentiation. It is difficult to find industries in oligopoly without product differentiation. For even in pure oligopoly industries like cement, steel, aluminium, rubber tyre, etc., product differentiation is resorted to.

If there is no product differentiation there will be confrontation among the rivals on the basis of price competition. In Fig. 27.1 as a result of price war, the price has come down to QN. At this price the firm sells an output of OQ, earning just normal profit. This OQ output is the optimum output as it is being produced at the lowest average cost. If the firm raises the price beyond QN, it will lose all its customers because the product is not differentiated. It is assumed that the other firms will not increase their price. The firm will not be able to reduce the price below QN, as at that price it will not be able to get even normal profits and in the long run the firm will have to go out of business.

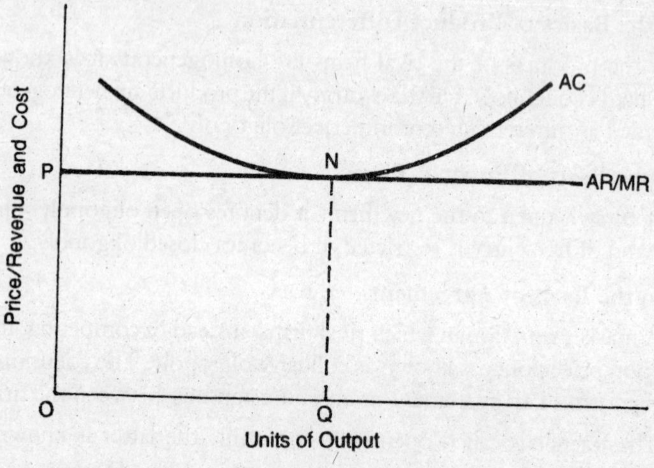

Fig. 27.1

EQUILIBRIUM WITH PRODUCT DIFFERENTIATION

Fig. 27.2 illustrates equilibrium with product differentiation under differentiated oligopoly.

Let us imagine that after the price war the price has settled down at OP and the firm is producing OQ level of output. The firm sells OQ output and earns just normal profit. Here the equilibrium is similar to that of the monopolistic competition. But it must be noted that the output will be noted less than the optimum level of OQ_1 (where the average cost is minimum).

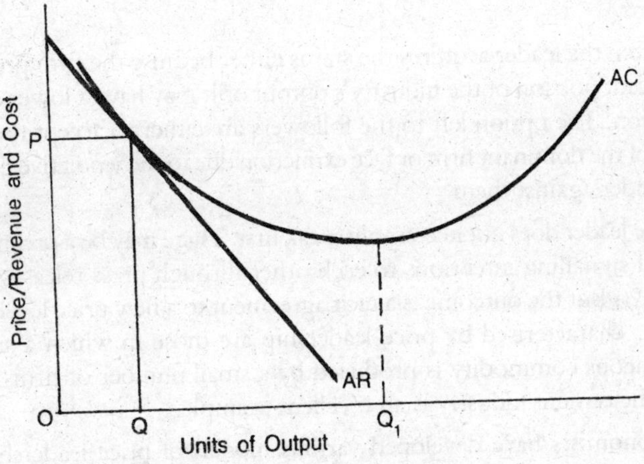

Fig. 27.2

The above discussion makes it clear that the price war ends in normal profit. It should, therefore, be in their interest to come to an understanding or agreement to avoid the price war. In practice, the final price in oligopoly with product differentiation will lie somewhere between the monopoly price and the competition price. It will vary from one case to another case and will be governed by the actual conditions prevailing in the market.

The important question that has to be answered is: How is the actual price fixed under oligopoly with product differentiation?

The main methods suggested by economists are as follows:

1. Pricing under imperfect collusion (price leadership)
2. Pricing under perfect collusion (cartels)
3. Pricing under non-collusive oligopoly (Kinked Demand Curve)

Let us discuss these models one by one.

PRICE LEADERSHIP

Oligopolists are keenly aware of their mutual interdependence. A careless pricing decision may lead to cut-throat price competition which lowers everyone's profit.[5] Price leadership is an escape route to avoid price war, which may be beneficial to all. A price leader is an oligopolist whose price changes are consistently imitated by other firms in the industry. The price leader keeps a sharp eye on market demand and costs that are common to all the firms; and its price increases and decreases are followed by all rival firms.

Often the leader acquires the status either because the firm produces a significant portion of the industry's output or it may have a lower cost of production. The option left to the followers are either to accept the price policies of the dominant firm or face extinction due to the vindictive policies of the leader against them.

The leader does not necessarily speak first. There may be a preliminary period of signalling intentions to each other through press releases or by other ways. But the outcome is a tacit agreement to a new price level.[6] The industries characterised by price leadership are those in which a simple, homogeneous commodity is produced by a small number of firms.[7] The steel or the cement industry is an excellent example.

Economists have developed various models of price leadership on the basis of assumptions regarding the behaviour of the price leader and his followers. The most common types are:

1. Price Leadership by a low-cost firm.
2. Price Leadership by a dominant firm.
3. Barometric price leadership.

PRICE LEADERSHIP BY A LOW-COST FIRM

Assumptions

1. The industry consists of two firms H and L. The firm L has a lower cost of production than firm H.
2. The product is homogeneous, and so, naturally the same price prevails in the market.
3. Each firm has an equal share in the market.

---

5. Robert Y. Ahw, *Micro Economics Theory and Applications,* John Wiley and Sons, New York 1976, p. 332.
6. Lloyd G. Reynolds, *Micro Economics*, 6th Edition, Universal Book Stall, New Delhi, 1988, p. 71.
7. K.E. Boulding, *Economic Analysis,* 4th Edition, Harper and Row, New York, 1969, p. 480.

In Fig. 27.3 AC_L and MC_L are the average and marginal cost curves of the low cost firm. AC_H and MC_H are the average and marginal cost curves of the high cost firm. DD is the market demand curve. dd is the demand curve for each firm. The corresponding marginal revenue curve for each firm is MR. Now given the demand curve and the cost curves each firm will like to produce a level of output and fix a price at which it can obtain the maximum profit. While fixing the price of the product the marginal rule of MC = MR is applied by both the firms. According to this principle, the firm H would like to produce OQ_1 output and charge OP_1 price. The firm L would like to produce OQ_2 output and charge OP_2 price. Since the largest firm L has the economies of scale its cost of production and price will be lower. Since the product is homogeneous, the high cost firm will be forced to accept the price charged by the low cost firm. In case it fails to do so, it will lose its customers to the low cost firm. Therefore, firm L is the price leader and firm H is the price follower.

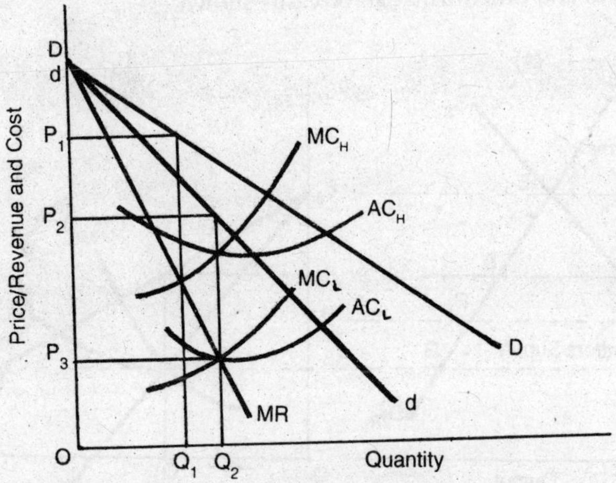

Fig. 27.3

If in this situation, the high cost firm does not want to become a follower, then the low cost firm can drive out the high cost firm from the market by fixing a price lower than the average cost of the high cost firm.[8] The above said price is shown in the figure at OP_3.

8. K.E. Boulding, *Economic Analysis,* Vol. I — 4th Edition, pp. 475-482.

PRICE LEADERSHIP BY A DOMINANT FIRM

A firm is said to be dominant when it has over half of the sales in the market and twice the size of the next largest firm.[9]

The assumptions of the dominant firm model are as follows:

1. The industry consists of one dominant firm and a competitive fringe of small firms.
2. The dominant firm sets the market price and allows the small firms to sell all as they wish at this price.
3. The market demand is assumed to be known to the dominant firm.
4. The small firms recognise their subordinate positions, and behave just like a firm in a perfectly competitive market. In other words, they assume that their demand curve is a horizontal straight line.

Given the above assumptions, the sharing of the market between the dominant firm and other firms can be easily shown.

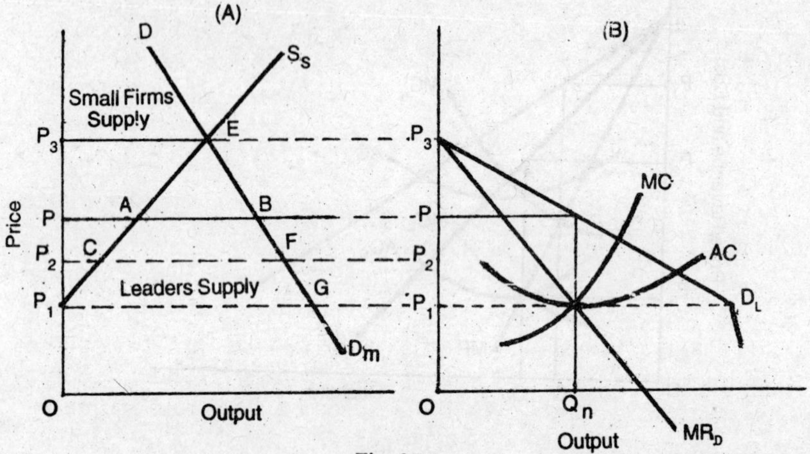

Fig. 27.4

Suppose the market demand curve is given by DD_M in part (A) of the Figure 27.4. The small firms are price takers, and the short run supply curve S_S is the horizontal sum of their marginal cost curves. The dominant firm estimates its net demand D_L by subtracting from the total market demand, how much other firms will supply at each possible price. The part

9. W.H. Locke Anderson — *Economics,* Prentice Hall, New Delhi, 1986, p. 122.

of the market demand not met by the small firms will be its own share. This is called the residual demand curve facing the leader. Thus the dominant firms quantity demanded D_L is given by

D_L = total quantity demanded in the market − quantity supplied by all small firms

Table 27.1

Price (1)	*Market Demand* (2)	*Quantity supplied by small firms* (3)	*Demand for Dominant firm (Column 2-3)*
OP_3	P_3E	P_3E	O
OP	PB	PA	AB
OP_2	P_2F	P_2C	CF
OP_1	P_1G	O	P_1G

The information so derived and plotted graphically gives $P_3 D_L$ as the demand curve for the dominant firm (Fig. 27.4 B) since the relation between MR and AR is known, MR curve for the dominant firm can be derived as MR_D. The dominant firm will set the price at which its MR = MC and its output is OQ_n. At price OP the total market demand is PB, and the part PA is supplied by the smaller firms while quantity AB = OQ_n is supplied by the leader.

The dominant firm maximises its profit by equating its MC to its MR, while the small firms which are price takers, may or may not maximise their profits depending on their cost structure.

Once the dominant firm sets its price at OP, the market demand curve for the smaller firms is the horizontal price line PB, because they can sell, at this price, as much as they can produce. As implied in the assumption the smaller firms consider PB as, the same as their AR = MR line and their supply curve P_1S_S intersects AR = MR at point A. The profit maximising output for the smaller firms will be PA.

We may conclude in the words of Prof. G.S. Maddala[10], "In actual practice the analysis of price leadership is more complicated. There can be more than one dominant firm. There could be product differentiation, geographical differences among sellers, and so on. It is impossible to say anything concrete when all these complications are introduced."

---

10. G.S. Maddala —*Micro Economics, Theory and Applications,* McGraw-Hill 1989, p. 407.

BAROMETRIC PRICE LEADERSHIP

Another form of price leadership is barometric price leadership in which an old and experienced firm which is able to forecast future developments in the market assumes the role of the leader. While it need not be the lowest cost firm in the industry, it certainly must be an efficient firm. The firm aims to protect not only its own interests but the welfare of all the firms in the industry. The price change announced by the leader serves as a "barometer that reflects the demand for the product and the cost of production. The price decision will not be forced upon others but others will accept it without any reservation. Unless the price leader sets the price that reflects with reasonable accuracy, the demand and supply conditions in the industry, it is not likely to continue its role as the barometric leader. A firm belonging to another industry may also be chosen as the barometric leader. For example, a firm in the steel industry may be agreed as the (barometric) leader for price changes in the motor-car industry.

Barometric price leadership may be established for various reasons.[11]

Firstly, rivalry between several large firms in an industry may make it impossible to accept one among them as the leader.

Secondly, followers may avoid the continuous recalculation of costs, as economic conditions change.

Thirdly, the barometric firm usually has proved itself as a 'reasonably' good forecaster of changes in cost and demand conditions in the particular industry and the economy as a whole, and by following it the other firms can be 'reasonably' sure that they choose the correct price policy.

Difficulties of Price Leadership

The operation of the price leader is not smooth in the real world. In practice, it has to face a variety of problems. Some are pointed out here below.

Firstly, there is no guarantee that the rival firms will follow the leader.

Secondly, the price leadership is rendered ineffective by the smaller firms by way of indirect price cutting such as offer of rebates, favourable credit terms, easy instalments with low rates of interest etc.

Lastly, if a leading firm loses its cost advantages, it loses its leadership also. Therefore there is a frequent "passing to-and-fro" of leadership among the competing oligopolists as a consequence of innovation in their products or processes.

---

11. A. Koutsoyiannis — *Modern Micro Economics*, 2nd edn., Macmillan Press, New York, 1983, p. 248.

CARTEL

A shared monopoly is another name for a cartel. Cartel is one of the ways to avoid the strains of rivalry. A cartel is a combination of firms whose object is to limit the scope of competitive forces within a market.[12] Producers in a cartel explicitly agree to co-operate in setting prices and output levels. The cartel becomes feasible only if the number of firms is not very large.

In the words of Prof. D.N. Hyman[13] "A cartel is a group of firms acting together to co-ordinate output decisions and control prices as if they were a single monopoly." Thus collusion refers to sinister secret cooperative agreements. According to Prof. Kamerchen[14] "A cartel is an organisation of independent producers intent on thwarting competition among themselves through joint regulation of market shares, production levels and prices." In some countries it is legal, in others, illegal. For example, after the passing of Sherman Anti-trust act in 1890, Cartels have become illegal in the United States.

The form of collusion may range from mere "gentlemen's agreement" to explicit collusion. Gentlemen's agreements are informal oral understandings among the oligopolists that they will maintain a certain minimum price. These agreements are often ratified by nothing more than a handshake over a lunch or dinner.

A cartel can be formed by producers within a country in which case it is called a domestic cartel or by producers (or governments) in different countries, in which case it is called an international cartel. OPEC is a classic example for an international cartel. The OPEC is a cartel of 13 oil producing countries. From 1973, its members meet regularly to set prices and output levels. Real OPEC revenues rose by 340 percent between 1974 and 1980. Yet almost from the start, many economists have predicted that OPEC, like most other cartels, would quickly collapse. In practice, one reason OPEC was successful for so long was the willingness of Saudi Arabia, the largest oil producer, to restrict its output further when smaller members insisted on their expansion. By 1986, however Saudi Arabia was no longer prepared to play these rules, and refused to prop up the price any longer.

---

12. C.E. Ferguson — *Micro Economic Theory* 1st edn., AITBS, Delhi, 1983, p. 333.
13. David N. Hyman, *Modern Micro Economics,* Mobsy College Publishing, St. Louis, 1989, p. 371.
14. Kamerschen McKenzie and Nardinelli, *Economics,* 2nd edn., Houghton Mifflin Company, Boston, p. 625.

The oil price collapsed from $ 30 to $ 9 for a barrel before recovering a little. In agriculture, cartel carries the name of co-operatives.

The twin functions of a cartel are price fixing and market divisions. There are two main requisites for a cartel to be successful. Firstly, the cartel organisation must be able to reach a collusive agreement. Secondly, once the agreement is reached the firms must be able to enforce it over a period of time. Many cartel agreements are, however, difficult to enforce, because they are considered illegal. Any action taken to punish the violator may expose the whole operation to the authorities.[15]

The chances for effective and lasting collusion decrease when there are:

1. Many sellers
2. Low entry barriers
3. Product heterogeneity
4. High rates of innovation
5. High fixed costs
6. Opportunities for cheating and
7. Legal restrictions.

Now the question is how long a cartel can last? This depends upon whether any member of the cartel cheats by reducing the price and thus, increases its market share. Once a few cheat, others follow suit. Chiselling (Price concessions made secretly or openly by a few mal-contents) makes inroads into the sales of the members who are stimulated to match them. Thus the ranks of the unfaithful are expanded, and ultimately the cartel breaks down completely.[16] Very few international cartels have managed to last for more than 5 years.

The life expectancy of a cartel depends on several factors.[17]

1. The Price Elasticity of Demand

If there are close substitutes for the cartel's product, then the life expectancy will be less. The copper cartel formed by Chile, Peru, Zaire and Zambia was unsuccessful because of the availability of close substitutes.

---

15. S.C., Maurice — *Micro Economics Theory and Applications,* Universal Book Stall, New Delhi, 1988, p. 247.
16. K.N. Prasad, *Advanced Lectures on Micro Economic Theory,* Himalaya Publishing House, 1987, p. 377.
17. G.S. Maddala, *Op. Cit.,* p. 402.

2. Stability of Demand

A stable demand is conducive to a cartel's survival.

3. The ability to control a substantial share of actual and potential output

The ability of a potential entrant also affects the power of the cartel. For example, as OPEC raised the price of oil, the quantity supplied from non-members increased dramatically. This increase undermined OPEC's power.

4. The political climate in the case of international cartels

The rivalry between Iran and Iraq has contributed to the instability of OPEC.

As mentioned earlier the two important functions of a cartel are price fixing and market sharing. Now let us discuss these functions in detail.

PRICE FIXING IN AN IDEAL CARTEL

Suppose a group of firms producing a homogeneous commodity form a cartel in order to reduce price competition and maximise their joint profit. A central management body is appointed, its main function being the determination of the uniform cartel price. The cartel can follow a monopolistic policy and adjust price and total output so as to maximise its total revenue.

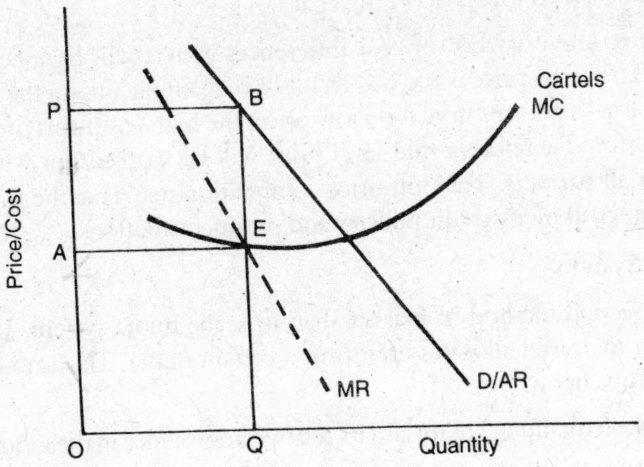

Fig. 27.5

In Fig. 27.5 the market demand and marginal revenue curve facing the cartel are labelled as AR and MR. If all firms in the cartel purchase all inputs in a perfectly competitive market, the cartel's marginal cost curve is simply the horizontal summing up of all firms' MC curves. The curve is labelled as cartel's MC. By equating the cartel's MR and MC, the profit maximising price and output is OP and OQ respectively. Thus the pricing process is similar to monopoly pricing.

Now the next question is the problem of allocating profits among cartel members. No simple solution to the problem of distributing profits among cartel members exists; the actual distribution depends upon their relative bargaining powers, influenced by such diverse factors as production costs, financial strengths, consumer attachment to each producers brand, and each firm's ability to inflict damages to others by refusing to join the cartel.[18]

CARTEL'S AND MARKET SHARING

Generally there are two methods of market sharing (1) Non-price competition and (2) Quota system.

1. Non-price Competition

Non-price competition is normally seen in "loose" cartels. The cartel sets a minimum price, and it is left to the whims and fancies of the firm to sell as much as they can. The only restriction is that firms are not allowed to cut prices below the cartel price. The best examples are haircutting, theatre tickets, medical services and legal services.

Due to the existence of cost differences cartels will be inherently unstable. The cartel price is the end result of bargaining among the firms. While the low-cost firms urge for a low price, the high cost firms press for a higher price. Therefore a mid-level price will be worked out with the consent of all partners. The non-price competition may take the form of advertising, customer's credit policies and product variations.

2. Quota System

The second method of market sharing is the quota system. Under this system the cartel allocates each firm a certain quota. The amount of quota depends upon

1. the bargaining ability and its relative importance in the industry.,
2. the relative sales of the firm in a pre-cartel base period and the productive capacity of the firm,

18. Robert Y. Ahw, *Op. cit.*, p. 338.

3. the relative advantage in geographical location.

Another method is to pool the orders, and allocate them on some pre-arranged system.

Let us assume that there are two firms and they divide the market.

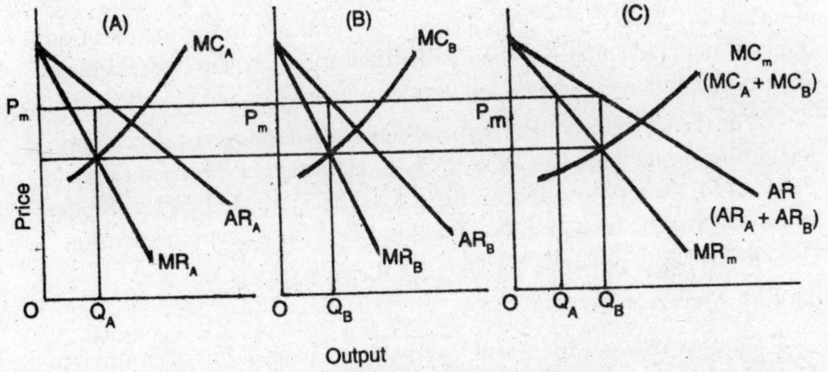

Fig. 27.6

Table 27.2
Quota Allocation under Cartel Agreement

	Firm A	*Firm B*	*Industry*
Average revenue curve	AR_A	AR_B	AR_m $(AR_A + AR_B)$
Marginal revenue curve	MR_A	MR_B	MR_m $(MR_A + MR_B)$
Marginal cost curve	MC_A	MC_B	MC_m $(MC_A + MC_B)$
Market share	OQ_A	OQ_B	OQ_m $(OQ_A + OQ_B)$

The fixation of price and output is based on the monopoly principle, Equilibrium is attained at the point where $MC_m = MR_m$. The cartels monopoly price is OP_m and the quotas will be

$$OQ_A + OQ_B = 1/2\ OQ_m$$

In the end, we may conclude that there is no guarantee that cartels create conditions for price stability in an oligopolistic market. New entrants free-riders and chiselers create instability in price and output.[19]

KINKED DEMAND CURVE

Several decades ago, economists believed that they had noticed something quite significant about oligopolies. For relatively long periods of time, prices in these industries seemed to remain more or less fixed. This observed "stickiness" of oligopolistic prices gave rise to the theory of the "kinked" demand curve — a theory that tries not to explain how prices are determined, but as to why they do not change very much.

The theory of the kinked demand curve was developed independently and almost simultaneously (1939) by R.L. Hall and C.J. Hitch in England and Paul M. Sweezy in America. But it was first outlined by Prof. Kaldor in 1934, while he reviewed the "Economics of Imperfect Competition." He called it as an "Imaginary Demand Curve."

Paul M. Sweezy's Version

Paul M. Sweezy of Harvard University in an article in the journal of political economy in 1938 argued that oligopolistic firms have "sticky" prices. Sweezy's kinked demand curve model attempts to explain why price stability or rigidity exists in oligopolistic firms. Sweezy writes, as oligopoly is the 'typical case' of most of the present day markets, a systematic inquiry into the nature of the demand curve is called for.

REASONS FOR PRICE RIGIDITY

The oligopolist may not like to vary the price due to several reasons.

Firstly, through experience he might have learnt about the futility of price wars.

Secondly, frequent changes in prices may irritate the consumers.

Thirdly, it avoids the unnecessary inconvenience of new price lists.

Fourthly, he may be satisfied with the existing level of price output and profit. So any change in price may result in a change in other variables too. So instead of inviting voluntary trouble, it is better to maintain the existing price.

Fifthly, the present price may have been established after a prolonged period of price war or collusion, and hence the firms may prefer to avoid a further confrontation.

---

19. Robert Y. Ahw, *Ibid.*, pp. 341-342.

Sixthly, when oligopoly firms are confronted with falling demand, instead of cutting prices they may intensify the sales promotion activities to increase demand.

Lastly, they may deliberately set a low price to block the entry of potential rivals into the industry.

The kinked demand curve as a tool of analysis can be traced from Chamberlin's intersection of the individual demand curve dd of the firm and its market share curve DD.

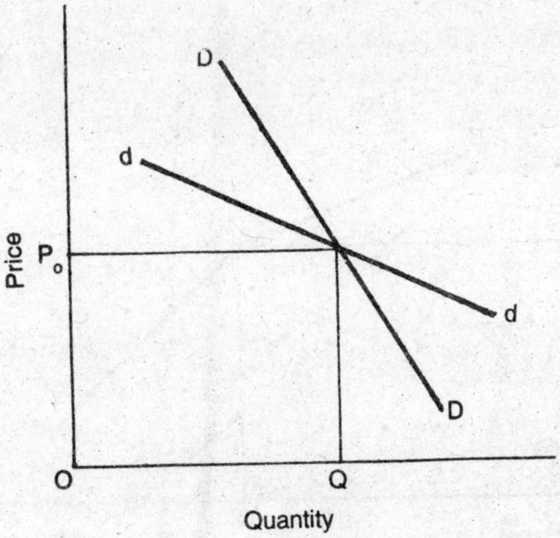

Fig. 27.7

In Fig. 27.7 dd is the demand curve that a particular oligopolistic firm faces if the other firms do not change their prices. DD is the demand curve the firm faces if all the firms charge the same price.

The demand curve of the oligopolist has a kink (at a point P in Fig. 27.8) reflecting the logical behavioural pattern of firms. When contemplating a change in price either upward or downward the seller must consider how his rivals will react. If he reduces his price he expects that his rivals will retaliate, by a matching price cut, so that, although the demand in the market increases the share of competitors remains unchanged. On the contrary, price increases do not usually invite such responses, because other firms will take the sales from the firm that raises its price. In other words, the kinked demand curve reflects the tendency of the competitors to follow price reductions than price increases.

In these circumstances, it will pay a firm to vary its price only under extreme provocation, that is, only if there is enormous change in its costs. For, the kinked demand curve represents a "head you lose, tails you lose" proposition in terms of any potential price change. If it raises its price, the firm will lose many customers (demand is elastic); if it lowers its price, the increase in quantity will be comparatively small (demand is inelastic).

AR curve = Dpd

MR curve = { DG corresponding to the segment DP of the AR curve
HJ corresponding to the segment pd of the AR curve }

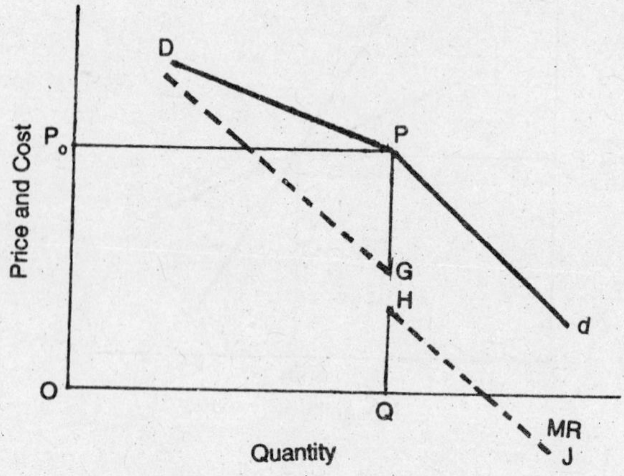

Fig. 27.8

If Fig. 27.8 the kink appears on the demand curve at p where the slope of the demand curve changes drastically. The prevailing price is OP_o and output is OQ. Dp portion of the demand curve is elastic, and so any increase in price will not only reduce his total sale but also his profits. On the other hand, pd portion of the demand curve is inelastic. Here any decrease in the price of the product will be counteracted by the rivals. So he may increase his sales but his net gain would be lesser than before. Thus the oligopoly price OP_o is determined for OQ output. Though Sweezy had mentioned the emergence of a kink and the consequent price rigidity, he conceded that sellers will provide secret concessions to their customers.

CHANGES IN COST

Sweezy assumes that as long as the marginal cost curve passes through the discontinuous portion of the marginal revenue curve, any fluctuation in the marginal cost is not likely to affect price and output. This is shown in the following Fig. 27.9.

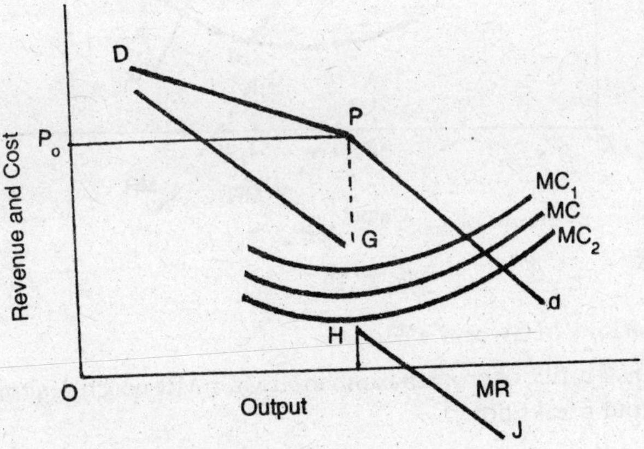

Fig. 27.9

The original marginal cost corresponding to OQ level of output is MC. If it shifts upward to MC_1 and downward to MC_2 as a result of changes in the marginal cost structure, the total output and price remains constant.

CHANGES IN DEMAND

Sweezy also assumes that a substantial change in demand may result only in a parallel horizontal shift in the demand curves, causing each firm's output to expand but the price to remain rigid at the level of the kink.

The original demand curve Dpd has the kink at p. Now due to some reason the demand curve shifts to dp_1d_1. The original price and output combination is OP_0 and OQ. The new relevant marginal revenue curve $DH_1G_1J_1$ has some gap in the H_1G_1 portion. The marginal cost curve still passes through the discontinuous portion of the marginal revenue curves. Now the profit maximising output is OQ_1 and the price is OP_0. Despite the change in demand, price is not changed by the firms.

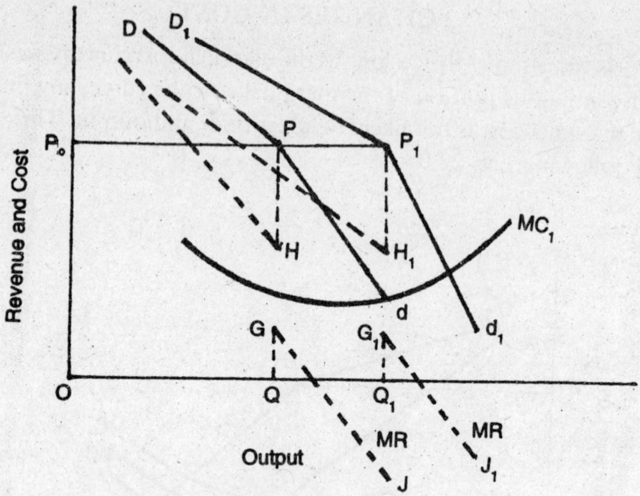

Fig. 27.10

Some Implications of Sweezy's Model

1. The equality rule of profit maximisation MC=MR which determines prices and output breaks down.

2. Shifts in the marginal cost curve will not affect the price or output within a given range. Therefore a general strike by trade unions can raise the wages without raising the prices.

3. Thirdly, since MC can shift up and down, MR remaining the same, it deviates from the marginal productivity theory, i.e., remuneration need not be equal to the value of marginal productivities.

Criticisms

The Sweezy model of the kinked demand curve is criticised on a number of aspects. While commenting on Sweezy's model Ferguson writes, "Sweezy's thesis must be regarded as an ex-post rationalisation rather than an ax-ante explanation of market equilibrium."[20]

Firstly, it is alleged that the model does not tell us how price and output are determined. In the words of Silberston "The most important and interesting question is not why prices are sticky in the short run," (if they are) but who decides what the price is to be, and on what principles."[21]

---

20. C.E. Ferguson — *Op.cit.*, p. 326.
21. Aubery Silberston, *Price Behaviour of Firms,* Economic Journal, 1970.

Secondly, George Stigler has empirically challenged the kinked demand curve as presented by Paul M. Sweezy. From his analysis of seven industries, cigarettes, automobiles, anthracite coal, steel, dynamite, gasoline and potash, he proved that the rivals follow price increases as readily as they match price cuts. Thus Stigler argues that, there is no objective basis to believe that any kink really exists in the oligopoly firm's demand curve.

Thirdly, the Sweezys model does not take into account the secret concessions, credit facility and easy returns that may be provided by rival sellers.

Fourthly, it is not applicable to cases of collusive oligopoly. If the rivals form a cartel and if the skepticism is removed the kink will disappear.

Lastly, Primeaux and Bomball examined electric utilities that are operated as a monopoly and those that are operated as duopoly and found that there was a greater price stability in monopoly than it was under duopoly.

However, the kinky demand curve analysis, as Prof. Baumol remarks, "does not show how the oligopolistic firms' view of competitive reaction patterns can affect the changeability of whatever price it happens to be charging."[22]

In the words of Prof. Peter Calvo, "The 'stickiness' of oligopoly prices provides atleast a partial explanation for the phenomenon that in times of economic recession and increasing unemployment (with substantial reduction in the level of output) there usually is no significant decline in prices."[23]

QUESTIONS

1. Explain why a demand curve can become kinked. What are the special features of oligopoly?
2. What is price-leadership under oligopoly?
3. What does the kinked demand curve explain?
4. What is the meaning of kinked demand curve in an oligopolistic market?
5. Define oligopoly and how price is determined under it:

   (*i*) with product differentiation, and (*ii*) without product differentiation.
6. What are the main types of collusion? Explain briefly the pricing problem of oligopoly under the centralized cartel and under market sharing cartel.
7. Why do oligopolistic firms have incentives to collude? What are the requirements for a successful cartel? Why are these requirements seldom met in practice?

---

22. William J. Baumol, *Op. cit.*, p. 414.
23. *Micro Economics*, Tata McGraw-Hill, New Delhi 1979, p. 209.

8. Explain briefly the functioning of dominant price leadership in an economy.
9. Explain the significance of kinked demand curve for price determination under oligopoly.
10. Write a note on cartels which aim at joint profit maximisation.
11. Do you agree with the view that price under oligopolistic competition is indeterminate.

❖ ❖ ❖

*** PART V ***

THEORY OF FACTOR PRICING

28

DISTRIBUTION

"***Economic and political theorizing, not based on facts and not controlled by facts, assuredly does lead nowhere.***"

— *Lord Beveridge*

MEANING OF DISTRIBUTION

The science of economics has been broadly divided into four basic divisions, namely, consumption, production, exchange and distribution. Distribution refers to that branch of economics which analyses how the national income of a country is divided among the various factors of production. "The economics of distribution," says Chapman "accounts for the sharing of the wealth, produced by a community among the agents, or the owners of the agents which have been active in its production."

FUNCTIONAL AND PERSONAL DISTRIBUTION

Functional distribution refers to the payments made to the factors of production for the contribution of those factors to National Income. Classical economists like Adam Smith and David Ricardo were concerned with the functional distribution of national income among the three basic factors of production — land, labour and capital.

Personal distribution refers to the income received by the individuals in a society.

In the words of Prof. Milton Friedman, "Personal distribution includes functional distribution, but not vice versa. The theory of personal distribution of income has therefore to explain not only how price or rewards for the services of factors of production are determined, but also how various people happen to own different quantities of these productive factors.[1]

In economic theory, we deal only with the functional distribution of income, though economists always comment on the personal distribution of income as well.

MARGINAL PRODUCTIVITY THEORY OF FACTOR PRICING

The theory of factor pricing is generally known as the marginal productivity theory of distribution. The origin of the concept of marginal productivity can be traced to the works of Ricardo and West. But J.B. Clark, Marshall and Hicks are the main exponents of this theory.

Statement of the Theory

According to J.B. Clark, "Under static conditions, every factor including the entrepreneur, would get a remuneration equal to its marginal product."

According to Prof. Mark Blaug,[2] "The marginal productivity theory contends that in equilibrium, each productive agent will be rewarded in accordance with its marginal productivity."

Meaning of Productivity

The demand for the factors of production is a derived demand; that is, the demand for such productive factors as labour and capital goods is derived from the demand for the final products that are produced by using these productive sources. For example, the demand for computer programmers, college professors and doctors is derived from the demand for computer services, educational services and health services respectively.

According to this theory, an entrepreneur will employ a factor till its marginal productivity is equal to its price.

Thus, MP_L = Price of labour.

THE CONCEPTS OF PRODUCTIVITY

1. Marginal Physical Product (MPP)

Marginal Physical Product is the physical addition made to the total product when one more unit of a factor is employed, keeping other factors constant.

$$MPP = TP_n - TP_{n-1}$$

1. Milton Friedman, *Price Theory — A Provisional Text,* Kalyani Publications, 1988, p. 15.
2. Mark Blaug, *Economic Theory in Retrospect,* Heinemann London, 1964, p. 44.

2. Marginal Value Product (MVP or VMP)

When we multiply price by MPP we get MVP. In other words, the MVP is the monetary representation of MPP.

$$VMP = MPP \times P$$

Where MPP stands for the marginal physical product of the factor, and P stands for the price of the product produced.

3. Marginal Revenue Product (MRP)

The marginal revenue product is the net addition to the total revenue by the employment of one additional unit of a factor, the quantity of other factors remaining constant.

$$MRP = MPP \times MR$$

Under perfect competition MR = AR. Therefore,

$$MRP = MPP \times MR \text{ or } MPP \times AR$$

Under imperfect competition MR < AR. Therefore MRP (MPP × MR) is less than VMP (MPP × AR).

4. Average Revenue Product

The average revenue product refers to the total revenue divided by the total number of units of that factor employed.

$$ARP = \frac{TR}{N}$$

Where ARP = average revenue product

TR = total revenue and

N = number of units of the factor employed.

Relationship between Average Revenue Product and Marginal Revenue Product

To a certain extent, the relationship between ARP and MRP is similar to the relationship between AC and MC. The only difference is that MC and AC are 'U' shaped while ARP and MRP are bell shaped (having the shape of an inverted 'U' or '∩').

The average and marginal revenue products depend upon the law of variable proportions, that is, they rise first, reach a maximum and then decline as shown in Fig. 28.1.

The measurement of some of the relevant concepts of productivity can be illustrated with the help of hypothetical data under perfect competition.

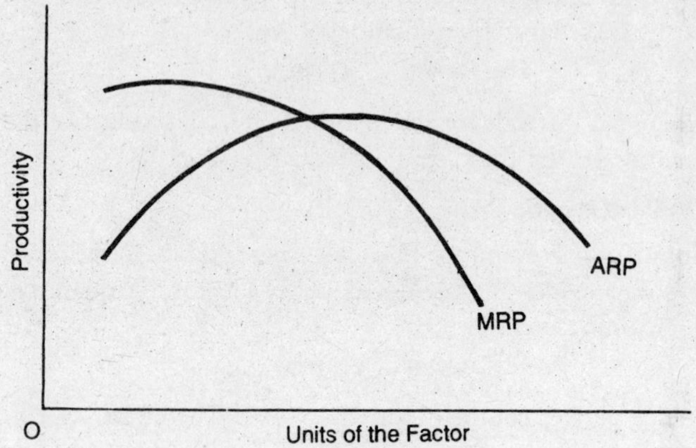

Fig. 28.1

Table 28.1

Value of Marginal product and a competitive firm's employment decision[2]

Quantity of input	*Marginal physical product (MPP)*	*Value of marginal product (VMP) (Rs. 5 × MPP)*	*Price of input*	*Optimal direction due to a change in input usage*
1	2	3	4	5
1	10	Rs. 50	Rs. 25	Increase
2	9	Rs. 45	Rs. 25	Increase
3	8	Rs. 40	Rs. 25	Increase
4	7	Rs. 35	Rs. 25	Increase
5	6	Rs. 30	Rs. 25	Increase
6	5	Rs. 25	Rs. 25	Do not change (equilibrium)
7	3	Rs. 15	Rs. 25	Decrease

Column (1) shows the amount of labour used per unit of time, say, per week. Column (2) shows the marginal physical product of the input. Assuming that the produced good sells at Rs. 5 per unit, the VMP is obtained by multiplying MPP × price. Column (4) indicates the price of the input, Rs. 25 per week.

2. Robert Y. Awh, *Micro Economics Theory and Applications,* John Wiley & Sons, New York, 1976, p. 387.

The firm will employ more units of labour as long as VMP is greater than the wage rate. Similarly, if VMP is less than the wage rate, the firm will reduce the use of labour. Thus, the equilibrium rate of employment is attained where VMP is equal to the wage rate. We must note that VMP is equal to MRP under perfect competition. Before proceeding further, even at this stage, it is worthwhile to introduce the concepts of average and marginal factor costs.

Average and Marginal Factor Costs

In a perfectly competitive factor market, the price of a factor is determined by the interaction of the forces of total demand and total supply of that factor. The firm can employ as many labourers as it wants at the prevailing market wage rate since it is one of the many firms. The factor supply curve is a horizontal straight line parallel to the X-axis. Since the factor price is assumed to be given and constant, the average factor cost (AFC) and the marginal factor cost (MFC) to the firm will be the same.

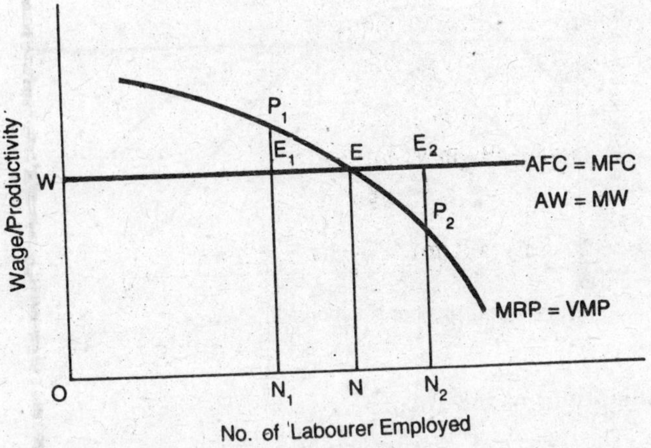

Fig. 28.2

A firm in the product market will be in equilibrium and will derive its maximum profit when MC = MR.

A firm in the factor market will be in equilibrium when MFC = MRP.

At the equilibrium point E, MRP = AW = MW. The number of labourers employed is ON. Suppose the firm employs ON_1 men, MRP (N_1P_1) will be greater than the wage rate N_1E_1. Therefore, the firm can increase its profits by employing more workers. On the contrary, if it employs ON_2 men, the marginal revenue product N_2P_2 will be less than the wage rate. The firm can therefore increase its profits by reducing the quantity of labour.

Industry's Equilibrium and Long Run Position

Though the firm is in equilibrium when MRP = MFC, it does not mean that the industry is in equilibrium. If a firm is able to make abnormal profits, new firms will enter into the factor market to buy labour. As a result, increased competition would tend to raise wages. Moreover with larger output in the market, there will be a fall in the price and a consequent fall in the marginal revenue product. This will continue till MRP = ARP = MFC. In this position, the firm neither incurs losses nor makes any abnormal profit.

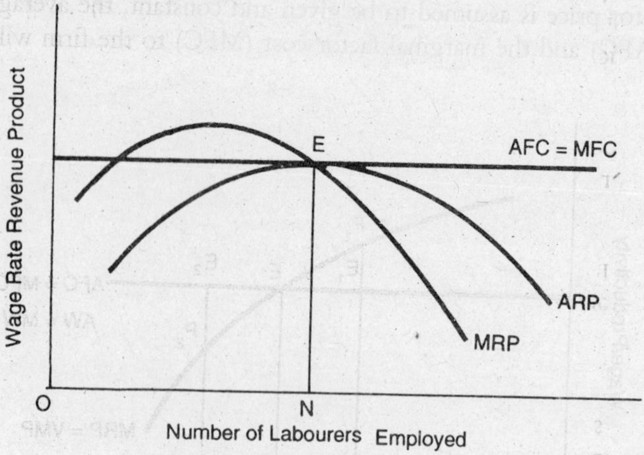

Fig. 28.3

Assumptions of the Theory

The marginal productivity theory of distribution rests on the following assumptions:

1. Perfect competition both in the factor and the product markets.
2. All the factor units are homogeneous.
3. The factors are divisible and substitutable.
4. Factors of production are mobile among the different uses.
5. The theory holds good only in the long run.
6. It is based on the law of variable proportions.

7. It is assumed that there is full employment.
8. Entrepreneurs are rational and they always try to maximise their profits.
9. There is no technological change.
10. There is no government intervention in the fixation of factor price.

Factor Pricing when there are many Variable Inputs

The logic of marginal productivity theory can be extended to inter-factor substitutions. The employer tries to achieve the least cost combination of factors. He attains equilibrium when marginal productivities of factors become proportional to their prices.

$$\frac{\text{MP of factor A}}{\text{Price of factor A}} = \frac{\text{MP of factor B}}{\text{Price of factor B}} = \frac{\text{MP of factor C}}{\text{Price of factor C}}$$

Critical Evaluation of the Marginal Productivity Theory

Though the marginal productivity theory is logically sound and perfect, it has its own drawbacks.

1. Perfect Competition

The theory assumes the presence of perfect competition. But in practice, perfect competition is a myth. If we drop the assumption of perfect competition, we cannot assert that the price paid to a factor would be equal to its marginal productivity.

2. Other Assumptions of the Theory are also Questionable

Firstly, the theory assumes that all units of a factor are homogeneous.

Units of labour differ in terms of their mental and physical abilities, training, motivation etc. Similarly, plots of land differ in fertility, and so on.

Secondly, the theory assumes full employment. But in real life, full employment is an exception rather than a rule.

Thirdly, the theory assumes perfect mobility of the factors, both geographically and occupationally. Land lacks mobility. Even the mobility of labour between different occupations and regions is restricted due to several social factors.

Fourthly, the theory assumes that factors are divisible. But certain factors like factory, machines etc., are indivisible.

Fifthly, the theory assumes profit maximisation as the only objective of a firm. But modern economists point out various other objectives for a firm.

3. Short Period Ignored

The theory holds good only in the long run. But in the long run, as Keynes rightly says "We are all dead." What is more important is the short run rather than the long run.

4. Objection of Keynes

According to this theory, the volume of employment can be increased by lowering wages. Prof. Pigou's policy of wage cut to solve the problem of unemployment is also based on the above view. But according to Keynes, the level of employment depends upon the level of effective demand, and not on the wage rate.

5. It is a Static Theory

The theory assumes that there is no change in technology. Therefore, the theory is not applicable to the present day world, which is dynamic in nature.

6. Theory of Exploitation

Bohm Bawerk criticized the theory since it justifies the unequal distribution of income and exploitation of the supra marginal units.

7. One-sided

The theory explains the demand side for factors. The supply side is ignored. The theory is, therefore, incomplete and one-sided.

8. Immeasurability

According to critics like Hobson, production is the outcome of the collective efforts of all the factors at a given time. Therefore, it is difficult to measure the marginal productivity of each factor separately.

9. The theory is basically explained for wage determination and is loosely extended for the pricing of other factors of production.

10. Normative Aspect is Ignored

It is a positive theory. It contains no ethical justification in determining factor rewards.

11. Reward Determines Productivity

According to this theory, the reward for a factor depends upon its marginal productivity. But as Prof. Sydney Webb says, enhanced wages will result in higher productivity. This may also be known as 'Shock effect.' Hence, reward is the cause and not the effect of wages.

12. Ignores Personal Distribution

The theory explains only functional distribution. The personal distribution aspect is not given importance.

While commenting on the theory, Prof. Samuelson writes, "It is simply a theory of one aspect of the demand for productive services by the firm."

On account of its various omissions, Prof. Nicholas Kaldor termed it as an "intellectual sterility."

QUESTIONS

1. What is meant by Distribution?
2. Distinguish between functional distribution and personal distribution.
3. Critically examine the Marginal Productivity Theory of Distribution.
4. Distinguish between marginal physical productivity and marginal revenue productivity.
5. Briefly state the classical theory of distribution.

❖ ❖ ❖

29

RENT

"It is cheaper to move than to pay rent."

—Joseph H. Peck

DIFFERENT CONCEPTS OF RENT

The term 'Rent' has different meanings and it is used in different senses.

(*a*) In ordinary language or as a layman's concept, rent is a price paid for the services of a durable good. It is known as contractual rent.

(*b*) In the Ricardian sense, rent is a payment by a tenant-farmer to the landlord, for the use of the land; and

(*c*) In the modern view, rent is a payment to any factor of production, over and above its transfer earnings.

RICARDIAN THEORY OF RENT

One of the oldest theories in economics, which have withstood the ravages of time, is Ricardo's theory of rent.

Ricardian theory of rent (1817) has an interesting antecedent.[1] In Britain, during the early part of the 19th century, food prices had greatly increased, partly due to the Napoleonic wars and partly due to increases in population. This caused a great deal of anxiety to the British government. The government therefore appointed a committee to report on the matter. The committee reported that food prices were high, because rents were high. But, Ricardo after carefully analyzing the problem pointed out the cause as otherwise. According to him, "rents were high because food prices were high."

Ricardian theory of rent is also known as the rent of productivity difference or the rent of fertility difference.

Ricardo defines rent as "that portion of the produce of the earth which is paid to the landlord for the use of the original and indestructible powers of the soil."

Ricardo considered payment of rent as an indication of the niggardliness of nature. This was contrary to the opinion of the French economists known as 'physiocrats' who considered rent as the result of the bounty of nature.

Assumptions

1. Specific Use of Land

1. Land has no alternative uses. At a given time a single agricultural commodity only is produced. The transfer price of land is therefore zero.

2. Rent depends upon two main qualities of land — fertility and location.

3. All the cultivable lands are owned by the landlords who rent out their lands to farmers. This means that no landlord is a farmer and no farmer is a landlord.

4. Differences in fertility: Land differs in fertility. Some lands are more fertile than others. If equal doses of labour and other supporting factors are applied on different grades of land, it results in a higher yield in some lands and lower yields in others.

5. Diminishing returns: According to Ricardo, the cultivation of land is subject to the law of diminishing returns.

6. Original and indestructible powers: Land possesses certain original and indestructible powers.

7. Perfect competition: The theory is based on the assumption of perfect competition. That is, there are a large number of landlords who want to give lands on rent and there are also a large number of farmers who wish to get lands on rent.

1. D.N. Dwivdi, *Principles of Economics,* Vani Educational Books, New Delhi, 1985, p.4.

8. Order of cultivation: Ricardo assumes an order of cultivation, i.e., the best land is cultivated first, and the next best is cultivated second and so on.

The theory assumes that rent is a surplus above the cost of production and, therefore, rent does not enter into the price of the product.

9. Marginal land: Ricardo assumes the existence of the marginal land or no-rent land, that is, the land from which the price that it secures for its product is exactly equal to its cost of production. There will be no surplus from this land.

10. Tendencies: Ricardian theory assumes the operation of two tendencies — the tendency of diminishing returns in agriculture and the tendency towards an increase in population.

How does rent arise?

Ricardo explained the emergence of rent with the help of a newly discovered island where people go to settle down first. Suppose there are three grades of land 'A', 'B' and 'C' arranged in their order of fertility. 'A' is the most fertile land and 'C' is the least fertile one. Suppose equal doses of inputs (labour, capital etc.,) are applied to these three grades of land. Let us further suppose that A grade land is cultivated first and the total yield from the A grade land is 1000 kg per hectare. If the price of the produce is Rs. 2 per kg., and the cost of cultivation is Rs. 2,000. 'A' will be a marginal land.

Table 29.1
Rent as a Differential Surplus

Grade of Land	*Cost of Cultivation (Rs.)*	*Production per hectare (kg.)*	*Value of output per hectare price Rs. 2 (per kg.)*	*Rent*
A	2000	1000	2000	No Rent — Marginal land

With the passage of time, the population of the island increases. Consequently, the demand for agricultural produce also increases. So, B grade land is now brought under the plough. Now the price rises to Rs. 3 per kg. and the total yield of the B grade land is 800 kg. per hectare. The cost of cultivation becomes Rs. 2,400.

Table 29.2

Grades of Land	*Cost of Cultivation (Rs)*	*Production per hectare (kg.)*	*Value of output per hectare price Rs. 3 (per kg.)*	*Rent*
A	2,400	1,000	3,000	600
B	2,400	800	2,400	Marginal land

Again, the population increases still further. The 'C' grade land also is brought under cultivation. Here, the cost of cultivation becomes Rs. 3,000; the yield from the 'C' grade land is 600 kg. and the price per kg. rises to Rs. 5.

Table 29.3

Grade of Land	*Cost of Cultivation (Rs)*	*Production per hectare (kg.)*	*Value of output per hectare price Rs. 5 (per kg.)*	*Rent*
A	3,000	1,000	5,000	2,000
B	3,000	800	4,000	1,000
C	3,000	600	3,000	Marginal land

The following diagram illustrates the concept of rent as a surplus.

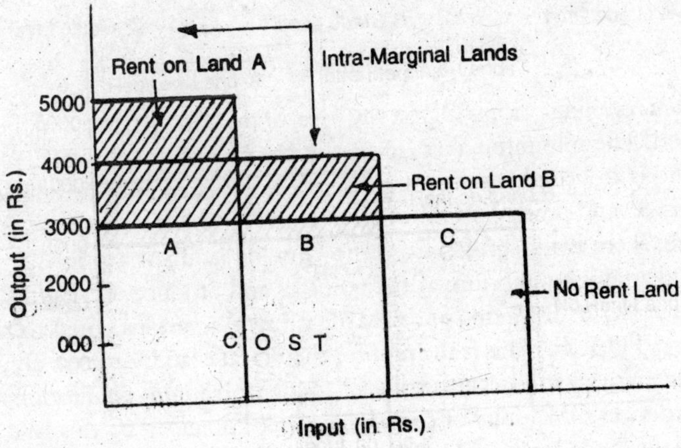

In the above diagram, the amounts of rent, earned by A and B grades of land are shown by the different shaded areas. C grade land just covers its cost. So, it is a 'No-Rent Land.' Hence, rent is a surplus between the production of the marginal and the intra-marginal lands.

Graphical Illustration of Ricardian Rent

The following three figures (A grade, B grade and C grade) illustrate the surplus arising in the superior A and B grades of land over the C grade of land, the yield from which covers just its cost of production. In all these figures, the curve AC is the average cost curve and the curve MC is the marginal cost curve.

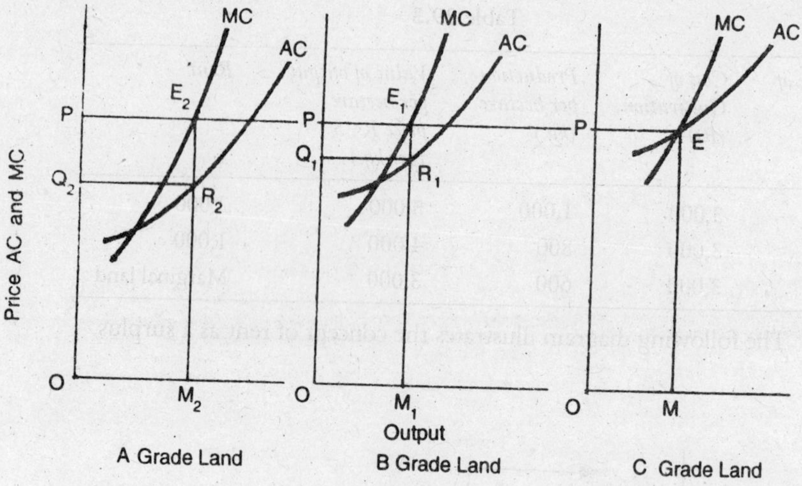

Fig. 29.2

The prevailing price is OP on the basis of the corn produced in the C grade land. The minimum average cost in the C grade land is ME. If C grade land is to be cultivated, the price of the produce must be equal to OP. C grade land produces OM units of corn. At E, MC = price = AC. Therefore, there is no surplus from the C grade land. At a price OP, B grade land attains equilibrium at the point E_1 and produces OM_1 units of corn. Since AC in B grade land is M_1R_1 it earns a surplus equal to the shaded area $PQ_1R_1E_1$. This is the rent for the B grade land. At price OP, A grade land enjoys a still larger surplus. A grade land attains equilibrium at E_2 and produces OM_2 units of corn. The surplus obtained by this land is shown by the shaded area is $PQ_2R_2E_2$. This is the rent for the A grade land.

Thus,

Rent in A grade land = $PQ_2R_2E_2$

Rent in B grade land = $PQ_1R_1E_1$

Rent in C grade land = Nil

INTENSIVE CULTIVATION

This is yet another type of farming. When the same plot of land is used over and over again with increasing inputs, it is known as 'intensive cultivation.' It is necessary to point out that Ricardo, used the assumption of the law of 'diminishing returns' in agriculture. It means that production increases at a diminishing rate when more and more units of labour and capital are employed on a given plot of land. The law helps us to come to the conclusion that rent also arises when all grades of land are alike in fertility and in their situation.

Instead of marginal land, now, we have the marginal doses of labour and capital. By the same logic, as in the case of extensive cultivation, the marginal dose should not yield any surplus.

Suppose a farmer Mr. X is cultivating a plot of 'A' grade land. To produce an increased output, he goes on adding additional doses of labour and capital in the same plot. The value of a dosc of labour and capital may be assumed to be Rs. 100. The first dose yields 400 kg. of sugarcane. The second dose gives him 200 kg. and the third dose only 100 kg. The marginal return from each dose goes on diminishing, because of the operation of the law of diminishing returns. The price of sugarcane is assumed to be Re. 1 per kilo. These facts can also be put in the form of a table as given below.

Table 29.4

Units of Labour and Capital	*Cost in Rs.*	*Marginal Production in units (in kg.)*	*Value of output at Re. 1 per kg.*	*Rent in Rs.*
1.	100	400	400	300
2.	100	200	200	100
3.	100	100	100	NIL (Marginal dose)

The table 29.4 explains that the 1st, and 2nd units earn rent, not due to differences in the fertility of land, but due to the law of diminishing returns on the same plot of land. The phenomenon of rent under intensive cultivation could also be depicted as in Fig. 29.3.

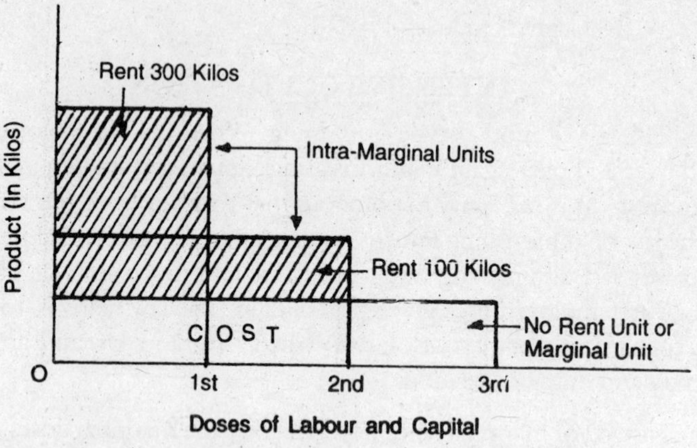

Fig. 29.3

SITUATIONAL RENT

Rent can also arise in cases of situational or locational advantage. As Ricardo pointed out "The most fertile and the most favourably situated land will be cultivated first. If all lands are equally fertile, rent will not arise unless a particular land enjoys the advantage of situation."

Let us assume that all lands are equally fertile. But some lands are situated near the market, while the others are located at a distance and away from the market. The yield from all lands per hectare may be 100 quintals. Here the lands located at a distance will not be cultivated first, because, in addition to the expenses due to doses of labour and capital employed, some extra expenditure has to be incurred in transporting the produce from the distant land to the market. The lands which are situated near the market need not incur the same expenditure. The better situated lands, therefore, yield rent.

CRITICAL EVALUATION OF THE RICARDIAN THEORY

Critics have lost no opportunity in placing a sharp finger at, the fallacies in the reasoning of Ricardo. Some of the major criticisms levelled against the Ricardian theory of rent are the following:

1. Ricardo's Concept of Land is Wrong

Ricardo's expression that rent is due to the "original and indestructible powers of the soil" is incompatible with modern scientific facts. The powers of the soil are neither original nor indestructible. Even fertile lands become barren by indiscriminate cropping. Likewise, by applying fertilizers and other improved techniques of cultivation, the fertility of the soil can be immensely increased. Similarly, in this nuclear age, nothing can be contended as indestructible. However, as Prof. Haney has remarked there are certain elements like rainfall, sunshine, climate etc., which cannot be substantially altered even with the present state of our knowledge.

2. No Historical Evidence

According to critics, Ricardo's order of cultivation, that is, the best fertile and most favourably situated land will be cultivated first is highly objectionable. An American economist Henry Carey, has pointed out, that the order of cultivation is just the reverse. For example, people from England, Holland, etc. have settled in the U.S.A. even from the beginning of the 17th century. But they occupied only the coastal area. It took them nearly two hundred years or more to move on to the west and occupy the most fertile areas of the United States, known as the 'Middle West'.[2]

This criticism is not sound. The order of cultivation is only an illustration and a method of presentation made by Ricardo just to explain that lands differ in their fertility. Ricardo's theory is not disproved even if the order of cultivation is reversed.

3. Assumption of Perfect Competition

The most damaging criticism against the Ricardian theory is that it is thoroughly hypothetical and unreal. It is based on perfect competition, which is unrealistic.

4. Rent Elements are found in all Factor Earnings

According to modern economists, it is not the supply of land only that is inelastic. This inelastic feature may be present in the case of labour and capital as well. Therefore, any excess income earned by a factor of production over and above its transfer price, is rent.

5. Multiple Factors Determine Productivity

Ricardo has used the concept of fertility of land in a very vague manner; fertility depends upon the location of land, agricultural practices of farmers, cropping patterns etc.

---

2. K.P.M. Sundhram, *Micro Economics*, 7th edn., Sultan Chand & Sons, New Delhi, 1988, P. 400.

6. No-Rent Land does not exist

The concept of marginal land is said to be theoretical, imaginary and not realistic. No-rent land is one which yields just enough to meet the expenses of cultivation, leaving no surplus. The use of this concept is not important for the study of the theory of rent. Even if a piece of land does not earn rent in any one use, it can be put to an alternative use where it can earn a surplus.

7. Scarcity Aspect is Ignored

Ricardo did not consider the scarcity aspect of land rent. According to Ricardo, rent would not arise if all lands were equally fertile. But as long as land is scarce, that is, demand for land is more than its supply, rent would arise. Therefore, the realistic approach to the problem of the emergence of rent should be studied through the scarcity pricing and not by the differential principle.

8. The Law of Diminishing Returns can be held in Abeyance

The theory assumes the operation of the law of diminishing returns. But with the advancement of science and technology, the operation of this law has been postponed not only in England but also throughout the continent of Europe. Ricardo could not visualize this phenomena.

9. Capital and Labour cannot be treated as a Single Homogeneous Factor

Ricardo in his analysis of rent treated capital and labour as a single homogeneous factor, and rent as a residual payment after the joint shares of capital and labour have been paid. But this seems to be absurd on two grounds. Firstly, labour and capital are separate factors that receive separate rewards, and secondly, Ricardo does not clarify the proportions in which capital and labour are used along with land.

10. Rent is a Cost Entering into Price

Ricardo's conclusion that rent does not enter into the cost of production and therefore, it does not enter into price, is erroneous. According to Ricardo, price determines rent. Rent is high when the price is high and rent is low when the price is low. This relationship between rent and price is not always true. Critics argue that the rent of land is a cost, and as such, enters into the price of the product. The error in Ricardo's conclusion crept in because he contemplated only one use for land, namely, cultivation.

Conclusion

Despite these drawbacks, the Ricardian theory of rent occupies a respectable place in economic literature. To Ricardo, rent was essentially an unearned income to the landlord without any effort. He is 'a parasite' and an interloper. It was on the basis of this theory that, an American writer Henry George in his book, 'Progress and Poverty' (1879) advocated a single tax proposal. Moreover, it brought into limelight the practical nature of landlordism. From the time of Ricardo, radical economists had started pleading for the confiscation of rent or nationalization of land by the state.

Karl Marx, the Father of Communism, with the help of his concept of surplus value and unearned income urged for the annihilation of landlords and capitalists who lived and thrived on surpluses. Thus, in the words, of Prof. Robertson, the theory has "by no means lost its validity and instructiveness."

QUASI-RENT

The term quasi-rent, which literally means semi-rent was introduced into economic literature by Marshall. It is an extension of the Ricardian concept of rent. In the words of Prof. K.N. Prasad[3] "The concept is a fortuitous gain like 'Consumer's surplus." The basic dividing line between rent and quasi-rent is that while rent is applied to income from land and other free gifts of nature, quasi-rent is the income derived from man-made machines and appliances.

There are some factors of production, whose supply in the long-run is elastic, but in the short-run is inelastic. Marshall terms these factors as 'machines and other appliances made by man.' The factors like ships, houses, machines etc. are fixed in supply in the short-run. When the demand for them increases, their supply being fixed, they earn a surplus which is not rent but is similar to rent. Marshall preferred to call it quasi-rent. In other words, quasi-rent is earned during a period when the supply of man-made factors cannot be adjusted in response to an increase in the demand for them. Quasi-rent is a short-run concept. It vanishes with an increase in the supply of such inputs in the long-run.

Quasi-rent has also been defined as the excess of total revenue earned in the short run over and above the total variable cost.

$$QR = TR - TVC.$$

3. K.N. Prasad, *Lectures on Micro-Economic Theory*, Himalaya Publishing House, Mumbai, 1986, p. 462.

In the short-run, a firm under perfect competition must cover its prime or variable costs. Variable costs are payments for raw materials, fuels, depreciation associated with the use of the plant and equipment, most of the labour costs, excise taxes etc. The firm can continue to produce the product even if it is able to cover the cost just equal to AVC and none of its fixed cost (in the hope of recovering both the costs in the long period). If the price of the product is less than the AVC, the firm will shut-down its business and if the price of the product rises to more than the AVC, there will rise a surplus which is termed as quasi-rent. In the long-run the distinction between fixed costs and variable cost disappear and all costs become variable costs and so, the firm must cover both the costs; otherwise the firm will cease to exist. Since there is no fixed cost in the long-run, quasi-rent does not arise in the long-run.

Quasi-rent can be defined as "the short-run earnings of machines minus the short-run costs of keeping it in running order."

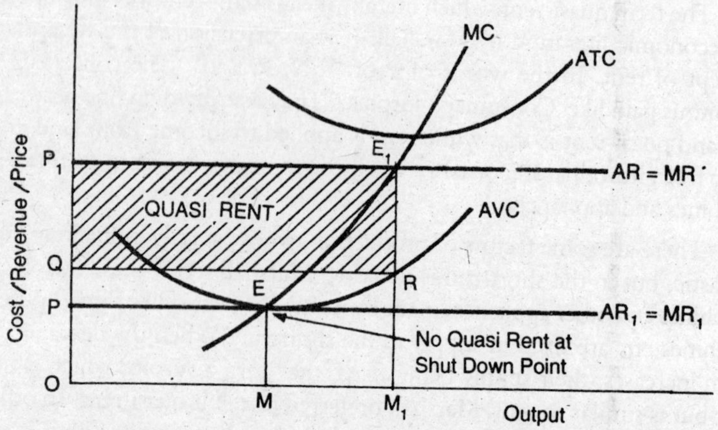

Fig. 29.4

In Fig. 29.4, suppose the market price is OP. At point E, MC becomes equal to the price. The output of the firm is OM. The price OP covers just the average variable cost. It is the critical shut-down point. Suppose the market price is OP_1. At point E_1, MC becomes equal to the price. The price OP_1 not only covers the average variable cost but also leaves a surplus. At OM_1 level of output, the average variable cost is M_1R. The price OP_1 (or M_1E_1) is greater than the average variable cost of M_1R.

Here, total receipts at OM_1 output $= OM_1E_1P_1$

The total variable cost $= OM_1RQ$

Therefore, quasi-rent $= OM_1E_1P_1 - OM_1RQ$

$= QRE_1P_1$

The quasi-rent of Marshall can be illustrated in many ways.

During the world war II, there was a sudden increase in the demand for shipping. But the supply of ships could not be increased overnight. Since there was acute shortage of shipping space during the war time, the freight charges went up. Not only the existing ships earned enormous income, but old and discarded ships which were pressed in to service, also earned abnormal freights. Thus, the ships earned a surplus over their normal income. In the long period, new ships were constructed and shipping charges came down. Hence the quasi-rent earned by the ships in the initial periods of war, disappeared altogether.

Differences between Rent and Quasi-rent

Rent	*Quasi-rent*
1. Permanent phenomenon.	A temporary phenomenon.
2. Accrues to land and other free gifts of nature, whose supply is fixed in the short as well as in the long period.	Accrues to factors (other than land and other free gifts of nature) whose supply is inelastic in the short-run, but elastic in the long-run.
3. It is a payment to induce the owners to offer their factors in the market.	It is not a payment to induce a factor to enter into the market.
4. Rent does enter into the price.	Quasi-rent does not enter into the cost and it is price determined.
5. Rent is the result of a differential surplus.	It is the result of the relative short term scarcity of a factor in relation to its demand.
6. It is a differential surplus of super-marginal land over marginal land.	It is an extra income over the normal earnings.

MODERN THEORY OF RENT OR DEMAND AND SUPPLY THEORY OF RENT

Modern economists have provided a better explanation of the phenomenon of rent. According to modern economists, rent arises due to the relative scarcity of land in relation to its demand. It is contrary to the view of Ricardo who held that rent arises due to the differential fertilities of land. The rent of land is obviously determined by the demand for and the supply of land. This is the reason why the modern theory of rent is also known as the demand and supply theory of rent.

Demand for Land

The demand for land is a derived demand. It is derived from the demand for the products of land. If the demand for products rises, the demand for land will also rise correspondingly. If the demand for products falls the demand for land will also decrease. This will lead to a corresponding increase or decrease in rent. For example, if the population of a country increases, the demand for land will also increase along with it. Consequently, the demand for land will increase leading to an increased rent.

We have already seen under the marginal productivity theory that the demand for a factor depends upon its marginal productivity, i.e., marginal revenue productivity. The MRP is subject to the law of diminishing returns. This is the reason why the demand curve for land slopes downwards from the left to the right.

Supply of Land

The supply of land is fixed for the community as a whole, but individuals can increase their own supply by acquiring more land from others or decrease supply by parting with land. In spite of the many reclamation projects (the effect of which on the total supply is negligible) the supply of land remains practically fixed. It is a case of perfectly inelastic supply, which means that whatever may be rent, the supply remains the same. This is the reason why land has no supply price.

Interaction of Demand and Supply

In Fig. 29.5, SS is the supply curve indicating fixed supply. DD is the total demand curve for land. Both the curves intersect at point E and

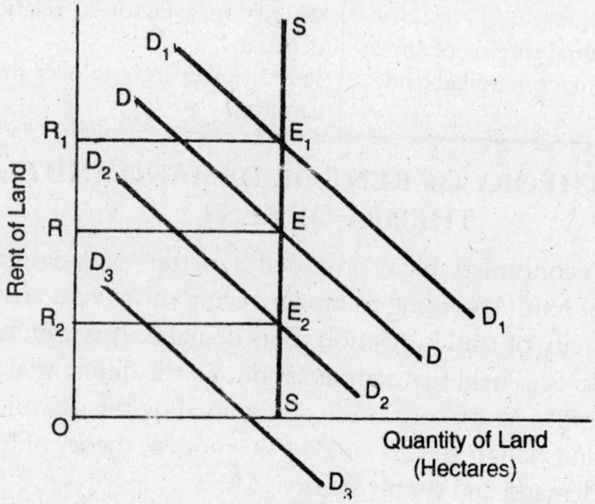

Fig. 29.5

the rent is fixed at OR. If the rent is less than OR, the demand for land will increase and make the rent rise again to OR. If the rent rises above OR, then the demand for land will decrease, and bring the rent back to OR.

Suppose due to an increase in population the demand for land has increased from DD to D_1D_1. The supply curve will still be the same as SS. The new point of intersection will be E_1 and the corresponding rent will be OR_1. If demand falls to D_2D_2 then the point of intersection of the two curves will be E_2 and the rent will be OR_2. When the supply of land is plentiful in relation to its demand, the land will not command a price and it will be a free commodity. This situation occurred in the free land era of American history. This condition is shown by D_3D_3.

In the above discussion, we have assumed that land is homogeneous. But in actual life, there may be different qualities of land. In such a case, each quality will have a separate demand curve and they will command different rates. Hence, this demand-supply theory explains the differential rent also.

In conclusion, we can say that, like the remuneration for other factors of production, rent also is determined by its demand and supply. In other words, it is the scarcity in relation to demand that determines rent.

Rent in a Particular Use

We have discussed above the total demand and the total supply of land for the community as a whole. Now, we shall discuss the demand and supply of land for a particular industry (firm) or for a particular use. The industry can get more supplies by offering more rent. So from the individual

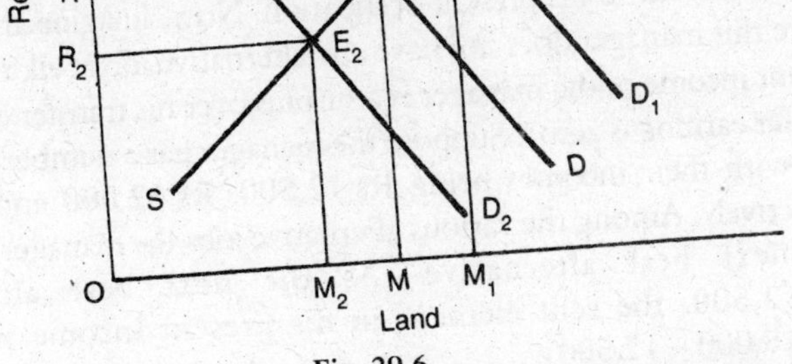

Fig. 29.6

or industry point of view, the supply curve will not be a vertical straight line. The supply curve will be elastic and it will be rising upwards from left to right as shown in the Fig. 29.6.

In Fig. 29.6 SS is the supply curve indicating that more will be available with increased rent. DD is the demand curve. The point of equilibrium is E and the corresponding rent is OR. At this rent OR, the firm uses OM quantity of land. Suppose, the demand increases to D_1D_1, the new point of equilibrium is E_1 and the rent rises to OR_1 and the quantity demanded becomes OM_1. Here MM_1 quantity of land has been withdrawn from its other uses and put to this use. Similarly when the demand decreases to D_2D_2 the rent will come down to OR_2 and the quantity of land will come down to OM_2. Here MM_2 land has gone out of this particular use, since the rent has fallen.

Modern economists are of the view that what is true of land is equally true of the other factors of production also.

Transfer Earnings or Opportunity Costs

Modern economists also evolved the concept of transfer earnings or opportunity costs while explaining rent. The modern concept of rent is applicable to all the factors of production including land.

Economic rent is the payment to a factor over and above what is necessary to keep the factor in its current use. In other words, the difference between what a factor actually earns and what it could earn in its next best possible, alternative use. A few examples will help to explain the concept clearly.

Labour

Suppose Mr. Dhanaraj is a Bank Manager whose present salary is Rs. 15,000. If he were to go to an alternative job, and if he again gets Rs. 15,000; then he does not get any surplus over his transfer earnings. Here his present earnings just equals his transfer earnings and hence there is no element of rent in his present occupation. Now, imagine an extreme case where this manager does not have any alternative job at all, then the entire present income of the manager is a surplus over his transfer earnings (here transfer earning is zero). Suppose the manager has a number of alternative jobs with their incomes being Rs.12,500, Rs.12,000 and Rs. 10,000 respectively. Among the various alternative jobs the manager will consider the next best alternative. As the next best alternative is Rs. 12,500, the rent element in his present income is Rs. 2,500 (Rs. 15,000 – 12,500).

Land

Suppose a piece of land is allotted to the cultivation of cotton by which the owner of land earns a sum of Rs. 2,000. In its next best alternative use, say cultivation of onion, it can fetch only Rs. 1,600. Now it earns Rs. 400 more than its transfer earnings, which is a surplus, this is the economic measure of rent.

Capital

Suppose one is getting a 20 per cent interest in a private chit company on his capital. If the next best alternative investment is a fixed deposit in a commercial bank from which he can get only 13 per cent. Here, the present investment gives an excess of 7 per cent over its transfer earnings. This is economic rent.

Thus the concept of rent is applicable to all the factors of production.

In the words of Joan Robinson[4], "The essence of the conception of rent is the conception of a surplus earned by a particular part of a factor of production over and above the minimum earnings necessary to induce it to do its work."

What Determines the Size of Economic Rent?

The size of economic rent earned by a particular type of a factor depends upon the elasticity of supply of that factor and the way the particular type of factor is defined.

From the point of view of elasticity of supply, there are three possibilities.

1. When the supply is perfectly elastic.
2. When the supply is perfectly inelastic.
3. When the supply is imperfectly elastic.

1. When the Supply is Perfectly Elastic

If the supply of a factor of production is perfectly elastic, then the actual earnings will be equal to its transfer earnings because the price of the factor is fixed.

For example, under perfect competition, the supply of a factor of production for an individual firm is perfectly elastic.

In the above figure X-axis represents the units of labour and Y-axis represents the wage rate. Units of labour are assumed to be homogeneous. The demand for labour is DD and the supply of labour is SS and they intersect at point E. Now the wage per worker is OW = NE and the number of workers employed is ON.

---

4. *The Economics of Imperfect Competition*, Macmillan & Co. Ltd., London, 1965, p. 102.

Total remuneration = ONEW
Total transfer earnings = ONEW
Surplus or economic rent = Nil

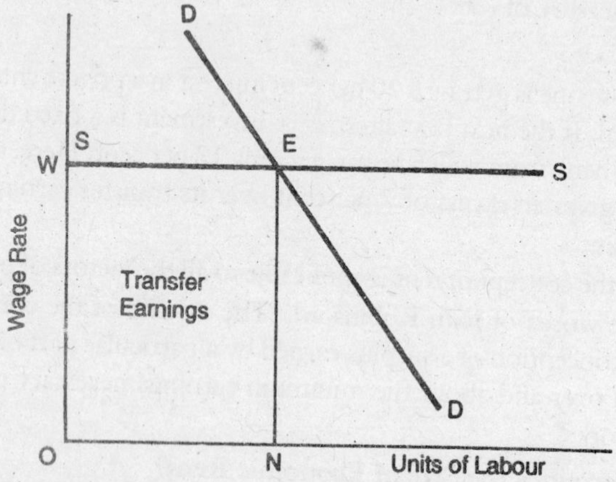

Fig. 29.7

Thus, when the supply of any factor is perfectly elastic, to a firm, or industry, the factor does not earn any rent.

2. When the Supply is Perfectly Inelastic

If the supply curve of a factor of production is perfectly inelastic, then its transfer earnings will be zero. This is illustrated in the following Fig. 29.8

Suppose there is only one use for a particular plot of land. Since the land cannot be shifted from its current location and there is no alternative use for the land, nothing extra has to be paid to retain it in its current use.

Total remuneration = ONEW
Total transfer cost = Nil
Surplus or economic rent = ONEW

Thus the return for a factor whose supply is completely fixed is often referred to as pure economic rent.

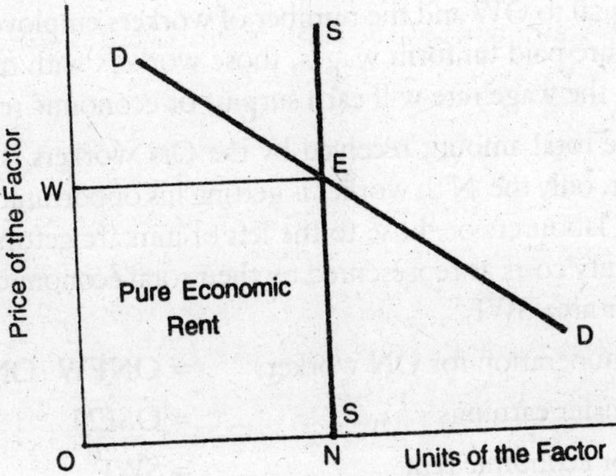

Fig. 29.8

3. When the Supply is Imperfectly Elastic

If the supply curve of a factor of production is elastic, but not perfectly elastic, then a part of the income (price) of the factor is rent.

Let us consider the supply of a particular kind of labour with a given skill in a particular industry. The workers may be heterogeneous from the point of view of other industries. Consequently, transfer earnings would also be different. The supply curve is upward sloping showing that additional workers will be available when higher wages are offered.

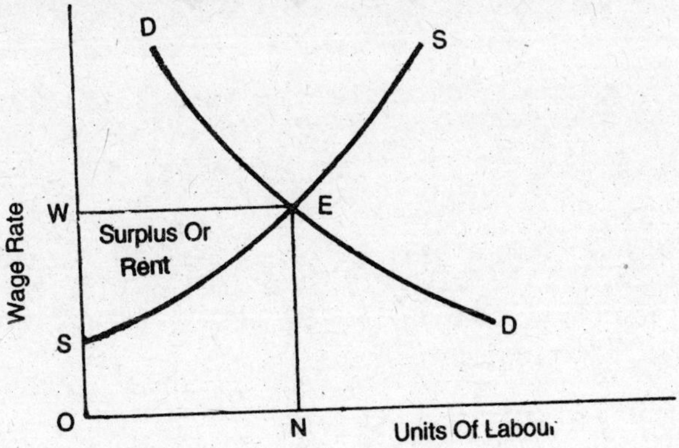

Fig. 29.9

Fig. 29.9 is a hypothetical model of the supply and demand for labourers under perfect competition. The equilibrium point is E. The wage rate is equal to OW and the number of workers employed is ON. Since all workers are paid uniform wages, those workers with transfer earnings of less than the wage rate will earn surplus or economic rent.

The total amount received by the ON workers is the area OWEN. However, only the 'N'th worker is getting his opportunity cost, those intra-marginal labourers or those to the left of him are getting more than their opportunity costs as represented by their total economic rent, namely, the triangular area SWE.

Total remuneration for ON workers	= ONEW (ON x OW)
Total transfer earnings	= OSEN
Surplus or economic rent	= SWE

QUESTIONS

1. What is quasi-rent?
2. What does Marshall understand by "Quasi Rent"?
3. What is no rent land?
4. Explain the concept of Transfer earnings?
5. Distinguish between rent and quasi-rent.
6. Distinguish differential rent from scarcity rent?
7. Critically examine the Ricardian theory of rent. Explain the limitations of the theory.
8. Examine Ricardo's Theory of Rent.
9. Discuss the modern theory of rent. What is the idea of transfer earnings in it?

❖ ❖ ❖

30

WAGES

"Wages are determined by the bitter struggle between capitalist and worker."
— Karl Marx, 1867

INTRODUCTION

The term 'wages' means payments made for the services of labour. Labour can be either 'mental labour' or 'physical labour.' According to T.R. Turner, "A wage is a price; it is the price, paid by the employer to the worker on account of labour performed."

NOMINAL WAGE AND REAL WAGE

It is customary to distinguish between nominal wages and real wages.

Nominal wages, also called money wages, refer to the amount of wages paid in money. For example, if Mr. X receives a sum of Rs. 2,000 per month, this amount is his nominal wage. Real wages mean conversion of money wages into real terms. It refers to the quantities of goods and services which can be bought with the money wage. But money wages do not reflect the real picture of the economic position of a worker.

FACTORS DETERMINING REAL WAGES

The factors determining the real wages of a labourer are the following:

1. Level of Money Wage

Other things remaining the same, the higher the money wage rate, the higher will be the real wage rate. As money wages rise, real wages also tend to go up.

2. Purchasing Power of Money

Purchasing power of money refers to the quantity of goods and services which a unit of currency can buy. The purchasing power of money varies inversely with the price level. A rise in the general price level leads to a fall in the purchasing power of money and consequently a decline in real wages and vice versa.

One hundred rupees in 1950 had a much greater purchasing power than in 1997. The cost of living varies in different regions and though money wages may be high in cities like Delhi and Mumbai, the real wage may be far less than what it would be in rural areas for the same level of money wages.

3. Opportunities for Supplementary Earnings

Certain occupations provide opportunities for supplementary earnings. A bearer in a five star hotel has an opportunity to supplement his wage with the tips he gets from his customers. A peon in a college has no such possibility. To that extent the hotel bearer's real wage is higher. Likewise professors earn additional income by valuing answer papers or setting question papers or from tuition fees and so on.

4. Additional Facilities

A worker in addition to his money wage may also receive some payments in kind. These may be called fringe benefits. For example, workers in estates may be provided with rent-free quarters, subsidized food, free fuel and other facilities. Provident fund contributions and bonus during services and pension after retirement must be counted while computing real wages.

5. Extra Work without Extra Payment

If workers are required to do extra work without compensation, their real wages will be less to that extent.

6. Nature of Employment

A worker's real wage also depends upon the regularity of his employment. Some jobs are permanent while some others are seasonal. In those occupations in which employment is regular or more secure, money wages may be lower but real wages may be higher. But irregular and insecure employments may carry higher money wages, but their real wages will be smaller. The wage covers a sort of a retaining fee for the time when the worker has nothing to do.

7. Strain of Work

Some occupations are risky, others are tiresome; some are healthier than others and so on. The work may be more pleasant or less pleasant, and so on. For instance, a pilot, or miner is paid a higher money wage than a clerk in a post office. All these things should be taken into account in estimating a person's real earnings.

8. Professional Expenses

A college lecturer who is interested in keeping abreast of in the day-to-day developments of the world for efficient teaching has to spend a handsome amount on books and services; while an accountant in a bank getting the same salary has no such expenses and to that extent the bank accountant's real wage is higher.

9. Cost of Professional Training

Some professionals such as technicians, computer and electronic operators, scientists, doctors spend huge amounts of money and spend a number of years on their training. Therefore, in calculating their real wage, we must deduct the cost of their training from their money wage.

10. Future Prospects

The anticipation of promotion, better treatment and higher wages in future may induce a person to accept a job for a low wage. So while calculating the wages of two persons, one with a higher wage and the other with a lower wage, an allowance has to be made to the present value attached to the anticipated increased earnings in the future.

11. Social Status

A manager working in a private company and an I.P.S. Officer may be having the same scale of pay and other facilities, but the I.P.S. officer has a social status which makes his real wage higher than that of the manager.

SUBSISTENCE THEORY OF WAGES

This is the oldest theory of wages, which was first given by physiocrats, a group of French economists and restated later by David Ricardo. Classicals called it the natural law of wages. The subsistence theory is based on two important assumptions. Firstly, population increases at a faster rate and secondly food production is subject to the law of diminishing returns. In the words of Prof. K.N. Prasad, "Ricardian wage theory was a successful marriage of the Malthusian population theory and the Ricardian rent theory."

According to this theory, just as the value of a commodity under perfect competition is determined by its cost of production, the value of the commodity, labour, is determined by its cost of production, i.e., the minimum subsistence amount required for the support of the labourer and his family in order to ensure a continuous supply of labour. In the long run, wages tend to become equal to the subsistence level. If at any time, the wages rise more than this subsistence level the workers are encouraged to marry and to have larger families. The larger supply of labour brings down wages again to the subsistence level. On the contrary, if wages fall below the subsistence level, there will be postponed marriages, starvation deaths and miseries leading to a fall in the supply of labour. The decrease in the supply of labour in this situation, pushes up wages again to the subsistence level. In short, population is responsive to wages. Thus in the long-run, wages will tend to stabilise at the subsistence level. No wonder the French socialist, Ferdinand Lassalse called it the "Iron law" or the "Brazen law" of wages because of the assumed rigidity of the principle. The main implication of the subsistence theory is that trade unions are not powerful organizations to raise the wage rates, so that they are not needed. At the best, it can disturb the subsistence wage level in the short-run, but in the long-run subsistence wage only will prevail. Professor Lewis', theory of economic development with unlimited supplies of labour is based on the assumption that in under developed countries the supply of labour is perfectly elastic at the existing subsistence wage rate.

Karl Marx, the father of scientific socialism, made the subsistence theory of wages the basis for his theory of capitalistic exploitation. Marx asserts that the growth of modern large scale industries and labour saving methods destroys the cottage and small-scale industries in a capitalistic system. The net result is the emergence of an industrial reserve army of unemployed people. Naturally the wage rate is prevented to rise above the subsistence level.

The subsistence theory may be applicable to a certain extent in under developed countries like India. In rural India the powerful landlords may be able to back-rent their tenants. In the context of the industrially advanced countries like America and England, the subsistence theory of wages has lost its relevance and significance completely.

The theory has been explained with the following Figure 30.1.

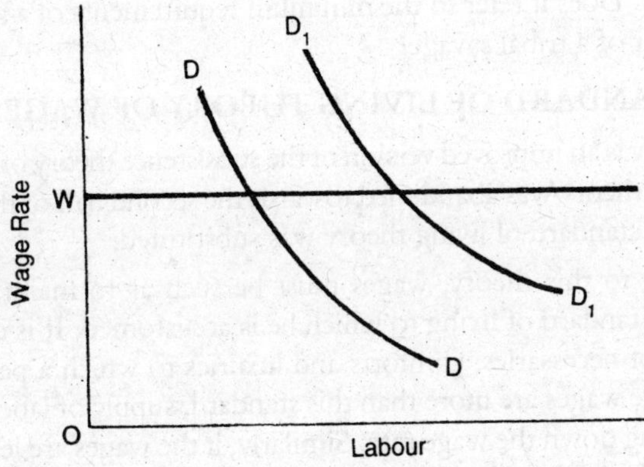

Fig. 30.1

In the above diagram wage rate is measured along the vertical axis and labour along the horizontal axis. OW is the subsistence level of wages. Since the supply of labour is perfectly elastic, wage rate can neither fall below OW nor rise above OW. Though demand increases from DD to D_1D_1 wage rate remains the same at OW level.

Criticism of the Theory

1. Firstly, this theory assumes that population is income elastic. But this is not correct. It is nonsense to say that every increase in wage is cancelled by an increase in population. In reality when a labourer gets higher wages, he will try to improve his standard of living, rather than have more children.

Secondly, this theory is pessimistic and devoid of justice. It predicts a dark future to labourers and says that there is no possibility for the lot of the labourers to improve.

Thirdly, the theory ignores the efficiency of workers.

Fourthly, the theory fails to explain the existence of different wages in different occupations.

Fifthly, the theory is one-sided. It attempts to explain wages from the supply side of labour and the demand side is fully ignored.

Sixthly, the theory is applicable only in the long-run.

Seventhly, the theory ignores the power of the trade unions to increase the wages of workers.

Lastly, as Prof. Dewett points out the "subsistence minimum" is a very vague term. Does it refer to the minimum requirements of a modern scientific man or of a tribal savage?

THE STANDARD OF LIVING THEORY OF WAGES

This theory is an improved version of the subsistence theory of wages. The subsistence theory was abandoned towards the second half of the 19th century and the standard of living theory was substituted.

According to this theory, wages must be such as to maintain the labourer in the standard of living to which he is accustomed. It is defined as the amount of necessaries, comforts and luxuries to which a person is habituated. If the wages are more than this standard, supply of labour will increase, bringing down the wage rate. Similarly, if the wages are less than this standard, the supply of labourers will fall, leading to a rise in the wage rate.

Criticism of the Theory

Firstly, critics argue that labourers do not possess a fixed standard of living.

Secondly, it is true that wages are determined by the standard of living; it is also equally true that the standard of living is determined by the wages. Thus, it is difficult to find out which is the cause and which is the effect.

Lastly, it is a partial theory, as it explains only the supply side of labour.

THE WAGES FUND THEORY

This theory was propounded by J.S. Mill. According to this theory, every employer sets apart a given amount of capital for payment to the labourers, known as the wages fund. It is called fund because it is fixed. The average wage of a worker can be calculated as follows:

$$\text{Average wage per worker} = \frac{\text{Total wage fund}}{\text{Number of workers}}$$

Wages therefore can rise only when the wage fund increases or the number of workers decreases. Since the wage fund is fixed, the average wage is governed by the number of workers. The alternative available to raise the wage rate is to cut down the size of the family members. According to the proponents of this theory, the workers are poor because they are too many in numbers. This theory is an attempt on the part of the classical economists to defend the exploitative capitalistic system. According to this theory, the trade unions are futile because under no circumstances can they increase the wages of workers. Further, a general wage increase without any increase in wages fund or reduction in the number of workers is possible, only at the expense of interest or of profits. But it would eventually lead to the withdrawal of some capital and enterprise from the industry, the demand for labour would decrease and wages would again fall to the original level.

Criticism of the Theory

The theory of the wages fund is open to numerous objections.

Firstly, critics like Lange argue that, the theory does not explain how the wage fund arises and why it remains fixed.

Secondly, the theory does not explain the difference in wages in different occupations.

Thirdly, the wage fund theory is unscientific and illogical. It assumes that the employer will fix the wages fund first and determine wages later. But in actual life, the wage per worker is of utmost importance to calculate the wages fund.

Fourthly, the assumption that wages can increase only at the expense of interest and of profit is not borne out by facts. In times of prosperity in business, both wages and profits may increase.

Fifthly, wages in one industry can be increased only at the expense of a decrease in another industry is also not proved by facts.

Sixthly, wages fund theory has been vehemently attacked by the trade unions for its implication that wages cannot be increased through collective bargaining.

J.S. Mill accepted a majority of criticisms levelled against his theory and he tried to reformulate the theory. But he abandoned it altogether in his next edition of the book.

RESIDUAL CLAIMANT THEORY

This theory was developed by the famous American economist F.A.Walker in 1875, in his book *Political Economy*. According to Walker wages are the residue left over after other factors of productions have been paid.

In the words of Stanley Jevons "The wages of a working man are ultimately coincident with what he produces after the deduction of rent, taxes, and the interest on capital." Walker is of the view that rent and interest are governed by contracts and profit is governed by definite principles. But the theory states no such principle with regard to wages. Therefore, after rent, profits and interest have been paid, the remainder goes to the workers as wages.

Unlike subsistence theory and wages fund theory, which are pessimistic, this theory is optimistic. It is optimistic in the sense that it admits the possibility of increase in wages through an increase in the efficiency of labour.

Criticisms of the Residual Claimant Theory of Wages

This theory has been criticised on the following grounds:

Firstly, in the real life it is not the labourer but the entrepreneur who is the residual claimant. In fact, the worker is paid much in advance and even before the product is sold.

Secondly, it does not take into account the supply side of labour.

Thirdly, it does not explain how trade unions can secure higher wages for workers.

Fourthly, it fails to explain, why the general theory of pricing based on demand and supply cannot be extended to wages as well.

MARGINAL PRODUCTIVITY THEORY OF WAGES

The marginal productivity theory of wages, is an application of the general marginal productivity theory (discussed earlier).

The origin of the concept of marginal productivity can be traced in the works of Ricardo and West. The theory was put forth by Jevons in the 19th century. It was latter developed by Wickstead, Walras and J.B. Clark, among whom the credit for the systematic formation of the theory goes to Prof. Clark.

According to this theory, the wages of a labourer should be equal to his marginal productivity. In the short run, the wages may be more or less than marginal productivity, but in the long run the wages must equal the value of the marginal productivity of labour. The employer demands labour not for its own sake, but because labour is productive. Just as a consumer demands a commodity in the market on account of its utility to him, the producer also demands labour for its productivity. In the process of purchasing, a consumer does not pay a price more than the marginal utility of the commodity. In the same manner, an employer does not pay wages to workers in excess of their marginal productivity. Therefore in equilibrium

$$VMP_L = OW \text{ (price of labour)}$$

Where VMP_L = value of marginal product of labour

OW = Wage Rate

In the product market a firm's price output equilibrium is attained at the point where MC=MR. Likewise, in the factor market a firm attains equilibrium and maximum profit at the point where marginal cost of each factor is equal to its marginal revenue product. Thus at the point of equilibrium $VMP_L = OW$.

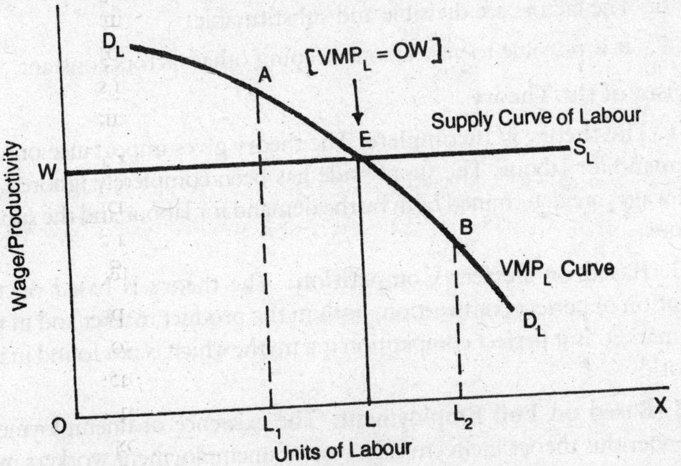

Fig. 30.2

Here WS_L is the supply curve of labour which is horizontal because all labour units are homogeneous and there is perfect competition in the market. $D_L D_L$ is the VMP_L curve which is negative in slope because of the diminishing marginal productivity of labour. Point E is the equilibrium point where $VMP_L = OW$. Now the firm employs OL units of labour and pays OW wage.

At point A we find that

$VMP_L > OW$ — therefore, the firm can increase its profit by employing more units of labour. Though the rate of profit will be diminishing, the total profits will be increasing.

At point B, we find that

$VMP_L < OW$ — here the firm is incurring a loss. So it will benefit by reducing the units of labour. Thus in the long run $VMP_L = OW$ must hold good.

Assumptions of the Theory

The theory rests on the following assumptions:

1. Perfect competition both in the labour and product markets.
2. There is free entry and exit of the firms.
3. There is full employment.
4. All the units of labour are homogeneous.
5. The law of diminishing returns is applicable to production.
6. The factors are divisible and substitutable.
7. It is possible to vary labour keeping other factors constant.

Criticism of the Theory

1. The theory is Incomplete: The theory gives importance only to the demand for labour. The supply side has been completely ignored. In reality wages are determined both by the demand for labour and the supply of labour.

2. Based on Perfect Competition: The theory is based on the assumption of perfect competition, both in the product market and in the factor market. But perfect competition is a myth, which is not found in the real world.

3. Based on Full Employment: The existence of unemployment may render this theory ineffective. In case of unemployment workers may accept a rate of wage that is less than the marginal revenue product.

4. Long-Run: According to critics, the theory offers an explanation only for the long-run. It throws no light on the determination of wages in the short run.

5. Difficulty in Measuring Productivity: According to critics like Hobson, it becomes difficult to find out the marginal productivity of labour when the production is being carried out on a large scale.

6. Wage Differentials: The theory fails to explain the existence of wage differentials. Wages differ from place to place, from person to person and from employment to employment.

7. Productivity: Professor Dobb argues that the demand for labour does not depend upon productivity but on the willingness of the capitalists to save, which depends on previous profits and on previous wage bargains.[1]

DISCOUNTED MARGINAL PRODUCTIVITY THEORY

The American economists, Taussig, has given a modified version of the marginal productivity theory of wages. He thinks that, capitalist production is a round about production and it takes a long time to produce and sell the commodity. During this period the labourers have to be supported by an advance payment of wages. The employer deducts a certain percentage from the value of the final output as a means of compensation. This deduction is made at the current rate of interest.

Recognizing the weakness of the theory, Taussig admits that this theory is "a dim and abstract one, remote from the problem of real life."

MODERN THEORY OF WAGES

Though marginal productivity theory of distribution provides a reasonable explanation of determination of wage, it is a one-sided theory. It does not take into consideration the supply side of labour which is equally important as that of demand. By giving equal importance to demand and supply aspects of labour, the modern theory provides a satisfactory explanation of wage determination. Aptly this theory is termed as the "Demand and Supply theory."

Although labour possesses certain unique peculiarities and cannot, therefore, be regarded as a commodity, yet wages are largely determined by the interaction of the forces of demand and supply.

Demand for Labour

The demand for labour is a derived demand. It is derived from the commodities it helps to produce. If the demand for the product increases, the demand for labour required for making it also increases. Moreover it is ex-ante demand and not expost demand for the product that determines the demand for labour. The elasticity of demand for labour depends on the elasticity of demand for the product.

The demand for labour depends on the prices of the co-operative factors. Suppose the machines are costly, certainly more labour will be employed. Likewise the greater the demand for co-operating factors, the greater will be the demand for labour.

1. H.S. Agarwal, *Micro Economics,* 1983, p. 499.

Still another factor influencing the demand for labour is the technical progress. For example, the introduction of computers reduces the demand for labour.

Apart from the factors discussed above, a fundamental factor determining the demand for labour is its productivity. Just as there is a demand price for commodities, there is also a demand price for labour. The demand price of labour depends upon the marginal productivity, i.e., marginal revenue product of labour. Since all labour units are assumed to be homogeneous, what is paid to the last labourer will be paid to all labourers. So long as the marginal revenue product of labour is more than the wage rate, it is, profitable to employ more labour, for it adds more to revenue than to costs. But the law of diminishing marginal productivity will operate when more and more labourers are employed. The employer will stop employing additional workers at the point at which the cost of employing a worker just equals the addition made by him to the value of the total net product.

Figure 30.3(A) depicts the position of a firm regarding the demand for labour. When the wage is OP, the firm is in equilibrium at the point E and the demand for labour is ON. Similarly at OP_1 wage, the demand is ON_1 and at OP_2 wage, the demand is ON_2. Thus as the wage falls, the demand for labour will increase. The marginal revenue productivity curve of a factor is in fact the demand curve of the firm for that factor.

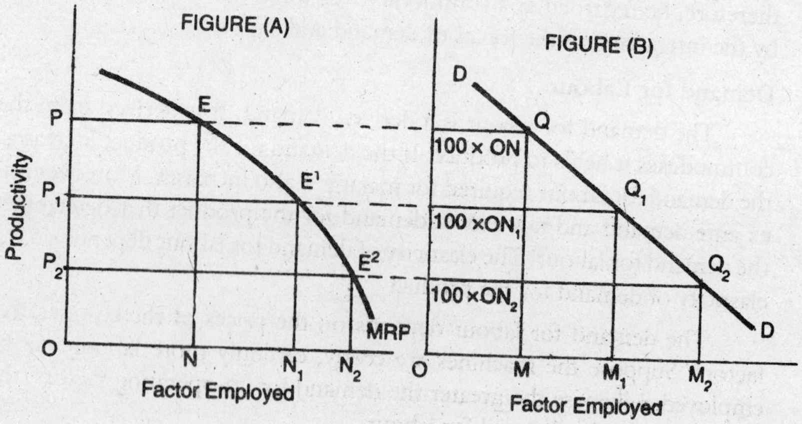

Fig. 30.3

The total demand curve of the industry is derived by the lateral summation of the marginal revenue productivity curves of all the individual firms. The industry's demand curve for the factor is DD. We know that the demand for the factor at OP price is ON units, at OP_1 price ON_1 units and at OP_2 price ON_2 units. If there are 100 firms in the industry the total demand for labour can be obtained by multiplying the individual firm's demand with 100.

Thus the industry's demand for labour is as follows:

at OP price	$= ON \times 100 = OM$
at OP_1 price	$= ON_1 \times 100 = OM_1$
at OP_2 price	$= ON_2 \times 100 = OM_2$

It may be seen that the curve slopes downwards from left to right because it is based on MRP curve which also slopes downwards.

Supply of Labour

By supply of labour we mean the number of men offered for work at various wage rates. Supply of labour may mean three things.

1. Supply of labour to a firm.
2. Supply of labour to an industry and
3. Supply of labour to the entire economy.

1. Supply of Labour to a Firm

To a given firm under perfect competition, the supply of labour is perfectly elastic because at the current wage rate the firm can engage as many workers as it wants. The demand of the firm will constitute a very negligible fraction of the total supply of labour.

2. Supply of Labour to the Industry

To the industry as a whole the supply of labour is not infinitely elastic. If it wants more labour, it can attract labour from other industries by offering a higher wage rate. It can also work with the existing labour force by making them work overtime which in effect will imply an increase in labour supply.

3. Supply of Labour to the Entire Economy

The supply of labour to the entire economy depends upon economic, social and political factors, institutional factors, attitude of women towards work, working age, school and college age, and possibilities of part time employment, size and composition of the population, cost of education, training, labour efficiency, sex distribution, attitude to marriage, size of the family, birth control, health and sanitation standards, mobility of labour etc.

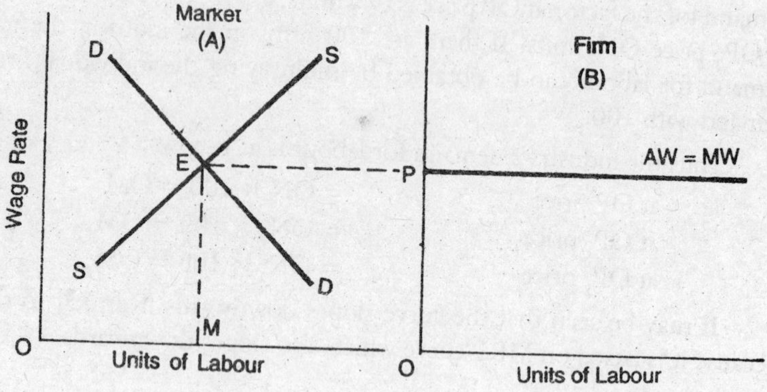

Fig. 30.4

Determination of Wages

We have already discussed the demand and supply aspects of labour. The interaction of the two determines the wage rate. The Fig. (39.5) illustrates demand and supply curves for the market and how the wage rate is determined.

In the above diagram market (Figure 30.4(A)) wage is determined at ME. In this case no employer will like to pay more than OP wage (MW) and no worker will be prepared to accept less. The supply curve of labour for the individual firm will be horizontal. This represents the average wage (AW) and the marginal wage (MW) of labour for the firm.

Relation between Wage and Productivity

In the long run under competitive conditions, wages will be equal to both the marginal revenue product and the average revenue product. If the wage rate is less than the average revenue product, the firms would be getting super normal profits in the short-run.

If the existing firms are earning super normal profits in the short-run, new firms will enter into the industry and the demand for labour will increase which will push up the wage rate so as to be equal to the average revenue product.

On the contrary, if the existing wage rate is more than the average revenue product, the firm will be suffering losses in the short-run. As a result, some firms will leave the industry and the demand for labour will decrease which will lead to a decrease in the wage rate.

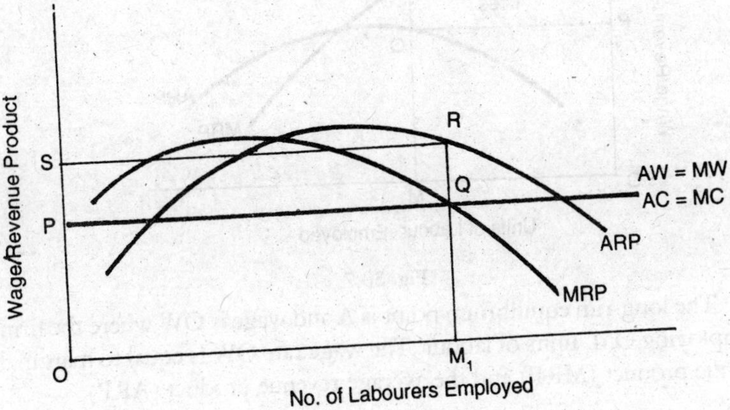

Fig. 30.5

Long-run Equilibrium under Perfect Competition

Thus in the long run under perfect competition

$$\text{Wage} = \text{MRP} = \text{ARP}$$

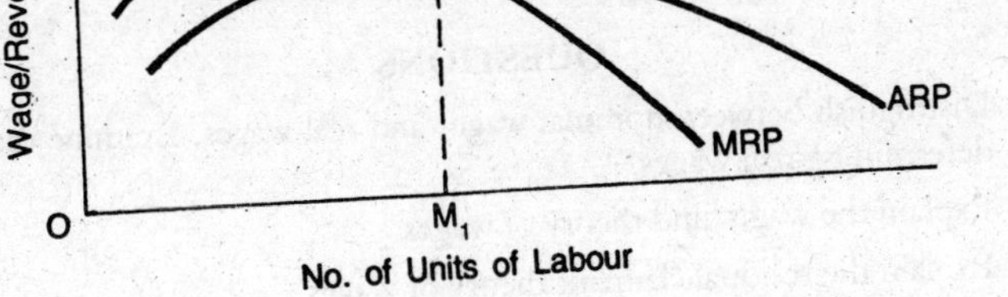

Fig. 30.6

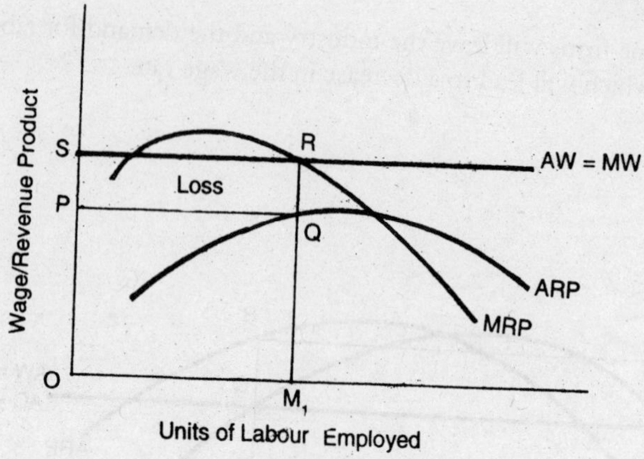

Fig. 30.7

The long-run equilibrium point is A and wage is OW where the firm is employing OM_1 units of labour. The wage rate OW is equal to marginal revenue product (MRP) and the average revenue product (ARP).

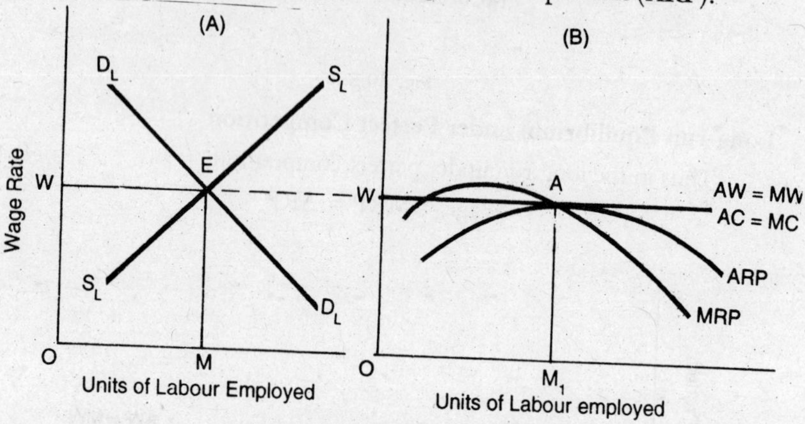

Fig. 30.8

QUESTIONS

1. Distinguish between nominal wages and real wages. Examine the factors determining real wages.
2. Explain the wage fund theory of wages.
3. Explain the residual claimant theory of wages.
4. State the modern theory of wages. How far is it true to say that the theory of wages is an application of the general theory of value?

❖ ❖ ❖

31

INTEREST

"Few topics in Economics, in fact, have received as varied a treatment as the theory of interest."

— Harold Somers

INTRODUCTION

Interest is one of the most controversial topics in economics. The Greek philosophers like Plato, Aristotle and even the great Kautilya had condemned usury. Pointing out that money is "barren", Aristotle said, it was unfair to charge a positive interest for loans. Many sophisticated medieval school thinkers followed him in his view that interest represents unjustified usury. The Bible was the source of inspiration to the Greek philosophers and the ancient Romans. According to them, people used to borrow money to meet their consumption needs, and therefore, from a moral point of view, they should not be required to pay interest. The Islamic religion also prohibits interest payment strictly.

But these views have undergone a tremendous change. In the words of Prof. P.A. Samuelson,[1] "The biblical utterances against interest and usury clearly refer to loans made for consumption rather than for investment purposes."

Nowadays, modern business centres around capital, and interest acts as a boon to savers.

1. P.A. Samuelson, *Economics*, McGraw-Hill, International Edition, 1983, p. 563.

DEFINITION OF INTEREST

In ordinary language, interest is a premium which is paid on capital that is borrowed. As there is no cat without a grin, so there is no capital without interest.[2]

Prof. Benham has defined interest as follows: "Interest is the price paid for a loan. If you borrow £ 100 and promise to pay back £105 at the end of twelve months, you are promising to pay a rate of interest at 5 per cent per annum." In economics, interest does not refer to the total amount paid by a borrower, but to that part of his payment which can be attributed to the use of capital only, and for nothing else.

According to Knut Wicksell, "Interest is a payment made by the borrower of capital, by virtue of its productivity, as a reward for his abstinence."

GROSS INTEREST AND NET INTEREST

The gross interest means the total amount which a creditor gets from the debtor. It is a composite item which includes the following elements.

1. Pure or Net Interest

It is the payment made for the use of capital only. This is the interest in the true economic sense.

2. Insurance Against Risk

The lender is exposed to risk when he lends money. Marshall divided these risks into two parts. Trade risks, which depend upon the nature of the business in which the capital is used. Personal risks which are due to the dishonest or unreliable character of the borrower himself. The lender, therefore, expects a reward in proportion to the degree of risks involved.

3. Wages for Management

Every lender has to incur some expenditure on management of loans. He buys accounts books and even maintains staff. Modern money lending involves a complex system and is a whole time job. Therefore, the lender expects some reward for this kind of work.

4. Reward for Inconvenience

When a lender lends money, he loses his command over it for a certain period. During this period, it cannot be used in more profitable ways. The compensation for such inconveniences is added to the interest charged.

---

2. K.N. Prasad, *Lectures on Micro Economic Theory*, Himalaya Publishing House, 1987, p. 529.

Gross Interest = Net interest +
Insurance against risk + Wages for
management + Reward for inconvenience.

Why Interest is Paid?

Economists have developed various theories to answer the question, why interest has to be paid?

MARGINAL PRODUCTIVITY THEORY OF INTEREST

This theory was initially developed by Bohm Bawerk in 1884. Later, economists like J.B. Say, Knies and Menger, have elaborated on this theory.

According to this theory, interest is paid because capital is productive. Capital co-operates in the production of more wealth, and, therefore, something must be paid for its use to its owner. This something is interest. The basis of the determination of the rate of interest is the productivity of the marginal unit of capital.

If the rate of interest is less than the marginal product of capital, there will be greater demand for capital, since it will be useful for the entrepreneurs to substitute capital for other factors of production, and, consequently, the rate of interest will rise. Conversely, if the rate of interest is higher than the marginal productivity of capital there will be less demand for capital, and consequently the rate of interest will fall. Thus, the rate of interest will stabilise itself at a level where it will be equal to the marginal productivity of capital.

Criticism

This theory is subject to the following criticisms:

1. First, it is not the productivity, but scarcity of capital which explains interest. This theory is one sided, because it concentrates on the demand side, and the supply side has been completely ignored.
2. Secondly, if interest depends merely on productivity, interest rates should vary in proportion to the productiveness of capital. But in actual practice, this does not happen.
3. Thirdly, loans utilised for consumption purposes are not productive, yet interest has to be paid for them.
4. Lastly, the rate of interest does not depend on productivity only but upon a number of other factors also like supply of capital, the monetary policy of the Central Bank, and so on.

ABSTINENCE OR WAITING THEORY

The abstinence theory of interest was developed by the famous English economist, N.W. Senior. While the marginal productivity theory attempted to explain the payment of interest from the demand side, this theory explained interest from the supply side.

According to this theory, interest is a reward for saving. In other words, interest accrues due to saving. Every act of saving involves abstinence from present consumption. Abstinence involves self-denial, pain or sacrifice, for which the payment of interest is a compensation.

The abstinence theory is weak in many respects.

First, rich people save without any sacrifice. In the words of Prof. Keirstead, "If interest is a reward for abstinence, it is paid to the wrong people."

Likewise, the theory has no relevance to voluntary savers who can save more even as the interest rate declines.

Secondly, it is difficult to measure the intensity of sacrifice which is the base for interest. There is no method for calculation of pains and sacrifices.

Thirdly, this theory neglects the demand side, and is, therefore, incomplete.

Lastly, saving by itself, cannot result in interest unless the saved money is lent also.

Marshall substituted the term "waiting" for abstinence and treated interest as the reward for waiting. Saving implies waiting. When a person saves he does not refrain from consumption for all time; he merely postpones present consumption to a future date. Meanwhile he has to wait. Interest is the inducement or reward for waiting.

AGIO THEORY OF INTEREST[3]

This theory was first propounded by John Rae in 1934, but the final shape was given by Eugen Von Bohm Bawerk of the Austrian school of economics.

According to this theory, interest arises because people prefer present goods to future goods, and therefore there is an 'agio' or premium on present goods. Interest is a reward which should be paid to induce people to lend their money and postpone their present consumption to a future date. One bird in the hand is said to be worth two in the bush. Therefore, present gratification is given greater importance than future satisfaction.

---

3. It is also known as Psychological Theory of Interest.

In the words of Bohm Bawerk, "Interest is the reward of acting contrary to the agio to present goods."

Why do people prefer present satisfaction to future satisfaction? Bohm Bawerk gives three reasons.

1. Present wants are felt more keenly than future wants.
2. Prospective underestimation of the future because of
   (*a*) Deficiency of imagination, i.e., myopia in respect of future.
   (*b*) Limited will power; and
   (*c*) The shortness and uncertainty of life.
3. Technical superiority of present over future goods, which means that the present goods can be used as capital to have a larger bundle of goods in near future.

Assumptions

The theory is based on two assumptions

1. The purchasing power of money is assumed to be constant.
2. The tastes, preferences and attitudes of the capital owners remain the same.

Criticisms

1. Agio theory fails if the above said assumptions are invalid.[4] For example, if money is expected to buy more in the future, than it does at present, or if the lender expects to lead relatively a simpler life in future, the assumptions are violated and the agio theory becomes inapplicable.

2. Secondly, it ignores completely the demand side.

FISHER'S TIME PREFERENCE THEORY

In his book 'The Theory of Interest' Irving Fisher gave a modified version of Bohm Bawerk's theory, known as the time preference theory. It is based on the fundamental idea that people prefer present income to future income even when the future income is equally certain.

According to Fisher, a man attaches greater importance to the present than to future, not only because of the uncertainty of the future, but also because of the natural tendency to enjoy the present satisfaction in preference to the future. This tendency is known as 'Time preference.'

4. P.L. Mehta — *Essentials of Micro Economics,* Sultan Chand & Sons 1988.p. 441.

Fisher defined interest as "an index of the community's preference for a dollar of present over a dollar of future income." In other words, the rate of interest is the outcome of the trade-off between present and future incomes by the individuals of a society.

According to Fisher, the intensity of the people's preference for present income depends upon a host of subjective and objective factors. These factors are grouped into:

(1) Willingness and (2) Opportunity. Thus, Fisher based his theory of interest on two principles, viz.,

(*a*) The impatience or the willingness principle.

(*b*) The investment opportunity principle.

1. WILLINGNESS PRINCIPLE

The impatience or willingness principle depends upon:

1. The size of the income,
2. The distribution of income,
3. The composition of income,
4. The certainty of income in future,
5. Personal traits of individuals, such as foresight, self-restraint, consumption etc.

1. The Size of the Income

If a person is rich, time preference will be low, because most of his wants are already satisfied. A poor person will have a high time preference because he will need the whole or a major portion of his income for his present consumption.

2. The Distribution of Income

The distribution of income may take place in three different ways:

(*a*) If a person's income remains constant throughout his life, then his impatience to spend will be determined by the size of his income, his character and foresight.

(*b*) If a person's income increases with the passage of years, then his impatience to spend will be high because he discounts the future in comparison with the present.

(*c*) If a person's income decreases with the passage of years, his time preference will be low and he will save.

3. The Composition of the Income

The individuals real income consists of items like food, clothing, house, shelter etc. Reduction in any one of these will have some effect on his time preference in the same way as a fall in his total income.

4. The Certainty of Income in Future

If an individual is certain to receive his income regularly in future, then he will not be inclined to save for the future.

5. Personal Traits of Individuals

A prudent person will save for the rainy day. On the other hand, some persons are of the happy-go-lucky type and they believe in "eat, drink and be merry." Such persons will have a high time preference.

When the rate of willingness is determined in this way, it tends to equal the rate of interest. When the rate of time preference of an individual is higher than the market rate of interest, he will borrow and use this amount to satisfy his more pressing wants. On the contrary, if the rate of time preference or willingness is lower than the market rate of interest, he will lend his income and gain thereby. This process of lending or borrowing will continue, till his rate of willingness equals the rate of interest.

In the words of Prof. Fisher, "Only time preference could account for interest, for where one was indifferent as to the present and future, interest could not arise."

2. INVESTMENT OPPORTUNITY PRINCIPLE (OR) MARGINAL RATE OF RETURN OVER COST

Investment opportunity principle refers to the rate of return over cost. To explain this principle, let us assume that an individual is faced with alternative investment proposals, which imply two income streams that are substitutes. Here "cost" implies the loss of withdrawing from one income stream and "returns", the gain from substituting one income stream for another. The rate of return over cost is, therefore, the rate of discount which equalises the present net values of the investment opportunities. Whenever the discount rate exceeds the market rate of interest, one of the two proposals must be rejected.

Thus each individual in the society will try to satisfy the following conditions.

1. Willingness = Market rate of interest
2. Marginal rate of return over cost = Market rate of interest

Which implies that under equilibrium conditions

Willingness = Marginal rate of return over cost
= Market rate of interest.

The market will be in equilibrium when the total amount offered by the lenders equals the total amount demanded by the borrowers. Fisher calls this, the market equilibrium principle.

Criticisms

Fisher's time preference theory has been hailed by J.A. Schumpeter as "the peak achievement, so far as perfection when its own frame is concerned, of the literature on interest." But the theory is subject to the following criticisms:

Firstly, contrary to reality, this theory assumes constant purchasing power of money.

Secondly, the theory is general in nature, and it fails to show the influence of the banking system on the rate of interest.

Thirdly, the theory gives undue importance to consumption out of a given income.

Fourthly, the theory assumes the position and character of the consumer as constant in the present as well as in future. But this is also not true.

Fifthly, the theory is silent about the impact of expectations on interest rates.

Lastly, Keynes has shifted the emphasis from time preference to liquidity preference.

THE CLASSICAL THEORY OF INTEREST (OR) THE SAVING-INVESTMENT THEORY OF INTEREST (OR) THE DEMAND AND SUPPLY THEORY OF INTEREST

In reality, there is no accepted 'classical theory' of interest. According to Keynes, the classical theory of interest refers to the views of Marshall, Cassel, Taussig, Walras etc. Keynes provides an excellent summary of the classical theory of interest in his famous book "The General Theory of Employment, Interest and Money."

This theory is also known as the demand and supply theory of interest because it deals with the demand side as well as the supply side.

This theory is in fact a synthesis of "Marginal Productivity Theory (on the demand side) and "Waiting Theory." (on the supply side). The classical theory is a real theory because it seeks to explain the determination of the rate of interest by real factors like productivity and thrift.

Demand for Capital (Investment Schedule)

Capital is demanded by entrepreneurs because it is productive. Marginal productivity of capital is the addition made to the total product by employing one more unit of capital asset, keeping other factors constant. The marginal productivity of capital diminishes as more capital is employed in the production process. The marginal revenue productivity curve therefore slopes downwards from left to right. There is an inverse relationship between the rate of interest and the demand for capital. In other words, higher the rate of interest, lower will be the investment or demand for capital. Lower the rate of interest, greater will be the investment, or demand for capital. Thus investment is interest-elastic. This is shown in Fig. 31.1.

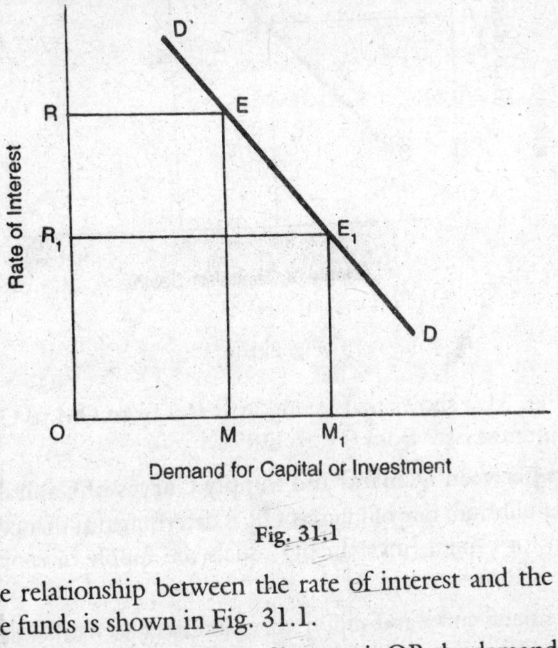

Fig. 31.1

The relationship between the rate of interest and the demand for investible funds is shown in Fig. 31.1.

In Fig. 31.1 when the rate of interest is OR the demand for capital is OM. When the rate of interest falls to OR_1, the demand for capital increases to OM_1.

Supply of Capital (Saving Schedule)

The funds which are used for investment are made available through savings. Savings are made by households and individuals in a community. The volume of savings depends upon a host of factors like, the level of income, the distribution of income, the standard of living, saving habits, family affection, farsightedness, political and social climate, inflation rate etc. The most important factor which determines the supply of savings is the rate of interest. Saving is an increasing function of the rate of interest. Since, rate of interest is an incentive to save, higher the rate of interest, higher will be the volume of savings and vice versa.

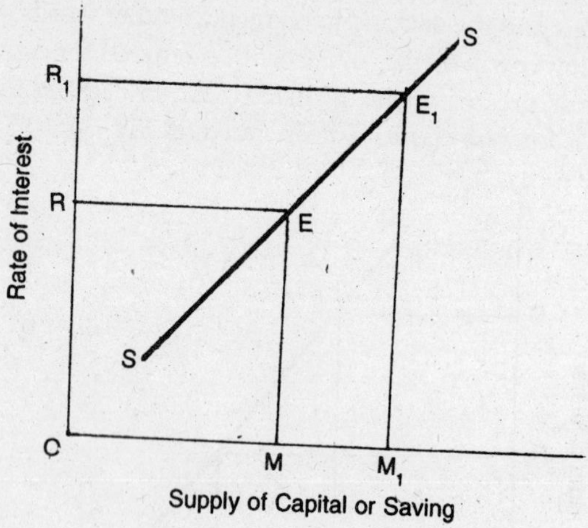

Fig. 31.2

The Fig. 31.2 shows that saving increases from OM to OM_1, when the rate of interest rises from OR to OR_1.

Interaction between Demand and Supply Curves of Capital

The equilibrium rate of interest OR is determined at that point where the demand for capital (investment) equals the supply of capital Saving (ON). This is shown in Fig. 31.3.

The demand curve and supply curve intersect each other at the point E. Therefore OR is the equilibrium rate of interest. If the rate of interest is greater than OR, the supply of capital will exceed the demand for capital and consequently the equilibrium rate of interest will be OR_1, then the supply of saving will be R_1B_1 whereas the demand will be R_1A. Supply exceeds demand. The rate of interest will fall. If on the other hand, the rate of interest is lower than OR, the demand for capital will exceed the supply of capital and consequently once again the equilibrium rate of interest of OR will be attained. For example, if the rate of interest is OR_2, the demand for capital will be R_2D_2, whereas the supply will be R_2C. Demand exceeds supply. The rate of interest, therefore, moves upwards to OR.

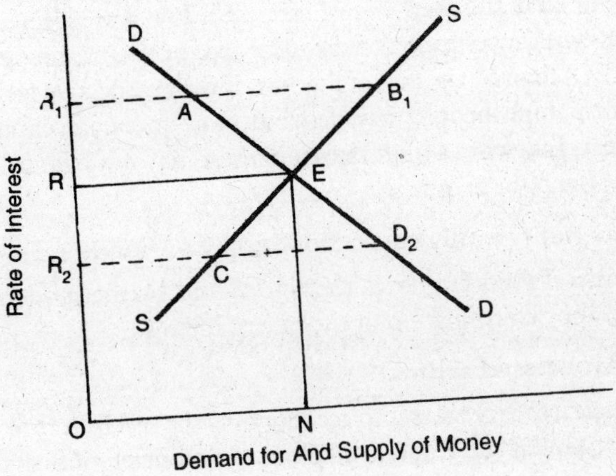

Fig. 31.3

Criticism of the Classical Theory of Interest

The Classical Theory of interest has been criticised by many economists including Prof. J.M. Keynes on the following grounds.

1. Full Employment Assumption

The Classical Theory is based on the assumption of full employment of resources. But this assumption is unrealistic, imaginary and not applicable to the real world. As Prof. Dudley Dillard remarks[5] "Within the framework of a system of theory built on the assumption of full employment, the notion of interest as a reward for waiting or abstinence is highly plausible. It is the premise that resources are typically fully employed that lacks plausibility in the contemporary world."

2. Changes in Income Level Ignored

In Keynes' view, the most fundamental defect is its neglect of the influence of changes in income levels on saving and investment. According to him, the equilibrium between saving and investment is not made through the variations in the interest rate, but through the changes in the levels of income.

3. Relationship between Investment and Rate of Interest

Classical theory assumes investment as interest elastic. In other words, the most important determinant of investment is the rate of interest.

5. D. Dillard: *The Economics of John Maynard Keynes,* Vikas Publishing House Pvt. Ltd., New Delhi, 1977, p. 162.

Investment will be high when rate of interest is low and vice versa. But according to Keynes, investment is more influenced by the marginal efficiency of capital (MEC) than by the rate of interest. If the prospective yields from an investment is high people may demand more money even at higher rates of interest. Likewise, a high rate of interest may not help to increase the savings of the poor people in a country.

4. Savings are not the only sources of Supply of Funds

The Classical theory ignores the role played by the modern credit institutions in the determination of the rate of interest.

5. Neglects Monetary Factors

The Classical theory takes into account only the real factors like thrift, productivity of capital etc. It totally neglects the monetary influence. The classical economists believed that money is merely a medium of exchange, a 'veil' over real goods and services. They failed to take into account the store of value function of money.

6. Saving and Investment Schedules are not Independent

The classical theory treated the demand and supply as independent of each other. But this is a serious error in the theory.

7. No Automatic Mechanism to bring Equality between Equilibrium and Market Rates of Interest

According to the classical view, any discrepancy between the natural and market rates of interest is purely accidental and only a temporary phenomenon which would disappear in the long run. Keynes, however, does not regard the discrepancy between the two as accidental or temporary. To him, it is due to monetary policy changes.

8. Definition of Interest

Contrary to the classical theory which states that interest is determined by the demand for money and supply of money, Keynes states interest is a reward of parting with liquidity for a specified period.

9. Variations in the Rate of Interest

The Classical theory fails to explain why fairly short-term variations in the rates of interest occur.

LOANABLE FUNDS THEORY OF INTEREST

Loanable funds theory was developed independently by Knut Wicksell in Sweden, Sir Dennis Robertson in Britain and H.J. Davenport in the United States. Top honour, however, goes to Wicksell for both priority and profoundity. Other notable contributors to this theory of interest are Ohlin, Pigou, Viner etc.

According to this theory, interest is the price paid for the use of loanable funds and as such, it is determined by the demand and supply of loanable funds. Demand for loanable funds is inversely related to the rate of interest, while the supply of loanable funds is positively related to the rate of interest.

There are several sources for both supply and demand of loanable funds which are discussed below.

Supply of Loanable Funds

The supply of loanable funds is derived from four sources, namely,

(*a*) Savings,
(*b*) Dishoarding,
(*c*) Bank Credit and,
(*d*) Disinvestment.

(a) Savings

Savings by individuals or households form the most important source of savings. Savings may be of two types, planned and unplanned. Planned saving is called ex-ante savings. The individual plans his savings before the actual expenditure takes place, and he sets aside a sum to save money. The unplanned saving is known as ex-post savings. It is in this sense that Robertson has used the word savings. It is the difference between the income of the preceding period and the consumption of the present period. Savings depend on the level of income. But given the level of income, savings vary with the rate of interest.

Like individuals, business firms also save. The undistributed profits of a business firm constitutes the corporate savings. Instead of approaching the loan market for loans, their own saving can be used for investment.

(b) Dishoarding

When the idle cash balances of the past become active balances in the present, and become available for investment, it is called dishoarding. If the rate of interest is low, dishoarding would be negligible. If the rate of interest becomes high more money will be dishoarded.

(c) Bank Money

Bank money is another component of the supply of loanable funds. Credit creation is one of the fundamental functions of the modern banks.

Modern banks are compared to a factory manufacturing credit. Banks can increase or reduce loanable funds by the process of credit creation. Normally, banks will lend more money when the rate of interest rises.

(d) Disinvestment

Disinvestment is the opposite of investment. Disinvestment takes place when the stock of existing machines is allowed to wear out, without being replaced. Such a disinvestment takes place because of structural changes. When the rate of interest is high, some of the current capital may not produce a marginal revenue product to match this rate of interest. In this situation, a part of the revenue from the sale of products, instead of going into capital replacement flows into the market for loanable funds.

The total supply curve of loanable funds is obtained by the lateral summation of the four curves, savings (S), dishoarding (DH), disinvestment (DI) and bank money (BM).

Thus $S_L = S+DH+BM+DI$

The supply curve for loanable funds slopes upwards to the right showing that more will be supplied at higher rates of interest and vice versa. At higher rates of interest people hoard less money.

Demand for Loanable Funds

The demand for loanable funds arises mainly from three sources — investment, consumption and hoarding.

(*a*) Investment demand,

(*b*) Consumption demand

(*c*) Demand for hoarding.

(a) Investment Demand

The bulk of the demand for loanable funds comes mainly from business concerns for investment purposes. Business firms demand loanable funds up to the point at which the expected net rate of return on capital goods becomes equal to the rate of interest. The demand for loanable funds for investment purposes is interest elastic and it varies inversely with the rate of interest.

(b) Consumption Demand

Consumers borrow mainly to finance the purchase of durable goods like automobiles, refrigerators, television sets, washing machines, room coolers etc. A low rate of interest encourages consumers to borrow more money funds.

(c) Demand for Hoarding

Hoarding signifies keeping idle cash balances. People prefer to hold money when they feel that the current rate of interest is not enough to induce them to part with their money and that in the near future they will be able to make better use of their hoarded balances.

By a horizontal summation of the three curves of investment (I), consumption (C) and hoarding (H) we get the demand curve, D_L for loanable funds.

Thus $D_L = I + C + H$

The demand curve for loanable funds slopes downwards to the right showing that more will be demanded at lower rates of interest and vice versa.

Determination of the Rate of Interest

According to the loanable funds theory, the equilibrium rate of interest is determined at a level where the demand for and the supply of loanable funds are equal.

$$S + DH + DI + BM = I + C + H$$

The determination of the rate of interest according to the loanable funds theory is illustrated with the help of Fig. 31.4.

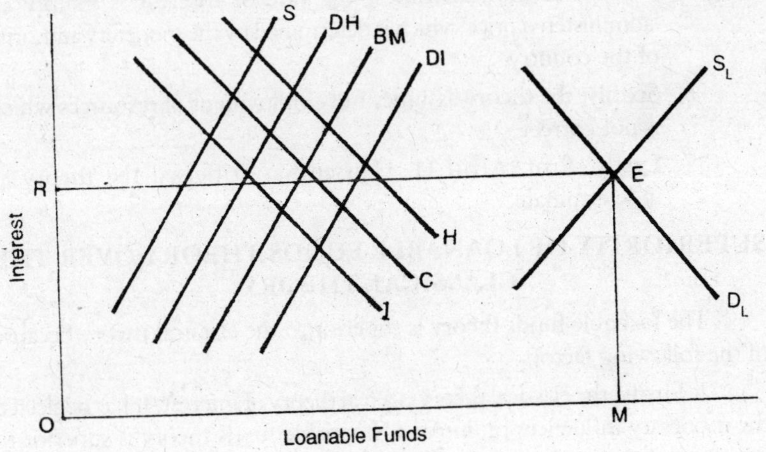

Fig. 31.4

In Fig. 31.4 S_L is the supply curve of loanable funds and D_L is the demand curve for loanable funds. The curves I, C and H refer to the components of demand and S, DH, BM and DI refer to the components of supply — their slopes indicating their relationship with the rate of interest.

The total demand cu. .e D_L and the total supply curve S_L intersect each other at the point E. The equilibrium rate of interest is OR. At this rate, the loanable funds supplied are equal to the loanable funds demanded.

Criticism of the Theory

Prof. Robertson considers, the loanable funds theory as a "common sense explanation" of the determination of the rate of interest. But the theory was the target of criticism for Lord J.M. Keynes and his followers.

1. Firstly, according to critics, this theory is simply an extension of the classical theory.
2. Secondly, the theory gives undue importance to the rate of interest on savings.
3. Thirdly, Keynes refutes the relationship between the rate of interest and investment as postulated by the theory. According to him, investment in an economy depends more upon the marginal efficiency of capital than upon the rate of interest.
4. Fourthly, critics have objected to the way the monetary factors have been combined with the real factors in the theory.
5. Fifthly, in modern times, the rate of interest is mainly an 'administered price' which is determined by the monetary authority of the country.
6. Sixthly, the theory assumes full employment of resources which is not correct.
7. Lastly, Prof. Alvin H. Hansen has criticised the theory as indeterminate.

SUPERIORITY OF LOANABLE FUNDS THEORY OVER THE CLASSICAL THEORY

The loanable funds theory is superior to the classical theory because of the following factors:

1. Firstly, the classical theory is a real theory of interest. It has neglected the monetary influences on interest. Loanable funds theory is superior to the classical theory, because it includes both monetary and real factors.

2. Secondly, the classical economists have failed to take note of bank credit which is a major determinant of the rate of interest.

3. Thirdly, the classicals also do not consider the role of hoarding. By giving an important place to hoarding, the loanable funds theory brings us nearer to the Keynesian liquidity preference theory.

4. Lastly, in the classical approach, money is merely a 'veil' and a passive factor influencing the rate of interest. In the loanable funds approach, money acts as an active factor in the determination of the rate of interest. It is determined by the demand for and the supply of money.

LIQUIDITY PREFERENCE THEORY OF INTEREST

In his magnum opus book "The General Theory of Employment, Interest and Money" Keynes gives a new idea about interest. Keynes points out that interest is purely a monetary phenomenon.

According to Keynes, interest is the reward for parting with liquidity for a specified period. Keynes defines interest as "the premium which has to be offered to induce people to hold their wealth in some form, other than hoarded money.[6] In other words, interest is the opportunity cost of holding wealth.

A man with a given income has to make economic decisions or calculations at two levels. At the first level, he decides how much to consume and how much to save out of his current income. At the second level, he decides how much of his savings he should hold in the form of money and how much of it he should invest in the form of liquid assets like bonds. The first level of decision depends upon the "marginal propensity to consume" and the second level depends upon "liquidity preference."

Meaning

Liquidity means power to convert assets into money. It is a measure of the ease and cheapness with which an asset may be exchanged for any other asset. Liquidity preference means the desire of the public to hold cash. Money is demanded because, it is the only perfectly liquid asset.

The desire to hold ready money arises out of three motives:

(*i*) the transactions motive,

(*ii*) the precautionary motive, and

(*iii*) the speculative motive.

1. Transactions Motive

In the words of Alvin H. Hansen "The transactions motive relates to the need for cash for the current transactions of personal and business

6. Alvin H. Hansen: *A Guide to Keynes,* McGraw Hill Book Company, NewYork 1953, p. 141

exchanges." Individuals hold cash in order "to bridge the interval between the receipt of income and its disbursement."

A person who gets his salary once a month must keep enough cash in his hands to meet payments of everyday transactions. Therefore a man has to keep a certain amount of money in liquid form to spend on food, health, clothing, bus fare, entertainment, education etc. This amount will depend upon the size of the individual's income, the interval at which his income is received and the methods of payments current in the locality.

The business exchanges also require cash "to bridge the interval between the incurring of costs and the receipt of sale proceeds." Keynes calls this motive as 'business motive.' The amount of money, under business motive depends upon the business turnover.

2. Precautionary Motive

The precautionary demand for money is for holding a reserve against unforeseen and contingent liabilities. People hold a certain amount of money to provide for the danger of unemployment, sickness, accidents and for other more uncertain pursuits.

In the words of Stonier and Hague, "money held under the precautionary motive is rather like water kept in reserve in a separate tank."

Money held under this motive will depend on the circumstances under which a person lives, and his own nature. Like individuals, business concerns also face emergencies and have contingent and unforeseen liabilities, therefore they also keep a portion of their income in the form of reserve to meet sudden unforeseen expenditure.

According to Keynes, the transactions and precautionary motives are relatively interest-inelastic, but are highly income elastic. The amount of money held under these two motives (M_1) is a function (f) of the level of income (Y) and is expressed as $M_1 = f(Y)$.

3. Speculative Motive

The speculative motive relates to the desire of the people to hold resources in liquid form, with a view to take the advantages of market movements. According to Keynes, speculative motive is for "securing profit from knowing better than the market what the future will bring forth."

Individuals and firms hold liquid cash in order to take advantage of the price movements of income earning assets, known as bonds.

This tendency, is the common feature of the stock exchange markets. In stock exchange markets, sales and purchases of shares, bonds and securities take place.

Sometimes, there will be an excessive purchase or excessive sale of securities in the stock exchange market. The tendency for excessive purchase of securities is known as the "Bullish sentiment" and the tendency for aggressive sale of securities is known as the "Bearish sentiment." The person who joins hands in these tendencies are called the members of the 'Bull' brigade and the 'Bear' brigade respectively.

The amount of money held under the speculative motive depends upon the rate of interest. Bond prices and the rate of interest are inversely related to each other. Low bond prices are indicative of high interest rates and high bond prices reflect low interest rates. Let us suppose that an individual wants to purchase a bond of Rs. 1,000 which carries 4% interest. Now on this bond, he earns an income of Rs. 40. When the rate of interest goes up to 5 per cent, to earn the same income of Rs. 40, an investment of Rs. 800 will be sufficient. It means that bond prices decrease with an increase in the rate of interest and vice versa. This shows that when the rate of interest is high, people will have a desire to hold less money for speculative purposes. When the rate of interest decreases, the bond holders sell their bonds and hold liquid cash. It means that lower the rate of interest, greater will be the liquidity preference. Thus people will prefer to hold more or less cash depending on the future changes that are likely to take place in the prices of assets.

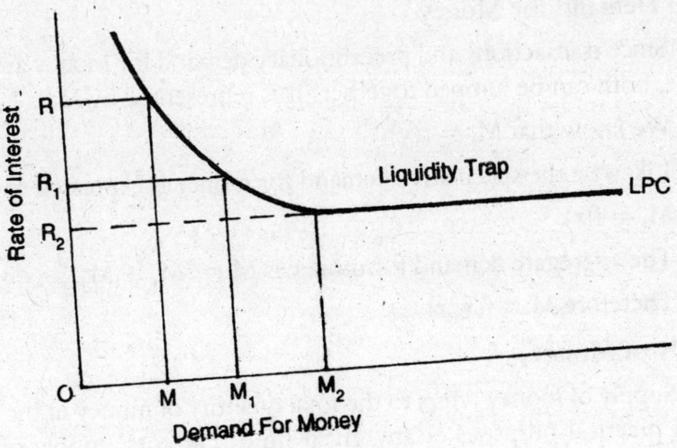

Fig. 31.5

Thus higher the rate of interest, the lower will be the speculative demand for money and vice versa. Geometrically, it is a smooth curve which slopes downwards from left to right, indicating that more money will be held at a lower rate of interest. Algebraically, the speculative demand for money is expressed as $M_2 = f(r)$.

According to Keynes, Liquidity preference curve (LPC) becomes perfectly elastic at a certain rate of interest, such as OR_2. At a very low rate of interest people prefer to keep money in cash rather than lend it.

The argument is that at abnormally low interest rates virtually everyone would expect the interest rate to rise towards its normal level in the near future. In this situation, virtually, everyone would be expecting a fall in the price of bonds and therefore, capital losses are expected for bond holders.

The flat portion or the perfectly elastic portion of the liquidity preference curve is known as the liquidity trap.

Implications of Liquidity Trap

The concept of liquidity trap has certain important implications.

Firstly, the monetary policy is out of commission. It cannot influence the rate of interest by following a cheap money policy. In this extreme case, the velocity of circulation falls as all increases in the money supply are added to 'idle' balances and the monetary policy is helpless as it cannot cut down the interest rate any further.

Secondly, the rate of interest cannot fall to zero.

Lastly, the policy of a general wage cut cannot be effective in the perfectly elastic portion of the liquidity preference curve.

Total Demand for Money

Since transactions and precautionary demand for money are income elastic, both can be lumped together. It is represented by M.

We know that $M_1 = f(y)$

Likewise the speculative demand for money is expressed as M_2.

$M_2 = f(r)$

The aggregate demand for money is $M = (M_1 + M_2)$

Therefore $M = f(y, r)$

Supply of Money

Supply of money refers to the total quantity of money in the country for all practical purposes at any given time. The total supply of money consists of legal tender money and credit money or bank money. Money supply is a policy variable, and its supply is determined by the central bank of a country. At any particular point of time the supply of money is fixed. Given the supply of money, the rate of interest is determined by the demand for money.

Determination of Rate of Interest

According to Keynes the rate of interest is determined by the interaction of the forces of demand for and the supply of money. The determination of the rate of interest is illustrated by the Fig. 31.6 given below.

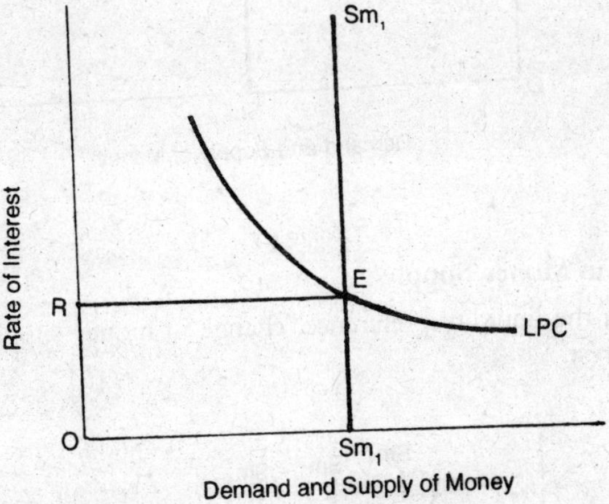

Fig. 31.6

Money supply is shown by a vertical straight line SM. The downward sloping LPC represents the liquidity preference demand for money. The demand curve intersects the supply curve at point E. Thus OR is the equilibrium rate of interest.

A Change in Liquidity Preference

A shift in liquidity preference may also bring about changes in the rate of interest.

The supply of money remaining constant, a change in LPC changes the rate of interest. An upward shift of liquidity preference curve (LPC_1) raises the rate of interest to OR_1 given the money supply. On the other hand, the downward shift of liquidity preference curve (LPC_2) decreases the rate of interest to OR_2 given the supply of money.

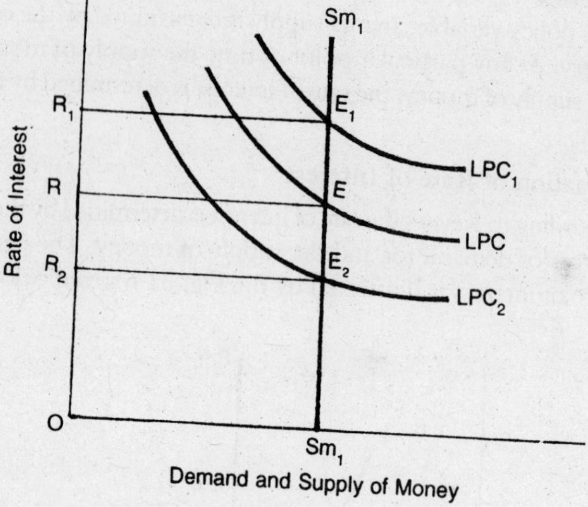

Fig. 31.7

A Change in Money Supply

Given the liquidity preference, change in money supply alters the rate of interest.

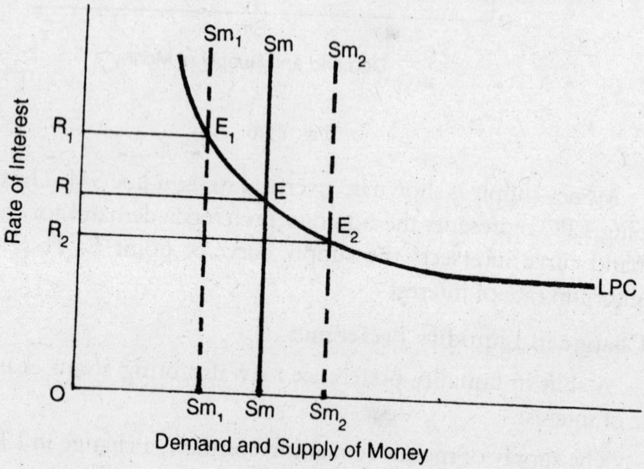

Fig. 31.8

If the supply of money increases from Sm to Sm_2, the liquidity preference schedule remaining the same, the rate of interest will come down to OR_2. With a fall in money supply, Sm_1 on the other hand, the rate of interest will go up to OR_1.

Thus according to Keynes, interest is purely a monetary pheno-menon.

Criticism of the Liquidity Preference Theory

The Liquidity Preference theory has several weaknesses. The theory has been heavily attacked by Hansen, Robertson, Hazlitt, Hutt and others.

1. College Bursar's Theory

According to Robertson Keynes' assumption that all non-money financial assets are only bonds is an over simplification that makes the analysis unrealistic. A theory of money which insists on working everything through the bond market is a college bursar's theory.

2. Indeterminate

Keynes says that the liquidity preference and the supply of money determine the rate of interest. To find the rate of interest, we need to know the supply of money available for the speculative purposes, but that cannot be known unless we know the rate of interest.

In the words of Prof. Hansen, "Keynes' criticism of the classical theory applies equally to his own theory."

3. Ignores 'Real' Factors Altogether

It is pointed out that the main fallacy in the Keynesian theory of interest is that it ignores the influence of real factors in determining the rate of interest. To Keynes, interest is a purely monetary phenomenon. Therefore, he fails to take into account thrift, marginal productivity of capital and abstinence which are needed for saving.

In the words of Robertson, the theory is "at best an inadequate and at worst a misleading account of the whole matter."

4. No Liquidity without Saving

Keynes considers the rate of interest as the reward for parting with liquidity and not as a return for saving. Without previous saving there can be no liquidity to part with. In Jacob Viner's words, "Without saving there can be no liquidity to surrender. The rate of interest is the return for saving without liquidity."

5. Liquidity has not been Clearly Explained

In Keynes' analysis, the term 'liquidity' has not been clearly explained. It is more confusing and less illuminating. It is not only vague but also self contradictory. Suppose a man having money in the form of time deposit or short term treasury bills is paid interest. In such a case he is getting interest and possesses 'Liquidity' also. Hazlitt asks 'what becomes, then, of Keynes theory that interest is the 'reward' for parting with liquidity'?

6. Motives

According to Keynes the desire for liquidity arises due to three motives. But critics point out that in addition to the three motives mentioned by Keynes, there are several other motives which are not stressed by Keynes.

7. Changes in Money Supply

Keynes' theory states that the rate of interest can be reduced by increasing the supply of money. The rate of interest will remain the same if the liquidity preference also increases in the same proportion.

8. Incomplete Theory

According to Prof. Hansen the rate of interest along with the level of income is determined by four factors:

(*i*) the investment function,

(*ii*) the consumption function,

(*iii*) the liquidity preference function, and

(*iv*) the quantity of money function.

Keynes takes only the liquidity preference function and the quantity of money function in explaining the phenomenon of interest and ignores the first two functions. Thus Keynes fails to provide an integrated and determinate theory of interest.

9. The Theory Ignores Long Period

Keynes' theory furnishes an explanation of the rate of interest in the short run. It gives no clue to the rates of interest in the long run.

10. Existence of different interest rates

The theory also fails to explain why in the market one witnesses the co-existence of a number of interest rates.

11. Notion of Liquidity Trap

According to critics the notion of liquidity trap itself is wrong. They argue that in reality the liquidity preference schedule may be perfectly inelastic rather than elastic at a low rate of interest. During the period of depression all expectations are extremely pessimistic. It is, therefore not correct to argue that expectation with regard to the rate of interest will be that it will go up.

12. Applicability in less Developed Countries

Keynesian theory of interest has little relevance to the underdeveloped countries.

MODERN THEORY OF INTEREST

Keynesian Liquidity preference theory of interest gave undue weightage to the monetary factors in the determination of the rate of interest. This is in contrast to the classical theory which stressed the importance of real factors. Neither the monetary factors, nor the real factors by themselves can determine the rate of interest. It is argued that like the classical theory of interest, the liquidity preference theory of Keynes is also indeterminate. An adequate theory must take into consideration both the monetary and real factors that influence the interest rate.

Modern economists like J.R. Hicks and A.H. Hansen, have therefore made an attempt to provide us with a determinate theory of the rate of interest by reconciling both the monetary and real factors.

The modern theory has successfully combined the four variables — savings, investment, liquidity preference and money supply.

According to A.H. Hansen, "the neo-classical (loanable fund) formulation and the Keynesian formulation, taken together do supply us with an adequate theory of the rate of interest."[7]

Professor Hick's theory of interest can be explained with the help of the IS and LM curves. The IS curve shows the equilibrium in the real sector, while the LM curve represents the equilibrium in the monetary sector.

The IS Curve

The IS curve is the locus of the various combinations of income and the rate of interest in which saving is equal to investment. This curve will reflect equilibrium in the goods market and can be derived from a family of saving curves in the following manner.

In Fig. 31.9(*a*) we have drawn an investment curve II and a family of saving curves S_1, S_2, S_3 and S_4 corresponding to Y_1, Y_2, Y_3 and Y_4 levels of income respectively. If,

$Y_4 > Y_3 > Y_2 > Y_1$ then the position of savings curves will be in the order as shown in the diagram.

Since income is increasing, the saving schedule will shift towards the right. It is also clear from the diagram that as the saving curve shifts to the right (or as the income increases from Y_1 to Y_2, Y_3, Y_4 etc.) the rate of interest falls from r_4 to r_3, then to r_2 and so on. Thus there is an inverse relationship between the level of income and the rate of interest. This is shown in Fig. 31.9(*b*).

7. *A Guide to Keynes, op. cit.*, pp. 143-146.

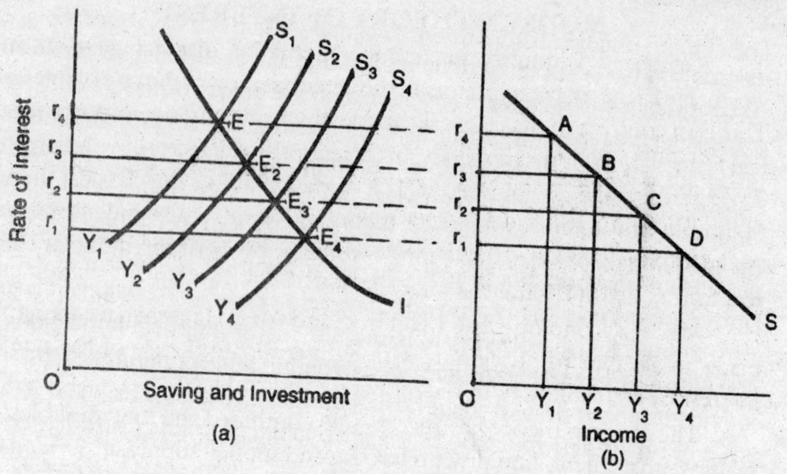

Fig. 31.9

The LM Curve

The LM curve is derived from the liquidity preference theory. The LM curve is the locus of the various combinations of levels of income and rates of interest in which the demand for money is equal to the supply of money. The LM curve reflects the equilibrium in the money market and can be derived from a family of liquidity preference curves as shown in Fig. 31.10(*a*) and (*b*).

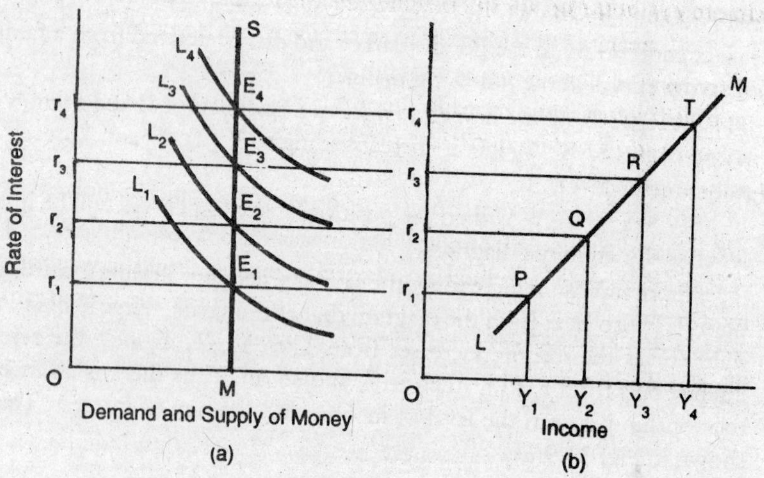

Fig. 31.10

Let us suppose that income increases from Y_1 to Y_2, Y_3, Y_4 etc. As liquidity preference is a function of income, the liquidity preference shifts from L_1 to L_2, L_3, L_4 etc. As a result the rate of interest would increase from r_1 to r_2, r_3, r_4 etc. Thus it is possible to draw a curve depicting the relationship between income and rate of interest which equates the demand for and the supply of money. This is shown in Fig. 31.10(*b*).

Equilibrium

Now the IS and LM curves, taken together, can determine the equilibrium rate of interest as well as the equilibrium level of income simultaneously.

In Fig. 31.11 IS and LM curves intersect each other at the point E. Therefore OY and OR are the equilibrium levels of income and rate of interest respectively.

Changes or shifts in the IS or the LM curves or in both, change the equilibrium position and the rate of interest is determined accordingly.

Thus at the point of equilibrium

$$S = I \text{ and } M = L$$

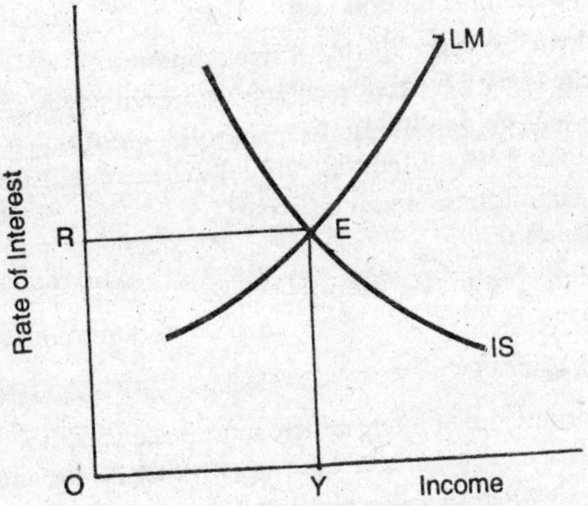

Fig. 31.11

DIFFERENCES BETWEEN LOANABLE FUNDS AND LIQUIDITY PREFERENCE THEORIES

We may notice the following differences between the loanable funds and liquidity preference theories.

Loanable funds theory	*Liquidity preference theory*
1. According to this theory, interest is a reward for the use of loanable funds.	According to this theory, interest is a reward for parting with liquidity.
2. Interest is determined by the demand and supply of loanable funds.	Interest is determined by monetary factors.
3. Supply of money is fixed.	Supply of money is interest elastic.
4. Money is considered as a flow in the loanable funds theory	Money is assumed to be a stock in the liquidity preference theory.
5. There is no belief in liquidity trap with respect to the rate of interest.	Believes in liquidity trap.
6. Role of expectation is not given much importance.	Role of expectation is given a due place.

QUESTIONS

1. What is interest? Distinguish between gross interest and net interest.
2. Define the term interest and give a brief description of the various theories developed to determine interest rate.
3. Explain the loanable funds theory of rate of interest.
4. "Interest is the reward for time preference." — Discuss.
5. Explain the concept of liquidity trap.
6. "Interest is the reward for parting with liquidity." — Discuss.
7. What is the significance of liquidity trap?
8. Write short notes on:
   (*i*) Interest is the reward for waiting
   (*ii*) Time preference.
   (*iii*) Liquidity trap.
9. At the equilibrium rate of interest there must be equality not only between the supply and demand, for money but also between saving and investment. Explain with the help of a diagram the theory which attempts to satisfy both the conditions.
10. Give an account of the classical theories of interest.
11. Make a critical analysis of the modern theory of interest.
12. Discuss Keynes' theory of interest.
13. Examine the liquidity preference theory of interest.
14. "Both the classical and the Keynesian theories of interest are indeterminate and therefore incomplete." — Discuss the truth of this statement.

❖ ❖ ❖

32

PROFIT

"Profitability is the Sovereign criterion of the enterprise."

—Peter Drucker, 1967

INTRODUCTION

The share of income that the entrepreneurs receive in the process of distribution is known as profit.

Profit differs from the return on other factors, in three important aspects.

First, profit may be negative whereas rents, wages and interests are always positive.

Secondly, profit fluctuates more than the other rewards. While wages and interest are adjusted over time, it is profit which feels the immediate impact of booms and slumps.

Thirdly, profit is a residual income while rents, wages and interests are contractual payments.

To get an accurate picture of profit, it is necessary to distinguish between gross profit and net profit.

Gross Profit and Net Profit

Gross profit is the surplus of total return to the entrepreneur after paying rent, for land, interest, for capital and wages, for the labourers employed. In ordinary parlance profit means only gross profit.

Net profit is the reward to the entrepreneur for his risk-taking function and his bargaining skill.

Gross profit is made of various constituents of which net profit is one. Gross profit comprises of

(1) Reward for the factors of production supplied by the entrepreneur himself.

(2) Charges of maintenance such as

 (*i*) Depreciation charges and

 (*ii*) Insurance charges

(3) Extra personal gains: It may take two forms (*i*) Monopoly gains and (*ii*) Windfall gains

(4) Net Profit: It is the reward for two main functions: (*i*) Reward for risk-taking and (*ii*) Reward for bargaining skill.

Therefore,

Gross Profit = Total revenue – Total explicit cost

Net Profit = Total revenue – (Total explicit cost + Total implicit cost)

= Gross Profit – Total implicit cost

RENT THEORY OF PROFIT

This theory is associated with Francis Walker. Walker's treatment of profit is similar to the theory of rent as advanced by David Ricardo.

In the words of J.S. Mill "the extra gains which any producer obtains through superior talents of business or superior business arrangements are very much similar to rent."

Just as there are different grades of land, there are different grades of entrepreneurs. Just as rent arises on account of differences in the fertility of land, profits arise on account of differences in ability. To use Walker's own words "Profit is the wage of entrepreneurs, which accrues to him on account of his special ability. Just as rent on superior lands is measured by the difference in the productivity of the marginal and intramarginal lands, in the same way the profits of the superior entrepreneurs are determined by the differences in the ability of the marginal and intra-marginal entrepreneurs. Like marginal lands, which yield no rent there exists marginal entrepreneurs with no profit." According to this theory, marginal entrepreneurs get only wages of management. Profits are thus like rent and like rent, they do not enter into the price of the product.

Criticisms of the Rent Theory of Profit

(1) Though it is true that there are similarities between rent and profit, both are not identical in all aspects. Dissimilarities between the two concepts are more pronounced than the apparent similarities.

(2) The theory provides no explanation to the share of profits of the shareholders of joint-stock companies.

(3) According to critics, there cannot be a perfect similarity between rent and profit. Rents can never be negative while profits can be negative when the entrepreneur suffers losses.

(4) It is wrong to say that profit does not enter into the price of the commodity. This may be true only in the short period; but in the long period, profit must enter into price.

(5) Walker has explained surplus profit. He has nothing to say about other types of profit and the size of the profit.

(6) Profit is not always the reward for entrepreneurial ability. It may arise also on account of the monopoly power of the firm, favourable chances available to the entrepreneur etc.

(7) The concept of a no-profit entrepreneur is wrong. If, an entrepreneur earns no profit, he will leave the industry and try his luck elsewhere.

WAGE THEORY OF PROFIT

This theory was advanced by the American economist Prof. Taussig.

According to Taussig, "Profits are best regarded simply as a form of wages." The theory states that profit is also a form of wage which is given to the entrepreneur for the services rendered by him in the process of production. The theory has been criticised on the following grounds:

1. There are basic differences between wages and profits. Wages are fixed and are a stipulated income, while profits are uncertain and are residual incomes.
2. It is the entrepreneur who undertakes risks in any production process while the wage earner is free from undertaking any such risks.

3. The theory fails to explain the reason as to why the shareholders of a company receive profits while they do not put in any labour.

DYNAMIC THEORY OF PROFIT

J.B. Clark propounded his dynamic theory of profit in 1900. The distinction between a static and a dynamic economy is fundamental to this theory of profit. According to Clark, profits are exclusively the result of dynamic changes.

No Profit in a Static Economy

Clark defined profit as the difference between the selling price and cost. It is a surplus above costs. According to this theory, under static conditions in a stationary state where no change in demand and supply occur, profits do not arise. In a static state, there is no increase in either population or capital, methods of production do not improve, the forms of industrial organisation do not change and the wants of the consumers do not multiply. In a static state, prices of goods are equal to costs of production and there can be no profit. In a static society, since payments are made on the basis of marginal productivity, the total product will be distributed between wages and interest. In such an economy the share of profit is zero. The only income of the entrepreneur is his wages for management or for co-ordination, or for his routine work of supervision.

In the words of Prof. F.H. Knight[1], "In a static state each factor secures what it produces, and since the cost and the selling prices are always equal, there can be no profit beyond wage for the routine work of supervision."

Thus in a static economy everything is known and knowable. There is no risk and no uncertainty; and hence there are no profits.

The long period competitive equilibrium is a good example of a static economy.

The long-run equilibrium is attained at point E where the price of the product OP (=ME) is equal to the cost of production which includes normal profits. So profit or loss does not exist in such a society.

---

1. F.H. Knight, *Risk Uncertainty and Profit,* University of Chicago Press, Chicago, 1971.

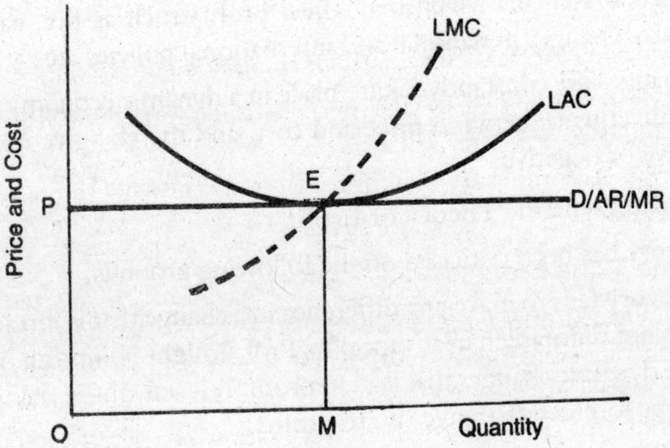

Fig. 32.1

Profits Arise in a Dynamic Economy

Clark says that our society is a dynamic one and changes take place in it every moment. He mentions "five generic changes" which may occur in a dynamic economy to give rise to profit opportunities.

1. Changes in the size of population
2. Changes in human wants
3. Changes in production techniques
4. Changes in the forms of industrial organisation
5. Changes in the supply of capital

The first two of these changes affect demand, while the last three changes affect the supply.

The changing world offers enormous opportunities to the farsighted and clever entrepreneurs who can anticipate a world of changes and adjust their activities accordingly and earn extra profits.

The world is dynamic due to two sets of factors.

(A) Internal

Internal factors are certain changes which the entrepreneur himself brings about such as new discoveries, new inventions and new innovations.

(B) External

The external changes may take two forms:

(*a*) regular changes like trade cycles which may affect profits.

(*b*) irregular changes which may affect profits such as fire, earthquake, changes in national and international policies etc.

Thus changes are constantly taking place in a dynamic economy and they create a divergence between price and cost, and thereby give rise to profits, positive or negative.

Criticism of the Dynamic Theory of Profit

This theory has been criticised on the following grounds:

1. The theory fails to make any difference in a change that is foreseen and one that is not unforeseen in advance. As Prof. Knight points out, it is not all types of dynamic changes that lead to profit. It is only those changes which cannot be foreseen that give rise to profits.

2. Profits may also emerge in the absence of Clark's five principal of dynamic changes.

3. Lastly, as Prof. Taussig points out, Clark's dynamic theory creates an artificial distinction between profits and wages of management.

RISK THEORY OF PROFIT

The risk theory of profit was propounded by an American economist, Prof. F.B. Hawley, in 1907. According to this theory, risk bearing is the most important function of the entrepreneur and profit is a reward for it. Risks are common in all types of production. Risks are both unpleasant and irksome. Therefore, no one would like to undertake risks unless he gets a reward for it. The theory predicts a positive relationship between risk and profit. Higher the risk greater is the possibility of profit.

In Hawley's[2] words "The profit of an undertaking, or the residue of the product after the claims of land, capital and labour are satisfied, is not the reward for management or co-ordination, but of risks and responsibilities that the undertaker subjects himself to."

Criticism of the Risk Theory of Profits

This theory has been criticised on the following grounds:

1. The theory disregards many other factors such as superior organsational ability, monopoly power etc. and just concentrates on risks.
2. According to Prof. Carver, profit is the reward for risk avoidance, rather than for risk-taking.

2. *Enterprise and the Productive Process,* 1907.

3. There can be no functional relationship between risk and profit. Those who undertake high risks in certain business may not necessarily earn high profits.
4. According to Prof. Knight, profit cannot be attributed to all types of risks. While predictable risks are insurable, unpredictable risks are not. In fact it is the uninsurable risk which is uncertain that gives rise to profit.

UNCERTAINTY-BEARING THEORY OF PROFIT

This theory was developed by the American economist, Prof. Knight in 1921. According to Prof. Knight, it is uncertainty-bearing rather than risk-bearing which is the most important function of the entrepreneur which leads to profit.

Knight made a distinction between risk and uncertainty. According to him, risks inherent in any business activity are of two kinds: (*i*) insurable and (*ii*) non-insurable. The distinction between insurable risks and non-insurable risks is a very important one and it is the real basis of the theory.

Insurable Risks

Insurable risks are those whose possibility of occurrence can be statistically calculated and can be insured against with an insurance company. They are of two kinds.

1. Risks of loss of property due to earthquake, fire, flood and other natural calamities; and
2. Risks of dishonesty such as loss due to theft, robbery, burglary etc.

Though it is not possible for the insurance company to predict which particular man will die or which specific firm will catch fire, it can tell very accurately how many men died or how many firms caught fire in a particular year. This fact enables the insurance company to fix the premium to be charged. The insurable risks are not the responsibility of the entrepreneur, because by paying the insurance premium he is absolved of the worry. The premium paid for insurance is included in the cost of production.

However, there remains an area of risks in which the probability of risk occurrence is not susceptible to measurement. He calls them 'uncertainty.' It is in this area that the responsibility of an entrepreneur is unique. In other words, uncertainty-bearing expects rare human abilities.

Non-Insurable Risks

The non-insurable risks are as follows:

1. Competition Risks: Competition risks are those which arise when more rival firms enter into the industry.

2. Technical Risks: Technical risks arise from the possibility of machinery becoming obsolete due to the discovery of a new process. The old firms may not be in a position to follow the new process and may thus suffer a heavy loss.

3. Risks of Government Policy: Government policy regarding business activities undergoes a change over time, some of which cannot be accurately predicted. These may relate to price control, foreign trade policy, corporate taxation etc.

4. Business Cycle Risks: Business cycle risks occur when a major part of the business sector is in the grip of a recession. In such a case, the effective demand for the product may be reduced. Moreover the fall in prices may be higher than the decline in costs.

It is the lure of profits which induces the entrepreneurs to produce goods for an uncertain market. People who are both prepared to bear the risk and possess capital for investment earn profits. If his decisions are proved correct by the subsequent events, the entrepreneur makes profit, and vice-versa.

(*i*) The profits may arise as a result of decisions concerning the state of the market (*ii*) decisions which result in increasing the degree of monopoly (*iii*) decisions with respect to holding stocks that give rise to windfall gains when prices increase; and (*iv*) decisions taken to introduce new techniques or innovations that give rise to profits.

Criticism of Knight's Theory of Profit

1. Uncertainty bearing is not the only function of the entrepreneur, though it is an exertion of rare human qualities. There are other functions like co-ordination, innovation, etc., for which he gets profit.

2. Knight's uncertainty theory lacks scientific precision.[3] According to Prof. Taussig, though certain risks are in the area of uncertainty many are not. For example, a person is betting in a horse race. If he has the knowledge of the age, training, rearing etc. of different horses and their jockeys, he would be operating in a region of risk. And if he does not have the knowledge about the horses and jockeys participating in the race, he would be regarded as operating in the area of uncertainty. But, if he has some knowledge about the horses and/or jockeys, it will be difficult to decide whether the person is operating in the area of risk or in the area of uncertainty.

3. D.N. Dwivedi, *Principles of Economies,* vani Educational Books, New Delhi, 1985, p. 433

3. The theory throws no light on monopoly profit. Monopoly firms earn profits not due to the presence of any uncertainty.

4. Moreover, the uncertainty element cannot be quantified to impute profit.

5. The theory assumes uncertainty bearing as an independent factor of production. But it depends upon the business ability of the entrepreneur. The more efficient an entrepreneur, lesser will be the uncertainty and vice versa.

6. Lastly, the theory fails to separate the two functions in modern business, namely, ownership and control. Nowadays ownership rests with the shareholders of the company and control lies in the hands of the salaried managers. Therefore, the concept of profit and the precise function of the entrepreneur have not been clearly explained in this theory.

INNOVATION THEORY OF PROFIT

The innovation Theory of Profit was developed by Joseph A. Schumpeter. His theory of profit is more or less akin to the dynamic theory of profit. Instead of five "generic changes" of Clark, Schumpeter resorts to innovations to explain the emergence of profits. According to this theory, innovation is a distinctive function of an entrepreneur for which he gets profit.

For example, Steven Jobs, the founder of Apple Computer Company became a millionaire in the course of a few years by introducing the Apple Computer in 1977.

Meaning of an Innovator

An innovator is a person with vision, originality and drive.[4] The entrepreneur is one who innovates. Entrepreneurship and his endeavour lies in introducing innovations. The entrepreneur is an aggressive innovator who introduces improved techniques of production or who alters the production function in other ways.

The entrepreneur may not be a scientist who invents new products or processes but the man who successfully introduces them in the production process. The person who undertakes the risk of introducing the idea in mass commercial use is the entrepreneur and it is he who gets the profit for it. The scientist or technician gets only a fixed sum or a percentage by way of royalty. Thus profit is due only to the entrepreneur.

---

4. P.L Mehta — *Essential of Micro Economics*, Sultan Chand & Sons, New Delhi. 1998 p. 457

The role of the entrepreneur is quite distinct from that of the capitalist. The entrepreneur innovates and does not undertake any risk. Risk taking is the function of the capitalist or the banks that provide credit. Thus profit is a reward for innovation rather than for risk-taking.

Meaning of Innovation

Any new measure or policy designed by the entrepreneur to reduce costs of production or to increase the demand for his product is known as innovation.

Innovations may be divided into two broad categories.

***(i)* Those innovations which reduce the cost of production**

The cost of production may be reduced by the introduction of a new machine, new and cheaper techniques of production, exploitation of a new source of raw material, new and better methods of organising the firm etc.

***(ii)* Those innovations which change the demand or utility function**

The utility or demand may be increased by the introduction of a new product, a new design in the market, attractive and efficient methods of advertisement, discovery of new markets for the product etc.

Whenever a new innovation is introduced, it reduces the cost of production below the existing price and results in the emergence of profit.

According to Schumpeter, profits are temporary in nature. A change is followed by another change. A new innovation gives profit to a particular firm. Soon this profit is wiped out because others imitate that innovation. Thus, there is a "swarm like appearance of entrepreneurial activity." So the profit "slips in time through their fingers and bestows itself on all members of the society." Profits are thus unstable and temporary. But it should be noted that when one source of innovational profit disappears some other new innovation may appear. Hence, innovational profits have a tendency to disappear and reappear.

Criticism of Innovation Theory of Profit

The theory has been criticised on the following grounds:

1. A Special Case of Knight's Theory

According to critics, Schumpter's theory is nothing else than the uncertainty theory, for innovations are one of the causes for uncertainty, although a deliberately created uncertainty.

2. Role of Risk-bearing

The theory does not consider profit as the reward for risk-bearing. According to Schumpeter "The entrepreneur is never the risk-taker. The one who gives credit comes to grief if the undertaking fails." This is not true.

3. Relation between Innovational Ability and Profit is not Correct

According to Schumpeter the profit of an entrepreneur depends upon his ability to innovate and reduce the cost of production. But in actual practice, a number of ordinary businessmen obtain a lot of profit which is in no way correlated to their innovational capacity. The windfall gain and loss aspects have also been ignored by the theory.

4. Ignores the Long Period

The theory states that profit is a temporary phenomenon, because in the long run innovation gets itself reduced to that of a routine. Thus this theory fails to explain the determination of profit in the long run.

5. An Institutional Theory

The theory is not based upon economic factors. It elevates the position of an entrepreneur to that of an institution. Therefore, it is more sociological in nature than economics.

MARGINAL PRODUCTIVITY THEORY OF PROFIT

The chief exponents of the marginal productivity theory of profit are Edgeworth, Chapman, Stigler and Stonier and Hague. In simple terms, the theory states like the payment for other factors of production, the remuneration of the entrepreneur, i.e., profit will be determined by the marginal productivity of the entrepreneur.

But the real problem with regard to this theory is the difficulty of calculating the MRP of the entrepreneur. Since there is only one entrepreneur in a firm, the principle of marginal analysis may not be valid. But this difficulty can be avoided by taking an industry where the number of firms can be varied. As more and more firms enter into the industry, the marginal revenue productivity of entrepreneurship decreases. Thus, the slope of MRP curve can be got which will be negative as shown in Fig. 32.2. The demand curve (MRP curve) and supply curve intersect at point E where all entrepreneurs make normal profits OS (=EM) in the long run. In the short run, the number of entrepreneurs being OM_1 instead of OM, they make a supernormal profit of E_1M_1. But this theory is not a systematic theory.

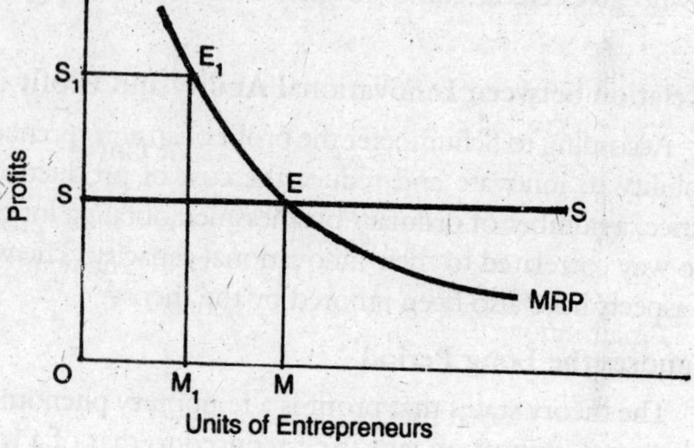

Fig. 32.2

QUESTIONS

1. Define profit. Distinguish between Gross Profit and Net Profit.
2. "The theory of profit is at present the most controversial and unsatisfactory branch of economic theory." Examine the statement critically.
3. Explain innovation theory of profits.
4. "Profits are the surplus of the intramarginal over marginal producers." — Comment.
5. "Profit is the reward for uncertainity bearing." — Discuss.
6. "Profits cannot exist in a stationary state." — Comment.
7. Write notes on:
   (*a*) Innovation
   (*b*) Stationary state
   (*c*) Risk and uncertainty
   (*d*) Wage theory of profit
8. What do economists mean when they describe profit as a dynamic surplus?
9. "Profits are dynamic in origin and institutional in appropriation" — Discuss.

❖ ❖ ❖